P9-DTW-868

THE SIERRA CLUB GUIDE TO THE NATURAL AREAS OF CALIFORNIA

The Sierra Club Guides To The Natural Areas Of The United States

The Natural Areas of California

The Natural Areas of Colorado and Utah

The Natural Areas of Idaho, Montana, and Wyoming

The Natural Areas of New Mexico, Arizona, and Nevada

The Natual Areas of Oregon and Washington

The Natural Areas of Florida

The Natural Areas of New England

The

Sierra Club

Guide

to the

Natural Areas of

California

John Perry & Jane Greverus Perry

with revisions by Roger Rapoport,
Linda Cohen, and Nancy Madway

SIERRA CLUB BOOKS · SAN FRANCISCO

AND OTHER MEN AND WOMEN

WHO CARE FOR OUR FORESTS,

PARKS, AND PRESERVES

The Sierra Club, founded in 1892, has devoted itself to the study and protection of the earth's scenic and ecological resource-mountains, wetlands, woodlands, wild shores and rivers, deserts and plains. The publishing program of the
Sierra Club offers books to the public as a nonprofit educational service in the
hope that they may enlarge the public's understanding of the Club's basic concerns. The point of view expressed in each book, however, does not necessarily
represent that of the Club. The Sierra Club has some sixty chapters coast to
coast, in Canada, Hawaii, and Alaska. For information about how you may par-
ticipate in its programs to preserve its wilderness and the quality of life, please
address inquiries to Sierra Club, 85 Second Street, San Francisco, CA 94105.

http://www.sierraclub.org/books

Library of Congress Cataloging-in-Publication Data
          Perry, John, 1914-
          The Sierra Club guide to the natural areas of
                California.
          Includes bibliographical references and index.
          1. Outdoor recreation — California — Guide books.
          2. Natural history—California. 3. Natural areas —
          California — Guide-books. 4. California — Description
          and travel — 1981- -Guide-books. 1. Perry, Jane
                Greverus. II. Title.
          GV191.42.C2P47   1983   917.94   82-16936
                          ISBN 0-87156-850-0

Production by Janet Vail
Cover design by Bonnie Smetts
Book design by Mark Ong
Maps by Tom Camara

Printed in the United States of America on acid-free paper containing a minimum of 50% recovered waste paper, of which at least 10% of the fiber content
is post-consumer waste

10 9 8 7 6 5 4 3 2 1

CONTENTS

THE NATURAL AREAS OF CALIFORNIA

INTRODUCTION

This is a guide to California's quiet places, where plants grow, birds sing, and the signs of humans are few.

It is true that some of the quiet places have been overrun. One must make reservations weeks ahead to enter a wilderness. Beach parking is full by midmorning in summer. Noisy off-road vehicles have driven off wildlife and hikers.

The western landscape has been much changed since we first saw it 50 years ago. Many hillsides have been stripped of timber, tundra trails beaten into muddy ditches by many boots, deserts permanently scarred by vehicle tracks.

Yet we have no difficulty finding quiet places. In the last phase of our research, we traveled 8,000 mi., camping every night. On most nights we were alone or with few neighbors. When we were too late for a backcountry permit at Yosemite, we found a lightly used trail in the nearby National Forest.

People congregate. Most seem to prefer the developed recreation sites, the publicized trails. Most come at certain seasons. Those who seek solitude can find it, often nearby. They may find a very popular site more peaceful at another time of the year. We camped alone in a vast marsh less than an hour's drive from a major city.

In the East, less than 10% of the land is publicly owned. Almost half of California remains in federal ownership, and the state has extensive landholdings. Most of these public lands are in the mountains and deserts, although California has kept much of its seacoast in public ownership.

Almost every description of California begins by remarking on its contrasts and extremes. The highest point in the conterminous United States is 14,495-ft. Mount Whitney. The lowest point, in Death Valley, is only 85 mi. distant. Temperatures have ranged between –45°F and +134°F. A desert rain gauge has recorded zero for a full year; one in a rain forest accumulated 161 in. One can ski in the mountains and swim in the ocean on the same day, or lunch at Fisherman's Wharf and hike in a wilderness that afternoon.

The state is 800 mi. long, but its coastline measures 1,340 mi. The Coast Range parallels the shore from the Oregon border to just N of the Los Angeles basin. These mountains rise abruptly from the sea or from a narrow coastal plain, not to the heights of the Sierra Nevada, although some peaks in the N exceed 8,000 ft. In the N, the Coast Range merges with the Cascade Range, forming a high, rugged area more than 200 mi. wide.

California's Cascades rise to peaks and ridges 5,000 to 10,000 ft. high, Mount Shasta towering over them at 14,161 ft. To the SE the Cascades merge with the Sierra Nevada, the largest mountain mass in the United States, more than 400 mi. long, 60 to 80 mi. wide. Elevations increase from N to S. In the N, few peaks exceed 8,000 ft., while S of Yosemite National Park the crest is above 11,000 ft.

The Coast Range and the Sierra are separated by a broad, flat valley, from which the Sierra foothills rise gradually. The W slopes are generally moderate, cut by many rivers and streams. The high country is not a single ridge but many ridges, some paralleling the main crest, others branching away from it. This is a spectacularly rugged region of mountain meadows, glacial lakes, ice fields, and tundra flowers, deep in snow for most of the year. The E slope drops steeply.

East of Bakersfield the Sierra meets the Tehachapi Mountains, which trend SW, meeting the Coast Range and closing the S end of the Central Valley. Beyond, minor ranges extend SE to Mexico. The mountain barrier denies rainfall to the land on the E side. The SE quarter of California is a vast and fascinating desert.

The Sierra is a formidable obstacle to travel as well as to moisture. From Lake Tahoe to the S tip of the mountains, no all-year road crosses the range. Highway maps show the few existing transmountain roads as "Closed in Winter." Strangers may not know that "winter" in this high country may extend to the Fourth of July. Don't expect to travel these roads in April!

California has 5,000 lakes, 30,000 mi. of rivers and streams, more than 40 million acres of forest land. California also has more participants in outdoor recreation than any other state. We were told that one household in three has some kind of recreation vehicle. Unfortunately, many of them are off-road vehicles (ORVs): 254,591 dirt bikes, 321,300 4-wheel drives, 14,331 dune buggies, 52,168 3x4-wheel utility vehicles, 12,566 snowmobiles. Their damage to flora, fauna, and artifacts is widespread and increasing. Control efforts are opposed by a vociferous, well-financed lobby.

Even wilderness areas may be crowded in California. So many fragile places have been trampled that access to some areas is now rationed. More and more campgrounds are now available by reservation only.

All true, but, wherever we traveled in California, we found the quiet places.

How We Selected Sites

We use the "natural area" broadly, generically. A few specialists have objected. They have appropriated the term and devised narrow definitions. "Federal Research Natural Areas," for example, are "lands on which various natural features are preserved in an undisturbed state solely for research and educational purposes."

We look for places where a visitor can enjoy nature. The majority of such places are not pristine. Some have been logged, farmed, mined, or otherwise disturbed, but the healing processes of nature are at work. Most wildlife refuges are not "natural" because their ponds and marshes are maintained by dikes and crops are planted to support waterfowl. Without such places few waterfowl would travel the flyways. When tens of thousands of geese and ducks endorse these places, they're good enough for us.

Large National Forests and National Parks were automatic selections. More than 20 million acres—one-fifth of California—is in 19 National Forests. Sites administered by the National Park Service total 6 million acres, National Wildlife Refuges another 0.25 million.

The state has many splendid sites and is acquiring more. The largest is 550,000-acre Anza-Borrego Desert State Park. The Providence Mountains State Recreation Area has only 5,250 acres, but it is surrounded by a sweeping landscape of public lands, and no boundaries are visible.

California has been more determined than most states to maintain public ownership of and access to its ocean beaches, despite pressures for commercial development. Near cities and resorts, beaches are often unpleasantly crowded. But the coast still has fine, unspoiled areas. The largest, wildest, and most remote is the King Range in zone 1.

We studied smaller sites more critically. For example, we do not include a state park planned for intensive recreation unless, in addition to a developed area, it has a few hundred roadless acres of interest to hikers and birders.

In studying a small site, we considered its setting. A small seaside park may provide access to a dozen miles of uncluttered ocean beach. A park with little more than a campground may be a wilderness trailhead. A sit that is intolerably crowded on the Fourth of July may offer splendid solitude in December.

The revised edition of our book was researched and prepared for publication by Roger Rapaport and his staff at RDR Books in Berkeley.

The Public Domain

When we had screened every National Park, National Forest, and National Wildlife Refuge, we had 17.2 million acres of federal land left over, what remains of the original public domain. It sprawls over the landscape, sometimes in huge, solid blocks, sometimes in a checkerboard of 1-mi. squares, alternating with state and private land. It includes mountains, plains, canyons, rivers, lakes, and wetlands, but most of it is in the California Desert.

Its boundaries are not marked. It is not divided into neat packages, such as parks and forests. We looked for outstanding features, such as a mountain or canyon, then studied the surrounding area. Finally, we fixed arbitrary boundaries enclosing areas that seemed to fit together.

The U.S. Bureau of Land Management (BLM) manages the public domain. Our entries for BLM sites have local names and unmarked boundaries. The visitor will find no signs, no gates, and—except at a few recreation sites—no facilities. Only by chance will a BLM staff member be present. It is almost as unlikely that he or she will encounter other visitors.

These tens of millions of acres are yours to enjoy. Here you can drive, hike, backpack, ride horseback, and camp almost anywhere, hunt and fish subject to state laws. Except in a few developed recreation areas, you are unlikely to meet other visitors.

Much of this land has been leased, usually for grazing, and some of it is fenced by cattle ranchers. This does not shut you out. Where public land is fenced and gated, you have the right to enter—and close the gate behind you.

How do you know you are on public land? In some areas, private and public land are intermixed. Our entries are for areas with few private inholdings. If you have doubts or concerns, visit or telephone the BLM District Office.

What if a rancher tells you to get off his place? Go quietly. You could have strayed onto private land. But some ranchers have used the public land for so long that they consider it their own. Perhaps previous visitors have misbehaved. However, such confrontations are rare even on private land. Should you have one, the BLM office would like to know about it.

Other Public Lands

We reluctantly decided to omit most county and regional parks. Inquiries convinced us that gathering the required data would be impossible, as few could supply what we needed, and some were simply unwilling to do that—noting that their parks are for local taxpayers, not outsiders. We have included a few such entries, when an area seemed to hold unusually broad appeal or offered something unique in a broad geographic area and when park officials were receptive to its inclusion.

We have included no military reservations. Some of these are large, and many permit limited public use. However, the limits are usually strict, and they often change from day to day. The base nearest our home has a special number to call in order to hear whether visitors are permitted today. Most public use of these reservations is by hunters and fishermen, but if there is one near you, inquire. Some reservations have naturalists or wildlife managers who can tell you what's there and who may even offer a guided tour.

Private Lands

Some of the largest private holdings are those of timber companies. In the past some companies permitted or invited public use. We wrote to the largest and asked if this is still the case. Only two replied. Both asked that we not mention their lands. Neither answered our question.

Off the record, company official said, "We allow public use, but we don't want publicity. If many more people come, we'll have to close the gates. And we must be able to close them at any time, without notice, for operating reasons."

A state wildlife official confirmed this. Most timber company lands are used by hunters and fishermen, he said, and sometimes by hikers. Some owners require permits. A few charge fees. He advised prospective visitors to inquire at the nearest federal or state forestry office. Our advice: Forget it, unless you have a special interest in an area.

The Nature Conservancy
Western Regional Office
201 Mission St., 4th Floor
San Francisco, CA 94105
(415) 777-0487

The Conservancy is a national nonprofit organization devoted solely to the acquisition and management of ecologically significant land. It has helped preserve over 2 million acres of such land.

TNC preserves are, for the most part, small and fragile. Few have full-time managers, and visitors are asked to write or call for permission.

Unique in our entries, Audubon Canyon Ranch (See entry zone 3) is a private, nonprofit environmental organization founded specifically to protect nesting colonies of birds in two California counties. Though sponsored by several chapters of the National Audubon Society, the ACR is not directly affiliated with the Society and must depend largely upon public donations to support the Preserves and the educational functions they serve.

How to Use This Book

We divided the state into zones. Zone boundaries generally follow county lines. A map showing these zones appears on page ix. An alphabetical list of the sites appears in the index.

At the beginning of each zone section is a zone map on which sites are spotted, with key numbers. Sites are listed in numerical order.

- If you plan to visit an area, find the corresponding zone and see what other sites in the zone would interest you.
- If you plan to visit—say—a National Park (NP), locate its key number on the zone map and see what other sites are nearby.
- Entries are arranged alphabetically within zones.
- Information in entries is presented in a standard sequence.

Site Names

Parks are for people. Most parks have formal entrances. Most parks are closed to logging and hunting. Most parks have developed recreation sites. Parks have more facilities, more supervision, more rules, and more visitors than forests or refuges. ·

Forests are for trees and water. National Forests are managed for wood, water, wildlife, and recreation, although critics charge imbalance. Timber is often harvested on the more humid western slopes, vegetation maintained in semiarid areas. Hunting and fishing in National Forests are governed by state law. Recreation has a high priority in many National Forests. Although there are campgrounds, one can make camp almost anywhere.

Wildlife management areas, state operated, are for birds and beasts, fishes included. In the past, most visits were by hunters and fishermen, whose license fees supported the state system. Now visits by "nonconsumptive users," such as hikers and birdwatchers, are welcomed, especially outside hunting season.

National Wildlife Refuges are also for birds and beasts, but many have visitor facilities: auto tour routes, exhibits, information centers. Hunting is usually permitted, though often restricted to certain parts of the refuge and with special rules.

Public domain lands, managed by the BLM, have many uses, including grazing, mining, forestry, and geothermal development. Most areas are open to public use. Large areas are far from any paved roads, and access often requires 4-wheel drive or a sturdy pickup truck. In the many roadless areas, travel is by foot or horseback. Most BLM lands are arid or semiarid.

The Pacific Crest National Scenic Trail (PCT), a 2,638-mi. wildland route connecting Mexico with Canada, holds carefully to the crest of the mountain ranges of California, Oregon, and Washington. It is largely routed over public lands, crossing or touching 33 federally designated Wildernesses, 24 National Forests, 7 National Parks, as well as 5 State Parks and county land. The PCT also crosses some private lands, but landholders have made the route available by right-of-way agreements with the federal government. Elevations range from 140 to 13,200 ft.

Administering Agency

Entries name the agencies with management responsibility, not parent departments.

Acreage

Many National Forests and some other sites have "inholdings," privately owned land within their boundaries. If these are significant, the entry gives both the acreage within the boundaries and the acreage of publicly owned land.

How to Get There

Routings begin from points easily found on ordinary highway maps. For large sites, the route is one most visitors use.

Open Hours

Most National Parks are open 24 hours. Many State Parks are closed at night, though campers may be able to leave or enter. National Wildlife Refuges and many state wildlife management areas are closed at night. Forests don't have gates.

Symbols

Symbols tell at a glance if a site offers camping, swimming, etc. Most symbols have obvious meanings:

 Used for both hiking and backpacking.

 In addition to canoeable and kayakable waters, this symbol is also used for white water requiring rafts.

 Used for ski touring, usually includes snowshoeing.

 We used this for birding and wildlife viewing.

In many cases, the symbols correspond to items in the "Activities" part of the entry. If there is no useful information to report, the symbol stands alone.

Description

Each site is briefly characterized: terrain, main physical features, climate, vegetation, wildlife. Subheads such as *"Plants"* and *"Birds"* do not appear in all entries, usually because no one has studied these areas.

Even if complete flora and fauna lists were available, reproducing them would require a library, rather than a volume. Using whatever data we could gather, we have made selections of species, attempting to characterize the principal plant and animal communities. In some cases this has seemed best achieved by listing the most common species. In others it seemed useful to mention rarities.

Comprehensive mammal lists were less often available than bird lists. Information on reptiles and amphibians was scarce.

In entries, the singular is used to signify single species. Plurals signify more than one species. Example: ". . . mountain bluebird, woodpeckers . . ."

Note: Authorities often decree changes in common names. "Myrtle warbler" and "Audubon's warbler" have become "yellow-rumped warbler." But "Traill's flycatcher" has been split into "willow flycatcher" and "alder flycatcher." Most species checklists supplied to us include some of the old names. Our purpose has been to use the names most readers now use.

Features

Noted first are wilderness areas, primitive areas, and other large and noteworthy portions of sites. Wilderness areas are closed to virtually all entry except by visitors on foot or horseback.

This portion of the entries also mentions other prominent site features, such as waterfalls, canyons, major rivers, and caverns. It also mentions the principal recreation sites.

Because our concern is with natural areas, we give little or no attention to forts and other historical features.

Interpretation

Here we note visitor centers, museums, nature trails, campfire programs, guided hikes, and other naturalist programs.

Activities

Camping: Entries note numbers of sites, seasons of operation, and whether reservations are required. (Reservation requirements and systems change from year to year.)

Camping in parks is usually limited to campgrounds. Check with Park Headquarters on site.

One can camp almost anywhere in National Forests. But along some heavily traveled routes, camping is restricted to campgrounds. In some National Forest areas, camping is prohibited during periods of high fire danger.

One can camp almost anywhere in the public domain.

Most National Wildlife Refuges prohibit camping. Some state wildlife areas permit it. In some cases, hunters are allowed to park RVs overnight in parking areas.

Can one "camp"—park an RV overnight—in highway rest stops or roadside pullouts? *In California, no.*

Hiking, backpacking: The backpacking symbol is used where hiking with trailside camping is permitted and attractive. It is used for some small sites that serve as trailheads.

Trails in Parks are more likely to be marked and maintained than trails in Forests, although many National Forests have extensive trail systems. In California, many National Parks and Forests have connecting trails.

Over most of the public domain, you're on your own, although there are numerous unmapped trails and tracks.

If you plan a backcountry trip, visit the nearest ranger station or BLM District Office for useful advice on routes, trail conditions, and whether many hikers are on the trail. You may be shown trail maps, even photographs of your destination.

The hiking season in the high country is short. Trails may be blocked by snow into July, and new snow may fall in Sept. Trail maintenance can't be performed until soil is reasonably dry, so expect problems if you follow the melt too closely. Streams one can ford later may be dangerous torrents during the runoff.

Some western hikers scorn all but the high country—and thus spend most of the year indoors! One can find delightful trails in any season. Spring and fall are the best times on the lower slopes and in the green valleys. Beach hiking can be good in any season.

Hunting: Except for the Parks, portions of some Wildlife Refuges, and recreation areas, public lands are generally open to hunting. State regulations apply everywhere, as do federal regulations on migratory species. Wildlife management areas often have special rules limiting the number of hunters or permitting hunting only on certain days.

Fishing: Entries report whether fishing is possible and name the principal species. In some National Parks, stocking has been discontinued, in keeping with the policy of maintaining near-natural conditions.

Swimming: We report what we were told. Swimming from many Pacific beaches is said to be cold, rough, and dangerous. In some State Parks, swimming is permitted only when lifeguards are present. Responses from National Forests and BLM sites often failed to mention swimming even though lakes and rivers are present. Management is permissive: Swim where you wish, at your own risk.

Boating: The symbol is not used for bodies of water smaller than 100 acres.

Canoeing, kayaking, drift boating, rafting: It seemed impractical to have symbols for each, although each is the choice for certain streams. Usually the text makes the distinction.

Horse riding: The symbol is used where pack trips and other trail riding were reported. Horses can be ridden in many other places: on any suitable trail in a National Forest, for example, or anywhere on BLM land. If horse rentals were said to be available, this is noted in text, but the reader is warned that such enterprises come and go.

Skiing: Downhill ski areas are mentioned when they are on public land. Many ski areas are operated by concessioners.

Ski touring: Usually one can ski cross-country wherever there's enough snow. We note where this was reported as a popular activity.

Snowmobiling: Noted where reported. Many National and State Parks restrict or prohibit snowmobiles. They are banned in wilderness areas.

Rules and Regulations

All sites have them. Parks have the most.

Pets: In Parks, the general rule is that pets must be leashed. They are often prohibited on trails and beaches and in buildings. California requires proof of rabies vaccination, and pets must be confined to a tent or vehicle at night. A fee is charged for each dog.

Refuges and wildlife areas generally require that dogs be leashed, except while used in hunting.

Some sites ban pets altogether, and entries note this.

Cautions

Some site managers thought you should be warned—about ocean currents, summer thunderstorms, rattlesnakes. We report their warnings. But keep in mind that other managers didn't mention similar hazards.

Publications

Entries list publications issued by sites or about sites. If a site has a descriptive leaflet, you may be able to have it sent to you, but fewer and fewer sites have sufficient staff to respond to such requests. Most leaflets, species checklists, nature trail guides, etc., are available only on site.

California's State Parks now charge for leaflets, except where old leaflets are still in stock. We paid 50 cents for most, $1.00 for a few.

National Forests will send maps by mail. When we checked, the price was $3.22.

"Checklist available" usually means copies can be obtained. Not always. At some sites we found supplies exhausted but were allowed to study file copies.

What's Not in the Entries

Entries do not include information about:

Picnic grounds. One can picnic almost anywhere.

Campground facilities. Excellent directories are published.

Cabins, inns, lodges. It was difficult to distinguish among lodgings on public land, lodgings on private inholdings, and lodgings just outside.

Restaurants and snack bars presented the same difficulty. Also, many close when crowds are absent.

Playgrounds, golf courses, etc.

Admission fees. Most Parks charge fees. Fees change from year to year. At the National Parks, frequent park users, senior citizens, and blind and disabled patrons should inquire about the Golden Passport, which offers special rates. At State Parks, seniors and disabled patrons may be eligible for discounts. Park toll booths are often closed when visitors are few.

Rock climbing, rockhounding, spelunking, and scuba diving are too specialized for a general guide.

Changes

These are hard times for the public lands. For years budgets failed to keep pace with increasing public use. Now federal and state agencies' budgets have been cut, in some cases savagely. The permanent damage thus inflicted on precious natural resources is of deep concern to us, but beyond the scope of this book. Readers will encounter many reductions in opportunities and services:

- Publications may be out of print. Others, once free, will be sold.
- Campfire programs, guided walks, and other interpretive programs may be curtailed.
- Some campgrounds may be closed, others operated for shorter seasons. Facilities may be reduced. Broken or vandalized equipment may not be replaced.
- Some wildlife refuges may be closed, perhaps seasonally or on certain days. Visitors may be restricted to smaller portions of refuges.
- Maintenance of hiking trails may be reduced.
- Snow plowing may be discontinued on some park roads.

Pathfinding

To travel California, the first need is an ordinary highway map. The state is so large, one needs larger-scale maps to find the way locally. A fine series of regional maps is available to members of the American Automobile Association (California State Automobile Association, 150 Van Ness Ave., San Francisco, CA 94101; or Automobile Club of Southern California, 2601 S. Figueroa St., Los Angeles, CA 90007). The Los Angeles office also has 11 maps of the southern counties.

Most surfaced roads shown on such maps are suitable for ordinary cars, except mountain roads in winter. Map legends for other roads should be heeded, especially "graded dirt," "dirt," and "poor or doubtful." Washouts, mudslides, and other interruptions are common. Inquire locally about the condition of unpaved roads, especially if you are driving an RV or towing a trailer.

These maps do not show road networks in National Forests. Each National Forest has its own map.

Pathfinding in the public domain can be adventurous. Here you may find paved and maintained roads, unmaintained dirt roads, and miles of washes an ORV can negotiate in dry weather. Backcountry travel can be hazardous. Some of the sites we describe can't be visited casually. One needs good maps, a reliable vehicle, local advice—and common sense. Especially in desert travel, two vehicles are far safer than one. If you travel alone, it's wise to drive in no further than you'd be able to walk out.

Agency Offices and Publications

Federal Agencies

U.S. Forest Service
Pacific Southwest Region
630 Sansome St.
San Francisco, CA 94111
(415) 705-2874

Publications Include:

Brochures: Central Coast; Central Valley; Deserts; Gold Country; High Sierra; Inland Empire; Los Angeles County; North Coast; Orange County; San Diego County; San Francisco Bay Area; Shasta Cascade.

Celebrating an American Treasure.

Driving Tips for National Forest Roads.

An Enduring Resource of Wilderness.

Fact sheets on wilderness regulations and permits, backcountry safety tips, ORV use, and hunting.

Federal Recreation Passport Program.

Find Yourself . . . on the Pacific Crest Trail.

The Fish Habitat Relationships Program of the U.S. Forest Service.

Fishing Your National Forests.

Forest for the Future: Highlights in the History of Forest Conservation.

A Guide to National Forest Wilderness in California.

A Guide to Your National Forests.

Highlights in the History of Forest Conservation.

Living with California Mountain Lions.

National Wilderness Preservation System map.

Noxious Weeds: A Growing Concern.

Partners in Wild Turkey Management on Your National Forests.

Recreation Opportunities on Public Lands.

Watershed and Air Management.

Wetlands Role of the Forest Service.

National Park Service
Western Regional Office
Fort Mason, Bldg. 20
San Francisco, CA 94123
(415) 556-4122/0560

Publications Include:

Backcountry Travel in the National Park System.

Camping in the National Park System.

National Recreation Trails.

Maps and brochures of all National Parks.

U.S. Fish and Wildlife Service
Regional Office
911 N.E. 11th Ave.
Portland, OR 97232-4181
(503) 231-6121

U.S. Bureau of Land Management
2800 Cottage Way
Sacramento, CA 95825
(916) 978-4754

Publications Include:

BLM in California.

BLM Trails and Rivers.

List of BLM campgrounds

BLM National Recreation Guide map

Maps and information on BLM wilderness areas

State Agencies

California Department of Parks and Recreation
1416 9th St.
Sacramento, CA 95814
(916) 653-6995

Publications Include:

Leaflets describing each State Park. Most are now 50 cents; a few are $1.00.

The Official Guide to California State Parks, $2.

Rules and Regulations.

Campground Regulations.

Color map of State Park locations, $2.

Note: Campground reservations are necessary for popular parks in season. The list of parks requiring reservations and their reservation seasons change from year to year. When we gathered our information, the following numbers were used:

National Forests: (800) 280-CAMP; TDD (800) 879-4496

National Parks: (800) 365-2267 (DESTINET)

State Parks: (800) 444-7275; reservations can be made up to 7 months in advance.

California Department of Fish and Game
1416 Ninth St.
Sacramento, CA 95814
(916) 653-7664

Publications Include:

How the DFG Works.

Sport fishing regulations.

Hunting regulations.

Public Access Projects (list and map).

California Department of Forestry
1416 Ninth St.
Sacramento, CA 95814
(916) 653-7772

THE SIERRA CLUB GUIDE TO THE NATURAL AREAS OF CALIFORNIA

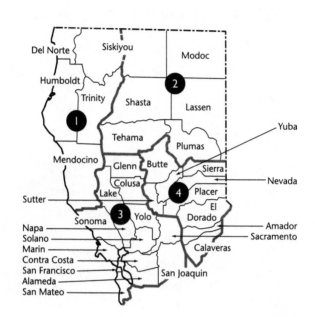

Del Norte

Siskiyou

Modoc

Humboldt

Trinity

Shasta

Lassen

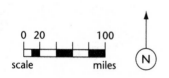

Tehama

Yuba

Plumas

Mendocino

Glenn

Butte

Sierra

Colusa

Nevada

Lake

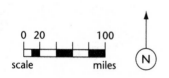

Placer

Sutter

Yolo

El
Dorado

Sonoma

Napa

Amador

Solano

Sacramento

Marin

Calaveras

Contra Costa

San Francisco

San Joaquin

Alameda

San Mateo

0 20   100

scale   miles

N

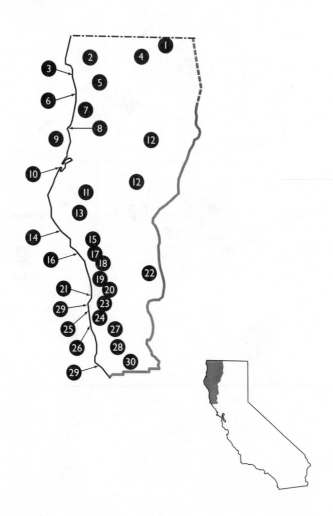

ZONE 1

Includes these counties:

Del Norte	Humboldt	Mendocino
Siskiyou (W of I-5)	Trinity	

From Gualala N to Rockport, Hwy 1 is a scenic highway along a splendid coast: rocky headlands, sheer cliffs, haystack islands, sheltered coves, long sand beaches backed by dunes, salt marshes, shallow bays. Through traffic uses US 101 inland. The Coast Hwy is narrow, and it can be congested on holiday weekends, but, much of the time, driving can be relaxed and delightful. It's a trip to make without haste, for there are many places to stop for views of the coast, a stroll along the headlands, or a hike up a moist canyon. Several State Parks are along the way. Points of interest include ancient marine terraces, a pygmy forest, groves of Coast redwoods.

Near Rockport, Hwy 1 turns inland, ending at its junction with US 101. For the next hundred-odd miles, the terrain was too forbidding to build a coastal road. This is California's "Lost Coast," remote, rugged, with only a few points reachable by any kind of road. Don't rely on your ordinary highway map here. See the entries for King Range, Sinkyone Wilderness, and Humboldt County Beaches.

Groves of Coast redwoods can be seen S of San Francisco, and several fine ones lie between Hwy 1 and US 101 before they join. From here N, however, their numbers increase. Redwood parks described in entries include Standish-Hickey, Smithe, Richardson, and Humboldt, largest in this area. Humboldt Bay is worth exploring before proceeding N of Eureka. Now US 101 becomes the Coast Hwy, at least the road nearest to the coast, passing a number of State Beaches before arriving at Redwood National and State Parks.

In the N part of CA, the Coast and Cascade Ranges merge, creating a rugged, mountainous area more than 200 mi. from W to E. From the

OR border S, most of the mountains in zone 1 are within National Forests: Six Rivers, Klamath, Shasta-Trinity, and Mendocino.

Admiral William Standley State Recreation Area

California Department of Parks and Recreation
45 acres.

From Laytonville on US 101, W on Branscomb Rd. 14 mi.

A small park on a lightly traveled road. Fine stand of Coast redwoods. Over 3,000 ft. along the headwaters of the South Fork of the Eel River. No fishing: spawning grounds. Elevation 1,700 ft.

No Facilities.

Information
(707) 925-6482 or (707) 247-3318.

Del Norte Coast Redwoods State Park

See Redwood National and State Parks.

Grizzly Creek Redwoods State Park

California Department of Parks and Recreation
400 acres.

35 mi. SE of Eureka. From US 101 near Alton, 17 mi. E on Hwy 36.

Smallest and farthest inland of the state redwood parks, seldom crowded, visited chiefly by campers. Area also includes Cheatham Grove. In Van Duzen River Valley, near base of the Coastal Range. Elevation 375 ft. Almost 1 mi. of river frontage.

Plants: About 85% forested. Several groves of Coast redwood, mostly virgin stands. Other tree species: Douglas-fir, lowland fir, California bay laurel, tan oak, cottonwood, bigleaf maple. Understory includes thimbleberry, huckleberry, Oregon grape, poison oak, ceanothus, salal, oxalis, ferns.

Mammals: Although the park is small, the surroundings are sufficiently undeveloped to support populations of deer, skunk, raccoon, pine squirrel, and river otter, as well as seldom-seen bobcat, mountain lion, black bear, and porcupine.

Interpretation

Visitor center has information on local wildlife.

Campfire programs 4–5 times weekly, mid-June to Labor Day.

Guided hikes daily in summer. Children's programs.

Nature trail, ¾ mi., self-guided.

Activities

Camping: 30 sites, plus 6 environmental sites at Cheatham Grove, all year. Reservations Memorial Day—Labor Day.

Hiking: 4½ mi. of trails, longest 1¼ mi.

Fishing: Stream. Salmon, steelhead, trout.

Swimming: Stream, unsupervised.

Headquarters

CA Dept. of Parks and Recreation, 16949 Hwy 36, Carlotta, CA 95528; (707) 777-3683.

Heath and Marjorie Angelo Coast Range Preserve

U.S. Bureau of Land Management and the University of California 4,055 acres each.

From US 101 at Laytonville, W on Branscomb Rd. about 18 mi. N on Wilderness Lodge Rd. to HQ.

This was The Nature Conservancy's first CA project, established in 1956. In 1994 TNC transferred this area to the University of California. Only 480 of TNC's 4,000 acres had been logged when it acquired the site. On the South Fork of the free-flowing Eel River. The boundaries contain several watersheds. One, Elder Creek, is completely within the Preserve and virtually pristine. Terrain is hilly to mountainous, elevations ranging from about 1,200 to 4,209 ft. in the BLM section. The two streams above and Fox Creek have white water, cascades, and falls.

The only practical access to the BLM land, which includes the higher elevations, is through the UC site; even this is difficult because the terrain is rugged and there are no trails. Except for the elderly and disabled, visitors may not drive into the Preserve. They park outside and hike in. The interior road is narrow and winding, not suitable for vehicles with low clearance, high tops, or dual wheels.

Plants: 85% forested. Several thousand acres of old-growth Douglas-fir, undisturbed. Understory includes madrone, tan oak, California bay laurel, Oregon white oak, black oak, hazel, huckleberry. Also some black oak forest, knobcone pine community, chaparral, redwood groves, and meadows. Over 450 species of flowering plants have been identified, including various orchids, monkeyflower, brodiaea.

Birds: Checklist available. 120 species recorded. In fall and winter, ripening fruits of coffeeberry, poison oak, honeysuckle, and madrone attract many band-tailed pigeon, varied thrush, cedar waxwing, purple finch. Forest species include ruby-crowned and golden-crowned kinglets. Townsend's warbler, chestnut-backed chickadee, Hutton's vireo. Golden-crowned sparrow and dark-eyed junco are among the species frequenting the meadows. The checklist notes both seasonal abundance and favored habitats.

Mammals: Checklist of 42 species available. Often seen: river otter, black bear, cottontail, skunk, squirrel. Present but seldom seen: mountain lion, mink, gray fox.

Reptiles, amphibians: Checklist on request.

Interpretation

Small *visitor center* has displays.

Sugar Creek Nature Trail, ⅛ mi., with printed guide.

No pets, firearms, radios, ORVs. No hunting, fishing, or collecting.

Heavy rain can make winter visit inadvisable. High fire danger in summer/fall.

Publications

Leaflet with map.

Bird checklist.

Mammals of the Northern California Coast Range Preserve.

Field Guide to the Shrubs of the Northern California Coast Range Preserve.

Field Guide to the Trees of the Northern California Coast Range Preserve.

Nature trail guide.

Miscellaneous natural history pages.

Headquarters

Bureau of Land Management, 42101 Wilderness Rd., Branscomb, CA 95417; (707) 984-6653.

Hendy Woods State Park

California Department of Parks and Recreation
816 acres.

From Cloverdale on US 101, NW about 37 mi. on Hwy 128, then left on Greenwood Rd. ½ mi. to Park entrance.

Two virgin redwood groves. Park is on N slope of Greenwood Ridge, elevation 200 ft. Navarro River runs the length of Park, quiet in summer, a torrent after heavy winter rains. N portion of Hwy 128 is a scenic drive.

Plants: Big Hendy (80 acres) and Little Hendy (20 acres) have enormous old-growth redwoods, up to 16 ft. diameter, over 300 ft. tall. Other species include Douglas-fir, California bay laurel.

Birds: Include Steller's jay, varied thrush, olive-sided flycatcher, pileated woodpecker, great horned owl.

Interpretation

Campfire programs, guided walks, and *Junior Rangers* in summer.

Activities

Camping: 92 sites, all year. Reservations May 15–Sept. 30.

Hiking: 5 mi. of trails.

Fishing: Steelhead, salmon in fall and winter. Downstream of Philo-Greenwood Bridge.

Swimming: Marginal. River is too low by late summer.

Publication
Map with rules and directory of area businesses.

Headquarters
CA Dept. of Parks and Recreation, c/o Mendocino Area, Star Rt., Mendocino, CA 95460 (18599 Philo-Greenwood Rd., Philo, CA 95466); (707) 937-5804.

Humboldt Bay National Wildlife Refuge
U.S. Fish and Wildlife Service
2,110 acres.

The visitor facilities are located 7 mi. S of Eureka on US 101. Exit US 101 at Hookton Rd., go 1.2 mi. on Hookton Rd. Follow Watchable Wildlife signs to Hookton Slough trailhead.

Humboldt Bay, one of the most important stopover points along the Pacific Flyway, is the winter home for thousands of migratory ducks, geese, swans, and shorebirds. More than 200 bird species regularly feed, rest, or nest on the bay or in adjacent marshes and willow groves. The bay, which ranges from ½ to 4 mi. wide and 14 mi. long, consists of two shallow tidal basins, connected by a relatively narrow channel.

Habitat diversity in and around the bay is varied and includes mudflats, eelgrass beds, diked seasonal wetlands, sand spits, uplands, salt marsh, brackish marsh, and freshwater marsh. The eelgrass beds, along with extensive mudflats, provide habitat for large concentrations of waterbirds, especially black brant, which depend on Humboldt Bay in the fall, winter, and spring.

Wildlife viewing: Shorebird and waterfowl watching is excellent from late Oct.–April. Black brant and migratory shorebird populations peak from mid-March to late April. Summer visitors see many gulls, terns, cormorants, and pelicans, as well as resident egrets and herons. Harbor seals and small numbers of deer are visible year-round.

Activities

Camping: No campground on the Refuge, but public and private campgrounds are available within a 30-min. drive.

Hiking: Two interpreted trails—Hookton Slough and Shorebird Loop—are open to visitors; both are subject to seasonal, temporary closure. During peak waterbird migration, special winter tours may be arranged to areas without developed trails.

Fishing: Humboldt Bay and tidal sloughs are open to fishing year-round. Hookton Slough Trail is open to shore fishing; access to other areas is by boat. Surf fishing is available at nearly Table Bluff County Park.

Boating: Field Landing boat ramp is 3 mi. N of the Refuge office. Exit US 101 at Fields Landing.

Nearby

Arcata Marsh and Wildlife Sanctuary.

Samoa Dunes National Recreation Area.

Publications

General brochure with maps.

Hunting maps.

Headquarters

U.S. Fish and Wildlife Service, 1020 Ranch Rd., Loleta, CA 95551; (707) 733-5406.

....

Humboldt County Beaches

California Department of Parks and Recreation

See also entries for King Range National Conservation Area, Patrick's Point State Park, Redwood National and State Parks (this zone).

Hwy 1 turns away from the coast near Humboldt County's S border. The next 90 mi. N are California's "Lost Coast." Mountains rise steeply from the sea, so rugged as to discourage roadbuilding. Hillsides are forested, although some slopes have been logged or burned in recent years.

From Garberville, a steep but well-kept paved road crosses the mountains to Shelter Cove. From Dyerville, also on US 101, a longer paved road crosses the Humboldt Redwoods State Park, passes through Honeydew and Petrolia, and meets the coast S of Cape Mendocino. Near the Cape it turns inland again, rejoining US 101 NE of Ferndale.

The beach is wilderness, with few access points. Impassable below Shelter Cove, it can be hiked N, although some points are blocked by very high tides. Much land above the high-tide mark is privately owned, although undeveloped, but other sections are within the King Range National Conservation Area.

From Ferndale to Trinidad, a coastal plain extends as much as 5 mi. inland, with extensive salt marshes at Humboldt and Arcata bays.

Near Trinidad, the hills again come down to meet the sea. US 101 follows the coast to Orick. Beyond, to the county's N boundary, the coast is within redwood National and State Parks.

Includes

Eel River Wildlife Area (California Department of Fish and Game): 168 acres. S of Eureka. From US 101, Loleta exit. W on Cannibal Rd. to Crab Park; boat necessary to cross McNulty Slough. Or hike S along beach from Table Bluff, about 2 mi.

Narrow spit of land, about 2¼ mi. long, between the ocean and slough, at mouth of Eel River. Dunes to 25 ft. high. Much large driftwood. Many waterfowl in season, including pintail, wigeon, teal, scaup, scoter, loon. *Hiking, hunting,* and *fishing.*

Caution: 4-wheel-drive vehicles and dune buggies can often travel the beach from Table Bluff, but abrupt dropoff on surf side, rising tides, and sand traps are hazards.

Clam Beach/Little River State Beach: About 13 mi. N of Eureka, on US 101. Marked exits from US 101 lead to a parallel service road back of the dunes. Numerous trails cross the dunes, some of which are almost 100 ft. high. Dune vegetation includes brush, scrub trees. Sea is cold; few people swim. Fishing is said to be good in Little River, and children splash in the lagoon. Beach is undeveloped but popular on warm weekends. *Hiking* and *fishing.*

Trinidad State Beach: 159 acres. At Trinidad, on US 101. Popular small park in busy resort community, crowded with picnic parties on fine weekends. Sandy beach backed by high bluffs. Pewetole Island is close to the shore. Two short trails to scenic coves. Headlands overlook sea lion rock and puffin rookery, whale migration route. *Fishing.*

Humboldt Lagoon State Park: 1,500 acres. Includes Big, Dry, and Stone Lagoons. On US 101, 31 mi. N of Eureka. 5 mi. of sand beach, including long sand spit enclosing Big Lagoon. Much driftwood. Agate and black jade sometimes found. Surf usually heavy. *Hiking,* beach trails, S toward Patrick's Point State Park, N toward Redwood Creek; *fishing,* surf and lagoon. Boat in at Stone and Dry Lagoons.

Headquarters

CA Dept. of Parks and Recreation, N. Coast Redwoods District, 600 A West St., Eureka, CA 95501; (707) 445-6547.

Humboldt Redwoods State Park

California Department of Parks and Recreation
50,692 acres.

On US 101 45 mi. S of Eureka.

Largest of the redwood State Parks, and, in relation to its size, relatively underused. Most visitors see the Avenue of the Giants Parkway, a 33-mi. route paralleling US 101 along the South Fork of the Eel River. Many of the principal redwood groves, as well as campgrounds, are on or near this route. Most of the park acreage is W of US 101, crossed by a single secondary road and several trails.

Much of the forest is open and sunlit, mixed conifers and oaks. Entering a redwood grove, one is suddenly in deep shadow. The giant trees grow close together, the canopy blocking off the sun.

Elevation at the Avenue is about 150 ft. Highest point is Grasshopper Peak, 3,379 ft. Rainfall averages 64 in. per year, most of it Nov.–April. The river runs high and muddy until April, but as it clears it may be good for salmon and steelhead fishing. From April into early summer the river can be great for kayakers and canoes with ranger-led float trips. Snow is a rarity; winter temperatures are usually above freezing.

Park officials would like to encourage greater use of the backcountry, to relieve visitor pressure on redwood groves close to main highways.

Plants: Chief interest is the Coast redwood, many specimens over 300 ft. high, occurring both in pure stands and with other tree species such as Douglas-fir, lowland white fir, madrone, tan oak, bigleaf maple, California bay laurel. Spring flowers include dogwood, azalea, rhododendron, trillium, oxalis, fairy lantern, calypso orchid.

Birds: Include great and snowy egrets, great blue heron, golden eagle, turkey vulture, raven, osprey, common merganser, dipper, Steller's jay, varied and hermit thrushes, brown creeper, towhees, dark-eyed junco, pine siskin, winter wren, hermit warbler. Occasional sighting of wild turkey.

Mammals: Include mule deer, bobcat, skunk, raccoon, tree and ground squirrels, ringtail, river otter, chipmunk. Cougar, mink, fisher considered probable.

Reptiles, amphibians: Mountain and common kingsnakes, Pacific rattlesnake, common garter snake, Pacific giant salamander, clouded salamander, western fence and alligator lizards, California and rough-skinned newts, red-legged and yellow-legged frogs, tree frog.

Features

Rockefeller Forest, 9,000 acres, largest of the groves, includes one of the world's tallest trees at 362 ft.

Founder's Grove is dedicated to the early leaders of the Save-the-Redwoods League, organized in 1918.

Other groves along the Avenue of the Giants and elsewhere in the Park are named for sponsoring organizations and individuals.

The Bull Creek area, upstream, was outside the Park and had been logged. Damaging floods demonstrated that redwoods in the Park could not be saved unless the upper watershed was rehabilitated. Most of the watershed has been acquired, young redwoods planted. It is now good deer habitat.

Luke Prairie, an open, grassy ridge, has fine spring wildflowers, is a good place to look for hawks.

Interpretation

Visitor center has natural history exhibits, information, publications. Naturalist on site all year.

Campfire programs and *guided hikes* are offered occasionally in June, regularly July 1–Labor Day. Schedules are posted.

Nature trail at Founder's Grove.

Activities

Camping: 3 campgrounds, at least one open all year, 247 sites. Reservations May 1–Sept. 15.

Hiking: 55 mi. of trails, most shown on Park leaflet map. Grasshopper Peak trail is a 12-mi. round-trip from E. Backpacking has been prohibited, but is under consideration on a trial basis.

Fishing: Winter steelhead and salmon runs.

Swimming: River, unsupervised.

Horse riding: About 30 mi. of old logging and fire roads. Group horse camp.

Bicycling: On "bikecentennial" route. Hike and bike camp near Weott.

Boating: Kayaks and canoes are popular on ranger-led float trips in the spring and early summer.

Auto tour: Pick up brochure at either end of the 33-mi. tour of the Avenue of the Giants.

Publications

Leaflet with map.

Founder's Grove Nature Trail guide.

Species checklists.

Headquarters

CA Dept. of Parks and Recreation, P. O. Box 100, Weott, CA 95571; (707) 946-2409.

....

Jackson Demonstration State Forest

California Department of Forestry
50,000 acres.

Along Hwy 20; E of Fort Bragg on Hwy 1, W of Willits on US 101.

Mountainous; elevations from 200 to 1,948 ft. 90% forested: Coast redwood, Douglas-fir, tan oak, madrone, hemlock, beach and Bishop pines, red alder. Two areas of old-growth redwood. Logging has been continuous since the 1850s.

A Forest map is essential. Forest roads are not shown on highway road maps, and no signs on public roads identify the Forest land or Forest roads. The office is at Fort Bragg, not in the Forest.

Several streams, notably the South Fork of the Noyo River and North Fork of Big River.

Condition of Forest differs from area to area because of past and current logging. However, recreation is one of the management considerations, and logging is planned to maintain scenic, wildlife, and general recreation values.

Plants: Coast redwood, Douglas-fir, grand fir, hemlock, Bishop pine, tan oak, alder, madrone, bay, and wax myrtle. Shrubs include ceanothus, manzanita, huckleberry, rhododendron, sword and five-finger ferns, and poison oak. Flowers include wild iris, redwood sorrel, trillium, columbine, and golden yarrow.

Birds: List available. Osprey, turkey vulture, red-tailed hawk, California quail, spotted and screech owls, pileated woodpecker, raven, and wrens.

Mammals: Complete booklet available. Black bear, black-tailed deer, bobcat, mountain lion, raccoon, jackrabbit, skunk, wood rat, and other rodents.

Amphibians: Complete list available. Include giant salamander, red-bellied newt, and yellow-legged frog.

Fish: Coho salmon, steelhead trout, sculpin, and stickleback.

Features and Interpretation

Pygmy Forest, a Registered Natural Landmark, an area of cypress and pine stunted by high soil acidity and poor drainage.

Demonstration trails: 3 demonstration trails—Chamberlain Creek Demonstration Trail, Tree I.D. Trail, and Forest History Trail—with trail guides inform visitors about the history, management, and ecology of the forest.

Note: No motorized vehicles are allowed behind closed gates, barricades, or where posted. Campsites and roads may be closed anytime for maintenance, seasonal restrictions, or other reasons.

Activities

Camping: 2 campgrounds, 65 sites. All year; some seasonal. Permit must be obtained from camp hosts at Camp 1 (west end) or Dunlap Camp (east end). Outhouses. No potable water. Almost all sites near streams. Pets must be leashed in campgrounds. *Crowding is probable on opening weekend of deer season* in early Aug. and on major holidays.

Hiking: Chiefly on Forest and old logging roads.

Hunting: Deer. With permit, in season.

Mountain biking: Chiefly on Forest roads.

Horse riding.

Swimming.

Nearby

Russian Gulch State Park, Jug Handle State Reserve (see entries this zone). Both have common boundaries with the Forest, but no formal trails link them. Also see entries this zone for MacKerricher and Van Damme State Parks.

Publications

Forest leaflet with map.

Jackson State Forest at a Glance.

Forest History Trails.

Forest Management Demonstration Trail Guide.

Headquarters

CA Dept. of Forestry, 802 N. Main St., Fort Bragg, CA 95437; (707) 964-5674.

Jedediah Smith Redwoods State Park

See Redwood National and State Parks (this zone).

Jug Handle State Reserve

California Department of Parks and Recreation
1,800 acres.

From Mendocino, N about 6 mi. on Hwy 1.

Parking area on W side of highway, just S of bridge over Jug Handle Creek. Highway sign reads Ecological Staircase and Beach Parking. Trail from parking lot to small, sandy beach.

Exhibit explains that the "staircase" is a series of uplifted marine terraces, each about 100 ft. above the one before. Each step has a distinctive plant community. Unusual pygmy forest appears at fourth step.

Guided hikes upon request, check with HQ: (707) 937-5804.

Hiking: About 5 mi. of trails. Staircase trail from parking area goes underneath highway bridge. Trail map on bulletin board. Water on trail made boots a necessity.

Publication
Ecological Stairs: Self-Guided Tour of Jug Handle Reserve

King Range National Conservation Area

U.S. Bureau of Land Management
60,000 acres.

From US 101 just N of Garberville, W through Redway and about 20 mi. toward Shelter Cove.

On California's "Lost Coast," where rugged topography forces Hwy 1 far inland. The King Range extends about 35 mi. between the Mattole River and Whale Gulch. For most of this area, the coastal mountains rise steeply from the sea. The Lost Coast has miles of sandy beaches, some strewn with boulders, about a dozen coves where streams flowing through canyons meet the sea, and rocky headlands where breaking waves send spray high on the cliffs.

Hwy 1 crosses the ridge to Shelter Cove, a small seaside resort community. Grades are steep, but the road is paved and well maintained. Near the crest, it meets Kings Peak Rd., running N along the ridge, and Chemise Mountain Rd., running S. Both are classed as all-weather surfaces. Neither is suitable for trailers or large RVs. Both are scenic. Two BLM campgrounds are on each of them. Just outside the site boundary the Kings Peak Rd. meets Wilder Ridge Rd., which ends at Mattole Rd. in the town of Honeydew. A right turn leads through Humboldt Redwoods State Park. Those who like adventures on wheels should turn left. The 45 mi. from the Humboldt Redwoods to Ferndale is a scenic route known to a few Californians who would prefer others not know about it. Mountain driving.

Highest point in the King Range area is Kings Peak, 4,087 ft. The crest is generally above 2,000 ft., numerous peaks are higher than 2,500 ft. Terrain is rugged, the mountains deeply cut by drainages. On the W slopes, many short streams drop rapidly to the sea. Many cliffs, huge rock slides, talus piles. The E slopes, although also steep and rugged, are not so precipitous as the W side. Here streams drain into the Mattole River.

From Oct. to April, the King Range is one of the wettest places on the Pacific Coast, receiving about 100 in. of rain per year, more at higher elevations. Yet the appearance is not that of rain forest. Indeed, only three-fifths of the acreage is forested. The area has broad expanses of grass, especially in the N, and slopes are covered with coastal chaparral. The vegetation is the product of thin soils, rapid runoff, and long, hot summers. Winter temperatures rarely drop below freezing. Snow sometimes falls on the higher slopes but little accumulates.

Most of the site is N of the road to Shelter Cove. Only two all-weather roads descend to the coastline. Most of the area between the sea and the upper slopes is roadless, the shoreline a true wilderness beach.

The late Congressman Clem Miller introduced the legislation to preserve this wild area, legislation that was enacted in 1970, after his untimely death. The BLM is authorized to buy most of the private inholdings if owners offer to sell or exchange. The legislation restrains conflicting uses of tracts remaining in private hands.

Plants: Forest is mixed conifers and hardwoods. Principal species are Douglas-fir, tan oak, madrone, California bay laurel. Understory includes ceanothus, manzanita, black huckleberry, poison oak, ferns. The area includes a number of old-growth Douglas-fir and a unique stand of mature sugar pine on the E slopes. We asked about a burn near the Shelter Cove road and learned it had covered 14,000 acres, since replanted in Douglas-fir.

Plants of the coastal grassland and chaparral include wild oats, poison oak, filaree, annual rye. Beach strand has mostly annual forbs, sand verbena. Succulents along W-flowing streams with some alder and willow.

Prominent flowering species include ceanothus, madrone, dogwood, poppy, monkeyflower, lupine.

Birds: The BLM office has a bird list. Nearly 300 kinds of native and migratory birds have been spotted, including blue grouse, band-tailed pigeon, Steller's and scrub jays, kinglets, gnatcatchers, flycatchers, golden eagle, spotted owl, turkey vulture, red-tailed hawk, towhees, osprey, California murre, pigeon guillemot, mountain and California quail, brown pelican. Bald eagle occasionally seen on offshore rocks.

Mammals: Species recorded include Columbian black-tailed deer, raccoon, black bear, coyote, marten, weasel, ground squirrels, river otter, mink; Roosevelt elk S of Shelter Cove. Present but seldom seen: mountain lion, ringtail, bobcat, gray fox. Offshore: Steller sea lion, harbor seal, porpoise, gray and killer whales. Offshore rocks at Punta Gorda are a rookery for Steller sea lion and marine birds.

Reptiles, amphibians: Species include Northern Pacific rattlesnake, gopher snake, kingsnake, garter snake, rubber boa, yellow-bellied racer, Pacific giant salamander, speckled black salamander, rough-skinned newt, Pacific mud turtle, tailed frog.

Activities

Camping: 5 campgrounds, 48 sites. Primitive. Camping elsewhere on BLM land is permitted, unless signed otherwise, but suitable level sites are few.

Hiking, backpacking: Hiking the wilderness beach is one of the main attractions. The BLM recommends hiking N to S with the prevailing winds. From Mattole River trailhead to Telegraph Creek, near Shelter Cove, is 24 mi. Several points cannot be passed at very high tides. Rattlesnakes are common in driftwood and rocky areas. Several parcels of private lands are located on the beach. Please respect landowners' privacy. King Crest Trail is part of a trail system in the high country. Several trails connect the King Crest to the beach, offering loops of various lengths up to 34 mi. These trails are long, extended grades. Water is scarce and hard to find on the upper slopes, as are level campsites. Treat all water before drinking.

Hunting: Chiefly deer, bear.

Fishing: Saltwater angling for salmon, bottom fish, rock fish. On-shore fishing for perch and cod.

Boating: Launching at Shelter Cove, one of the few protected harbors along the coast.

Note: Off-road vehicles only along King Range coastline between Black Sands Beach and Gitchell Creek. Also, some dirt roads required 4-wheel-drive vehicles. *All dirt roads should be approached with caution in wet weather. Winter driving can be hazardous because of extremely high rainfall, slides, washouts, mud, occasional snow.* Vehicles should be in excellent condition, as repair facilities are miles away.

Nearby

Sinkyone Wilderness State Park (see entry this zone).

Publication
Map.

Headquarters
Bureau of Land Management, Arcata Resource Area, 1695 Heindon Rd., Arcata, CA 95521; (707) 825-2300.

....

Klamath National Forest

U.S. Forest Service
1,671,053 acres; 1,891,724 acres within boundaries. (Additional 26,564 acres in OR.)

From the OR border S, occupying most of Siskiyou County W of I-5. Another large section is E of Yreka on US 97.

Part of a huge complex of National Forests and other public lands covering much of N CA. The Klamath Forest is mountainous. It includes portions of the Klamath, Salmon, Siskiyou, Marble, Scott, and Cascade ranges. It adjoins the Shasta-Trinity National Forest on the S, Modoc National Forest on the E, Six Rivers National Forest on the W, and two OR National Forests, Rogue River and Siskiyou, on the N.

Elevations range from about 600 ft. to over 8,500 ft. The mountain ranges are generally narrow ridges, 5,000–8,000 ft., separated by deep canyons with steep walls. Principal rivers are the Klamath, Scott, and Salmon, listed as part of the Federal Wild and Scenic River System. River rafters and commercial outfitters migrate yearly to these rivers for class II–VI rafting and kayaking opportunities.

The rivers are fed by swift streams flowing through rugged canyons and mountain valleys. The Forest has many lesser streams and small, clear lakes.

Climate is generally moderate. Below-freezing temperatures are common in winter, especially at higher altitudes. Snowfall in the valleys is usually light. Some of the high passes have snow from early Nov. to mid-May, but roads are usually kept open. June–Oct. weather is usually fine: bright, warm days and cool nights.

Plants: The complex terrain produces a mosaic of life zones. Principal timber trees are ponderosa, sugar, western white, and Jeffrey pines, Douglas-fir, white and red firs, incense cedar, lodgepole pine, Port

Orford cedar. Other tree species include vine, dwarf, and bigleaf maples, live, Oregon white, and California black oaks, box, red, and white alders, Brewer and Engelmann spruces. Other plant species range from sagebrushes of dry slopes to ferns and mosses of moist canyons.

Birds: 284 species identified. Waterfowl include grebes, whistling swan, Canada, white-fronted, Ross's, and snow geese, wigeon, shoveler, blue-winged, green-winged, and cinnamon teals, wood duck, redhead, canvasback, bufflehead, scaups, common, red-breasted, and hooded mergansers. Many shorebird species. Birds of prey include bald and golden eagles, Cooper's, sharp-shinned, rough-legged, ferruginous, red-tailed, red-shouldered, and Swainson's hawks, and northern harrier. Broad-tailed, calliope, Anna's, Allen's, rufous, and black-chinned hummingbirds. Many woodpeckers, sapsuckers, swifts, flycatchers, swallows, jays, chickadees, nuthatches, thrushes, blackbirds, orioles, sparrows, wood warblers.

Mammals: Include elk, mule deer, mountain lion, bobcat, black bear, wolverine, coyote, red and gray foxes, otter, mink, marten, fisher, numerous shrews, moles, bats, squirrels, gophers, mice, voles, etc.

Features

Marble Mountain, Russian, Siskiyou, and Salmon–Trinity Alps Wildernesses: Almost a fourth of the Forest is wilderness. The Klamath contains all or part of four wilderness areas, totaling 387,000 acres. Most of the trail system accesses and traverses the Forest's extensive wilderness system. There are over 1,000 mi. of trails, including 116 mi. of the Pacific Crest Trail.

Activities

Camping: 32 campgrounds, 378 sites. Few open year-round; most open Memorial Day–Labor Day. Most campgrounds are located adjacent to Hwy 96, Scott River Rd.; others are along Salmon River Rd. and the Callahan-Forks of Salmon Rd. Camping is also at large.

Hiking, backpacking: Over 1,300 mi. of trails and more than 4,000 mi. of Forest roads that provide additional access for public use. High elevations normally snow free by mid-July, but this can vary.

Hunting: Principally deer, bear, small game.

Fishing: Klamath is best known as fishing country. Salmon and steelhead in the principal rivers fall and winter, rainbow trout in summer. Many smaller trout streams.

Swimming: River swimming at several campgrounds and at numerous trails leading to remote beaches along rivers.

Canoeing, kayaking, rafting: Klamath River. Class III water from Ash Creek Bridge to Beaver Creek; class II to confluence of Scott River; class III to Happy Camp, except class IV at points near Hamburg and Fort Goff. Careful trip planning recommended. The Salmon and Scott Rivers frequently retain higher class ratings but are dependent on snowpacks and rainfall to affect velocity and river flow.

Horse riding: A number of trails offer exceptional rides. Corrals at some trailheads. Contact HQ for locations.

Publications

Forest map.

Marble Mountain Wilderness map.

Russian Wilderness map.

Trinity Alps Wilderness map.

General Information.

Campground information.

Camping on the Klamath.

Packers' List for Outfitter-Guides.

Klamath Boating and Rafting Guide.

Checklists of birds, plants.

Available from CA Dept. of Fish and Game:

Anglers' Guide to the Klamath River.

Anglers' Guide to the Lakes and Streams of the Marble Mountains.

Anglers' Guide to the Lakes and Streams of the Salmon and Scott Mountains.

Headquarters

U.S. Forest Service, 1312 Fairlane Rd., Yreka, CA 96097; (916) 842-6131.

Ranger Districts

Goosenest R.D., Star 3, Box 175, Weed, CA 96094; (916) 398-4391 or 4343. Happy Camp R.D., Happy Camp, CA 96039; (916) 493-2243. Oak Knoll R.D., Klamath River, CA 96050; (916) 465-2241. Scott River R.D., Fort Jones, CA 96032; (916) 468-5351. Ukonom R.D., Somes Bar, CA 95568; (916) 469-3331.

MacKerricher State Park

California Department of Parks and Recreation
1,700 acres.

On Hwy 1, 3 mi. N of Fort Bragg.

Seacoast. 7 mi. of varied ocean frontage: some sheer cliffs, rocky areas, broad sandy beaches. Highest point about 50 ft. Many tidepools. Several miles of sand dunes N of the developed area, reached by hiking along beach.

Coastal prairie along the headlands. 25-acre Lake Cleone is within the developed area. About 20% of the site, on higher ground, is forested.

Plants: Great variety of wildflowers in season, including sea rocket, yellow sand verbena, baby blue eyes, ice plant, sea pink, cinquefoil, California poppy, paintbrush, wallflower, iris, buttercup. Forest species include Bishop, shore, and Monterey pines, tan oak, wax myrtle. Understory includes salal, thimbleberry, huckleberry, blackberry.

Birds: Checklist available. Park is not on a main flyway, but about 100 species recorded. Migratory sea- and shorebirds, many visiting Lake Cleone. Upland species include quail, scrub and Steller's jays, osprey, white-tailed kite, northern flicker, mountain bluebird, kingfisher, Wilson's and Audubon's warblers.

Mammals: Harbor seal live on the rocks just offshore, not far from the Seal Watching Station on the headland. Gray whale seen during migration. Deer, raccoon, striped skunk, weasel, gray fox, jackrabbit, gray and ground squirrels.

Tidepools: Great variety of marine fauna and flora, including sea and brittle stars, sea anemone, sea urchin, hermit crab, turban snail, limpet, chiton, abalone, periwinkle, mussel, kelp crab.

Interpretation

Scenic drive: A former logging road along 7 mi. of beach and dunes is open to pedestrians and bicyclists. The trestle across Pudding Creek is expected to reopen (foot and bike only) in 1998.

Nature trail around Lake Cleone, half of it usually under water in winter, early spring.

Campfire programs weekly in summer. *Guided hikes* and *tidepool walks* once or twice a week in summer. Notices posted. *Junior Ranger* program.

Activities

Camping: 142 sites. Reservations May 1–Sept. 30. Campground usually full from end of school to mid-Sept.

Hiking: Beach and headlands.

Fishing: Surf. Lake stocked with trout.

Horse riding: Trail along beach. But horses may not be kept in park.

Canoeing, kayaking: Nonmotorized boating at Lake Cleone.

Bicycling

Caution: High winds can cause tree hazards. Portions of campground may be closed during high winds, most common winter and spring.

Publications

Leaflet with map.

Bird checklist.

Headquarters

CA Dept. of Parks and Recreation, Mendocino Area, P.O. Box 440, Mendocino, CA 95460; (707) 937-5804 or 964-9112.

Mailliard Redwoods State Reserve

California Department of Parks and Recreation
242 acres.

From Cloverdale on US 101, 20 mi. NW on Hwy 128; left on Fish Rock Rd.

200-acre grove of Coast redwoods. Forested site crossed by creek that is source of Garcia River. Elevation 1,000 ft.

Nearby

Hendy Woods State Park (see entry), another small park with redwood groves, and Paul M. Dimmick Wayside Campground, which has large second-growth redwoods, are also along this route from Cloverdale to the coast.

Call (707) 937-5804 for general information.

Mendocino County Beaches

See also entries this zone for MacKerricher State Park, Russian Gulch State Park, Van Damme State Park.

From the county's S boundary, Hwy 1 closely follows the coast. Most through traffic uses US 101, farther inland, leaving the coastal route to those with time to enjoy its spectacular views of the sea.

For much of the distance, headlands rise abruptly from the shore. Sandy beaches are isolated between rocky points. Back of the headlands is a plateau, often quite narrow, usually grassy, occasionally wooded, hills rising to the E. At times a fringe of trees forms a screen between the road and the sea, but soon the road is again near the edge. Close to shore are many small islands that attract seals, sea lions, and seabirds.

Large sections of the plateau are privately owned and posted against trespassing. Although there are available routes to many beaches, the scalloped shoreline limits hiking; rocky points are effective barriers. A few beaches are more extensive, offering opportunities to hike for several miles. In several places, headlands are replaced by sand dunes.

Coastal hillside forests include such species as Bishop pine, madrone, and Coast live oak. River canyons are moister; here are Coast redwood with dense growths of ferns and mosses.

Includes

Gualala Point Regional Park: 150 acres. 1 mi. S of Gualala on Hwy 1. Sand spit at mouth of Gualala River. *Camping:* 18 sites.

Manchester State Beach: 760 acres. Central area, including campground: from Manchester, 1 mi. N on Hwy 1 then W on Kinney Lane. Dunes area: about 1 mi. S of Manchester, then W on Stonesboro Rd. Alder Creek area: about 2 mi. N of Manchester, then NW on Alder Creek Rd. *Camping, fishing, swimming, boating.*

3½ mi. of sand beach. Much driftwood. Sand dunes, stabilized by plants, slowly evolving into prairie grassland. Spring wildflowers include sea pinks, poppies, lupines, baby blue eyes, wild iris. Central portion is popular picnic area, often crowded on weekends. *Camping:* 46 sites; *hiking; fishing.*

Mendocino Headlands State Park: 131 acres. Coast, at town of Mendocino. Wave action has cut deeply into the headlands, forming caves, arches, and small islands separated from the mainland and each other by narrow channels. Waves pile high in these channels, breaking over the lower islands, sending white water high on the cliffs. Prairie back of the headlands is trampled in places, elsewhere has abundant wildflowers. Sweeping vistas up and down the coast. Essentially a town park, but scenic, a pleasant place to walk a mile or so. *Hiking* and *fishing.*

Westport–Union Landing State Beach: 41 acres. 1½ mi. N of Westport on Hwy 1. About 2½ mi. of moderately rugged coast. Long roadside parking area, an extended overlook. No facilities. At the time of our visit, no sign identified this as state land. No signs prohibited roadside camping, and several RVs had parked overnight. *Fishing.*

Mendocino National Forest
U.S. Forest Service

About 170,000 acres of this Forest are in zone 1, but the entry appears in zone 3, where most of the Forest is located. The zone 1 portion is on the W slope of the Coast Range, chiefly in Mendocino County, crossed by a secondary road E from Covelo.

Montgomery Woods State Reserve
Cailfornia Department of Parks and Recreation
1,142 acres.

From Ukiah on US 101, about 11 mi. NW on Comptche Rd.

On Big River headwaters. One of the finest groves of Coast redwoods. No development except trails. An exceptional display of woodwardia ferns, 7–8 ft. tall. Road continues 34 mi. to Van Damme State Park (see entry).

Information:
(707) 937-5804.

Patrick's Point State Park

California Department of Parks and Recreation
640 acres.

25 mi. N of Eureka on US 101.

Headland of forest and meadow with broad, sandy beach jutting into the sea. Main portion is up to 200 ft. above the sea. Steep bluffs, constantly eroded by sea, rain, wind. Agate Beach, reached by short, steep trail, extends 2 mi. N. Semiprecious stones often found. Much driftwood. To S are steep, craggy inlets, rugged promontories. Steep trails down the cliffs.

Temperature moderate all year, but ocean too cold for swimming.

Plants: Forest of spruce, hemlock, pine, fir, red alder. Dense understory of salal, huckleberry, blackberry, azalea, rhododendron.

Birds: Include Steller's jay, Wilson's warbler, chestnut-backed chickadee, wrentit, many shorebirds.

Mammals: Include sea lions on islands close inshore, black-tailed deer. Gray whales often seen during migration.

Features and Interpretation

Ceremonial Rock, viewpoint, 100-ft. climb from meadow. Trails to promontories: *Wedding Rock, Rocky Point, Abalone Point, Palmer Point.*

Naturalist programs, mid-June through Labor Day. *Nature trail.*

Restoration of *Yurok Village.*

Activities

Camping: 3 campgrounds, 124 sites. All year. Reservations Fri. before Memorial Day–Labor Day, (800) 444 7275.

Hiking: 2-mi. Rim Trail, Forest trails. Agate Beach.

Publication

Leaflet with map.

Headquarters

CA Dept. of Parks and Recreation, 4150 Patrick's Point Dr., Trinidad, CA 95570; (707) 677-3570.

Prairie Creek Redwoods State Park

See Redwood National and State Parks.

Redwood National and State Parks

U.S. National Park Service

Del Norte Coast Redwoods State Park
Jedediah Smith Redwoods State Park
Prairie Creek Redwoods State Park

California Department of Parks and Recreation
110,246 acres.

US 101 between Orick and Crescent City.

These four redwood parks are contiguous, and a single Park leaflet describes all four areas. The great Coast redwoods once covered about 2 million acres. Fewer than 135,000 acres of original growth remain. The Save-the-Redwoods League, organized in 1918, raised sufficient funds to preserve over half of this remaining acreage, now in these and other State Parks. In 1994, a Memorandum of Understanding between the National Park Service and the CA Department of Parks and Recreation was signed. The two agencies work together in all aspects of Park management. The Parks are a World Heritage Site and International Biosphere Reserve protecting resources important to many nations.

The Park area is long and narrow with about 3½ mi. of coastline. Rolling hills and coastal bluffs. Some sandy beaches, others rocky and inaccessible. Numerous streams, including Redwood Creek, Prairie Creek, Smith River. Climate is mild and humid. Annual precipitation is 80–100 in., most of it Nov.–March.

Many of the magnificent redwood groves can be seen from US 101 and US 199, or by a short stroll from a parking area. Much more can be seen away from these main highways. Although there is no wilderness area, one can find quiet trails.

Plants: Redwoods occur both in pure stands and with other species. Redwoods grow rapidly, live up to 2,000 yeas. Average mature trees are 200–240 ft. tall, 10–15 ft. in diameter. Exceptional specimens attain 350 ft. in height, diameter over 20 ft. Coast redwoods are the world's tallest trees. In groves they grow surprisingly close together, their canopy casting deep shade on the forest floor.

Associated species are Douglas-fir, western hemlock, tan oak, madrone, California bay laurel. Inland, redwoods are replaced by Douglas-fir or Jeffrey pine. Understory includes redwood sorrel, rhododendron, huckleberry, salal, many ferns. Prairies, naturally occurring "balds," form openings on hillsides favorable for wildlife.

Rivers and streams are often lined with alder, bigleaf and vine maples. Coastal scrub vegetation is diverse, including wild strawberry, lupine, cow parsnip, paintbrush, stonecrop, silk tassel, ceanothus, coyote brush, with thick stands of red alder, Sitka spruce.

Birds: Checklists available for Redwood National and State Parks and Prairie Creek Redwoods State Park. Common residents include pied-billed grebe, cormorants, mallard, cinnamon teal, common merganser, white-tailed kite, northern harrier, Cooper's and red-tailed hawks, kestrel, blue grouse, California quail, great blue heron, Virginia rail, black oystercatcher, killdeer, spotted sandpiper, western gull, common murre, pigeon guillemot, Cassin's auklet, marbled murrelet (see over Boyes Prairie July, Aug., early Sept.), screech, great horned, and barn owls, northern flicker, black phoebe, Steller's jay, raven, chestnut-backed chickadee, winter, Bewick's, and marsh wrens, robin, varied thrush, purple and house finches, savannah and white-crowned sparrows. Many migrants.

Mammals: Checklist available. Includes among common residents: various species of shrew, Townsend mole, little brown myotis, brush rabbit, beaver, ground squirrel, Townsend chipmunk, pocket gopher, various mice, porcupine, coyote, gray fox, raccoon, skunks, bobcat, mountain lion, Roosevelt elk, mule deer, some black bear. Also harbor seal, river otter. Regular visitors include elephant seal, California sea lion, Steller sea lion.

Elk herd often seen along highway and near campground at Prairie Creek Redwoods State Park.

Tidepools: Variety of marine fauna and flora seen at low tides, including sea cucumber, crab, snails, etc.

Features

Tall Trees Grove, reached by Redwood Creek Trail or, in summer, by shuttle bus. *Lady Bird Johnson Grove* on Bald Hill Rd. Several groves in Prairie Creek Redwoods State Park reached by short trails from parking lot near main entrance. Many other groves along highway and foot trails. Jedediah Smith Redwoods State Park has 36 memorial groves, including 5,000-acre *National Tribute Grove.*

Fern Canyon, reached by Davison Rd., near coast, has 50-ft. walls, masses of ferns. Nearby is *Gold Bluffs Beach.*

Scenic drives, in addition to US 101 and US 199: *Bald Hill Rd.,* N of Orick, E of US 101; *Davison Rd.,* to Fern Canyon; *Coastal Drive,* about 8 mi., from US 101 S of Klamath; *Requa Rd.,* W of US 101, to trailhead for Coastal Trail, exhibits; *Enderts Beach Rd.,* S of Crescent City, to Crescent Beach, Enderts Beach; *Howland Hill Rd.,* in Jedediah Smith Redwoods State Park, through old-growth redwood forest. Several of these roads are unpaved, narrow, unsuitable for trailers, large RVs.

Interpretation

Information at ranger information station on US 101 S of Orick; open daily, 8–5, until 8 P.M. in summer. Exhibits, publications.

Park HQ is at Crescent City, Second and K Sts.; open weekdays 8–5; daily April–Nov.; until 7 P.M. in summer.

Hiouchi Ranger Station on US 199, open 8–7 in summer only.

Prairie Creek HQ also has information, exhibits.

Nature trails: at Lady Bird Johnson Grove; Yurok Loop Trail near Lagoon Creek; Revelation Trail, near Prairie Creek HQ, for both blind and sighted people.

Campfire programs and *guided hikes* at campgrounds in summer. Notices posted.

Shuttle bus tours in summer.

Activities

Camping: In State Parks only. 4 campgrounds, 378 sites. All year. Reservations May 25–Oct. 1. *Campgrounds generally full July–Sept. 15.*

Hiking, backpacking: Limited backpacking opportunities; inquire. Over 150 mi. of foot trails, round-trips of a few minutes to 8 hr. Trails through redwood groves, other forest, along bluffs, beach. Leaflets of all 4 parks show some trails; trail map for sale.

Fishing: Surf, river. Steelhead, salmon, trout.

Swimming: Smith River, in Jedediah Smith.

Canoeing, kayaking: Seasonally in Smith River. Organized daily kayak trips in summer.

Adjacent
Six Rivers National Forest (see entry this zone).

Publications
Leaflets with maps, all 4 units.

Trail map.

Redwood National Park Visitor Guide, published seasonally.

Nature trail guides, available at sites.

Interpretive folder.

Forest rehabilitation folder.

Headquarters
Del Norte Coast Redwoods State Park, P.O. Drawer J, Crescent City, CA 95531; (707) 458-3115. Jedediah Smith Redwoods State Park, P.O. Drawer J, Crescent City, CA 95531; (707) 464-9533. Prairie Creek Redwoods State Park, Orick, CA 95555; (707) 488-2171. Redwood National Park, 1111 Second St., Crescent City, CA 95531; (707) 464-6101.

Richardson Grove State Park
California Department of Parks and Recreation
1,500 acres.

8 mi. S of Garberville, on US 101.

Fine groves of giant redwoods, the tallest 337½ ft., diameter of 13 ft. About 200 mi. N of San Francisco on US 101. The Park attracts half a million visitors annually. Campground often fills during the summer. A store and gift shop and a visitor center are located in old lodge building. Many trails, including Durphy Creek, Woodland, Lookout Toumey, and Settler's, lead visitors through this beautiful area.

Plants: Trees include Douglas-fir, tan and canyon oaks, madrone, bigleaf maple, red alder. Understory of huckleberry, salal, and California bay laurel. Wildflowers include calypso orchid, bush monkeyflower, inside-out flower, trillium, redwood lily, firecracker flower, fairy bells, and oxalis. Ferns are 3–4 ft. tall.

Birds: Osprey, great blue heron, dipper, bald eagle, merganser, robin, varied thrush, western meadowlark, western tanager, black phoebe, California towhee, brown creeper, chestnut-backed chickadee, dark-eyed junco, hermit thrush, pileated woodpecker, northern flicker, and belted kingfisher.

Mammals: Pacific and other shrews, long-eared bat, gray fox, ground squirrel, deer mouse, brush rabbit, black-tailed jackrabbit, redwood white-footed mouse, Townsend chipmunk, chickaree, western gray squirrel, pocket gopher, flying squirrel, otter, spotted skunk, raccoon, mule deer, coyote, mink, bobcat, and mountain lion.

Reptiles, amphibians: Northern Pacific rattlesnake, California king snake, common king snake, rubber boa, several types of garter snake, salamanders, newts, lizards, and frogs.

Interpretation
Visitor center (books and other related publications); *guided hikes; children's* and *campfire programs.*

Activities
Camping: 3 campgrounds, 169 sites. One campground open all year. All 3 open in summer. Reservations May 1–Sept. 30th.

Hiking: Guided hikes, 3 days a week, 4 hiking trails, varying in length from 1 to 3 mi.

Fishing: River. Mainly for squaw.

Swimming: In the water hole. No lifeguard on duty.

Other Units
Benbow Lake State Recreation Area; Smithe Redwoods State Reserve and Standish-Hickey State Recreation Area (see entries this zone).

Publication
Park map, $1.50.

Headquarters
CA Dept. of Parks and Recreation, Richardson Grove State Park, 1600 US 101 #8, Garberville, CA 95542; (707) 247-3318.

Rogue River National Forest

U.S. Forest Service
54,016 acres in CA.

No practical road access from CA.

Most of this 630,000-acre Forest is in OR. A portion extends into CA, where it has a common boundary with the Klamath National Forest (see entry this zone). A section of the Pacific Crest Trail lies along this boundary. Only foot and jeep trails enter from CA. Best access is from OR Hwy 238, turning S at Ruch, entering the Forest at McKee Bridge, and continuing S into CA to the trailhead at Cook and Green. The campground here is a popular base for backpacking, trail riding, and hunting.

The region is mountainous. The highest peaks, 6,000 to 7,000 ft., are on the boundary between the two National Forests. Numerous creeks and intermittent streams flow generally N.

Publication
Forest map, $3.25.

Headquarters
U.S. Forest Service, P.O. Box 520, Medford, OR 97501; (541) 858-2200.

Russian Gulch State Park

California Department of Parks and Recreation
1,209 acres.

2 mi. N of Mendocino on Hwy 1.

Remarkable diversity in a relatively small area: coastal headlands, sand beach, redwood forest, fern canyon, abundant wildlife. Site is a long oblong extending inland for about 3 mi. along Russian Gulch. Broken headlands, cliffs up to 100 ft., fine views up and down the coast. *Devil's Punch Bowl:* a sea-cut tunnel about 200 ft. long has collapsed at inland end to form a blowhole—although "blowing" occurs only in storms. Some tidepools.

Plants: Canyon is deep, moist, with second-growth, large Coast redwood and Douglas-fir. Associated species: tan oak, hemlock, California bay laurel; alder and bigleaf maple beside stream. Many rhododendron, ferns, spring wildflowers.

Birds: Include osprey, red-tailed hawk, kingfisher, band-tailed pigeon, great blue heron, California quail, raven, Steller's jay, sea- and shorebirds.

Mammals: Include raccoon, rabbit, chipmunk, mule deer, skunk, bobcat, gray fox.

Feature
Russian Gulch Falls, 36 ft., reached by Fern Canyon Trail.

Activities
Camping: 30 sites. April–Oct. Reservations.

Hiking: Several trails can be combined in a 9-mi. loop, through canyon, forest.

Fishing: Ocean.

Swimming: Sheltered beach. Cold water.

Bicycling: Canyon Bike Trail, ½ mi.

Adjacent
Jackson Demonstration State Forest (see entry). No formal trails link the two sites.

Nearby
Jug Handle State Reserve, Van Damme State Park (see entries this zone).

Publication
Leaflet with map.

Headquarters
CA Dept. of Parks and Recreation, P.O. Box 440, Mendocino, CA 95460; (707) 937-5804.

Shasta-Trinity National Forests

U.S. Forest Service
2,132,892 acres. 2,862,101 acres within boundaries.

NE and S and W of Redding. W portion is crossed by Hwy 299, E portion by Hwy 89. Many access routes E and W of I-5.

A vast area, part of a complex of 5 contiguous National Forests in northern CA. Several large sections of the Forest are a checkerboard, with private and Forest lands alternating in 1-mi. squares, but this is not conspicuous on site. Forest roads and foot trails cross both private and public land. An occasional house or commercial establishment is the principal indication of inholdings.

Terrain includes gently rolling plateaus, river valleys, steep-walled canyons, ridges, high mountains. Highest point is Mount Shasta, 14,161 ft. Forest includes 131 natural lakes, 11 reservoirs, 1,900 mi. of fishable rivers and streams. Although the Forest receives over 5 million visitors annually, they concentrate in several popular recreation sites in the warm months. At any season it is possible to find quiet, secluded areas.

Climate in lower sections is moderate: warm, dry summers; cool, wet winters. More than half the annual precipitation is in Dec.–Feb. Snowfall is light; depth of 6 in. is seen only once in 25 years. Much more cold and snow at higher elevations.

Whiskeytown-Shasta-Trinity National Recreation Area has 3 units. Clair Engle and Lewiston Lakes unit and Shasta Lake unit are within National Forest boundaries and are administered by Forest Service. Whiskeytown unit (see entry zone 2) is outside the boundaries and is administered by National Park Service.

Plants: Ponderosa pine and Douglas-fir are the principal tree species of the Forest, but many other conifer species occur. Gray pine, for example, is found below 4,500 ft. elevation, incense cedar at 3,500 to 6,000, Jeffrey pine 3,500 to 7,000, knobcone pine 1,000 to 5,600, whitebark pine 7,000 to 10,000. Others, also with characteristic ranges, are foxtail pine, lodgepole pine, mountain hemlock, Pacific yew, Port Orford cedar, red fir, sugar pine, western juniper, western white pine, white fir. Hardwood species include black oak, white oak, tan oak, canyon live oak, bigleaf maple, black cottonwood, Pacific madrone.

Widely distributed shrubs include ceanothus, deer brush, snow bush, mountain lilac, poison oak. Many wildflower species, including tiger lily, pitcher plant, columbine, Indian pink, Indian paintbrush, spreading phlox, bleeding heart, fireweed, shooting star, mountain pennyroyal, mountain violet, buttercup, monkeyflower. Great variety of alpine plants; over 400 species identified on Mount Shasta.

Birds: No checklist available. Common species include bald eagle, osprey, red-tailed, red-shouldered, Cooper's, and sharp-shinned hawks, goshawk, kestrel, turkey vulture, raven, Steller's and scrub jays, red-winged blackbird, acorn, hairy, downy, and Lewis' woodpeckers, robin, California and mountain quails, savannah, rufous-crowned, white-crowned, golden-crowned, fox, song, and house sparrows, dark-eyed junco, western tanager, black-capped, mountain, and chest-nut-backed chickadees, Nashville, yellow, hermit, Wilson's, and McGillivray's warblers, calliope, Anna's, and rufous hummingbirds, killdeer, great blue heron, dipper.

Mammals: No checklist available. Include black bear, mule deer, rac-coon, ringtail, beaver, striped skunk, bobcat, mountain lion, coyote, gray fox, Townsend chipmunk, golden-mantled, gray, and northern flying squirrels, chickaree.

Features

Yolla Bolly–Middle Eel Wilderness: 111,000 acres. Includes a portion of the Mendocino National Forest (see entry this zone). Wild, rugged country on the headwaters of the Middle Fork, Eel River, bounded by the North and South Yolla Bolly Mountains. Mountains are rounded, heavily forested. The area is scenic, though not dramatic. Average elevations 2,000–4,000 ft., with peaks over 8,000 ft. For those who seek solitude, this area is choice. Visitor use is light. Yet most of the area is open for hiking by late May, earlier than most CA wildernesses. Ridges have a mixture of dense stands of pine and fir with open meadows. Lower slopes are a combination of conifers and chaparral. Good fishing in several creeks, but water is generally scarce and springs are usually dry by late summer. Trail map available. Wilderness permit required.

Trinity Alps Wilderness: 225,200 acres. Along the headwaters of the Salmon and Trinity Rivers in the NW sector of the Forest, partially within the Klamath National Forest (see entry this zone). Various access routes from Hwy 299 and Hwy 3 near Weaverville. This is the second-largest wilderness area in CA. Spectacular scenery. High, rough mountain ridges, deep glacial canyons, peaks 7,000–9,000 ft. Mixed stands of timber; some brush-covered slopes; huge talus boulders above timberline. Annual precipitation is about 50 in.; snowfall in some high places up to 12 ft. Frost-free period is usually July 1–Sept. 15. Wildflower blooming peak July–Aug. Many lakes and streams. *Good hunting, fishing. Wilderness permit required.*

Mount Shasta: 14,162 ft., rising over 10,000 ft. from its base, 7,000 ft. higher than nearby peaks in the Cascade Range. Everitt Memorial Hwy, from Mount Shasta City, 14 mi. to just below the 7,800-ft. level. Timberline at about 8,000 ft. About 16,700 acres, largely above timberline, proposed for wilderness status. Area includes 5 living glaciers, hot spring, Shastina Crater, Clarence King Lake. A variety of *hiking trails* to the top. Map information available at Ranger District office.

Castle Crags Wilderness: 7,300 acres. Noted for the unique granite spires found here and in adjacent Castle Crags State Park. Numerous streams, 6 alpine lakes. Wide range of elevation; highest point 7,078 ft. Near Pacific Crest Trail.

Medicine Lake Volcanic Highlands: NE sector. A 2-hr. drive from McCloud to Medicine Lake. Miles of colorful volcanic formations. Volcanic glass mountain, spatter cones, ice caves. Fine vista from fire tower on Little Mount Hoffman. Check at ranger station in McCloud before entering the Highlands sector.

Shasta Lake: California's largest artificial lake, with a 370-mi. shoreline. Water-based recreation attracts many visitors, and shore points reached by road are crowded in season. However, regulations have kept the water clean, and it is one of the few large CA lakes where *shoreline camping* is permitted away from established campgrounds. More than 20 Forest Service *campgrounds* around the shoreline, including 4 that can be reached only by boat. Several foot trails leave from or link shore points. *Houseboating* is popular. *Fishing* is popular, best in cool weather.

Clair Engle Lake, with 150 mi. of shoreline, is also a focus for *water-based recreation.* Nearby, smaller *Lewiston Lake* is mostly for *fishing,* boat speed limited to 10 mph. The lakes are the center of the Trinity unit, National Recreation Area. *Many campgrounds.* Trails lead into the nearby Trinity Alps Wilderness.

Black Butte, 6,325 ft., N of Mount Shasta, is a cinder cone. 2½-mi. trail leads past various volcanic formations to fire lookout at peak. Visitors welcome but must bring own water.

Castle Lake is 11 mi. from Mount Shasta City by adequate road. *Camping, fishing.* Short trail to Little Castle Lake, scenic area. Pacific Crest Trail is nearby.

Scenic drives: Many Forest roads have high scenic value. Outstanding is Hwy 299 along the Trinity River.

Interpretation

Interpretive programs chiefly at the two National Recreation Areas, Shasta Lake and Trinity.

Visitor information at U.S. Forest Service, Weaverville. *Visitor center* at S end of Clair Engle Lake, Trinity area. At Lake Shasta, visitor information at Shasta Lake Ranger District, Mountain Gate exit from I-5.

Campfire programs at several campgrounds in Recreation Areas. Schedules posted. Also *guided hikes, nature trails.*

Activities

Camping: More than 75 campgrounds, 1,393 sites. Most sites open May 15–Sept. 15, and, according to Forest Service, "as needed or as the weather permits during the balance of the year." Forest has several campgrounds available on National Recreation Reservation System: (800) 280-CAMP; inquire if you plan summer visit. Camping outside campgrounds is permitted, subject to area restrictions and required fire permit.

Hiking, backpacking: About 3,100 mi. of trails. 150 mi. of Pacific Crest Trail. Trail is generally E-W, elevations 2,400–7,200 ft. Crosses Trinity Alps Wilderness where wilderness permit is required. Trail map shows current trail conditions. 400-mi. trail system in Trinity Alps area. Yolla Bolly area also has many trails. Topo maps of both available. Many trails for day hiking; those most heavily used begin at the National Recreation Areas. An interesting new trail, Sisson-Callahan, begins at Siskiyou Lake, SW of Mount Shasta City, follows North Fork of Sacramento River W, meeting Pacific Crest Trail near Deadfall Lakes. Map available.

Weaverville Ranger District office has a large loose-leaf book describing trails and destinations: topo maps, color photos, precise information on trail conditions, water, campsites. Many destinations are small lakes.

Backpacking begins in spring, but snow limits access to high country.

Forest map does not show contours. Forest Service Wilderness maps are topos, essential for backcountry travel. Points that appear close together on Forest map may be separated by sawtooth ridges, a difficult day's climb.

Hunting: Deer, bear, small game.

Fishing: Many opportunities: lakes, rivers, streams. Trout, bass, other species.

Swimming: Mostly in lakes. Unsupervised.

Boating: Marinas, ramps, rentals, other facilities at Shasta and Clair Engle lakes. Small motors, 10 mph limit, on Lewiston Lake.

Canoeing: On smaller lakes, some rivers. Whitewater opportunities on South Fork of the Trinity River.

Pack trips, horse riding: Forest Service says, "Six pack stations serving the area." If you bring your own stock, consult District Ranger; it may be necessary to carry feed. Hundreds of miles of trails are suitable for horses.

Ski touring: Special area on Mount Shasta. Elsewhere as conditions permit.

Snowmobiling: Good terrain in McCloud-Mount Shasta area.

Note: In dry periods, when fire hazard is high, special restrictions apply. Under extreme conditions, some Forest areas are closed; low-risk areas are exempt.

Adjacent:
Klamath, Mendocino, Six Rivers National Forests (see entries this zone). Castle Crags State Park, Lassen (see entries zone 2).

Nearby
Whiskeytown unit, Whiskeytown-Shasta-Trinity National Recreation Area (see entry zone 2).

Publications
Forest map, $3.25.

Visitor information map.

Campground information and directory.

Information sheets for Yolla Bolly-Middle Eel and Trinity Alps Wilderness areas.

Leaflets

Trees of the Trinity.

Wildflowers of the Trinity.

Birds of the Trinity.

Wildlife of the Trinity.

Geology of the Mount Shasta Area.

Shasta Lake Recreation Area.

Trinity Recreation Area.

Mount Shasta, A Climber's Guide.

Pacific Crest Trail, current information, trail maps.

Sisson-Callahan Trail map.

Mount Shasta Ski Park brochures.

Headquarters
U.S. Forest Service, 2400 Washington Ave., Redding, CA 96001; (916) 246-5222.

Ranger Districts
Big Bar R.D., Big Bar, CA; (916) 623-6106. Hayfork R.D., P.O. Box 159, Hayfork, CA 96041; (916) 628-5227. McCloud R.D., P.O. Box 1620, McCloud, CA 96057; (916) 964-2184. Mount Shasta R.D., 204 W. Alma, Mount Shasta, CA 96067; (916) 926-4511. Shasta Lake R.D., 14225 Holiday Dr., Redding, CA 96001; (916) 257-1587. Weaverville R.D., P.O. Box 1190, Weaverville, CA 96093; (916) 623-2121. Yolla Bolly R.D., Platina, CA 96076; (916) 352-4211.

Sinkyone Wilderness State Park
California Department of Parks and Recreation
7,312 acres.

Usal Beach Campground entered from Hwy 1 at milepost 90.88 via Mendocino County Rd. 431. Needle Rock entered via Briceland Rd. in Redway.

Rugged, undeveloped coastline; steep coastal mountains. About 5½ mi. of seacoast.

Plants: Coastal bench is grassland; inland areas are heavily forested with mixed conifers and Coast redwood; understory contains white-thorn, chamise, huckleberry.

Mammals: Herd of 50–60 Roosevelt elk; mule deer, fox, squirrels, raccoon, porcupine, occasional black bear. Seals and sea lions common. Gray whales are seen migrating N in spring.

Activities

Camping: Car camping at Usal Campground. Hike-in camping at many locations. Primitive campsites have picnic table, fire ring, and pit toilets. Group camping facilities at Usal Beach. Bring your own water and firewood. Fees vary.

Hiking, backpacking: 16.7-mi. Lost Coast Trail.

Fishing: Surf.

Mountain biking: 7½-mi. bike trail.

Horse riding: Horses are permitted on roads as well as equestrian trails. Horse camping at Usal, Needle Rock, and Wheeler Trail Camps.

Dogs are permitted only in certain camping areas and on certain trails. *They must be on leash at all times.*

Caution: The last 15 mi. of access road are narrow and unpaved. *Trailers, motor homes, and pickups cannot negotiate this road. In wet weather, 4-wheel-drive vehicles may be necessary.* For road and trail conditions, call (707) 986-7711.

Nearby
King Range National Conservation Area (see entry this zone).

Publication
Park brochure, $1.50.

Headquarters
CA Dept. of Parks and Recreation, Sinkyone Wilderness State Park, P.O. Box 245, Whitethorn, CA 95589; (707) 986-7711.

Six Rivers National Forest

U.S. Forest Service
958,470 acres. 1,092,170 acres within boundaries.

From OR border to point E of Garberville. Crossed by Hwys 199, 96, 299, and 36.

Reaching S from the OR border in a long and narrow 140-mi. band, this Forest offers an unparalleled range of river experiences for water enthusiasts and other recreationists. The Forest contains over 1,500 mi. of permanent waterways, of which 366 are wild, scenic, or recreational rivers; this represents 35% of California's Wild and Scenic Rivers. Congressionally designated 305,000-acre Smith River National Recreation Area (NRA) highlights the Smith River, the last major undammed and undiverted river in CA and one of the largest Wild and Scenic River Systems in the U.S. Coastal mountains are cut by the valleys of 6 major rivers: Smith, Klamath, Trinity, Mad, Van Duzen, and Eel. Elevations range from near sea level to just over 7,000 ft. along the E boundary. Ruth Lake is 9 mi. long, 1,150 acres. There are 4 wilderness areas: Trinity Alps, Siskiyou, Yolla Bolly, and North Fork. These include more than 60 small natural lakes and ponds. All mechanical vehicles including mountain bikes are prohibited within wilderness areas. With the exception of the Trinity Alps, these wildernesses are lightly visited. Wilderness permit required for entry to Trinity Alps; campfire permits required for all others.

Plants: Diverse vegetation featured in 6 very unique botanical areas—North Fork Smith River, Broken Rib, Myrtle Creek, Bear Basin Butte, Horse Mountain, and Lassics—which protect and highlight rare plants, wildflowers, conifer tree diversity, and distinctive plant communities. Predominant tree species is Douglas-fir. Others: Jeffrey, sugar, and ponderosa pines, white and red firs, Port Orford and incense cedars, tan oak, madrone, canyon live oak. Many wildflowers March–April. Poison oak is common. Good fall colors late Sept.–Oct.

Birds: Checklist available. Common and abundant residents include turkey vulture, red-tailed hawk, kestrel, California and mountain quail, band-tailed pigeon, mourning dove, screech owl, nighthawk, Vaux's swift, Anna's and Allen's hummingbirds, kingfisher, northern flicker, acorn and hairy woodpeckers, flycatchers, swallows, jays, raven, chickadee, red-breasted nuthatch, wrentit, winter and Bewick's wrens, robin, golden-crowned kinglet, vireos, warblers.

Watchable wildlife: Ruth Lake is the Forest's designated viewing area. Nearly 200 species of birds, including nesting bald eagles and osprey; river otter sightings. Approximately 194 bird, 74 mammal, 20 amphibian, and 18 reptile species may be observed within the Forest when conditions and circumstances are right.

Mammals: Common and abundant species include Trowbridge shrew, Townsend mole, little brown myotis, silver-haired bat, black bear, mule deer, porcupine, raccoon, striped skunk, coyote, gray fox, ground squirrel, gray and golden-mantled squirrels, Townsend chipmunk, chickaree, black-tailed jackrabbit, brush rabbit, mice, voles.

Reptiles, amphibians: Common and abundant species include pond turtle, western toad, Pacific tree frog, bullfrog, rough-skinned newt, salamander, western fence lizard, alligator lizard, gopher snake, racer, garter snake.

Interpretation

Smith River Scenic Byway: 33 mi. along Smith River corridor on Hwy 199.

Trinity Scenic Byway: 150 mi. from the coast to Redding along Hwy 299.

Forest Route 1: Travels along the ridge of South Fork Mountain and offers incredible views of Trinity Alps peaks and the Pacific Ocean.

Highway 96: Scenic route following the winding course of the Klamath River.

Smith River NRA Information Center: Offers exhibits, information, brochures, maps.

Horse Linto Creek Interpretive Trail: Short trail highlighting salmon habitat, restoration, and natural history. Interpretive brochure available.

Myrtle Creek Trail: 2-mi. trail interpreting rare plants, unique geology, and gold mining history. Brochure available.

Smith River NRA: Interpretive signs at various locations.

Other attractions: Historic fire lookouts, 1930s Civilian Conservation Corps architecture, mining sites, old homesteads, barns, native American cultures, Gambi waterwheel.

Activities

Camping: 16 campgrounds, several fully accessible. 370 sites. Reservations must be made for Patrick's Creek, Panther Flat, and Grassy Flat. All other campgrounds are on a no-reservation basis. Some open year-round. Primitive camping is allowed in most areas outside of campgrounds, unless prohibited. Fire permits required for any fires, camp stoves, or hibachis if outside a campground or picnic area.

Watersports: Major recreational draw. Waterskiing, windsurfing, sailing, motorboating, canoeing, kayaking at Ruth Lake. Nonmotorized boating only on Fish Lake. Canoeing, kayaking, rafting on the main rivers, chiefly Trinity and Klamath; technical kayaking on the Smith. Commercial outfitters and guides under permits offer services and rentals. Jet ski use allowed on lower Trinity River.

Fishing: Salmon, steelhead, trout, and bass.

Swimming, scuba diving, snorkeling: No lifeguards.

Hiking, backpacking: 220 mi. of trails in wilderness and general forest areas. Forest is not heavily used, so it is a good alternative when trails in other areas may be busy. Most trails are open for mountain biking (except in wilderness areas), foot, and pack use. Check trail conditions at district office. Three National Recreation Trails: Horse Ridge, Salmon Summit, and South Kelsy National Historical Trail.

Hunting: Forest has one of the highest deer-hunter success rates in the state. Other plentiful species include quail, grouse, pigeon, and squirrel.

Ski touring: Snow at high elevations most years. Main areas with easy access are South Fork Mountain off Hwy 36, and Horse Mountain off Hwy 299.

Motorized recreation: In addition to the Scenic Byways and scenic routes identified, over 2,000 mi. of Forest roads to explore. Opportunities for sport utility vehicles, four-wheel drives, trail bikes, and all-terrain vehicles. The newly established Backcountry Discovery Trail will run through part of the Forest on unpaved roads. Site specific maps and other information available.

Adjacent
Klamath, Shasta-Trinity, Mendocino National Forests, Redwood National and State Parks, Humboldt Bay Wildlife Refuge, Hoopa Valley Indian reservation.

Publications
Six Rivers National Forest map, $3.25.

Six Rivers National Recreation Area map, $3.25.

Adventure Outdoors: A Visitor Guide to the Six Rivers National Forest.

Traveling through Time.

Horse Linto Creek Interpretive Trail: A Salmon Success Story.

Smith River NRA brochures: *Camping, Backroads Discovery, Hiking, River Recreation, National Recreation Guide.*

Headquarters
U.S. Forest Service, Forest Supervision's Office, 1330 Bayshore Way, Eureka, CA 95501-3834; (707) 442-1721.

Ranger Stations
Smith River NRA, P.O. Box 228, Gasquet, CA 95543-0228; (707) 457-3131. Lower Trinity R.S., P.O. Box 68, Willow Creek, CA 95573; (916) 629-2118; Mad River R.S., Star Rt., P.O. Box 300, Bridgeville, CA 95526; (707) 574-6233. Orleans R.S., Drawer B, Orleans, CA 95556; (916) 627-3291.

....

Smithe Redwoods State Reserve
California Department of Parks and Recreation
822 acres.

4 mi. N of Leggett on US 101.

On the South Fork of the Eel River. A splendid grove of giant redwoods is on W side of highway. Short trails through the grove and to the river. This is a small portion of the site, but a nice rest stop along the Redwood Hwy.

Nearby
Standish-Hickey State Recreation Area, Richardson Grove State Park (see entries this zone).

Standish-Hickey State Recreation Area
California Department of Parks and Recreation
1,012 acres.

2 mi. N of Leggett on US 101.

A redwood park, where the oldest tree is the Miles Standish-Hickey tree. Scarred by fire and saw cuts, this tree stands 225 ft. tall and 13 ft. in diameter. The Park is located along the South Fork of the Eel River. Visitors who plan on staying only one night tend to find themselves returning again and again.

Plants: Forest of Coast redwood, old-growth Douglas-fir, tan oak, California bay laurel, Oregon and other oaks, bigleaf maple, alder. Shrubs include toyon, manzanita, huckleberry, ceanothus. Many ferns. Wildflowers include brodiaea, Indian pink, redwood sorrel, shooting star, lupine, buttercup, tiger lily, calypso orchid, chaparral pea, and fetid adders-tongue.

Birds: Include Steller's jay, raven, quail, junco, osprey, merganser, great blue heron, and, in winter, bald eagle.

Mammals: Include mule deer, raccoon, bobcat, ground squirrel, gray squirrel, mountain lion, black bear.

Interpretation
Campfire programs, 3 evenings weekly in summer.

Junior Ranger programs in summer.

Litter Getter programs.

Guided nature walks and *self-guided nature trails.*

Activities
Camping: 3 campgrounds, 162 sites. One campground open all year. Also Hike and Bike camping. Reservations May 25–Sept. 3.

Hiking: 4 loop trails, longest 4.7 mi. Steep sections.

Fishing: Steelhead and salmon Oct. 1–March 31. Summer fishing only for squaw.

Swimming: River. No lifeguard on duty. Deep holes.

Publication
Leaflet with map.

Nearby
Richardson Grove State Park, Smithe Redwoods State Reserve (see entries this zone).

Headquarters
Ca Dept. of Parks and Recreation, 69350 US 101, Leggett, CA 95585; (707) 925-6482.

Van Damme State Park

California Department of Parks and Recreation
2,070 acres.

3 mi. S of Mendocino on Hwy 1.

Coast, extending about 3 mi. inland. Ocean beach, forest, river canyon, meadows, bog. Once a virgin redwood forest, but logged off; sawmill was closed in 1893.

Plants: Second-growth forest now has trees of impressive size. Coast redwood, Douglas-fir, Pacific hemlock, Bishop pine, shore pine, lowland fir. In *Fern Canyon,* luxuriant growth of trees and ferns: sword, five-finger, lady, licorice, wood, bird's-foot, deer. Many rhododendrons, spring wildflowers. *Pygmy Forest,* reached by Fern Canyon Trail, has mature cypress and pine trees stunted by acid soil. Pygmy Forest can also be reached by Airport Road, S of Park. *Cabbage Patch* is a bog with skunk cabbage.

Tidepools can be seen at low tide. Beach is used for picnicking, beachcombing, scuba; swimming is inadvisable, with water seldom above 52°F.

Interpretation

Visitor center program, "Living Under the Sea." Open daily 10–4, April–Sept. Weekends rest of year.

Activities

Camping: 74 sites. All year. Reservations May 1–Sept. 30.

Hiking: Fern Canyon Trail, 2½ mi. from campground to junction with Old Logging Trail. 6 mi. round trip. Bog Trail near visitor center.

Nearby

Jackson Demonstration State Forest, Russian Gulch State Park (see entries this zone).

Publications

Leaflet with map.

Fern Canyon Discovery Trail.

Pygmy Forest Discovery Trail.

Headquarters

CA Dept. of Parks and Recreation, P.O. Box 440, Mendocino, CA 95460; (707) 937-5804.

ZONE

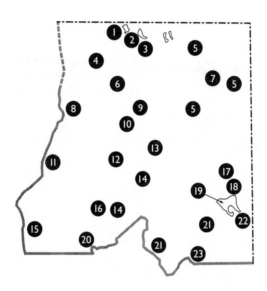

ZONE 2

Includes these counties:

Siskiyou (E of I-5)	Lassen	Plumas
Shasta	Tehama	

The Cascade Range extends into this zone from the N, the Sierra Nevada from the S. In the SW is the upper part of the Sacramento Valley and the E slope of the Coast Range. The far NE is within the Great Basin.

The forests, parks, and wildlife areas described in these entries make up more than half of the zone's land area. Most of the remainder is crop and grazing land, much of it in the fertile Sacramento Valley. By far the largest public areas are the National Forests, and these, for the most part, occupy the mountains.

Elevations range from around 200 ft. in the Valley to 14,161-ft. Mount Shasta. Although there is much rugged terrain, the mountain slopes are generally less steep than in the Sierra to the S, and the high country is not quite as high.

In the far N are wetlands that attract vast numbers of waterfowl. The zone has many lakes, rivers, and streams, as well as semiarid regions where travelers must bring their own water.

Some mountain areas are open for hiking by late May; others are blocked by snow until July. Snow closes some passes. The road through Lassen Volcanic National Park is usually closed by snow from the end of Oct. until early June. Snowfall is generally light at lower elevations.

The zone offers a great array of scenic features: volcanic craters and peaks, lava caves, waterfalls, cascades, virgin forests, seasonal wildflower displays. Hiking trails range from easy to difficult. Quiet isolation in splendid surroundings is available to anyone willing to walk a few miles. The National Forests have large wilderness areas, and some of the long trails have only moderate grades. Many trails are suitable for horses.

Many popular resorts are within the zone, and some public recreation areas are crowded at times. A few wilderness trails have become so popular that some fragile areas are now closed to overnight camping.

Ordinary road maps will take you to the zone. Within the zone, National Forest maps are indispensable.

Biscar Wildlife Area

California Department of Fish and Game
548 acres.

From Susanville, E and N on US 395 about 35 mi. SW on county road through Karlo. Site boundary just beyond SP railroad tracks.

Isolated, high desert country, seldom visited except by hunters in season. Sweeping plateau cut by steep-walled canyon of Snowstorm Creek, an intermittent stream. Canyon walls are lava rimrock. Annual precipitation about 10 in., winter snowfall scant. Impoundments.

Plants: Typical of Great Basin: scattered juniper, rabbitbrush, sage, black greasewood, saltbush. Less common: bitterbrush, curl-leaf mountain mahogany, squaw apple.

Birds: Chukar, quail, sage grouse, dove; migrant waterfowl on creek.

Mammals: Cottontail, black-tailed jackrabbit, coyote, bobcat, badger, marmot. Summer antelope range. Some mule deer.

No campground, no sanitary facilities. Travel over much of the area on foot only.

Bring your own water.

Winter road conditions variable. Advisable to consult BLM office in Susanville (916) 257-5381, or Fish and Game in Redding (below).

Headquarters

CA Dept. of Fish and Game, 601 Locust St., Redding, CA 96001; (916) 225-2300.

Castle Craggs State Park

California Department of Parks and Recreation
6,216 acres.

6 mi. S of Dunsmuir, or 20 mi. N of Lake Shasta on I-5.

In the Klamath Mountains, along the Sacramento River. Group of soaring crags, with elevations ranging from 2,000 ft. along river to 6,000 ft. at the top. Crags have sheer faces with rounded domes. 2-mi. frontage on the river, across from I-5 and the main portion of the Park.

Plants: 80% forested: valley oak, red fir, Jeffrey pine, Pacific yew, Port Orford and incense cedars, black and valley oaks, sugar and ponderosa pines, Douglas-fir, white fir, vine maple, dogwood. Flowering plants include azalea, tiger lily, pitcher plant, several kinds of ceanothus and manzanita.

Birds: Steller's jay, robin, Brewer's blackbird, western meadowlark, raven, western bluebird, red-tailed and Cooper's hawks, and great blue heron.

Mammals: Black-tailed deer, coyote, black bear, raccoon, gray squirrel, ground squirrels, gray fox, bobcat, fisher. Present but seldom seen in the higher elevations, mountain lion.

Interpretation

Campfire programs, summer months.

Ranger-guided walks and *talks.*

Activities

Camping: 64 sites. All year. Reservations recommended summer months, (800) 444-7275.

Hiking, backpacking: 24 mi. of improved trails. Indian Creek Trail, 1 mi., self-guided; Crags Trail/Indian Springs Trail, 2.7 strenuous mi.; Root Creek Trail, 1 mi., moderately strenuous; Pacific Crest Trail, 10 mi., easy walking. *Hikers are warned not to go beyond trails: some cliffs have sheer drops of almost 2,000 ft.—there are no markers or warning signs.*

Fishing: River, April–Nov.

Swimming: River.

Canoeing, kayaking: River navigable for canoe or kayak from late spring to early or midsummer, depending on runoff.

Horse riding: Allowed only on designated riding trails.

Adjacent
Shasta-Trinity National Forest (see entry this zone).

Publications
Information sheet with map.

Checklists of birds, plants.

Headquarters
CA Dept. of Parks and Recreation, P.O. Box 80, Castella, CA 96017-2684; (916) 235-2684.

Doyle Wildlife Area
California Department of Fish and Game
13,975 acres.

From Doyle on US 395 (SE of Susanville), N on Herlong Rd. Area adjoins US 395, N and E of Doyle.

Foothills and flatland on Long Valley Creek. Creek, in a deep cut, flows N to Honey Lake, dry only in extreme drought. Wildlife Area was established to provide winter deer habitat. Purpose now is to maintain all wildlife resources. Climate is dry, about 10 in. of precipitation a year; hot summers, cold winters.

Plants: Typical of Great Basin. Exclusion of domestic livestock has brought recovery of browse species, notably bitterbrush. Also curl-leaf mountain mahogany, big sage, California juniper.

Wildlife: Include mule deer, coyote, bobcat, badger, raccoon, skunk, cottontail, mourning dove, chukar, California quail, various raptors and passerines, some waterfowl.

No campground or sanitary facilities. Hunters need to obtain regulations. *Vehicles must stay on maintained roads. Soft sand.*

Nearby
Plumas National Forest (see entry this zone).

Publication
Leaflet with map.

Headquarters
CA Dept. of Fish and Game, 601 Locust St., Redding, CA 96001; (916) 225-2300.

Honey Lake Wildlife Area
California Department of Fish and Game
7,840 acres.

From Susanville, N on US 395 through Litchfield. 3 mi. beyond Litchfield, right 2 mi. on Mapes Rd., then left 1 mi. to HQ.

Two units, both on N shore of Honey Lake. Lakes is in a large natural sink. Surface water is from the Susan River and drainage from irrigated farmland. Surrounding area was once largely wetlands, supporting vast waterfowl populations. Honey Lake Wildlife Area now provides nesting, resting, and feeding habitat. Impoundments and cultivation of feed crops increase carrying capacity.

Elevation is 4,000 ft. Ponds and marshes, plus cropland.

Birds: More than 150 species recorded. Nesting area of Canada goose, only goose nesting in CA. Snow, white-fronted, cackling, and Ross's geese are migrants. Mallard, pintail, and cinnamon teal are common nesting species. In addition, sandhill crane, avocet, and black-necked stilt are common nesting and wading birds. Pheasant introduced. Said to provide spectacular opportunities to observe newly hatched geese and ducks.

Mammals: Include mule deer, muskrat, mink, beaver, weasel, porcupine, raccoon, coyote, bobcat, occasional pronghorn.

Activities

Camping: 15 sites. Limited facilities. Water in summer only. Obtain use permit on arrival.

Hiking: In designated areas. Always be aware of hunters during hunting season.

Hunting: In designated areas, on designated days in season; number of hunters limited. Waterfowl, pheasant, quail, dove.

Fishing: Termed "modest." Bass, catfish, sunfish, mostly fall and spring.

Capacity crowds on opening weekend of waterfowl hunting season and pheasant season. Must have hunting license and area permit to enter on hunt days.

Nearby

Lassen National Forest (see entry).

Publication

Leaflet with map.

Headquarters

CA Dept. of Fish and Game, 700-628 Fish and Game Rd., Wendel, CA 96136; (916) 254-6644.

....

Klamath Basin National Wildlife Refuges: Tule Lake and Lower Klamath Units

U.S. Fish and Wildlife Service
85,700 acres.

From Tulelake on Hwy 139, W on East-West Rd. 5 mi. to Hill Rd. Left to HQ and Tule Lake. For Lower Klamath, NW from Tulelake about 4 mi. on Hwy 139, then W on Hwy 161 10 mi. to beginning of tour route.

The Klamath Basin, almost a million acres in CA and OR, was once a region of vast shallow lakes and marshes, one of the world's chief waterfowl areas. Dams, ditches, and other alterations have eliminated most of the wetlands. Lower Klamath became a Refuge in 1908, Tule

Lake not until 1928. Clear Lake, a storage reservoir, was not brought into the system in 1911.

Reclamation drastically altered the Lower Klamath, and for a time two federal agencies, the Reclamation Service and the Biological Survey, fought angrily over water management. Eventually they compromised and cooperated. Although the basin as a whole will never be restored to its primitive condition, the 6 units of the Klamath Basin Refuge—3 of them in Oregon—support great numbers of waterfowl and bald eagles. Both the Tule Lake and Lower Klamath units support peak waterfowl populations of more than a million.

Lower Klamath includes water, marsh, and upland. Marshes are maintained by water pumped from Tule Lake by a 6,600-ft. tunnel through an intervening ridge and by water diverted from the Klamath River. Part of the upland is farmed by permittees who must leave one-third of the grain crop for waterfowl.

Tule Lake is surrounded by rich grainlands that were once part of the lakebed. The original 100,000-acre lake is now only 13,000 acres, but it produces a rich crop of aquatic plants and attracts vast numbers of waterfowl.

Birds: Spring is a fine season here, the population of migrants usually peaking in early March, but the fall migration is phenomenal, producing the largest concentration of waterfowl on the North American continent. The 5 Klamath units are likely to have 1 to 2 million birds, including 500,000 pintail, 100,000 mallard, 200,000 wigeon, 100,000 white-fronted goose, 100,000 cackling Canada goose, 200,000 snow goose. An estimated 70–80% of all the waterfowl on the Pacific Flyway pass through here.

More than 275 bird species have been recorded, including 170 nesting on one or more of the units. The complex produces 50,000 to 70,000 ducks and geese per year. Many redhead nesting. Also gadwall, mallard, cinnamon teal, ruddy duck; lesser numbers of shoveler, pintail, scaup, and canvasback. In July and Aug., broods can be observed from Hwy 161.

Duck populations usually peak in the last half of Oct., geese 1 to 2 weeks later.

Up to 1,000 bald eagles winter here. Sandhill crane nest at Lower Klamath. Eared, western, and pied-billed grebes nest at Tule Lake and Lower Klamath.

The Refuge checklist includes many shorebirds, hawks, owls, woodpeckers, and songbirds.

Mammals: Include mule deer, coyote, pronghorn, marmot.

Auto tour routes are available on both units. Lower Klamath has two, 6 and 16 mi. Tule Lake has a 10-mi. tour. All are on graded gravel roads. Your car is a good blind.

Activities

Hiking: On unpaved roads, some of which are on the auto tour route.

Hunting: Designated areas; special rules. Inquire.

Wildlife photography: Very popular. To help the nature photographer, 8 wildlife blinds have been made available, 5 on Tule Lake and 3 on Lower Klamath. Available during daylight hours and by reservation only. Reservations can be made in person or by telephone at the visitor center, (916) 667-2231.

Interior roads may be in poor condition in wet weather. Inquire.

Nearby

Lava Beds National Monument (see entry this zone).

Publications

Leaflet with map.

Bird checklist.

Klamath Basin National Wildlife Refuges.

Upper Klamath Canoe Trail.

Common Wildlife of Klamath Basin National Wildlife Refuges.

Sheepy Ridge Wildlife Trail Guide.

Bald Eagles of the Klamath Basin.

Hunting: Lower Klamath and Tule Lake National Wildlife Refuges.

Photo blind information (leaflet).

Headquarters

U.S. Fish and Wildlife Service, Rt. 1, Box 74, Tulelake, CA 96134; (916) 667-2231.

Klamath National Forest

See entry in zone 1.

Lassen National Forest

U.S. Forest Service
1,060,588 acres. 1,375,067 acres within boundaries.

Surrounds Lassen Volcanic National Park (see entry this zone). Crossed by Hwys 89, 44, 36, 32.

Lassen Peak, in the National Park, is the S outpost of the Cascade Range. The N tip of the Sierra is near Lake Almanor, SE of the Park. In the National Forest, although elevations range to 9,000 ft., peaks are rather widely separated and most slopes are moderate. Steeper slopes occur in the SW sector, but even these are less rugged than many to the S and N. The Forest sits at the intersection of the Sierra Nevada and the Cascade Mountains and of the Modoc plateau and the Great Basin.

Because of inholdings, the Forest land is patchy in a few sectors, and there are scattered bits on the periphery. However, there are large, solid blocks, largely N of the Park, but also to the E, S, and SW.

Some frontage on Lake Almanor, almost 15 mi. long, and along the shore of Eagle Lake. Numerous smaller lakes and ponds, many formed by volcanic action. Streams, mostly small (except for Mill, Deer, and Hot creeks), some intermittent.

Plants: Largely forested, up to timberline. In general, lower slopes have white fir, ponderosa and Jeffrey pines, hemlock, some Douglas-fir, sugar pine, incense cedar. Higher, red fir, dense stands of lodgepole. Alder, willow, aspen along streams. Common shrubs include ceanothus, mountain mahogany, manzanita. Some open meadows with grasses, bromegrass, meadow barley, sedges, rushes.

Wildflowers include lupines, buttercup, filaree, violet, penstemon, aster, yarrow, dandelion.

Birds: Canada goose common on lakes in summer. Other waterfowl include mallard, teal. *Osprey Management Area* at Eagle Lake. Several hawk species, golden eagle. Bald eagle rare but present. Some California and mountain quail. Turkey introduced. Band-tailed pigeon, mourning dove. Numerous blackbirds, woodpeckers, Steller's jay, killdeer. No checklist.

Mammals: Include mule deer, pronghorn, coyote, fox, cottontail, bobcat, jackrabbit, chipmunk, gray squirrel. Uncommon: black bear, mountain lion.

Features

Thousand Lakes Wilderness: 16,335 acres. Access from 4 trailheads on Forest roads. Popular area for short trips; long trail across the area is about 6 air mi. Open enough for off-trail hiking, with topo and compass. Elevations 5,000–9,000 ft. Open and barren above timberline, forest and meadow below. Some gentle slopes with recent lava flows, sparse vegetation. Thousand Lakes Valley is the principal attraction, a level, glacier-carved valley with many small lakes and ponds. Difficult trail to top of Magee Peak, 8,550 ft.

Caribou Wilderness: 20,625 acres. On E boundary of National Park. Access from 3 trailheads on Forest roads. Gently rolling forested plateau with many tree-fringed lakes. Trails well maintained. Highest point is Red Cinder Cone, 8,370 ft. Forest cover mostly Jeffrey and lodgepole pines, with white and red fir, western white pine, hemlock, on lower slopes.

Cinder Butte Roadless Area: 15,500 acres. NW corner of Forest, E of Burney. Encompasses, almost entirely, a volcano active within the past 2,000 years. Numerous cinder cones, caves, shallow water-filled potholes. Rising River, large volcanic spring, near NW corner.

Cinder Butte is 4,288 ft., highest point, panoramic views. Vegetative cover is sparse, as is wildlife. Ground surface is rocky, irregular.

Ishi Wilderness: 41,600 acres. SW corner of Forest. Transition zone between Sacramento Valley and upper slopes of Sierra. Elevations 2,000–3,000 ft. Network of steep ravines separated by sharp ridges. Most slopes have annual grasses or dense brush with scattered digger pine, black oak. Several small, flat plateaus have stands of ponderosa pine. Drained by Mill Creek. Jeep and foot trails.

Timbered Crater: Candidate for Research Natural Area, 1,777 acres. Near SE corner of Siskiyou County. Three parcels of Forest land adjacent to a larger area, administered by the BLM. Also being considered for wilderness status. Timbered Crater rim elevation almost 4,000 ft. Area elevations 3,600–3,900 ft. Lava flows and shallow depressions are principal landscape features. Sparse vegetation.

Eagle Lake: Forest Service campgrounds, boat rentals.

Subway Cave: On Hwy 89 near junction with Hwy 44. Lava tube 1,300 ft. long, formed less than 20,000 years ago. Stairs at both ends, but no lights; bring your own. Rough floor. Low ceiling in places, but only tall people need to stoop. Always 46°F.

Antelope Mountain lookout: W of Eagle Lake, reached by gravel road from Eagle Lake Rd. Mountain is 7,684 ft. Lookout station open 8–5 during fire season.

Scenic drives: Many attractive routes including the Lassen Scenic Byway, a 185-mi. double-loop byway on Hwys 44, 89, 36, and 147. Dogwood and redbud blooms in spring. Many gravel roads in Forest for backcountry travel, plus many roads requiring 4-wheel drive.

Activities

Camping: 39 campgrounds, 997 sites. Campgrounds vary in size (4 to 182 units) and facilities. A few have no water or only water taken from stream or lake. Seasons vary. Some are open all year. Others open March 1–June 1, close Oct. 1–Nov. 30.

Hiking, backpacking: Trails and unpaved roads. Pacific Crest Trail runs roughly N-S, through center of Forest, also crossing center of Lassen Volcanic National Park (see entry this zone). The PCT follows the ridges, where snow limits travel to season beginning mid-July, ending Oct. Trail elevations 2,900–7,000 ft.

Many trails and back roads are good hiking possibilities in addition to the PCT and wilderness routes. Examples include 26-mi. Bizz Johnson National Recreation Trail from Westwood to Susanville; 6-mi., paved Eagle Lake South Shore Trail; and paved, 8½-mi. Lake Almanor Trail. Several trails link the Forest and National Park.

Trailside camping is permitted almost everywhere. Special permit required in wilderness areas. Campfire permit is required for any type of fire, including stove, outside campgrounds.

Hunting: Deer, bear, game birds. Not outstanding.

Fishing: Lakes and streams.

Swimming: Beaches, unsupervised, at several campgrounds. Elsewhere as settings permit.

Boating: Lake Almanor, Eagle Lake. On Lake Almanor, most shoreline is privately owned, with much development. Most public land on Eagle Lake in a pristine setting.

Horse riding: Pleasant routes, most of them rather short. Because forage is limited, wilderness users must pack in feed for their stock.

Adjacent

Lassen Volcanic National Park, McArthur-Burney Falls Memorial State Park, Plumas National Forest (see entries this zone).

Publications

Forest map, $3.25.

Visitor guides for summer and winter recreation.

Thousand Lake Wilderness (leaflet).

Caribou Wilderness (leaflet).

Ishi Wilderness (leaflet).

Headquarters

U.S. Forest Service, 55 S. Sacramento, Susanville, CA 96130; (916) 257-2151.

Ranger Districts

Almanor R.D., P.O. Box 767, Chester, CA 96020; (916) 258-2141. Eagle Lake R.D., Eagle Lake Rd., Susanville, CA 96100; (916) 257-4188. Hat Creek R.D., P.O. Box 220, Fall River Mills, CA 96028; (916) 336-5521.

Lassen Volcanic National Park

U.S. National Park Service
106,000 acres.

Between Susanville and Redding. Access from Hwys 44, 89, 36, 32. Lassen Park Rd. connects with Hwy 89 and crosses the Park; mostly closed by snow from end of Oct. to early June.

Region of forest and lakes, dominated by 10,457-ft. Lassen Peak. Peak was formed by extrusion of lava from a vent in a larger extinct volcano. Beginning May 1914, eruptions occurred intermittently for more than 7 years. Other signs of volcanism: Cinder Cone, boiling springs, steaming fumaroles, sulfurous vents.

Lowest elevation is 5,200 ft. The Transition life zone, up to 6,500 ft., has snow 4–5 months a year. The Canadian life zone, up to 8,000 ft., is under snow 6–7 months a year with depths up to 20 ft. or more. The Hudsonian life zone, up to the timberline at 9,000 ft., has snow cover 8–9 months a year with depths to more than 27 ft. Above 9,000 ft. is the Alpine zone, buried under snow 9–10 months a year with some patches year-round. High winds; wide daily temperature fluctuations.

A major portion of the Park is roadless wilderness. 50 lakes, the largest about 1¾ mi. long. Numerous clear streams. Almost 50 peaks, many over 8,000 ft.

Although the Park is open all year, winter use is chiefly ski touring and skiing. From the NW entrance, the road is kept open a short distance to Manzanita Lake ranger station. Winter sports area is near the SW entrance.

Plants: The Park is at the S end of the Cascade Range, just N of the Sierra, W of the Great Basin. Thus there is intermingling of species. Because of comparatively recent volcanic action, the forest community is in an early stage of succession. Each life zone has typical species: TRANSITION ZONE: ponderosa pine with associated sugar pine, white fir, incense cedar. Typical wildflowers: snow plant, Washington lily, blue-eyed grass, dwarf larkspur, sneezeweed. CANADIAN ZONE: red fir with associated lodgepole, Jeffrey, and western white pines, bush chinquapin, Labrador tea. Typical wildflowers: Lewis monkeyflower, bog laurel, subalpine spiraea, western pasque flower, Lassen paintbrush. HUDSONIAN ZONE: mountain hemlock in lower portion, dwarf whitebark pine above. Shrubs: red and white heather, pinemat manzanita. Typical wildflowers: rose willow weed, phacelia, Shasta knotweed, Tolmie's saxifrage. ALPINE ZONE: low or creeping plants, often with hairy leaves: dwarf hulsea, golden draba, polemonium.

Birds: Checklist. Common species include Steller's jay, robin, dipper, Clark's nutcracker, Lewis's and three-toed woodpeckers, purple finch, pygmy nuthatch, Swainson's thrush, Nashville warbler, sharp-shinned hawk, Williamson's sapsucker, green-tailed towhee, fox sparrow. Species present but rare include bald eagle, peregrine falcon.

Mammals: Common species include chipmunk, golden-mantled ground squirrel, chickaree. Less often seen: black bear, pika, marmot, marten, weasel, coyote, mountain beaver, porcupine, mountain lion, flying squirrel, black-tailed deer.

Features

Wilderness area, where travel is by foot or horse only, is more than three-quarters of the Park. The Caribou Wilderness of Lassen National Forest is adjacent. This is a popular area, and regulations are designed to minimize environmental damage. A wilderness permit is required for overnight stays. Either Park or Forest will issue a permit good for the combined areas.

Lassen Park Road winds around three sides of the peak, offering many views of the mountain and the volcanic landscape. Features on or near the road include Manzanita Lake, Chaos Jumbles and Dwarf Forest, Devastated Area, Summit Lake, Lake Helen, Bumpass Hell, Sulphur Works. Color *Road Guide* available at entrances.

Unpaved roads from outside Park boundaries lead to Butte Lake, Juniper Lake, Warner Valley.

Interpretation

Loomis Museum (visitor center), NW entrance, open daily early June–late Sept. Information, exhibits, video program, publications.

Southwest information center, SW entrance, open daily late June–Labor Day. Information, publications.

Summer naturalist program.

Self-guiding nature trails at Bumpass Hell, Lassen Peak, Cinder Cone, Boiling Springs Lake, Sulphur Works.

Evening talks at Manzanita Lake and Summit Lake amphitheaters.

Activities

Camping: 7 campgrounds, 375 sites. Seasons differ: earliest opening sometime in May; latest closing Oct. 15. Contact Park for limits. No fires allowed outside designated areas.

Hiking, backpacking: 150 mi. of trails, throughout Park. 17-mi. section of Pacific Crest Trail. Other trail connections into Lassen National Forest. No trailside camping within 1 mi. of developed area or road or within ¼ mi. of a long list of areas considered fragile. Overnight permit required.

Fishing: Rainbow, brook, and brown trout. Some restricted zones.

Swimming: Especially at Butte, Bathtub, Juniper Lakes.

Canoeing: Canoes, other nonpowered craft permitted on all waters except Reflection, Emerald, Helen, Boiling Springs Lakes.

Horse riding: Pack and saddle stock may not overnight in Park except in corrals at Summit and Juniper Lakes. Reservations required. No grazing allowed. Wilderness permit required. A small corral near N boundary is available for those using Pacific Crest Trail.

Ski touring: Winter snow conditions usually good, but there is danger of avalanches.

   If planning a visit in May or Oct., inquire to make sure road is open.
   Visitor use is heavy, even in backcountry, during most of the June–Sept. season.

Adjacent
Lassen National Forest (see entry this zone).

Publications
Leaflet with map.
Backcountry Information.
Campground Information.
Lassen Park Guide.
Road Guide.
Lassen's Plants and Animals.
Bird checklist.

Headquarters
National Park Service, P.O. Box 100, Mineral, CA 96063; (916) 595-4444.

....

Latour State Forest
California Department of Forestry
9,033 acres.

50 mi. E of Redding. Hwy 44 E to Whitmore Rd., E on Whitmore to Bateman Rd. Normally accessible to vehicles late June to Nov. High winds, wet snow, extreme cold are common winter and spring.

On W edge of Lassen National Forest (see entry this zone), near Thousand Lakes Wilderness. Part of the Cascade Range, elevations 3,800–6,740 ft. Primarily forested, some brushfields and small meadows. Somewhat out of the way, it attracts more hunters than hikers or campers.

Plants: Pines: sugar, ponderosa, Jeffrey, western white, and lodgepole. Also white and red fir, Douglas-fir, incense cedar. Shrubs: mountain snowberry, manzanitas, chinquapin, serviceberry, mountain ash, Oregon grape, heathers, etc. Wildflowers include scarlet fritillary, Washington lily, fairybell, pussy paws, shooting star, anemone, star flower, slim solomon.

Birds: Resident species include goshawk, sharp-shinned hawk, blue grouse, mountain quail, screech owl, northern flicker, pileated, hairy, downy, and white-headed woodpeckers, scrub and Steller's jays, white-breasted nuthatch, California thrasher, golden-crowned kinglet, Cassin's finch, red crossbill, pine siskin.

Mammals: Resident species include shrews, mole, big brown bat, pika, snowshoe hare, mountain beaver, squirrels, marmot, porcupine, coyote, red and gray foxes, bobcat, mountain lion, black bear, fisher, weasel, striped skunk. Mule deer in summer.

Activities

Camping: 3 campgrounds. Primitive.

Hiking: No trails, but miles of forest roads.

Fishing: Rainbow and German brook trout.

Horse riding: Riders must bring own horse feed; grazing is limited.

Publication
Leaflet with map.

Headquarters
CA Dept. of Forestry, 1000 W. Cypress St., Redding, CA 96001; (916) 225-2508. Latour Station: (916) 474-3113.

Lava Beds National Monument
U.S. National Park Service
46,821 acres.

Near OR border. From Tulelake, 5 mi. S, then S on County Road 111. Open all year.

Rugged lava landscape; gentle slopes on the side of a dormant volcano; lava fields grading into high desert flats and honeycombed with lava tubes. Elevations 4,000–5,700 ft. Snow has been recorded in all seasons; but, because annual precipitation is only 15.4 in., accumulations are small. Summer climate is moderate.

Features are cinder and spatter cones, craters, lava-tube caves. Some tubes extend 1 mi. The most recent lava flow was about 950 years ago.

Plants: Grassland-sagebrush community at lower altitudes; juniper woodland above; small amounts of ponderosa pine higher. Semiarid species; over 200 recorded. Prominent species include western juniper, curl-leaf mountain mahogany, greenleaf manzanita, Great Basin sagebrush, gray ball sage, bitter cherry, rabbitbrush. Flowering plants include sagebrush buttercup, western blue flax, blazing star, desert phlox, gilia, phacelia, paintbrush, pussy paws.

Birds: Checklist available. Although the varied plant communities are generally rather dry, the Monument shares a long boundary with the Tule Lake National Wildlife Refuge (see entry this zone), which is mostly lake and marsh. The bird list carries a number of species, including bald and golden eagles, white pelican, bittern, and herons, which are most likely to be seen in the Refuge. Among the permanent residents in the Monument itself are sharp-shinned and red-tailed hawks, northern harrier, prairie falcon, kestrel, blue grouse, mountain and California quail, pheasant, barn, screech, great horned, saw-whet, and short-eared owls (as well as long-eared and burrowing owls, which are less likely to be seen). Also northern flicker, hairy and downy woodpeckers, horned lark, Steller's, pinyon, and scrub jays, black-billed magpie, raven, Clark's nutcracker, 3 nuthatches, brown creeper, Bewick's and canyon wrens, hermit thrush, western and mountain bluebirds, Townsend's solitaire, ruby- and golden-crowned kinglets, loggerhead shrike, yellow-rumped warbler, red-winged, tricolored, and Brewer's blackbirds, evening grosbeak, purple, Cassin's, and house finches, pine siskin, dark-eyed junco, song sparrow.

Summer residents include turkey vulture, Swainson's hawk, poorwill, nighthawk; several hummingbirds, flycatchers, swallows, vireos, house wren, blue-gray gnatcatcher, yellow-headed blackbird, Bullock's oriole, cowbird, black-headed and evening grosbeaks, lazuli bunting, green-tailed towhee, sparrows.

Many other species in migration.

Mammals: Mule deer common in winter and summer. Often seen: marmot, Belding and golden-mantled ground squirrels, chipmunk, cottontail, black-tailed jackrabbit, pika. Often seen along roads at night: porcupine, kangaroo rat, coyote, mice. Pronghorn, bobcat, mountain lion rarely seen.

Reptiles and amphibians: Western rattlesnakes fairly common: visitors are advised to watch their footsteps on trails early morning and evening, use light at night. 7 nonpoisonous snakes, 4 species of lizard, 1 frog, 1 toad recorded; most take shelter during summer middays.

Features

Wilderness areas include 28,460 acres, three-fifths of Monument. Travel by foot or horse only. Water must be carried. Cold weather is possible at any time. Register before entering.

Cave Loop Rd., near HQ, passes near many caves.

Symbol Bridge, ¾-mi. hike from Skull Ice Cave road, is site of Indian pictographs.

Mammoth Crater, source of lava, is near S boundary.

Schonchin Fire Tower, reached by ¾-mi. trail; viewpoint.

Interpretation

Visitor center with geology, history, and natural history exhibits and publications. 9 A.M.–6 P.M. in summer, 8–5 in winter.

Summer naturalist programs include cave walks, demonstrations, evening talks. Announcements posted.

Self-guiding interpretive trails at Captain Jack's stronghold and Petrograph Point.

Activities

Camping: One campground, 48 sites. All year, but no water Oct. 15–May 23.

Hiking, backpacking: 55 mi. of trails, chiefly in wilderness areas.

Only one cave is lighted. Adequate lights (more than one), good walking shoes, hard hats, and jackets are needed in caves. Lights and hats available at visitor center.

Crowding limited to occasional holiday weekends.

Adjacent

Tule Lake National Wildlife Refuge (see entry, Klamath Basin National Wildlife Refuges); Modoc National Forest (see entry this zone).

Publications

Leaflet with map.

Species checklists: plants, birds, mammals, reptiles and amphibians.

Wilderness Hiking and Camping (leaflet).

Cave Information (leaflet).

Captain Jack's Stronghold Historical Trail (pamphlet).

Rock Art (leaflet).

Summary of Geology (leaflet)

Headquarters

National Park Service, P.O. Box 867, Tulelake, CA 96134; (916) 667-2283.

Lower Klamath National Wildlife Refuge

See Klamath Basin National Wildlife Refuges (this zone).

McArthur-Burney Falls Memorial State Park

California Department of Parks and Recreation
853 acres.

From Burney, 11 mi. NE on Hwy 89.

Midway between Mount Shasta and Lassen Peak. Most visitors stop here to see the falls, once called by Theodore Roosevelt the eighth wonder of the world. The 129-ft. falls are supplied by giant springs a few hundred yards upstream, flowing full even in dry weather.

Almost 2 mi. frontage on 9-mi.-long Lake Britton and Burney Creek. Elevations from 2,762 to 3,140 ft.

Plants: Predominantly ponderosa pine forest with Douglas-fir, incense cedar, willows, aspen, black oak. Sparse understory includes manzanita, squaw carpet, squaw brush. Relatively few wildflowers.

Birds: 132 species recorded. Noteworthy are black swifts nesting in the cliff. Bald eagles nest. Others recorded include western, eared, and pied-billed grebes, great blue heron, Canada goose, mallard, common merganser, ruddy duck, barn and great horned owls, belted kingfisher, common flicker, black-headed and evening grosbeaks, dark-eyed junco.

Interpretation

Campfire programs and guided hikes. June–Aug.

Self-guided nature trail, 1 mi.

Activities

Camping: 2 campgrounds, 118 sites. All year. Reservations accepted May 25–mid-Sept.

Hiking, backpacking: 4 mi. of trails. Connection with Pacific Crest Trail; Park often used as stopover.

Fishing: Lake and stream. Bass, brown trout in lake. Streams have rainbow, brown, and brook trout.

Swimming: Lake. Unsupervised. Usual season June–Sept.

Boating: Ramp. Rentals.

Nearby

Portion of Shasta National Forest administered by Lassen National Forest. Forest map shows some primitive roads that may offer good hiking, but inquire.

Publications

Leaflet with map.

Nature trail guide.

Bird checklist.

Headquarters

CA Dept. of Parks and Recreation, 24898 Hwy 89, Burney, CA 96013; (916) 335-2777.

Mendocino National Forest

U.S. Forest Service

About 125,000 acres of this Forest, in Tehama County, is in zone 2. The largest part is in zone 3, where the entry appears.

Modoc National Forest

U.S. Forest Service
1.6 million acres National Forest. 337,000 acres privately owned. About 2 million acres altogether.

NE CA. Largest portion extends S from OR border, from Lava Beds National Monument on W to Goose Lake on E. Another block, from 5 to 15 mi. wide, extends 60 mi. S from OR border, E of Goose Lake. S portion is irregular, fragmented, with many inholdings. US 395 is between major sections. Forest is crossed by Hwy 299, Hwy 139.

Large, diverse scenic region of CA, less visited than mountain areas to the S. Dry summers to severe, moderately wet winters. Elevations from 4,200–9,892 ft. Mountain slopes from gentle to precipitous. Obsidian cliffs, crates, lava caves. Extensive forested plateaus, meadows, open rangeland. Lakes, reservoirs, and streams.

Doublehead Ranger District: NW sector, adjoins Lava Beds NM (see entry this zone) on W, S, and E, has similar volcanic features: glass and lava flows, caves, tubes, chimneys, craters. W portion has mountains with moderate to steep slopes. Sugar pine and red and white firs; understory of bitterbrush, manzanita. At higher elevations, pure stands of lodgepole pine. To the E, sagebrush and juniper slopes. Medicine, Little Medicine, Bullseye, and Blanche lakes offer the only fishing.

Devil's Garden Ranger District: W of Goose Lake, S to Pit River. Gentle to moderate slopes. Average elevation 4,800 ft. Although much of the district, like Modoc County as a whole, is semiarid, it contains the 6,000-acre Big Sage Reservoir and a number of smaller ones. It also contains some 34,000 acres of wetland habitat, 15,000 of which are permanent water and 19,000 are intermittent wetlands. The basins in this area are characterized by heavy clay soils, with meadow, grasses, forbs, and silver sage communities. The characteristic vegetation of the associated uplands is low sagebrush and bluegrasses; or juniper, low sagebrush, and grasses. These lands are being managed for wildlife, including pronghorn, feral horse, sage grouse, and waterfowl. Grazing is a continuing use. One of the largest continuous stands of juniper in the western U.S., 800 acres preserved in *Devil's Garden Natural Area*. Juniper areas have big, black, and silver sagebrushes; rabbitbrush, bunchgrass. Also stands of ponderosa and Jeffrey pines, with white fir and incense cedar on N slopes above 5,500 ft.

Big Valley Ranger District: SW and S central portions. Basalt-capped plateaus and steep, mountainous uplands. Elevations 4,500–7,000 ft. At lower elevations: sage, bunchgrass, juniper, with some bitterbrush, curl-leaf mountain mahogany. Higher, ponderosa and Jeffrey pines, with white fir and incense cedar on N slopes above 5,500 ft.

Warner Mountain Ranger District: includes *South Warner Wilderness* (see "Features" section). Mountain range moderately sloping on W side, very steep on E. Several high peaks, including 9,892-ft. Eagle Peak. Sage, bunchgrass, juniper at lower elevations, with bitterbrush and curl-leaf mountain mahogany. At intermediate altitudes: pure and mixed stands of ponderosa and Jeffrey pines, white fir. Above, lodgepole and western white pines. Small lakes, streams. The best fishing is outside the wilderness, at East Creek, Patterson, and Lily Lakes.

Plants: Ponderosa and Jeffrey pines, incense cedar, western juniper. Associated species include oaks, quaking aspen, mountain mahogany, manzanita, chokecherry and bitter cherry, blueberry, snowberry, currant, Sierra plum, mountain misery, fern bush, squaw apple, sagebrush, rabbitbrush, bitterbrush, squaw carpet, serviceberry. Wildflowers include wild onion, camas, Indian paintbrush, low larkspur, shooting star, daisy, strawberry, lupines, tarweed, bluebell, phlox, buttercup, pansy, wooly mule's ear. Monkeyflower, evening primrose, peony, gilia, fireweed are among the species less commonly seen.

Birds: List available. Common shorebirds and waterfowl include red-necked and pied-billed grebes, double-crested cormorant, great blue heron, Canada goose, mallard, gadwall, pintail, shoveler. Sandhill crane rare. Raptors include hawks, golden and bald eagles, osprey, and goshawk. Coot, killdeer, willet, greater and lesser yellowlegs; spotted sandpiper, American avocet, Wilson's phalarope. Black-necked stilt less common. Ring-billed gull, Forster's tern, and black tern are common, with Caspian tern less so. Owls, hummingbirds, woodpeckers, kingbirds, and flycatchers are represented by several species each. Six numerous swallow species.

Mammals: Common species include mule deer, pronghorn, coyote, striped skunk, raccoon, cottontail, muskrat, beaver, porcupine, feral horse, many mice, voles, and ground squirrels. Black bear, bobcat, cougar, badger, fisher, marten, mink, weasel, marmot, jackrabbit, snowshoe hare, and several squirrel species are here, but less common.

Features

South Warner Wilderness: 70,385 acres. Spectacular alpine and subalpine area. Highest point is Eagle Peak. Patches of timber, grassy basins, slopes, meadows. Tumbling streams, a few small lakes, many springs. Area is unusual in that the trails are designed for access only. Once in the area, travel is by bushwhacking, so topo map and compass are essential. Wilderness permit required. Subfreezing temperatures can occur any month. Thunderstorms common in summer; snow not uncommon late spring and early fall; strong winds late Aug. and Sept.

Medicine Lake Highlands: 9,000 acres. Lies within a loosely defined boundary S of Lava Beds National Monument. Points of interest are *Medicine Lake,* crystal-clear in an old crater; *Glass Mountain,* unique glassy dacite and rhyolitic obsidian flow estimated to be about 1,400 years old; *Burnt Lava Flow,* picturesque flow of jumbled black lava surrounding islands of timber; *Medicine Lake Glass Flow,* composed of dull, stony-gray dacite, which covers a square mile, and ranges 50–150 ft. in height; *Little Mount Hoffman Lookout,* a seldom-used lookout affording spectacular view N toward Lava Beds National Monument.

Activities

Camping: 20 campgrounds, about 320 sites. A few campgrounds are easily accessible, with vault toilets and piped water. Others are primitive, access roads not suitable for larger RVs. As in other National Forests, one can camp almost anywhere, subject to fire permits and special regulations. Camping season generally May 15–Oct. 1. Many campgrounds are on or near lakes or streams.

Hiking, backpacking: About 140 mi. of trails, 2,000 mi. of maintained Forest roads, all suitable for hiking. Off-trail is possible in many areas.

Hunting: Mule deer for both rifle and bow hunters; pronghorn, waterfowl, migratory birds other than waterfowl, quail.

Fishing: Variety of lakes and streams. Brook, German brown, and rainbow trout; bass, catfish, arctic grayling.

Swimming: Medicine Lake, Blue Lake, elsewhere. Water is usually very cold at higher elevations. No lifeguard on duty.

Boating, canoeing: Powerboating, rowing, and sailing on Blue, Big Sage, and Medicine Lakes. Canoeing on a few smaller lakes.

Horse riding: Some horse parties use the Forest, especially the South Warner Wilderness. Ask HQ about local outfitters. There are wild horses in the *Wild Horse Territory* in Devil's Garden and Doublehead

Ranger Districts. (The Modoc National Forest is legally obligated to manage the wild horses within the 258,000-acre Wild Horse Territory.)

Downhill skiing: Cedar Pass area.

Ski touring: In Warner Mountains and Medicine Lake Highlands.

Call HQ if planning a trip in May or after mid-Sept. for advice on late or early snow. If press reports forest fires, check HQ for possible closure.

Publications

Forest map, $3.25.

Off-road vehicle map.

South Warner Wilderness (brochure with map).

Medicine Lake Highlands (brochure with map).

Headquarters
U.S. Forest Service, 800 W. Thea St., Alters, CA 96101; (916) 233-5811.

Ranger Districts
Big Valley R.D., P.O. Box 159, Akin, CA 96006; (916) 299-3215. Devil's Garden R.D., 800 W. Thea St., Alters, CA 96101; (916) 233-5811. Doublehead R.D., P.O. Box 369, Tulelake, CA 96134; (916) 667-2246; Warner Mountain R.D., P.O. Box 220, Cedarville, CA 96014; (916) 279-6116.

Modoc National Wildlife Refuge
U.S. Fish and Wildlife Service
6,706 acres.

From just S of Alturas on US 395, E on County Road 56 for 0.6 mi., then S on County Road 115 and follow Refuge signs.

Open: Daylight hours. Dorris Reservoir closed Oct. 1–mid-Jan.

Waterfowl area 60 mi. SE of the Klamath Basin marshes. At W base of Warner Mountains. Elevation about 4,400 ft. Area is flat to rolling. Numerous lakes, ponds, with many islands for breeding. South Fork of Pit River flows through. Dorris Reservoir, about 3 mi. E of the main portion, supplies water by canal for irrigation. About 1,000 acres of impoundments, 1,500 of marsh, 2,200 of wetland meadows, and 50 of riparian; the balance is cropland and sagebrush-juniper. Area is semiarid, with dry summers.

Large concentrations of waterfowl spring and fall. Many nesting species, so birding is also good in summer.

Birds: More than 246 species recorded. Peak fall population about 4,000 geese, 25,000 ducks. Nesting flock of Canada goose as well as migrants. Other nesting waterfowl: eared, western, and pied-billed grebes, mallard, gadwall, pintail, ruddy duck, cinnamon teal, shoveler. Migrants include white-fronted and snow geese, wigeon, bufflehead. Sandhill cranes sometimes seen in courtship dance; approximately 35 pairs nest on the Refuge. White pelican present in summer, not nesting here. Whistling swans stop over during migration.

Snipe, avocet, willet, Wilson's phalarope, black-necked stilt, pheasant, bitterns, Virginia rail, owls, northern flicker, and many swallows nest here. Migratory species include long-billed dowitcher, greater yellowlegs. Other species often seen include such raptors as bald eagle, turkey vulture, sharp-shinned, Cooper's, red-tailed, and rough-legged hawks, kestrel, prairie falcon, and, occasionally, endangered peregrin falcon. Also egrets, flycatchers, mountain chickadee, mountain bluebird, warblers, sparrows.

Checklist available.

Mammals: Include mule deer, pronghorn, coyote, bobcat, badger, skunk, raccoon, mink, muskrat, ground squirrel, cottontail, black-tailed jackrabbit.

Entrance road overlooks several ponds. Birding, including upland species, is good in HQ area. Short *auto tour route* around a marsh.

Activities
Hunting: Waterfowl. Designated area. Special rules may change from year to year. Inquire.

Fishing: Dorris Reservoir: bass, catfish, trout.

Boating: April–Sept.

Nearby
Modoc National Forest (see entry this zone).

Publications
Hunting leaflet with map.

Wildlife leaflet.

Headquarters
U.S. Fish and Wildlife Service, P.O. Box 1610, Alturas, CA 96101; (916) 233-3572.

Plumas-Eureka State Park
California Department of Parks and Recreation
6,600 acres.
Within Plumas National Forest.

From Truckee, 50 mi. N on Hwy 89 to Graeagle, then 5 mi. W on CR A-14.

Scenic and historic Park on E slopes of the Sierra Nevada. Mountainous. Elevations from 4,000–7,500 ft. Eureka Peak, 7,447 ft., is the natural focal point of the Park. Two small lakes; several creeks. Cascades and falls on Jamison Creek. Park is open all year, campground seasonally.

Plants: Lower slopes forested, tree species include red and white firs, Douglas-fir, incense cedar, ponderosa, sugar, and Jeffrey pines, with alder, black cottonwood, aspen, willow along streams. Brushy areas, especially at higher elevations, have manzanita, chinquapin, ceanothus, buckthorn. No wildflower list, but local flora index is available at the museum.

Birds: Species noted include Steller's jay, band-tailed pigeon, robin, golden eagle, northern flicker, white-headed and pileated woodpeckers, red-tailed hawk, great blue heron, caliope hummingbird.

Mammals: Include deer, squirrels, chipmunk, gopher, raccoon, porcupine, striped and spotted skunks, muskrat, beaver. In more remote sections: coyote, mountain lion, bobcat, black bear, marten, weasel.

Features
Scenic drives: to parking area near Eureka Lake, 6,300-ft. elevation; Red Dirt Rd. into National Forest and to the isolated N section of Park.

Interpretation
Visitor center/museum: Natural and cultural history.

Campfire programs and guided hikes, June–Sept.

"Talking Forest" nature trail.

Activities

Camping: 67 sites. Approx. May 1st–Oct. 15. First come, first served basis. *Crowding* often occurs July–Aug.

Hiking, backpacking: Trails to Eureka Peak, around Madora Lake, along Jamison Creek to falls. Trails into National Forest backcountry. Trailside camping in the Forest.

Fishing: Rainbow, brook, brown trout.

Ski touring: 3 mi. of trail. Usual snow season: Dec. 15–March 15.

Publications

Leaflet with map, $0.50.

Flora and fauna list, $0.25.

Headquarters

CA Dept. of Parks and Recreation, 310 Johnsville Rd., Blairsden, CA 96103; (916) 836-2380.

Plumas National Forest

U.S. Forest Service
1,154,754 acres. 1,409,986 acres within boundaries.

US 395 approximates the NE boundary. Hwy 70 crosses the Forest from the E, approximating its W boundary just N of Lake Oroville. Bullards Bar Reservoir is at the S tip. Hwy 89 crosses, SE to NW.

Part of the huge block of public land in E CA, adjoining the Lassen National Forest on the N, the Tahoe National Forest on the S. In the transition zone where the Sierra Nevada and Cascade Range merge. Elevations from 1,000 to 8,372 ft. About 100 lakes, more than 1,000 mi. of streams with canyons, waterfalls, cascades. Forest, brushfields, meadows.

Our source at HQ commented that the area is not as popular as other National Forests along the Sierra, and that most people think it less scenic. Presumably the comment applies to the N portion, above

Hwy 70. The views may be less dramatic, but it's attractive country. Trails are not heavily traveled.

The Forest includes most of the Feather River watershed, and this area is undeniably popular. The quarter-million acres of Forest inhold-ings include numerous commercial resorts, summer homes, and tourist enterprises. Many of the lakes have developed private land as well as Forest land along their shores. Some parts of the Forest, espe-cially around lakes, are heavily used, and restrictions have been adopted to minimize damage to the environment.

The Forest map shows relatively few hiking trails but an extensive road network, including many miles of primitive roads, some of which are more suitable for quiet hiking than for driving with an ordinary car. The network also includes many miles of gravel and reg-ularly maintained dirt roads. Many of these follow streams. Some lead to relatively isolated lakeside campgrounds.

At Quincy, elevation about 3,500 ft., at the junction of Hwys 70 and 89, annual precipitation is about 43 in. per year, most of it in win-ter. Temperatures here are often below freezing in winter. Hwy 70 W of Quincy is below the snow line most of the time. On the higher slopes, of course, snowfall is heavier and freezing temperatures more common. Campgrounds at lower elevations are generally open in early May; those higher are usually open by Memorial Day weekend. High trails are usually open by mid-June.

Plants: About two-thirds of the area is forested, the other third mostly in manzanita, sagebrush, and sagebrush-juniper, with some meadows and rocky places. Of the forest area, mixed conifers dominate the zone from about 2,000–6,000 ft., red fir in the zone next above. Together these make up about half of the forested acreage. Ponderosa pine is on the hotter, drier slopes, white fir where conditions are somewhat cooler and moister. Other species include incense cedar, sugar pine, black oak. Douglas-fir in some areas. A rarity is the Baker cypress, found at 6,500–7,000 ft. on Wheeler and Eisenheimer peaks. The champion is a specimen 70 ft. high, 21 ft. in diameter. Virtually the entire forest has been logged from time to time, but isolated old-growth specimens remain.

No wildflower checklist available. Notable displays are redbud in April, dogwood in May and June.

Birds: Checklist on file at HQ. 223 species recorded, including com-mon loon, western, eared, pied-billed, and horned grebes, white peli-can, great blue heron, black-crowned night heron, great and snowy egrets, many waterfowl species, many birds of prey, blue and sage grouse, California and mountain quail, many shorebirds, many gulls and terns, 9 species of owl, 10 species of woodpecker, 12 species of fly-catcher, 6 swallow species, Steller's, scrub, and pinyon jays, black-billed magpie, Clark's nutcracker, black-capped, mountain, and chestnut-backed chickadees, 5 wren species, western and mountain bluebirds, northern and loggerhead shrikes, 12 wood warbler species, black-headed, evening, and rose-breasted grosbeaks, 15 species of sparrow and towhee.

Mammals: Checklist on file at HQ. Species recorded include black bear, raccoon, ringtail, bobcat, mountain lion, long- and short-tailed weasels, mink, pine marten, river otter, badger, striped and spotted skunks, red and gray foxes, coyote, mule deer, marmot, chickaree, ground squirrels, chipmunks, beaver, porcupine, mice, snowshoe and black-tailed hares; cottontail, pika, shrew, little brown bat, long-eared myotis.

Reptiles and amphibians: Include long-toed salamander, California newt, western toad, Pacific tree frog, California red-legged frog, mountain yellow-legged frog, 5 lizard species, 10 snake species includ-ing western ringneck, Pacific gopher, rubber boa, western rattlesnake.

Features

Feather Falls Scenic Area: 15,000 acres. Includes portions of Middle Fork of the Feather River and three tributaries. Wide variety of topog-raphy, vegetation, wildlife. Spectacular granite domes, picturesque waterfalls. *Feather Falls,* 640 ft., is sixth highest in continental U.S.; reached by self-guiding trail, 7 mi. round trip. Hiking and riding trails. *Caution: Sheer cliffs. Stay back of guard rails.*

Middle Fork, Feather River: 108 mi. long. Designated a National Wild and Scenic River. Designated land, a narrow band, along river includes 13,200 acres of National Forest land, 12,000 acres privately owned. Five zones include:

- *Bald Rock Canyon Wild River Zone:* Rugged, scenic. Massive boul-ders, cliffs, waterfalls, canyon walls. Access is difficult. End-to-end travel seldom possible, rarely accomplished. Portions can be visited by day or overnight hikes.
- *Upper Canyon Wild River Zone:* River is rugged, rocky. Slopes vege-tated but steep. Three trails to river for 4-wheel-drive vehicles or trail bikes. Also foot trails.
- *Milsap Bar Scenic Rive Zone:* Scenic, rugged. Car bridge crosses river within this zone; campground nearby. *South Branch Falls,* also known as *Seven Falls,* has 9 falls of 130–150 ft. About 1 mi. upstream from

campground, but no trail. A primitive road from Brush Creek is nearby. A scenic area, but rough country.

- *English Bar Scenic River Zone:* Scenic, less rugged than other zones. Timber stands closer to river. Car bridge crosses at Nelson Point. Access also from unimproved roads. Unimproved campsites.
- *Recreational River Zone:* Includes a variety of scenic types, notably Mohawk Valley. Many inholdings, commercial developments including motels, resorts, stables.

Caution: Wild River zones are not for the inexperienced, and Scenic River zones are not for the unprepared. Although portions of the river can be floated, sections are treacherous, and access in or out of some sections is nearly impossible. Check with rangers before undertaking a river trip.

Lake Davis Recreation Area: Elevation 5,800 ft. Camping, hiking, fishing, hunting, boating, ski touring, swimming.

Bucks Lake Recreation Area: Elevation 5,060 ft. Camping, hiking, fishing, hunting, swimming, boating, horse riding, and also ski touring. Commercial resorts and private homes occupy part of lakeshore. Good trails in area; Pacific Crest Trail is nearby. Brilliant red snow plant seen May–July. Beaver ponds and dams in Haskins Valley and Bucks Creek.

Bucks Lake Wilderness: 24,000 acres above the Recreation Area, allowing those who seek more solitude and primitive camping and hiking experiences to enjoy themselves. 41 mi. of trails ranging from well maintained to completely natural. As always in wilderness areas, leave no trace of yourself (or your horse) when you leave.

Little Grass Valley Recreation Area: Reservoir at 5,046-ft. elevation. Upper Canyon Wild River Zone of Middle Fork is N of lake. Feather River Falls Scenic Area is SW of lake. Camping, hiking, hunting, fishing, swimming, boating, ski touring. Although there are some inholdings, the entire shoreline is accessible.

Antelope Lake Recreation Area: Elevation 5,002 ft. Camping, hiking, hunting, fishing, swimming, boating. Scenic drive from here to timberline near crest of Diamond Mountain, ending at Red Rock Lookout; 25 mi. Road usually passable by late June.

Lakes Basin Recreation Area: Known for its scenic geological features, breathtaking scenery, and surrounding crystal lakes. Camping, hunting, picnicking, bird-watching, hiking, backpacking, boating, fishing, swimming, and nature study enjoyed in summer.

Cross-country skiing and snowmobiling in winter.

Includes:
Plumas-Eureka State Park (see entry this zone).

Activities

Camping: 47 campgrounds, 1,161 sites. Open Memorial Day weekend–Oct. 31; those at lower elevations may open mid–May. Camping is generally permitted elsewhere except for specified areas around lakes, subject to obtaining fire permit.

Hiking, backpacking: 73 mi. of Pacific Crest Trail are in the Forest. Trail guides available for this and other trails.

Hunting: Deer, bear, squirrel, rabbit, waterfowl, quail, chukar, dove.

Fishing: At many lakes and streams. Rainbow and brown trout, kokanee and coho salmon, bass, catfish, bluegill.

Swimming: Beaches at several lakes. Elsewhere as you choose.

Boating: Ramps on several lakes.

Canoeing, kayaking: Attempting the Middle Fork by raft or kayak is inadvisable. Tubing in the recreation zone and English Bar Scenic Zone is feasible in June and July.

Horse riding: Rentals at Blairsden, Gold and Bucks Lakes. Some trails are unsuitable for horses.

Mountain biking: 7 routes and trails, from 1-19 mi., easy to very difficult.

Adjacent
Lassen National Forest, Tahoe National Forest (see entries this zone).

Publications
Forest map, $3.00.

Forest information sheet.

Campground information.

Trail information: Quincy Ranger District.

Pacific Crest Trail route description (fact sheet).

Trail Guide: Feather River Canyon.

Leaflets with maps:

Feather Falls Scenic Area.

Middle Fork, Feather River.

Lake Davis Recreation Area.

Bucks Lake Recreation Area.

Little Grass Valley Recreation Area.

Antelope Lake Recreation Area.

Plumas National Forest off-road-vehicle control plan.

Headquarters:
U.S. Forest Service, Box 11500, Quincy, CA 95971; (916) 283-2050.

Information and Work Centers:
Challenge Visitor Center, 18050 Mulock, Challenge, CA 95925; (916) 675-1146. Greenville Information and Work Center, 128 Hot Springs Rd., Greenville, CA 95947; (916) 284-7126. Laufman Station, 446-525 Milford Grade, Milford, CA 96121; (916) 253-2223.

Ranger Districts
Beckwourth R.D., Box 7, Blairsden, CA 96103; (916) 836-2575. Feather River R.D., 875 Mitchell Ave., Oroville, CA 95965-4699; (916) 534-6500. Mount Hough R.D., 39696 Hwy 70, Quincy, CA 95971; (916) 283-0555.

Shasta-Trinity National Forest
U.S. Forest Service
See entry in zone 1. Although a large portion of the Forest is in zone 2, most is in zone 1, and a unified entry seemed best.

The Whiskeytown-Shasta-Trinity National Recreation Area has three units. Two of them, Clair Engle Lake and Shasta Lake, are within the Shasta-Trinity National Forest and are described in that entry. The Whiskeytown unit stands alone and is an entry below.

Skedaddle-Amedee Mountains
U.S. Bureau of Land Management
63,130 acres.

From Susanville, E 18 mi. on US 395, then E on Wendel Rd., the SW boundary. E boundary is Skedaddle Rd. Several dead-end roads lead N into the area.

Rugged vertical cliffs and canyons, peaks, and basins of the Amedee and Skedaddle Mountains. The high (up to 7,680 ft.) elevations of the Skedaddles support scattered aspen groves and patches of large shrubs on northern slopes. Riparian vegetation (willows, wild rose, berry shrubs) is found in the deep canyons, and small grass meadows in the basins. The rugged core unit is surrounded by open, sagebrush-covered flats from 4,000 to 4,600 ft. Numerous springs. *(Treat all drinking water.)* Unusual rock formations in scenic Wendel Canyon, Amedee Canyon, and Wendel Cliffs.

Wildlife abounds in the unit, including mule deer, pronghorn, and the seldom-seen mountain lion. Prairie falcon nests.

Hiking attractions include Wendel Canyon, two parallel canyons in Wendel Cliffs that offer challenging hiking and spectacular views across Honey Lake to the Sierra Crest. James and Amedee Canyons and the Summit Ridge best approached from the Bruback Springs Rd. pass.

Headquarters
U.S. Bureau of Land Management, Susanville District Office, 2950 Riverside Dr., Susanville, CA 92507; (916) 257-5381/0456.

Tehama Wildlife Area
California Department of Fish and Game
46,895 acres.

From Red Bluff on I-5, E 3 mi. on Hwy 99, then 15 mi. E on Hogsback Rd. Or 20 mi. N and E from Hwy 36 E to Paynes Creek, then S on Plum Creek Rd.

Winter range for Columbian black-tailed deer. Sierra Nevada foothills, a broad bench sloping from 4,000 ft. down toward the Sacramento River Valley, cut by steep-sided canyons with prominent rimrocks and lava outcroppings. Elevations in wildlife area vary from approximately 1,000–2,400 ft. The deer herd migrates over 100 mi. from summer range in and around Lassen National Park, arriving here mid-Oct. and remaining until early April.

Woodland, grass, and brush. Primary deer forage is wedgeleaf ceanothus, along with acorn mast, oak leafage, mountain mahogany, live oak, redberry.

A major portion of the Wildlife Area, S of Hogsback Rd., is closed Dec. 1 through first Friday in April to prevent harassment of the deer in the breeding season.

On the E, the area adjoins a lightly used section of Lassen National Forest. Map shows jeep roads crossing into the Forest.

Activities

Camping: 2 campgrounds. Primitive; no water.

Hiking: Trails and primitive roads. No maintained trails.

Hunting: Chiefly deer. Also feral hog, quail, turkey, squirrel. Poor water-fowl hunting.

Fishing: Rainbow and brown trout; bass in lower portion of Antelope Creek. Check regulations for special fishing and hunting restrictions: (916) 225-2867.

Caution: Visitors are advised to be extremely cautious using roads and trails. ORV use is prohibited.

Publication

Leaflet with map.

Headquarters

CA Dept. of Fish and Game, P.O. Box 188, Paynes Creek, CA 96075; (916) 597-2201.

Timbered Crater

U.S. Bureau of Land Management
18,690 acres.

From Fall River Mills on US 299, E 7 mi., then 8 mi. N on road to Day.

The Day road passes through private and National Forest land to an area of private land in Little Hot Spring Valley. This site lies to the W and adjoins Shasta National Forest land on the W and SE. It takes its name from a large crater on the W boundary, its slopes covered with grasses, manzanita brush, and ponderosa pine. Most of the area is a large lava flow that has not yet developed deep soil and is rocky, rough, and difficult to traverse. Terrain includes low buttes, shallow depressions, and drainages. Natural vegetation includes ponderosa and gray pines, oak, juniper, and dense to scattered mountain shrub. Much of the area sees wildfires during the summer.

The BLM reports that more than 200 bird species have been identified in the area, including bald eagle, mourning dove, band-tailed pigeon, California and mountain quail, wild turkey, pheasant, blue grouse. Mammals include black bear, black-tailed deer, mule deer, cottontail, gray squirrel, chickaree, mountain lion, Rocky Mountain elk. Wolverine reported. The site includes the *Baker Cypress–Lava Rock Natural Area*, 1,148 acres, designated to protect a stand of Baker cypress. Elevation here is 3,400–3,600 ft.

Most of the Timbered Crater area and adjoining National Forest land is up for wilderness review. Just S of the boundary, maps show a wetlands complex: Eastman Lake, Big Lake, Tule Lake, the Tule and Little Tule Rivers, swamp, and meandering creeks. The BLM bird information list includes waterfowl, and presumably this is where they occur. The area is said to be a combination of private and state-owned land. From Fall River Mills, Glenburn Rd. leads toward this area, and it would seem worth exploring, especially by birders.

Headquarters
Bureau of Land Management, Alturas Resource Area, 708 W. 12th St., Alturas, CA 96101; (916) 233-4666.

Tule Lake National Wildlife Refuge
See Klamath Basin National Wildlife Refuges (this zone).

Whiskeytown Unit, Whiskeytown-Shasta-Trinity National Recreation Area
U.S. National Park Service
42,503 acres.

From Redding, 8 mi. W on Hwy 299.

Other units of this National Recreation Area are within the Shasta-Trinity National Forest (see entry zone 1). This one stands alone.

Chief attraction is the 3,200-acre lake. Unlike Shasta and Clair Engle Lakes, it is not drawn down in summer. Thus it can have sandy beaches fine for swimming. Its size and shape favor canoeing and sailing rather than high-speed motorboating.

Surrounded by hills. Highest point 6,209 ft. The original forest was logged off in recent years with little heed for reforestation. Now under management, gradual recovery is occurring. Stands of young trees and extensive shrub cover have promoted development of wildlife populations.

People come here because of the lake. Few except hunters use the upcountry. The map shows no foot trails, but there are 50 mi. of backcountry dirt and gravel roads.

Interpretation

Evening *ranger programs.*

Junior Ranger programs.

Strike it rich: Information and history of gold panning.

Camden House tour.

Patio boat tours: Lectures about the natural and cultural history of the area.

Activities

Camping: Several campgrounds, 180 sites; 2 RV areas, 59 sites; 2 tent areas, 102 sites; 20 designated backcountry tent sites.

Hunting: Deer, bear, squirrel, rabbit, fox, dove, pigeon, quail, some waterfowl.

Fishing: Brown and rainbow trout, bass, bluegill, kokanee salmon.

Boating, canoeing: Ramps, marina, rentals.

Swimming: 2 sandy beaches.

Mountain biking: 8 trails from ¾ mi. to 7 mi.

Gold panning: There's a $1.00 permit fee.

Publications

Brochure with map.

Special interest information sheets.

Whiskeytown Nugget.

Headquarters:
National Park Service, P.O. Box 188, Whiskeytown, CA 96095; (916) 241-6584.

Woodson Bridge State Recreation Area

California Department of Parks and Recreation
428 acres.
From Corning on I-5, 6 mi. E on South Ave.

On the Sacramento River. Small park much used by local groups for nature study. Over 100 plant species identified. Prominent trees include valley oak, California black walnut, Oregon ash, black cottonwood. Many shrubs, wildflowers. Vivid fall colors.

Many bird species; checklist available. Deer often seen, as well as small mammals.

A portion of the site across the river, not accessible by land, has been set aside as a natural preserve.

Activities

Camping: 41 campsites and 1 group camp capable of holding 45 people. All year. Reservations available May 25–Sept. 14.

Fishing: Boat and bank. King salmon, shad, steelhead, striped bass, catfish, occasional sturgeon.

Boating: Ramp at adjacent county park.

Swimming.

Publication

Leaflet with map.

Headquarters

CA Dept. of Parks and Recreation, Rt. 1, Box 325, Corning, CA 96021; (916) 839-2112.

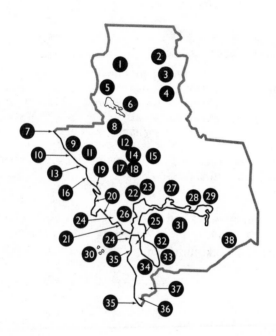

Z O N E

Includes these counties:

Glenn	Yolo	San Joaquin
Lake	Marin	San Francisco
Colusa	Solano	San Mateo
Sonoma	Sacramento	Alameda
Napa	Contra Costa	

Few cities have as much diverse, scenic, wild country nearby as does San Francisco. Zone 3 includes the Bay Area and the counties to the N and E. Those to the S are in zone 5.

The Bay itself is surrounded by fascinating wetlands, only a fraction of what was once here but none the less impressive. The largest, the Grizzly Island Wildlife Area, is relatively little known, but it is one of America's great marshes. Wetlands near the confluence of the Sacramento and San Joaquin Rivers are best explored by boat, although some areas are accessible by car and on foot.

The ocean beaches S of the city are attractive but heavily used, with few sections one could call natural. We have written a collective entry: San Mateo State Beaches. Inland are two of the redwood State Parks: Portola and Butano.

To the N is the Golden Gate National Recreation Area, at least a part of which merits the name "the wilderness next door." This National Recreation Area is a complex of city, state, and federal sites knitted together in an imaginative management scheme. Included are some of San Francisco's city parks. Across the bridge are the Marin Headlands, Muir Woods, Mt. Tamalpais, and other areas. Under the plan, development will be limited, large sections left wild. Adjoining is Point Reyes National Seashore, a large part of it wilderness.

Still farther N are Sonoma County Regional Parks at Bodega Bay and Sonoma Coast State Beach, a spectacular coastline. A big inland is another redwood State Park, Armstrong.

Directly N of the city, out Hwy 29, is the Napa Valley, famous for its wine grapes. Several State Parks offer easy and pleasant hiking: Annadel, Bothe-Napa Valley, Robert Louis Stevenson, with Boggs Mountain Demonstration State Forest a bit beyond. The valley floor is rolling rather than flat. The mountains on either side are not high but steep, with many canyons. Cross-mountain roads are likely to be scenic but steep and narrow.

W and N of Clear Lake, the W boundary of the zone is the crest of the Coast Range. These mountains largely constitute the Mendocino National Forest, a major part of which is in zone 3.

I-5, near the E boundary of the zone, runs through the Sacramento Valley. Once a great wetlands, supporting millions of waterfowl, the valley is now agricultural. In recent years, the swing has been to rice. Fields are surrounded by low dikes. Many operations are performed by low-flying planes. The Sacramento National Wildlife Refuges have the dual role of accommodating large numbers of wintering waterfowl and reducing their predation on farm crops.

Angel Island State Park

See Golden Gate National Recreation Area (this zone).

Annadel State Park

California Department of Parks and Recreation
Approximately 5,000 acres.

From Santa Rosa, E on Hwy 12 about 6 mi.; S on Los Alamos; W on Montgomery Dr.; S on Channel Dr.

A day-use park for hiking, about 50 mi. N of San Francisco. Flat to rolling terrain. Elevations from 300 to 1,887 ft. at top of Bennett Mountain. (The peak is just outside the Park boundary.) Some steep-sided canyons, rock outcroppings on knolls. Intermittent streams.

Includes 30-acre Lake Ilsanjo; 1½-mi. shoreline, a 35-acre marsh. A 30-ft. waterfall is usually dry. Parking, office, picnic facilities, trails. No other development.

Plants: About 70% forested: mixed evergreen and oak-deciduous. Trees include Douglas-fir, bay, madrone, California black oak, Oregon oak, Oregon ash, California buckeye, Coast live oak, bigleaf maple. Small stand of redwood, a few old growth. Understory includes wood fern, hazel, abundant poison oak. About one-quarter of the area is chaparral and includes manzanita, chamise, toyon. About 200 species of flowering plants such as brodiaea, lupine, California poppy, gold-fields, shooting star, linanthus, mule ears, iris, hound's tongue. The rare and endangered white fritillary blooms Feb.–April.

Birds: Checklist of 160 species available. Includes Cooper's hawk, great blue heron, screech owl, western bluebird, pileated woodpecker, white-crowned sparrow, wild turkey.

Mammals: Include fox, raccoon, muskrat, skunk, bobcat, black-tailed deer. Mountain lions have been sighted.

Reptiles and amphibians: Include western fence and alligator lizards, California newt, gopher snake, kingsnake, western yellow-bellied racer, rattlesnake (occasional), ring-necked snake.

Activities

Hiking, mountain biking: 39 mi. of trails. Bicycles yield to people and horses. Most trails have moderate grades. Ledson Marsh is a good birding area; at least 10 different plant community types.

Fishing: Black bass, bluegill.

Horse riding: Permitted on trails.

Drinking water only at park office and main parking lot. No fires allowed—this includes charcoal grills. Dogs prohibited except at parking lot and Channel Dr.

Publications

Park brochure, $1.00.

Trail map, $.75. Available by machine at park office.

Bird checklist, free.

Headquarters

CA Dept. of Parks and Recreation, 6201 Channel Dr., Santa Rosa, CA 95405; (707) 539-3911; fax (707) 538-0769.

Armstrong Redwoods State Reserve/Austin Creek State Recreation Area

California Department of Parks and Recreation
800 acres/5,800 acres.

W of Healdsburg. From Santa Rosa N on US 101 0.4 mi. then W on River Rd. to Guerneville. N. 2½ mi. on Armstrong Woods Rd.

Access to Austin Creek is through Armstrong. Armstrong is a popular, heavily used redwoods park. First- and second-growth Coast redwoods, the largest specimen 308 ft. tall, 14½ ft. in diameter.

The adjacent Austin Creek area is hilly, elevations 150 to almost 2,000 ft. Attractive canyons; many springs; several streams. Second-growth Coast redwoods, not so impressive as the Armstrong groves. Also Douglas-fir with madrone, oak, red alder, azalea, Oregon ash. Some open grassland. Annual rainfall about 55 in. Many wildflowers in the two areas, including hawkweed, balsamroot, heartleaf arnica, scarlet gilia, yellow globe lily, trillium.

Activities

Camping: 25 sites. All year. Trailers, RVs over 20 ft. can't use the access road, which may be closed to autos in bad weather. Also 4 primitive campsites for horse riders and hikers.

Hiking: 22 mi. of trails.

Horse riding: Horse trailer parking at entrance.

Headquarters

CA Dept. of Parks and Recreation, 17000 Armstrong Woods Rd., Guerneville, CA 95446; (707) 869-2015.

Audubon Canyon Ranch; Bolinas Lagoon Preserve

Audubon Canyon Ranch (a private organization)
2,000 acres.

3 mi. N of Stinson Beach on Coast Hwy 1.

Since 1962 this private environmental foundation has protected wildlife sanctuaries in Marin and Sonoma Counties such as the Bolinas Lagoon Preserve near Stinson Beach, the Cypress Grove Preserve on Tomales Bay in Marshall, and the Bouverie Preserve in Glen Ellen. The goals of the Ranch are to preserve and manage the properties as sanctuaries for native plants and animals, to educate children and adults about the value and protection of the natural environment, and to support research that enhances the preservation and management of the sanctuaries.

The *Bolinas Lagoon Preserve* is home to a nesting colony of great blue herons and great and snowy egrets. A ½ mi. trail to the overlook offers a view of the nesting birds. Also available are a display hall, a bird hide, and a nature bookstore. The Preserve is open to the public mid-March to mid-July, Sat., Sun., and holidays from 10 A.M.–4 P.M. and *open by appointment* Tues.–Thurs. 2–4 P.M. (After the end of May the weekday hours are usually 10:30 A.M.–4 P.M. by *appointment only.*) Once the Preserve closes in July, it remains closed to the public until the following March.

The *Bouverie Preserve* and the *Cypress Grove Preserve* are open by *appointment only.*

Plants: A mixed evergreen forest includes Coast redwood, cypress, and Douglas-fir. The grassy hillsides are coastal scrub and chaparral.

Birds: Great blue herons, great and snowy egrets; band-tailed pigeon, sandpipers, towhees, osprey, pelican, and hummingbirds.

Mammals: Mule deer, bobcat, badger, gray fox, raccoon, brush rabbit, meadow mouse, harbor seal.

Reptiles and amphibians: Several species of newt and lizard.

Interpretation
The Ranch sponsors a nature education program for greater Bay Area schools on weekday mornings March–June and Sept.–Nov.

Headquarters
Audubon Canyon Ranch, 4900 Hwy 1, Stinson Beach, CA 94974; (415) 868-9244; fax (415) 868-1699.

Boggs Mountain Demonstration State Forest

California Department of Forestry
3,493 acres.

From I-80, N on Hwy 29 through Napa to Middletown. Left on Hwy 175 through Cobb. Entrance is on Hwy 175, 1 mi. N of Cobb.

An experimental and demonstration Forest acquired in 1949 after all merchantable timber had been cut except a few seed trees and scattered, inaccessible patches. Under management, the Forest has regenerated and harvesting has resumed. Terrain is rolling to mountainous. Elevations from 2,400 to 3,750 ft. on Boggs Mountain, a viewpoint. Annual precipitation is about 70 in. Summers are dry. This is resort country; there are numerous developments along Hwy 175.

The Forest map is necessary as roads and trails are only sometimes marked, depending on the rates of vandalism and maintenance. When we visited in spring, roads were muddy. In extreme wet weather many are impassable. There are over 14 mi. of trails for non-motorized multiuse.

Plants: 90% forested: ponderosa and sugar pines, Douglas-fir. Understory includes manzanita, dogwood, coffeeberry, madrone, live oak.

Birds: No checklist. Species mentioned were mountain and California quail, band-tailed pigeon.

Mammals: Include gray squirrel, gray fox, coyote, raccoon, mink, bobcat, black bear, mule deer.

Activities

Camping: Two primitive campgrounds; one with 15 sites, one with 2. Camping is limited to the campgrounds. A permit from the HQ is needed.

Hiking, mountain bicycling, horse riding: Over 14 mi. of multiple-use trails for hiking, biking, and horse riding.

Hunting: Heaviest use is in deer-hunting season. Aug. 15–Sept. 15. Dates may vary from year to year.

Publication

Leaflet with map.

Headquarters
CA Dept. of Forestry, P.O. Box 839, Cobb, CA 95426; (707) 928-4378.

Bothe-Napa Valley State Park

California Department of Parks and Recreation
1,991 acres.

From St. Helena, N 5 mi. on Hwy 29.

The Park extends about 4 mi. W from the highway, primarily along the canyon of Ritchey Creek. About ½ mi. wide. All development is at the E end. Only foot, bike, and horse travel beyond the parking area and campground. The campground is popular, often used by people sightseeing in the Napa Valley and as a one-night stopover. Few campers use the trails.

Elevations from 320 to 2,000 ft. Steep hillsides. One of the most E stands of Coast redwoods. The original trees were logged off some years ago. Second-growth trees are now of good size.

Plants: In woodland areas: Coast redwood, Douglas-fir, Pacific madrone, bigleaf maple, and oaks: black, Oregon, Coast live, valley. Understory has poison oak, sweet shrub, oceanspray. In chaparral areas: chamise, ceanothus, manzanita, scrub oak. Some wildflowers.

Birds: About 100 species recorded, including turkey vulture, red-tailed and red-shouldered hawks, California quail, Anna's hummingbird, northern flicker, pileated, acorn, hairy, downy, and Nuttall's woodpeckers, black phoebe, olive-sided flycatcher, violet-green swallow, Steller's and scrub jays, chestnut-backed chickadee, plain titmouse, bushtit, brown creeper, varied and hermit thrushes, western bluebird, ruby-crowned kinglet, orange-crowned and Wilson's warblers, solitary vireo, pine siskin, chipping, golden-crowned, and song sparrows.

Mammals: Include squirrel, raccoon, mule deer, bobcat, gray fox, coyote.

Interpretation
Campfire programs and guided hikes in summer.

Activities

Camping: 50 sites. Reservations March 1–Oct. 31. Also hiker-biker camp.

Hiking: 10 mi. of trails.

Horse riding: 6 mi. of trails.

Publication

Leaflet.

Headquarters

CA Dept. of Parks and Recreation, 3801 St. Helena Hwy N, Calistoga, CA 94515; (707) 942-4575.

Brannan Island State Recreation Area

California Department of Parks and Recreation
336 acres.

3 mi. S of Rio Vista on Hwy 160.

The Park, on the Sacramento River just above its junction with the San Joaquin River, is not a natural area. Popular with swimmers, fishermen, boaters, campers, and sure to be crowded on any fine weekend. We include it because it's a good base for exploring the many channels and sloughs in the delta region.

Interpretation

Campfire programs once or twice weekly in summer.

Activities

Camping: 102 sites. All year. Reservations May–Sept.

Fishing: Striped bass, bluegill, crappie, perch, bullhead, largemouth bass, sturgeon.

Swimming: Beach, lifeguards in season.

Boating: 6-lane ramp; ample parking. 32 slips for overnighting. Walk-in camps available with slips.

Nearby

Franks Tract State Recreation Area: 3,838 acres. 5 mi. SE of Brannan Island by boat. Just N of Bethel Island. This was rich delta farmland

until the levee broke. Now most of the area is water. Boat access only.
Waterfowl, beaver, muskrat, fox, raccoon, river otter. *Delta Meadows
River Park:* 205 acres. Dredged slough adjoining a large natural area of
sloughs, tule marshes, meadows, and cottonwood and oak woodland.
Access via Hwy 160 near Locke or by boat from Snodgrass Slough.
Overnight mooring. Limit 30 days per year. Swimming, fishing, boat-
ing, wildlife viewing. Waterfowl, beaver, muskrat, river otter, fox,
raccoon.

Publication
Brannan Island leaflet with area map.

Headquarters
CA Dept. of Parks and Recreation, 17645 Hwy 160, Rio Vista, CA
94571; (916) 777-6671.

Butano State Park
California Department of Parks and Recreation
3,200 acres.

From Half Moon Bay, S 15 mi. on Hwy 1. Turn inland to Pescadero,
then S 5 mi. on Cloverdale Rd. From Santa Cruz, N 20 mi. on Hwy 1.
Turn inland on Gazos Creek Rd., then 3 mi. N on Cloverdale Rd.

A redwood park in the Santa Cruz Mountains, planned for hiking.
Includes most of the Little Butano Creek watershed. Park is about 4
mi. E–W, 1 mi. N–S. The developed area is at the W end. Elevations
from 220 to 1,714 ft.

Plants: Checklist available. The redwoods are mostly second growth
with some old growth. Also chaparral, grassland, riparian woodland.
Wildflowers include calypso orchid, trillium, iris, blue-eyed grass. Also
poison oak and stinging nettles.

Birds: Checklist available. 114 species recorded, including Steller's
jay, winter wren, varied thrush, great horned owl, red-tailed hawk,
California quail, chestnut-backed chickadee, marbled murrelet, Wilson's warbler, bank-tailed pigeon, black-headed grosbeak.

Mammals: Include gray squirrel, raccoon, coyote, gray fox, bobcat,
mule deer, assorted bats.

Reptiles and amphibians: Include California newt, ensatina, Pacific giant salamander, gopher snake, coast garter snake, ringneck snake, rubber boa, Pacific tree frog, California red-legged frog, western fence lizard.

Interpretation

Small *exhibit area* at HQ.

Campfire program Fri. and Sat. nights, Memorial Day–Labor Day.

Also *guided hikes,* Sat. and Sun. May–Sept.

Junior Ranger programs Sat. and Sun.

Annual "Leave It There" *Fungus Fair* in winter. Call HQ for date.

Activities

Camping: 39 sites, 19 of them walk-in. All year. Reservations Memorial Day–Sept. Campground is usually full Fri., Sat., and holidays May–Sept.

Fishing: Above Division Dam.

Hiking, backpacking: 20 mi. of trails. Trail camp with 7 sites for backpackers in old-growth forest. About a 5-mi. hike with elevation gain of 1,600 ft. Reservations required.

Dogs are permitted in campground and on fire roads, not on trails or in trail camp. There are ticks and yellow jackets.

Publication

Trail map.

Headquarters

CA Dept. of Parks and Recreation, 1500 Cloverdale Rd. #3, Pescadero, CA 94060; (415) 879-2040.

Caswell Memorial State Park

California Department of Parks and Recreation
258 acres.

From Ripon on Hwy 99, 6 mi. S on Austin Rd.

A small park with 4 mi. of frontage on the meandering Stanislaus River. Noted for a 138-acre stand of valley oak, remnant of the large hardwood forest that once covered much of the Central Valley's flood plains. Some trees with girths over 17 ft. Camping and day use areas are at the S end of the Park, foot trails beyond.

Oak Forest Nature Trail winds through the oak stand. Elsewhere are wild rose thickets, blackberry, wild grape, wild currant.

Camping: 65 sites. All year. Reservations recommended Memorial Day–Labor Day.

Publication
Leaflet with map, $.50.

Headquarters
28000 S. Austin Rd., Ripon, CA 95366; (209) 599-3810.

Cedar Roughs

U.S. Bureau of Land Management
7,183 acres.

N of Napa. About 2 mi. W of Rancho Monticello on Lake Berryessa, on the Berryessa-Knoxville Rd. No public road access. 1996 land acquisition provides legal access at NW corner of area. Ask at HQ for trail and access status.

A large serpentine mound extending NW–SE. Elevation of Lake Berryessa, near E boundary, is 440 ft. Site elevations from 1,000 to 2,287 ft. on Iron Mountain at SE corner. Trout Creek drains E slope. Noted for a large, almost pure stand of Sargent cypress. On the lower slopes, chaparral with scattered live oak, digger pine, native grasses.

Selected as a wilderness study area.

Headquarters
Clear Lake Resource Area, Bureau of Land Management, 2550 N. State St., Clear Lake, CA 95482; (707) 468-4000.

China Camp State Park

California Department of Parks and Recreation
1,512 acres.

From San Francisco, N on US 101 to San Rafael. Turn right at Marin County Civic Center, then 2.7 mi. on N San Pedro Rd. to campground, 5.2 mi. to Historic Area.

2 mi. of shoreline on San Pablo Bay. About 500 acres of salt marsh, 200 of grassland, 800 of forest. Elevations to 1,000 ft. Site includes China Camp Village Historic Area.

Forest tree species include California bay laurel, Coast live oak, valley oak, and madrone. Pickleweed, cordgrass, and saltgrass in marsh. No bird checklist; marshes attract waterfowl, shorebirds. Park ranger reports mule deer, gray fox, raccoon.

Activities

Camping: 30 developed sites with showers.

Hiking, horse riding, bicycling: Multiuse trails.

Fishing: Bay. Striped bass, flounder, sturgeon.

Swimming: Unsupervised.

Picnic and swimming areas sometimes crowded on weekends.

Headquarters

Rt. 1, Box 244, San Rafael, CA 94901; (415) 456-0766.

Clear Lake State Park

California Department of Parks and Recreation
565 acres.

From Cloverdale, N 51 mi. on US 101 to Hopland. E on Hwy 175 to Hwy 29 and S to Kelseyville. NE 3½ mi. on Soda Bay Rd.

Clear Lake, 45,000 acres, is the largest natural lake wholly within CA. A popular resort area, much of the shoreline developed. Vineyards and orchards around Kelseyville. The Park is also popular, the campground full on pleasant weekends, daily in summer. Hillside trails are not heavily used, especially fall to spring.

2 mi. frontage on the lake. Elevations from 1,320 to 2,800 ft. Site is 75% forested.

Plants: On high ground: gray pine, blue oak, valley oak. Lower: box elder, California sycamore, cottonwood, black walnut, California white oak, Oregon ash, California bay laurel, willow. Spring display of western redbud with California buckeye. Shrubs include manzanita, mountain mahogany, coyote bush.

Birds: Checklist available. Species "seen on most days" in season include pied-billed and western grebes, great blue heron, mallard, green-winged teal, ruddy duck, bufflehead, American coot, California and Bonaparte's gulls, red-tailed hawk, kestrel, turkey vulture, California quail, killdeer, Anna's hummingbird, belted kingfisher, northern flicker, acorn woodpecker, black phoebe, violet-green, tree, and barn swallows, plain titmouse, common bushtit, white-breasted nuthatch, mourning dove, ruby-crowned kinglet, western meadowlark, red-winged blackbird, house finch, lesser goldfinch, brown and rufous-sided towhees, dark-eyed junco, white-crowned and golden-crowned sparrows.

Mammals: Include black-tailed jackrabbit, brush rabbit, ground and gray squirrels, chipmunk, raccoon, mink, gray fox, mule deer. Occasional bobcat.

Interpretation
Nature trail.

Campfire programs and guided walks, July and Aug., as requested.

Activities
Camping: 3 campgrounds, 147 sites. All year. Reservations May 13–Sept. 7.

Hiking: 3 mi. of trails.

Fishing: Record-size bass, also catfish, bluegill, crappie.

Boating: Ramp.

Publications
Leaflet with map.

Bird checklist.

Nature trail guide.

Headquarters
5300 Soda Bay Rd., Kelseyville, CA 95451; (707) 279-4293.

Colusa National Wildlife Refuge

See Sacramento National Wildlife Refuges (this zone).

Cow Mountain Area

U.S. Bureau of Land Management
60,000 acres.

From Ukiah, 5 mi. E on Mill Creek Rd. to Mendo Rock Rd.

In the Mayacamas Mountains. Elevations from 800 to 4,000 ft. Steep chaparral-covered slopes with small stands of fir, pine, and oak. In 1927, Congress set aside 50,000 acres of Cow Mountain for hunting, fishing, public recreation, and watershed protection. Roads in the area are steep and narrow, not suitable for trailers and large RVs. Several perennial and intermittent streams. A number of small reservoirs. In summer, hot, dry days and cool nights. Winters are moderate with frequent rain. Annual rainfall is about 40 in.

The area has been divided into two parts. In the N, vehicles are limited to the main road. In the S, vehicles may use all designated roads and trails. There are 110 mi. of vehicle routes, 20 mi. of nonvehicular trails.

Birds: No checklist or detailed reports. Turkey vulture, hawks, owls, quail, dove, jays, swallows, woodpeckers, eagles.

Mammals: Black-tailed deer, black bear, mountain lion, bobcat, wild pig, coyote, raccoon, skunk, gray squirrel, jackrabbit.

Reptiles and amphibians: Garter snake, rubber boa, kingsnake, western rattlesnake, California newt.

Activities

Camping: 4 campgrounds, 23 sites with water, pit toilets. Some unimproved campsites. Trailside camping permitted.

Hiking and horse riding: 20 mi. of trails.

Hunting: Quail, dove, squirrel, rabbit, wild pig, deer, bear.

Publication

Map with visitor use information.

Headquarters

Clear Lake Resource Area, Bureau of Land Management, 2550 N. State St., Ukiah, CA 95482; (707) 468-4000.

Coyote Hills Regional Park

East Bay Regional Park District
994 acres.

From Oakland, Hwy 880 S to Hwy 84/Dumbarton Bridge, then W on Hwy 84 to first exit, R on Arden Wood Blvd. to Commerce, then L on Commerce to Park. On foot or bicycle, take Apay Way to the visitor center via the bridge over Hwy 84.

After centuries of native American habitation, farming, military use, duck hunting, and research, this East Bay landscape has become a wildlife refuge and environmental education center. The grassy hills, freshwater marshes, brackish marsh, willow runs, and fields are a major bird sanctuary, especially during the winter months. This is the largest swamp area in Alameda County. A variety of trails and interpretive displays make this creekside park popular with hikers, bikers, and equestrians. Boardwalks offer easy access. A shellmound village site shows where the Tuibun Ohlone lived for over two centuries.

Plants: Many wildflowers; also tules, pickleweed, bunch grass, willows.

Birds: Barn swallow, yellowthroat, marsh wren, great horned owl, black-shouldered kite. Canada geese nest here. Many ducks.

Interpretation

Weekend naturalist programs, birdwalks, and *workshops.* Reservations required. Schedules posted on Park bulletin board.

Activities

Camping: One group campground. Reservations required.

Hiking: Trails explore the wetlands, hills, and historic native American sites.

Horse riding: A number of trails can be used for riding.

Bicycling: Many trails are open to cyclists. The speed limit is 15 mph.

There's a parking fee of $3.00.

Publication

General brochure with map.

Headquarters

E Bay Regional Parks, 8000 Patterson Ranch Rd., Fremont, CA 94555-3502; (510) 795-9385.

Delevan National Wildlife Refuge

See Sacramento National Wildlife Refuges (this zone).

Del Mar Landing Ecological Reserve

California Department of Fish and Game
48 acres.

On the Pacific Coast about 3½ mi. S of the mouth of the Gualala River. From a marker on Del Mar Point S about 3,000 ft. Visitors need to request permission to enter through the private Sea Ranch development.

A relatively virgin bit of coastline. Exposed outer rocks, deep channels, tide pools. An undisturbed assemblage of plants and animals native to rocky shores. Harbor seals often seen on outer rocks.

Headquarters
CA Dept. of Fish and Game, 1419 Ninth St., Sacramento, CA 95814;
(916) 655-7203.

Don Edwards San Francisco Bay National Wildlife Refuge

U.S. Fish and Wildlife Service
21,000 acres.

From Hwy 84 (at E end of Dumbarton Bridge), exit at Thornton Ave.
Travel S on Thornton for 0.8 mi. to the Refuge entrance. Turn right and
follow Marshlands Rd. to stop sign. Turn left into parking lot.

Diking, dredging, and filling have greatly reduced the area of San
Francisco Bay, a rich estuarine system supporting large fish and
wildlife populations. Since 1972, South Bay wetlands have been
acquired for this Refuge, which one day will include 43,000 acres of
bay shore wetlands, open water, and uplands. Half of the authorized
acreage has been acquired.

Only selected portions are now open to visitors, including the visitor center, a 1½ mi. loop trail through a representative sample of the
habitat, and several miles of hiking trails. More trails are planned. The
site includes salt evaporator ponds, salt marsh, tidal mudflats, open
water, and small upland area. Pickleweed and cordgrass are the primary marsh vegetation.

Birds: Checklist of 248 species is a guide to the birds of the South Bay,
not just the Refuge. The South Bay wetlands are visited annually by
most of the shorebirds of the Pacific Flyway as well as many waterfowl. This is important habitat for four endangered bird species: California clapper rail, least tern, brown pelican, peregrine falcon. One
threatened species, the western snowy plover, nests here. Winter is
the best season for birding.

Interpretation
Docents present *nature walks* and *slide shows* to the public on weekends.

Base for extensive interpretive program: *Explore the Wild! Seminars,*
sponsored by San Francisco Bay Wildlife Society. Seminars require registration and fees. Most are for 1 or 2 days with field trips.

The *visitor center* is on a hill overlooking the Bay, near the Dumbarton Bridge toll plaza. Open 10 A.M.–5 P.M. Closed Mon. and most federal holidays. The *Environmental Education Center* in Alviso is open to the public from 10 A.M.–5 P.M. on weekends and offers *interpretive programs*.

Publications

Bird checklist.

Leaflets.

Newsletter.

Trail map.

Seminar program schedule.

Headquarters

U.S. Fish and Wildlife Service, P.O. Box 524, Newark, CA 94561; (510) 792-3178.

....

Farallon National Wildlife Refuge

U.S. Fish and Wildlife Service
211 acres.
In the Pacific Ocean about 30 mi. W of San Francisco.

A cluster of offshore islands with the largest continental colonial seabird rookery S of Alaska. All of the islands except Southeast Farallon Island have been designated wilderness areas. Upward of a quarter-million breeding birds each summer. Breeding species include western gull, Cassin's and rhinoceros auklets, common murre, Brandt's, double-crested, and pelagic cormorants, pigeon guillemot, tufted puffin, black oystercatcher. Breeding marine mammals include California and Steller sea lions, elephant and harbor seals. Northern fur seals and gray and humpback whales are occasionally seen around the islands. Leatherback turtles occasionally swim by.

Visitors may not go ashore. Bay area birding and whale protection organizations sponsor seasonal boat trips around the islands.

Publication

Wildlife checklist.

Headquarters
SF Bay National Wildlife Refuge Complex, 1 Marshlands Rd., Fremont, CA 94536. (By mail: P.O. Box 524, Newark, CA 94560.) (510) 792-0222.

Fort Ross State Historic Park

California Department of Parks and Recreation
3,315 acres.
12½ mi. N of Jenner on Hwy 1.
Visitor center open from 10–4:30.

Russians built a fort here in 1812. One original structure still stands; others have been restored or reconstructed. The fort is 90 ft. above the sea, below a cypress grove. One can hike over the grassy flat, down into the ravine where ships once landed. Fine views from the edge of the bluffs. Several steep trails down to rocky beaches with tide pools. Many wildflowers. *No dogs allowed.*

Headquarters
Fort Ross State Park, 19005 Coast Hwy 1, Jenner, CA 95450; (707) 847-3286 and 865-2391.

Golden Gate National Recreation Area

U.S. National Park Service
76,500 acres of federal land in 3 counties, 28 mi. of coastline.

In San Francisco, the city's N and W edge. Across the bridge in Marin County, most of the seacoast to Bolinas Bay and along Hwy 1 to Olema.

Golden Gate National Recreation Area is the world's largest urban park. Many areas are either undisturbed or returning to a natural state. This National Recreation Area is composed of municipal, county, and federal sites, transferred to the National Park Service for management. This entry describes the sites N of the Golden Gate

Bridge. The complex includes the Marin Headlands, Tennessee Valley, Muir Woods, Mount Tamalpais, Muir Beach, Stinson Beach, Olema Valley, and Fort Baker. The extensive Marin Municipal Water District lands, Samuel P. Taylor State Park, and Angel Island are nearby open space.

This National Recreation Area includes museums, the Cliff House and Alcatraz Island (once a prison), which are not natural areas, and are thus not within the scope of this guide.

Highest point in the area is Mount Tamalpais, 2,586 ft. The Marin Headlands rise steeply from the sea. Much of the terrain is rolling to mountainous, with many valleys and canyons. Especially near the city, many of the slopes are open, windswept, and grassy, with areas of brush and scattered trees. The Mount Tamalpais area includes open grasslands and redwood forests. Muir Woods is noted for its stand of gigantic Coast redwoods. The National Recreation Area includes no large lakes but has numerous streams, ponds, freshwater marshes, salt marshes, and several lagoons.

Immediately on crossing the Golden Gate Bridge, Vista Point is on the right. At the next right turn, a road loops back under the highway and to Conzelman Rd. This part of the Headlands was for many years the site of forts and guns defending the Golden Gate. The road is scenic, part of it one-way, steep, closed to trailers and RVs. After several turns, the route rounds Rodeo Lagoon and ends at a visitor center. One can return to Hwy 1 via Bunker Rd. Otherwise the area is roadless except for a stub road at the head of Tennessee Valley. This is hiking country, with coastal, valley, and steep trails, some to elevations 1,000 ft. above the ocean.

Backcountry *camping* is available all year in the Headlands at 3 *hike-in campgrounds*. There is *group camping* at Battery Alexander, up to 65 persons, all year. Kirby Cove has *4 group sites,* each also available for up to 65 persons, April 1–Oct. 31. Reservations required for all sites. Contact the Marine Headlands visitor center, (415) 331-1540.

Hwy 1, here called the Coast Hwy, turns seaward and follows the coast from Muir Beach to Stinson Beach and Bolinas Lagoon. It forms part of the SW boundary of Mount Tamalpais State Park (see "Features" section). An alternate route, Panoramic Hwy, follows part of the State Park's N boundary, passes the access road to Muir Woods (see "Features"), then cuts across the State Park on its way to the ocean. Trails from the Marin Headlands area link with the Mount Tamalpais trail system.

Beyond Bolinas Lagoon, Hwy 1 is the approximately boundary between Point Reyes National Seashore (see entry) and the upper end of the GGNRA in the Olema Valley. The valley itself is pastoral, and continuation of some cattle grazing is part of the land-use plan. The area also has forested canyons, tree-lined ridges, open grassy slopes. Fine hiking trails, some long and steep.

Plants: Described for all parts of GGNRA. Primary plant communities of the Headlands and similar areas are coastal scrub and grasslands. Common plants are coyote bush, sagebrush, lupines, poison oak, cow parsnip, blackberry, poison hemlock. Willow and elderberry are found along streams; trees in this area are exotics, planted around coast artillery installations.

Forest in the Mount Tamalpais area includes some virgin redwood in Steep Ravine Canyon. Generally mixed forest: Douglas-fir, California live oak, Sitka spruce, California bay laurel, western hemlock. Oak woodlands have interior live oak, tan oak, California bay laurel. The rare Sargent cypress is associated with serpentine rock formations. Also areas of chaparral: manzanita, ceanothus, chaparral pea.

Wildflowers include lupines, poppy, buttercup, shooting star, sticky monkeyflower, iris, hound's tongue, deer orchid, many others. 786 species of plants have been identified in the Mount Tamalpais area alone.

Birds: Again, general list here applies to all parts of GGNRA. The Marin Headlands visitor center has a birdlist. Many seabirds along the coast. Waterfowl and shorebirds in lagoons, marshes, ponds. Species noted include turkey vulture, red-tailed hawk, northern harrier, golden eagle, kestrel, scrub jay, northern flicker, goldfinch, wrentit, house finch, great and snowy egrets, great blue heron, cormorants.

Mammals: For all of GGNRA include deer mouse, pocket gopher, gray squirrel, jackrabbit, brush rabbit, striped skunk, ground squirrel, raccoon, gray fox, bobcat, badger, mountain lion, mule deer.

Reptiles and amphibians: For all of GGNRA include various salamanders, ensatina, rough-skinned newt, Pacific giant salamander, bullfrog, kingsnake, gopher snake, garter snake, rubber boa, striped racer, rattlesnake.

Features

Mount Tamalpais State Park: 6,233 acres. Long a popular sightseeing, hiking, and horse riding area. Scenic road to the summit. *Loop trail* around the peak. More than 200 mi. of marked trails. A *nature trail* begins behind the ranger station. Mount Tam has 16 family sites, 2 group sites, and 6 primitive sites for *camping.* The Park surrounds Muir

Woods. *Stinson Beach,* a crescent-shaped, sandy beach stretching a couple of miles, is below the Park. Swimming is popular during the spring and summer when lifeguards are on duty. Conditions may be hazardous at times due to riptides.

Muir Woods National Monument: 560 acres of old-growth Coast redwood forest with 2 mi. of level paved trails along Redwood Creek on the valley floor. Unpaved trails lead up and out of the canyon and connect with Mount Tamalpais S. P. and with Stinson Beach. Hours are from 8 A.M. to sunset. There is a visitor center. Park is usually crowded; best times to visit are Oct.–April.

Samuel P. Taylor State Park: 2,576 acres. From San Rafael, 15 mi. W on Sir Francis Drake Blvd. Two quite different sections on opposite sides of the road, one cool, damp forest, the other dry, sparsely vegetated hillside. Papermill Creek crosses the area, but is only knee deep in summer months. 60 sites for *camping, 2 group sites.*

Angel Island State Park: 750 acres. In San Francisco Bay. Ferries from Oakland, Alameda, Vallejo, Tiburon, and San Francisco. Private boats may only land at Ayala Cove, where there are finger piers. Trails to top of 781-ft. Mount Caroline and around island. Island is partially wooded but native trees were almost all cut years ago and exotics introduced. Visitor center, docent-led cultural and natural history tours. Tram tours available; check for schedules. Bicycles can be rented. Park is open 8 A.M.–sunset for day use. There are 9 *campsites,* reservations required (415) 435-1915.

Adjacent
Point Reyes National Seashore (see entry this zone).

Publications
Golden Gate National Recreation Area leaflet with map.

Guide to the Park.

Muir Woods Trail guide and map.

Mount Tamalpais State Park trail map, $1.00.

Mount Tamalpais leaflet, nature trail guide.

Headquarters
Golden Gate National Recreation Area, Bldg. 201, Fort Mason, San Francisco, CA 94123; (415) 556-0560. Angel Island State Park, P.O. Box 318, Tiburon, CA 94920; (415) 435-1915. Marin Headlands visitor center, National Park Service, Bldg. 948, Fort Barry, Sausalito, CA 94965; (415) 331-1540. Mount Tamalpais State Park, 801 Panoramic

Hwy, Mill Valley, CA 94941; (415) 388-2070. Muir Woods National Monument, Mill Valley, CA 94941; (415) 388-2595. Samuel P. Taylor State Park, P.O. Box 251, Lagunitas, CA 94952; (415) 488-9897.

Grizzly Island Wildlife Area

California Department of Fish and Game
72,250 acres.

From I-80, exit to Fairfield on Hwy 12. About 1 mi. beyond Fairfield, turn right on Grizzly Island Rd. About 9 mi. to HQ.

The Suisun Marsh is a remnant of the 750,000 acres of marshlands that once occupied the Sacramento–San Joaquin Delta. The marsh, encompassing 55,000 acres of wetlands and 29,000 acres of bays and sloughs, is the largest remaining contiguous area of coastal wetland in CA. A leaflet declares, "Although it lacks the national fame of the Everglades of Florida, the Dismal Swamps of Louisiana or the Bear River Marshes of Utah, in most ways it is the peer, and in many ways the superior, of these famous wetlands." Perhaps one reason for non-recognition is that most of the marsh is privately owned. Both federal and state governments have been seeking ways to preserve the remaining wetlands by purchase, easement, cooperative agreements, and other means.

Waterfowl are the principal attraction of the marsh, with up to 1.5 million birds feeding and resting here in winter. In dry years, one-quarter of California's entire wintering waterfowl population may be concentrated here.

Strictly speaking, the marsh is not an undisturbed natural area. More than three-quarters of the wetlands have been enclosed and protected by levees. Most of this area is at or slightly below mean tide level. The area is crossed by a network of sloughs and drainage channels open to the tidewaters. Roads run along many of the levees. In the late 1800s, extensive efforts were made to drain and reclaim the wetlands for farming. Poor drainage and salty soils doomed these efforts. A large part of the private area is now owned or leased by waterfowl hunting clubs. The principal threat to the marsh today is diversion of river water for agricultural, municipal, and industrial use, reducing by more than half the flow of fresh water to San Francisco

Bay. Thus salt water intrudes farther and farther into the marsh, increasing salinity beyond the tolerance of the food plants on which the waterfowl depend.

Grizzly Island Wildlife Area has 8 units totaling approximately 12,250 acres. The 2,137-acre *Joice Island Unit* has a special angling and bird-watching season from mid-May to mid-Aug. *Grizzly Island Unit,* 8,600 acres, is the main draw for visitors as it has a wealth of bird life and a herd of native tule elk. Both of these units are on Grizzly Island Rd. and border Montezuma Slough. Remaining units are relatively small with more difficult access and are usually only open for waterfowl hunting.

The Grizzly Island Unit is open to the public with seasonal restrictions for various hunting seasons and the spring nesting season, March 1–June 30. Waterfowl, pheasant, and elk hunting is by special permit.

Birds: About 220 bird species recorded. Checklist available. Ducks and geese begin to arrive in Aug. Some 200,000 may be present by mid-Sept. Most early arrivals are pintail. At peak population in midwinter, about 75–85% of the ducks present are pintail. Other species include gadwall, wigeon, green-winged teal, shoveler, and mallard. The marsh has relatively few diving ducks. Common winter species include white-fronted goose, eared and pied-billed grebes, great and snowy egrets, black-crowned night heron, American bittern, cinnamon teal, canvasback, goldeneye, bufflehead, black-shouldered kite, red-tailed and rough-legged hawks, barn, short-eared, and great horned owls, pheasant, California, ring-billed, and Bonaparte's gulls. Warblers are common. The birding here is good at any season.

Mammals: A small herd of tule elk. Numerous bat species, black-tailed jackrabbit, cottontail, pocket gopher, beaver, deer mouse, muskrat, gray fox, raccoon, weasel, mink, river otter, badger, spotted and striped skunks, bobcat.

Activities

Hiking: No special trails but many opportunities.

Hunting: Special rules; permit issued at HQ.

Fishing: Striped bass, catfish, crappie, sturgeon.

Publications

Bird checklist.

Hunting maps and regulations.

Headquarters
CA Dept. of Fish and Game, 2548 Grizzly Island Rd., Suisun, CA
94585; (707) 425-3828.

Lower Sherman Island Wildlife Area

California Department of Fish and Game
3,100 acres.

From W Pittsburg, E on Hwy 4, continuing N across Antioch Bridge and
Hwy 160 to Emmaton. Left on Sherman Island Rd. to parking area.

At the confluence of the Sacramento and San Joaquin Rivers. The
island is partially flooded, and there is boat access only beyond the
parking lot and boat ramp. Several past attempts to reclaim the area
with levees and cultivate the drained land failed. The state acquired
the island in 1920. Open water, extensive marshes, and a small area of
tidal flats at the tip. Willow thickets; dense stands of tule reeds.

The site is much used by waterfowl hunters. Needless to say, nonhunters should avoid the site in the waterfowl hunting season. Fishing is the largest use, with an average of more than 100 people fishing
per day.

Wildlife is abundant. No checklists are available, but 75–100 bird
species occur here, including many waterfowl, mourning dove, pheasant, and quail. Mammals include beaver, mink, muskrat, opossum,
raccoon, striped skunk, cottontail, and river otter.

Outside hunting season, it should be an interesting area to explore
by small boat or canoe, although visitors are warned that strong
winds often come up rapidly, especially in late afternoon, and there is
strong tidal action. The area has a maze of channels and shallows. The
N levee on the Sacramento River is a favorite picnic site.

Publication
Site map.

Headquarters
Region 2, CA Dept. of Fish and Game, 1701 Nimbus Rd., Suite A, Rancho Cordova, CA 95670; (916) 358-2900.

Mendocino National Forest

U.S. Forest Service
876,236 acres; 1,079,459 acres within boundaries.

From just N of Clear Lake, extends N about 65 mi. About 35 mi. wide. Access from I-5, to the E, or US 101, to the W, by secondary and Forest roads.

Southernmost of a continuous block of National Forests extending N into Oregon. Rolling to mountainous terrain on E side of the Coast Range. Elevations from 1,100 to 8,092 ft. About 65% forested, remainder brush-covered hills. Lake Pillsbury, about 2,000 acres; several smaller lakes, ponds. Numerous streams, including tributaries of Eel River. At lower elevations temperatures range from 20°F winter low to 110°F summer high; cooler in high country.

No main roads penetrate the Forest. There are several secondary roads, as well as Forest roads not shown on highway maps.

Plants: Principal tree species include Douglas-fir, white fir, ponderosa pine, incense cedar. Old-growth stands in Big Butte–Shinbone area and Yolla Bolly–Middle Eel Wilderness. Understory includes black oak, mixed conifers. Other tree species include Shasta red fir, Jeffrey, sugar, foxtail, gray, knobcone, and western white pines, Sargent and McNab cypresses, several live oak species and other oak, chinquapin, madrone, red alder, cottonwoods, willows. Chaparral species include chamise, mountain mahogany, toyon, cascara, bitter cherry, western chokecherry, wood and California wild roses, raspberry, blackberry, several manzanita species, many others. Long list of flowering plants includes golden fairy lantern, pussy ears, mariposa lily, several brodiaeas, false hellebore, several lilies, several orchids, buttercups, many more. Plant checklists available.

Birds: Checklist available. Residents include golden and bald eagles, Cooper's, sharp-shinned, red-tailed, and Swainson's hawks, merlin, kestrel, mountain and California quail, blue grouse, belted kingfisher, Anna's and calliope hummingbirds, white-breasted, red-breasted, and pygmy nuthatches, Bewick's and winter wrens, Hutton's vireo, American, lesser, and Lawrence's goldfinches, savannah and lark sparrows.

Mammals: Checklist available. Abundant and common species include mule deer, bobcat, coyote, porcupine, raccoon, gray fox, striped skunk, Douglas and gray squirrels, northern flying squirrel, Townsend, Sonoma, and yellow pine chipmunks, Heermann kangaroo rat, pocket gopher. Also mice: western harvest, deer, pinyon, brush, California meadow, long-tailed meadow, creeping meadow. Black bear, mountain lion, badger, tule elk, bison reported but rare or uncommon.

Reptiles and amphibians: Include western fence and alligator lizards, Pacific pond turtle, western skink. Also snakes: rubber boa, Pacific ringneck, California striped racer, sharp-tailed, California mountain kingsnake, rattlesnake. Reptile and amphibian checklists available.

Features

Yolla Bolly–Middle Eel Wilderness: 111,824 acres. Includes portion of Shasta-Trinity National Forest (see entry zone 1). Wild, rugged country on the headwaters of the Middle Fork, Eel River; bounded by North and South Yolla Bolly Mountains. Forest roads to trailheads are not the best, so visitor use is light. Average elevations, 2,000–4,000 ft., with peaks over 8,000 ft. Most of the area is available for hiking by late May, earlier than most other CA wildernesses. Fall storms common from early Oct., but heavy snows are rare before Dec. Ridges have dense stands of pine and fir; lower slopes are chaparral. Good fishing in several creeks, but water is generally scarce and springs usually dry by late summer. Trail map available. Wilderness permit required; obtain from HQ or Ranger Districts.

Snow Mountain Wilderness: 37,000 acres on Lake County–Colusa County boundary, E side of Forest. Snow Mountain is southernmost peak in N Coast Range; twin peaks, both over 7,000 ft. A minimum of 65 plant species here reach their S range limit. Near crests, open stands of red fir in protected areas; exposed sites treeless. Red and white fir, Douglas-fir, and ponderosa pine at middle elevations, chaparral, brush, and oaks below. Wildlife is abundant, with frequent reports of bear and mountain lion. This area also provides opportunity for early season activity.

Lookouts: Visitors are invited to fire lookouts when they are manned, daylight hours, June to mid-Oct. Several can be reached by road, in some cases with a short walk at the end. However, road conditions change seasonally, and it's advisable to ask about routing at any ranger office.

Recreation areas: At Letts Lake, Hammerhorn Lake, Plaskett Lake, Lake Pillsbury.

Interpretation
Nature trail ¾ mi., at Lake Pillsbury.

Activities
Camping: 24 campgrounds, 400 sites. Usual season June–Oct., but most campgrounds open all year. No reservations. Camping outside designated sites is permitted in most areas, but fire permit is necessary.

Hiking, backpacking: Over 160 mi. of mapped trails. Easy hikes of ½ to 4 mi. from recreation areas. Backpacking popular in the wilderness areas, but many other parts of the Forest offer attractive long hikes, on trails and lightly used unpaved roads.

Horse riding: No commercial packers or stables in the Forest. Camping along trails permitted, but horses are not permitted at campgrounds. Bring feed for entire trip; natural feed is insufficient. Good horse trails.

Hunting: Allowed in season except in State Game Refuge, recreation areas, near campgrounds. Mule deer, wild pig, squirrel, quail, pigeon, grouse, turkey, bear.

Fishing: Chiefly trout, lakes and streams.

Swimming: Streams and small lakes, chiefly at recreation areas. Unsupervised.

Boating, canoeing: Power boats on Lake Pillsbury only. Tubing on Stony Creek. Spring kayaking, Mill Creek Campground to Mine Camp. Rafting and canoeing on Eel River just outside Forest boundary.

Ski touring, snowmobiling: Forest Hwy 7 to snow line. Some ski touring. Snowmobiling from Covelo side in Mendocino Pass and Anthony Peak areas.

Trail motorcycling and 4-wheel vehicles allowed where posted.
Caution: Most Forest roads are unpaved; some are narrow, steep, rocky. Dust, mud, and snow are seasonal hazards. Be alert for logging trucks, cattle.
Poison oak is common, potent all year.

Adjacent
Six Rivers National Forest, Shasta-Trinity National Forest (see entries zone 1).

Publications

Forest map, $.25.

Wilderness map, $3.25.

Meet the Mendocino.

Fishing Your National Forests.

Plants and Animals of the Mendocino National Forest.

The Yolla Bolly–Middle Eel Wilderness, $3.25.

Trail map, Yolla Bolly–Middle Eel Wilderness.

Snow Mountain Wilderness map, $3.25.

Off Roading, map and regulations.

Headquarters

U.S. Forest Service, 825 N. Humbolt Ave., Willows, CA 94988; (916) 934-3316/7724. Recorded recreation message: (916) 934-2350.

Ranger Districts

Corning R.D., 22000 Corning Rd., Corning, CA 96021; (916) 824-5196. Covelo R.D., Route 1, Box 62 C, Covelo, CA 95428; (707) 983-2941. Stonyford R.D., 5171 Stony Ford–Elk Creek Rd., Stonyford, CA 95979; (916) 963-3128. Upper Lake R.D., P.O. Box 96, Upper Lake, CA 95485; (707) 275-2361.

Mount Diablo State Park

California Department of Parks and Recreation
19,500 acres.

E of Oakland. From Danville, E 5 mi. on Diablo Rd.

Many sightseers drive to the top of Mount Diablo for the view, said by some to encompass more land area than any other point in CA; others make the claim even broader. That's on a clear day, after a N wind has blown away the prevailing smog. Few people use the trails during the week, but don't expect solitude on a fine weekend. The peak's elevation is 3,849 ft., more than 3,600 ft. above the base.

Park hours all year are 8 A.M.–sunset. Entrance road gates are locked to incoming traffic at sunset. All vehicles must be out of Park half an hour past sunset.

Plants: Most of the hillsides are forested: Coast, blue, and black oaks and gray pine in open woodlands. On sunny slopes: madrone, California bay laurel, buckeye. In shady canyons: bigleaf maple, western sycamore, cottonwood, white alder. Wildflowers include wyethia, poppy, wallflower, trillium, fairy lantern, monkeyflower, giant red paintbrush, shooting star, wild rose, delphinium.

Birds: Checklist available. Species reported include barn, screech, and great horned owls, golden eagle, red-tailed hawk, kestrel, yellow-bellied sapsucker, horned lark, western tanager, violet-green and cliff swallows, Anna's hummingbird, cedar waxwing, western bluebird, blue-gray gnatcatcher, orange-crowned warbler, house finch. Peregrine falcon has been successfully reintroduced.

Mammals: Include squirrel, raccoon, brush rabbit, skunk, mule deer, bobcat. Mountain lion rarely seen.

Activities

Camping: 60 sites. All year, except in periods of high fire danger. First come, first served. Heated showers when water supply allows.

Hiking, horse riding: Over 50 mi. of trails.

All alcoholic beverages prohibited.

Publications

Leaflet with map, $0.25.

Trail map, $5.00.

Bird checklist, $0.75.

Headquarters

CA Dept. of Parks and Recreation, 96 Mitchell Canyon Rd., Clayton, CA 94517; (510) 837-2525.

Mount Tamalpais State Park

See Golden Gate National Recreation Area (this zone).

Muir Woods National Monument

See Golden Gate National Recreation Area (this zone).

Napa-Sonoma Marshes Wildlife Area

Mixed ownership. California Department of Fish and Game management 14,000 acres.

On the Napa River. Boat access only. Various sloughs on W side of river N of Hwy 37, Sears Point Rd.

A complex of sloughs, marshes, and islands. Many of the islands partially or wholly inundated by high tides. Portions of the area are privately owned so be aware of Fish and Game land versus privately owned property. Hunting is allowed Sept. 1–Jan. 31, with type B permits required in waterfowl season. Dogs allowed July 1–March 21, but must be under control of owner.

The *Coon Ecological Reserve*, 250 acres, is on the river at the N end of the area about 1¼ mi. S of the Southern Pacific Railroad bridge. Established to preserve a representative marsh area. Cordgrass on the frequently flooded areas. California bulrush, tule on slightly higher elevations. Pickleweed on land seldom flooded.

Birds: The marshes attract many waterfowl. Exposed mudflats are feeding areas for snowy and great egrets, great blue heron. Northern harrier, black-shouldered kite, and red-tailed hawk often seen. Also present, clapper rail.

Publication
Site map.

Headquarters
CA Dept. of Fish and Game, 1416 Ninth St., Sacramento, CA 98514; (916) 445-7613.

Palo Alto Baylands Nature Preserve

City of Palo Alto
2,000 acres.

From San Jose, US 101 N to Embarcadero Rd. Then go E 1 mi. on Embarcadero Rd. and follow signs to the Preserve.

Largely a salt marsh, these tidal wetlands are a key part of the San Francisco Bay food chain. An important stop on the Pacific Flyway, the baylands include four important habitats. Tidal salt marshes include hardy plants like cordgrass that can survive intensive saltwater flooding. Microscopic organisms found here are at the bottom of the Bay's food chain. Tidal sloughs are home to a variety of birds, fish, reeds, and, at times, a harbor seal. Marsh nutrients migrate into the Bay from these sloughs. Finally, freshwater marshes are found in a few baylands ponds.

An *interpretive center*, popular *duck pond*, hiking trails, and flood basin are all important observation points. Protected endangered species include the salt marsh harvest mouse and clapper rail.

Publication
Leaflet with map.

Headquarters
2757 Embarcadero Rd., Palo Alto, CA 94303 (mailing address: Palo Alto Baylands Nature Preserve, 1451 Middlefield Rd., Palo Alto, CA 94301); (415) 329-2506.

Point Reyes National Seashore
U.S. National Park Service
65,303 acres.

From Olema on Hwy 1, turn seaward on Bear Valley Rd.

The site is a rough triangle, about 18 mi. on its N–S base, its hooked tip projecting into the sea. The triangle is partially separated from the mainland by Tomales Bay, less obviously by the San Andreas Fault. Many bays, streams, and lagoons penetrate the triangle. The Inverness Ridge parallels the base, with elevations to 1,470 ft. on Mount Wittenberg. W of the ridge are rolling hills. The "Point" has tall cliffs rising from the sea. The S portion has five small lakes near the shore.

More than two-fifths of the area is classed as wilderness, open to foot, horse, and bicycle travel only. Outside this roadless area, several roads lead to the Point, to beaches, to overlooks on Pt. Reyes Hill and Mount Vision, and to other points of interest.

No car camping. Four campgrounds are available to hikers.

Warm, dry summers; cool, rainy winters. The exposed headlands and outer beaches have constant moderate to strong winds. The E side of Inverness Ridge is sheltered from the winds; the inland valleys have less fog; summer temperatures are usually 8°–10°F higher on the E side. In winter, night temperatures are usually higher along the beaches than inland. At the Point, rainfall averages about 12 in. per year. Dec–Feb. having the most. At Bear Valley, annual average is about 34 in.

Plants: Several habitats. On the ridge, stands of Douglas-fir and Bishop pine, not often found together. At lower elevations, groves of California bay laurel, madrone, tan oak, live oak, bigleaf maple, and wax myrtle, with many shrubs such as ceanothus, rhododendron, honeysuckle, wild rose, and huckleberry. Bordering the forest, an extensive belt of grassland with a scattering of California buckeye. Many wildflowers on the coastal dunes.

Birds: Checklist available at visitor center. Along the shoreline, curlew, oystercatcher, sandpipers, godwit, yellowlegs, as well as gulls, various waterfowl, white and brown pelicans. Egrets and great blue heron are among the marsh birds. Inland, red-tailed hawk, northern harrier, kestrel, black-shouldered kite, California quail, great horned owl.

Mammals: Include gray fox, raccoon, weasel, badger, striped and spotted skunks, mountain lion, bobcat, brush rabbit, black-tailed jackrabbit, mountain beaver, Sonoma chipmunk, southern pocket gopher, western gray squirrel, Point Reyes jumping mouse, mule deer, and two exotics: fallow and axis deer. Offshore: northern fur seal, Steller and California sea lions, harbor seal, elephant seal, gray whale in migration.

Features

Bear Valley, visitor center and Park HQ, near the entrance. *Earthquake Trail* along the San Andreas Fault. *Woodpecker Trail.* Also, replica of native Indian village.

Limantour Beach, swimming. Bird-watching at nearby Limantour Estero.

Point Reyes Beach, with two road access points, is fine for hiking and beachcombing, not swimming.

McClure's Beach is one of several with good tidepools.

Tule elk range has a small herd of free-ranging tule elk, reintroduced a century after they were eliminated here.

American Youth Hostel on Limantour Rd. For reservations: (415) 666-8811.

Activities

Backpacking, horse riding: Many miles of trails, especially in the central and S portions. Four *hike-in campgrounds.* Permits are required, and limit is one night per campground. Trail map shows trailheads, destinations, distances, the longest one-way route 13.1 mi. Fog, wind, and cold occur in July as well as Dec.

Swimming: The beaches N of the Point are unsafe. On the E side of the Point, Drakes Beach and Limantour Beach are sheltered.

Adjacent

Golden Gate National Recreation Area and Tomales Bay State Park (see entries this zone).

Dogs are prohibited in campgrounds, on designated beaches, and on trails. Elsewhere they must be leashed.

Publications

Leaflet with map.

Trail map.

Bird checklist.

Information pages on climate, vegetation types, wildlife, geology, gray whales, deer, harbor seals, tule elk.

Headquarters

National Park Service, Point Reyes, CA 94956; (415) 663-1092

Portola Redwoods State Park

California Department of Parks and Recreation
2,600 acres.

From I-280 W of Redwood City, exit W on Hwy 84 7 mi. to Hwy 35. S on Hwy 35 to Alpine Rd. W 3 mi. to Portola State Park Rd. S 3 mi. on Portola State Park Rd.

Just over the hill from the Bay Area, a redwood park in the rugged terrain of a deep canyon between Skyline and Butano ridges. The Park is a natural basin forested with Coast redwoods and associated flora. Elevations from 300 to 1,000 ft. Annual precipitation is about 48 in., chiefly in fall and winter. Peters Creek and Pescadero Creek flow in faults.

The Park is irregular in shape. Developments are clustered near the W boundary. For about 2 mi. to the E, the Park is roadless, open only to foot traffic.

Plants: Several groves of virgin Coast redwoods. Peters Grove, a strenuous 13-mi. hike, round-trip, has a 302-ft.-tall redwood. It's one of the largest in the Santa Cruz Mountains in a wonderful old-growth grove. The Park is almost entirely forested. Douglas-fir and tan oak on ridges and S slopes. Understory includes huckleberry, ferns. Wildflowers include redwood violet, trillium, hound's tongue, western azalea.

Birds: Checklist available, with habitats. All-year residents include marbled murrelet, red-tailed and Cooper's hawks, horned, screech, and pygmy owls, northern flicker, acorn woodpecker, Steller's and scrub jays, chestnut-backed chickadee, wrentit, dipper, pine siskin, band-tailed pigeon.

Mammals: Include raccoon, ringtail, coyote, bobcat, mule deer, mountain lion.

Reptiles and amphibians: Include western salamander, Pacific tree frog, garter snake, gopher snake, rubber boa.

Interpretation

Visitor center and *museum.*

Campfire programs, guided nature hikes, and *children's programs* seasonally.

Sequoia Nature Trail, ¾ mi.

Activities

Camping: 53 drive-in sites, 7 walk-in sites. All year. Reservations mid-May–Sept. 30, through DESTINET.

Hiking, backpacking: 14 mi. of trails, 5½-mi. Coyote Ridge–Slate Creek loop. Trails pass redwood groves, other points of interest. Trail camp for backpackers. Make reservations at Park.

Bicycling: 5-mi. trail.

Publication

Park leaflet with map and nature trail guide.

Headquarters

CA Dept. of Parks and Recreation, Box F, Rt. 2, La Honda, CA 94020; (415) 948-9098.

....

Robert Louis Stevenson State Park

California Department of Parks and Recreation
4,161 acres.

From Calistoga, 8 mi. N on Hwy 29.

Open: Daylight hours.

An undeveloped parkland; limited parking, no restrooms or water. Includes Mount St. Helena, 4,339 ft., highest point this close to San Francisco. The summit is private inholding, but public access is permitted at present. 9 mi. of trails, including trail to summit. Mostly steep, rocky, brush-covered slopes with wooded canyons. Some N-facing slopes are also wooded. A fire road, power line, and communications installation impair what is otherwise wilderness quality.

Plants: Only about 10% forested: Douglas-fir, tan oak, canyon live oak, ponderosa and knobcone pines, madrone. Mostly chaparral with manzanita, chamise, scrub oak, poison oak.

Birds: No checklist. Species reported include turkey vulture, red-tailed, Cooper's, and sharp-shinned hawks, kestrel, golden eagle, band-tailed pigeon, mourning dove, scrub jay, mountain quail, screech owl, peregrine falcon, white-throated swift, northern flicker, canyon wren, orange-crowned warbler, house finch, dark-eyed junco, rufous-crowned and sage sparrows.

Mammals: Include Sonoma chipmunk, spotted skunk, black bear, gray fox, black-tailed jackrabbit, western gray squirrel, ringtail, pocket mouse, bobcat.

Reptiles and amphibians: Include Pacific tree frog, western toad, Pacific ringneck snake, Mount St. Helena mountain kingsnake, Pacific gopher snake, California striped racer, rubber boa, Pacific rattlesnake.

128 CALIFORNIA

Publication
Part of Bothe-Napa Valley State Park leaflet.

Headquarters
CA Dept. of Parks and Recreation, 3801 N. St. Helena Hwy, Calistoga, CA 94515; (707) 942-4575.

Sacramento National Wildlife Refuges
U.S. Fish and Wildlife Service
24,000 acres.

For Sacramento National Wildlife Refuge, 6 mi. S of Willows on US 99 W, which parallels and is E of I-5.

The Sacramento Valley is the major wintering area for waterfowl of the Pacific Flyway. After most of the wetlands were drained and cultivated, waterfowl became dependent on farm crops. Beginning in 1937, these Refuges were established, attracting waterfowl so successfully that crop losses to ducks and geese are now minor. The Sacramento National Wildlife Refuge complex has 6 refuges: Sacramento, Colusa, Delevan, Sutter, Sacramento River NWR, and Butte Sink. Portions of all but the last are open to visitors. The CA Department of Fish and Game's Gray Lodge Wildlife Area (see entry zone 4) is nearby and serves the same general function.

Numbers of wintering waterfowl may exceed 2 million by Dec. 269 bird species have been recorded on the refuges since 1937.

Sacramento National Wildlife Refuge: 10,783 acres. The largest refuge, with headquarters. Hundreds of thousands of ducks and geese are here Sept.–Feb., marsh birds Aug.–April. About 6 mi. long, 3 mi. wide, the Refuge is divided by roads and ditches into ponds, marshes, and fields. Visitors can drive on a 6 mi. auto tour, hike on designated trails. When we visited, birding here was better than at any of the other refuges.

Colusa National Wildlife Refuge: 4,040 acres. On Hwy 20, ½ mi. W of Colusa. Long, rather narrow site, somewhat similar to Sacramento Refuge in managed habitats and species present. The auto tour route seemed to have fewer visitors. Hiking on designated trails.

Delevan National Wildlife Refuge: 5,794 acres. From Willows, 10 mi. S on US 99 W to Maxwell, then 4 mi. E on Maxwell Rd. No auto tour route. In hunting season, nonhunters are restricted to public roads bordering the site.

Sutter National Wildlife Refuge: 2,591 acres. From Yuba City, S to Oswald Rd., then W. Croplands and marshes. No auto tour route.

Hunters may prefer the smaller refuges. Other visitors should go first to the Sacramento Refuge, then consider visiting Colusa and the state's Gray Lodge Wildlife Area but ask for advice at Sacramento Refuge. There is good sightseeing and birding along the back roads of the area. To the E of Colusa are the *Sutter Buttes,* the highest 2,132 ft., a unique upthrust. W of the Buttes are about 10,000 acres of privately owned prime waterfowl habitat.

Birds: Checklist available. 269 species recorded. Ducks begin arriving during Aug., geese in Sept. Most commonly seen are pintail, mallard, wigeon, northern shoveler, gadwall, ruddy duck, and snow, Ross's, and white-fronted geese. Waterfowl numbers decrease in Feb. and March when birds return to their northern breeding grounds. Other birds include grebes, herons, white-faced ibis, cinnamon teal, turkey vulture, red-tailed hawk, northern harrier, kestrel, pheasant, greater yellowlegs, dunlin, black-necked stilt, avocet, long-billed dowitcher, moorhen, barn and great horned owls, western kingbird, tree, cliff, and barn swallows, yellow-billed magpie, marsh wren, ruby-crowned kinglet, American pipit, and many, many others. Songbirds are largely restricted to the cottonwoods and willows bordering irrigation ditches.

Waterfowl numbers gradually decline after early Jan., but a few thousand mallard, cinnamon teal, and other species nest. Shorebirds are present all year.

Mammals: Include opossum, black-tailed jackrabbit, Beechy ground squirrel, muskrat, river otter, black and Norway rats, raccoon, striped skunk, black-tailed deer, beaver. Ringtail, mink, coyote, red fox, California vole are present but uncommon.

Activities
Hunting: Portions of each Refuge are open to hunting in season. Inquire about special regulations, dates.

Nearby
Gray Lodge Wildlife Area (see entry zone 4).

Publications

Recreation Guide.

Bird checklist.

Young People's Bird List.

Hunting maps.

Hunting regulations.

Tour routes (Colusa).

Wetlands Walk Guide.

Headquarters

U.S. Fish and Wildlife Service, 752 County Rd. 99 W, Willows, CA 95988; (916) 934-2801.

Salt Point State Park

California Department of Parks and Recreation
4,114 acres.

20 mi. N of Jenner on Hwy 1.

On the coast. Hwy 1 runs about ⅒ to ½ mi. inland. The developed park area is on both sides of Hwy 1. A much larger area, with hiking trails and fire roads, is across the highway.

The coast includes protected, rocky beach coves as well as sharp bluffs and sheer sandstone cliffs plunging into the waves. Headlands are generally grassy, but in places the forest is near the sea. Inland, the terrain rises, coastal brush and grassland giving way to lush forest of Bishop pine, Douglas-fir, madrone, tan oak, and redwoods. At the top of the coastal ridge, about 1,000-ft. elevation, is a large, open "prairie" and pygmy forest, where stands of cypress, pine, and even redwood grow in stunted profusion.

From the highway, short access roads lead to campgrounds and parking areas. From the parking area, one can hike N along the coast, in several places dropping down to a beach or cove. Many tide pools. The site includes one of California's first underwater parks, where marine organisms are given special protection, although fishing is allowed.

Many wildflowers. Some, such as calla lily and red-hot poker, are signs of a former residence.

Birds: Include red-tailed hawk, kestrel, black-shouldered kite, northern harrier, various gulls, oystercatcher, pileated woodpecker, turkey vulture.

Mammals: Include mule deer, weasel, raccoon, coyote, bobcat, striped skunk, numerous rodents. Gray whales often seen offshore between Dec. and April.

Activities

Camping: 109 sites. All year. Reservations March 1–Oct. 31 by DESTINET.

Hiking: 14 mi. of trails, mostly inland. Coast trail to Kruse Reserve (see section headed "Nearby").

Swimming: Divers enjoy the underwater park.

Horse riding: Marked trails E of the highway.

Mushroom collecting.

Nearby

Kruse Rhododendron State Reserve is just N of the site. 317 acres. Second-growth redwood, Douglas-fir, tan oak, and an exceptional display of rhododendron, plants to 20 or more ft. tall, usually blooming April through early June. 5 mi. of trails.

Publications

Geology of Salt Point State Park.

Leaflet with map.

Mushroom Collecting in Salt Point State Park.

Headquarters

CA Dept. of Parks and Recreation, 25050 Hwy 1, Jenner, CA 95450; (707) 847-3221.

Samuel P. Taylor State Park

See Golden Gate National Recreation Area (this zone).

San Bruno Mountain State and County Park

San Mateo County Parks and Recreation Division
2,326 acres.

From SF, US 101 to Old Bayshore Blvd., turn R on Guadalupe Canyon
Pkwy. to Park entrance.

Adjacent to San Francisco's S boundary, this Park offers great views of
the city and the Bay Area. Steep slopes reaching a 1,314-ft. summit
host a variety of botanic resources including 14 rare and endangered
species, as well as endangered butterflies. Franciscan grassland, chaparral, and riparian habitat cover the mountain's shale and sandstone
bedrock.

It's a good spot for hiking and bird-watching, with trails of up to 3
mi. in length and open space just minutes from dense urban neigh-
borhoods in San Francisco and the northern peninsula. Bicycles are
allowed on several trails.

Publication
General brochure with map.

Headquarters
San Mateo Parks and Recreation Div., 590 Hamilton St., 4th floor, Red-
wood City, CA 94063; (415) 363-4020. Park site: 555 Guadalupe
Canyon Pkwy; (415) 587-7511.

San Francisco Bay National Wildlife Refuge
See Don Edwards San Francisco Bay National Wildlife Refuge (this
zone).

San Mateo State Beaches

California Department of Parks and Recreation
2,786 acres.

Seacoast, along Hwy 1, from Daly City to Año Nuevo Point, 27 mi. S of
Half Moon Bay.

State beaches occupy 19 mi. of this 51-mi. stretch of coast S of San
Francisco. These are not swimming beaches because of rough surf and
strong currents, and this somewhat limits the weekend crowds. Most
of the beaches are sand, backed by bluffs 10–200 ft. high. Some rocky
areas; some offshore rocks. Many of the beaches are at points where
creeks flow into the sea; here there are small coves and lagoons. The
principal units, N to S, are:

Gray Whale Cove State Beach: 93 acres. Surf fishing. Concession
operated.

Montara State Beach: 13 acres. Rather narrow, partially rocky, 11,000
ft. of ocean frontage, 4,287 ft. of sandy beach. Hiking.

Half Moon Bay State Beach: 170 acres. The HQ beach, and *the only
one with camping.*

San Gregorio State Beach: 165 acres. Creek, high cliffs, sand bar at
the creek mouth. 1 mi. of beach.

Pomponio State Beach: 80 acres. Over 1 mi. of ocean front. Small
lagoon.

Pescadero State Beach: 290 acres, adjoins the 584-acre *Pescadero
Marsh Natural Preserve,* one of the few remaining natural marsh areas
on the central CA coast. Good birding. Great blue heron rookery.

Bean Hollow State Beach: 44 acres. 2 mi. of ocean frontage. Only
1,300 ft. of sandy beach. Tide pools.

Año Nuevo State Reserve, 420 acres. Año Nuevo Point is the primary
mainland breeding ground of the northern elephant seal. Access in
breeding season (Dec.–April) is restricted to daily tours; reservations
required. For tour information: (415) 879-0226. 7½ mi. of ocean
frontage, including 3 mi. of sandy beach, open May 1–Dec. 1.

Año Nuevo Island, just offshore, has resident and migratory harbor
seals, California and Steller sea lions, many seabirds. No public access.

Other beaches: The units just mentioned account for about half the
acreage of state land. Other areas are undeveloped. Along the coast are

numerous unsigned, informal beach-access points where people pull off the highway and make their way down to secluded beaches. Some of these access points are on private land whose owners consent to public use, but land that is obviously private should not be crossed without the owner's consent.

Camping: Half Moon Bay, 50 sites. All year.

Headquarters
CA Dept. of Parks and Recreation, Bay Area District, 250 Executive Park Blvd., Suite 4900, San Francisco, CA 94134; (415) 726-8819.

San Pablo National Wildlife Refuge
U.S. Fish and Wildlife Service
13,190 acres.

On San Pablo Bay W of Vallejo. Part of the N boundary is Hwy 37.

Of the total protected acreage, 11,200 acres are leased from the state. Most of the acreage is open water and tide lands on the N shore of San Pablo Bay. Less than 50 acres are above maximum high tide. Nearly 5,000 acres are tidal mudflats; there are 1,700 acres of salt marsh, 300 acres of salt-brackish marsh.

Winter home for, on the average, half of the canvasbacks on the Pacific Flyway. Many loons, grebes, cormorants, terns, pintail, shoveler, wigeon, scaup, bufflehead, scoter, ruddy duck. Wading birds and shorebirds also winter here.

Sonoma Coast State Beach
California Department of Parks and Recreation
5,000 acres.

Pacific Coast, along Hwy 1, from Coleman Gulch N of Jenner S to Bodega Head.

The state owns most of these 17 mi. of spectacular coastline, one of the most scenic sections of the Coast Highway. Along it are frequent overlook points, some high above the sea. Rugged headlands with rocky bluffs and natural arches divide the coast into a series of beaches, some long enough for an hour of hiking, others small, secluded coves. Many offshore rocks. Many tidepools. The sea is not for swimming: heavy surf, strong undertow, sudden groundswells. Bluffs, slopes, and dunes have a hardy cover of shrubs, grasses, and wildflowers. Spring display of yellow and blue lupine, sea pink, Indian paintbrush, western wallflower, wild strawberry, monkeyflower. Many gulls, cormorants, pelican, other seabirds, as well as goldfinch, swallows, quail, raven, hawks, wrens. Mammals include raccoon, gray fox, cottontail, mule deer, skunk, ground squirrel.

Parking and trails to the beach have been provided at more than a dozen points. There are also many miles of trails, both in the backcountry and in the dune area.

Camping: Wright's Beach, 30 sites; *Bodega Dunes,* 98 sites. Also 2 primitive environmental campgrounds: *Willow Creek,* 11 sites; *Pomo Canyon,* 21 sites. Reservations all year through DESTINET.

Publication
Leaflet with map.

Headquarters
CA Dept. of Parks and Recreation, Salmon Creek R.D., 3095 Hwy 1, Bodega Bay, CA 94923; (707) 875-3483.

Sonoma County Regional Parks at Bodega Bay
Sonoma County Regional Parks Department

At Bodega Bay on Hwy 1.

On the N and W, the harbor is enclosed by a cape about 3½ mi. long ending in a high promontory, Bodega Head. On the S it is separated from the larger and more open Bodega Bay by a long sand spit. The harbor has a large fishing fleet.

A road leads along the N shore of the harbor to parking areas on the Head. Birding along the shore is excellent. In March we saw large numbers of loons, horned grebe, coot, bufflehead, marbled godwit, surf scoter. Fine views from the Head. The coast below is rocky, with tide pools. Good whale-watching in season.

One can also drive partway out on the S sand spit, where there is a campground and Coast Guard facility. Good birding here, too.

Activities

Camping: Doran Beach Park, 140 sites; *Westside Beach Park,* 40 sites.

Hiking: 5 mi. of dunes trails.

Swimming: At Doran Park.

Horse riding: The 5-mi. dunes trail system is open to horses.

Boating: Ramps at both county parks and at Spud Point Marina. Porto-Bodega party boat.

Fishing: Public and commercial fishing docks.

Handicapped access.

Headquarters

Sonoma County Regional Parks Dept., Doran Park, P.O. Box 372, Bodega Bay, CA 94923; (707) 875-3540.

Sugarloaf Ridge State Park

California Department of Parks and Recreation
2,700 acres.

From Santa Rosa, 7 mi. E on Hwy 12; N on Adobe Canyon Rd. Narrow, steep roads, not suitable for trailers or large RVs.

In the coastal mountains. Elevations from 600 ft. at the entrance to 2,729 ft. at the top of Bald Mountain. The office, campground, and other developments are clustered in the SW corner. Elsewhere the Park is open to foot and horse traffic only. Sonoma Creek, a perennial stream, begins in the Park and flows 3 mi. near its S boundary. There is a small waterfall.

Plants: Chaparral on the slopes and ridges: manzanita, chamise, ceanothus, poison oak, coyote bush, toyon, winebush. Meadows and groves of trees along the drainages. One of the state's largest bigleaf maples. Other tree species include Coast madrone, California bay laurel, gray pine, Douglas-fir, alder, California buckeye, Coast redwood, live oak. Wildflowers include poppy, cream cups, lupine, penstemon, mariposa lily, thistle, farewell-to-spring, brodiaea, Indian pink, buttercup, coralroot, orchid, camas, scarlet larkspur, mimulus, Indian warrior, iris, western azalea, spicebush, trillium, California fuchsia, shooting star, clarkia, fritillaria.

Birds: Checklist available. Species include great blue heron, turkey vulture, golden eagle, sharp-shinned, Cooper's, and red-tailed hawks, California and mountain quail, screech, great horned, and pygmy owls, Anna's, rufous, and Allen's hummingbirds, pileated and acorn woodpeckers, ash-throated, western, and olive-sided flycatchers, house and Bewick's wrens, varied, hermit, and Swainson's thrushes; Hutton's, solitary, and warbling vireos; orange-crowned, yellow, yellow-rumped, black-throated gray, hermit, and Wilson's warblers, black-headed grosbeak, lazuli bunting, purple and house finches, American and lesser goldfinches.

Mammals: Include rabbit, skunk, coyote, squirrels, weasel, raccoon, bobcat, gray fox, mule deer.

Reptiles and amphibians: Include rubber boa, kingsnake, gopher snake, ringneck snake, rattlesnake.

Activities

Camping: 49 developed sites without showers.

Hiking: 25 mi. of trails. Trail to tops of Bald, Red Mountains and Brushy Peaks.

Horse riding: Horse travel permitted on most trails, but restricted in winter.

Publications

Leaflet with map.

Bird checklist.

Headquarters

CA Dept. of Parks and Recreation, 2605 Adobe Canyon Rd., Kenwood, CA 95452; (707) 833-5712.

Suisun Marsh

See Grizzly Island Wildlife Area (this zone).

Sutter National Wildlife Refuge

See Sacramento National Wildlife Refuges (this zone).

Tomales Bay State Park

California Department of Parks and Recreation
1,078 acres.

On Point Reyes Peninsula. From Inverness, N 3 mi. on Sir Francis Drake
Blvd. Then right 1½ mi. on Pierce Point Rd.

On the W shore of Tomales Bay, its land boundaries common with
Point Reyes National Seashore (see entry this zone). Sheltered by the
Inverness Ridge, the Park's beaches are often warm and sunny while
the outer Point experiences wind and fog. Rolling hills with elevations to 565 ft. Deep, rugged canyons. Rocky headlands on the Bay.
Four sheltered beaches within the 2 mi. of waterfront. Four gently
sloping, surf-free beaches are the chief public attraction. The Park has
6½ mi. of hiking trails, much less than the larger, adjacent National
Seashore. For the naturalist, however, the Park has much to offer.

Plants: About 70% forested. The E slope of Inverness Ridge is steep,
heavily wooded, with thick underbrush. The 310 acres of Bishop pine
include one of the finest remaining virgin stands. The Jepson Trail
crosses this grove. About 210 acres of mixed evergreen forest, 130 of
oak-bay woodland, 160 acres of coastal scrub. Tree species include tan
oak, toyon, Coast live oak, madrone, red alder. In the understory:
ceanothus, huckleberry, hazel, salal, poison oak, coffeeberry, gooseberry, salmonberry, manzanita, mountain mahogany. Some shrubs
grow to tree size. The many ferns include woodwardia, swordfern,
deer fern, lady fern, maidenhair, gold-back, five-finger, polypodium.
About 300 species of spring wildflowers have been identified, including
lilies, fritillaria, poppy, wild strawberry, lupines, iris, monkeyflowers,

rein orchid, violets, pussy's ear, trillium, hound's tongue, slim solomon, fairy bells, columbine, larkspurs, bleeding heart, western wallflower, rosy arabis, Indian paintbrush, heliotrope.

Birds: No checklist. 5 species of owl, including spotted owl, nest here. Also murret, puffin, geese, scoters, pelican, grebes, goldeneye, buffle-head, ruddy duck, rails, sandpipers, band-tailed pigeon, horned lark, kingfisher, pygmy nuthatch, various warblers.

Mammals: Include gray fox, raccoon, badger, weasel, chipmunk, cottontail, skunk, wood rat, mule deer, bobcat, mountain lion.

Reptiles and amphibians: Granulated newt, Pacific giant salamander, slender salamander, garter snake, rubber boa.

Interpretation
Nature trail, ½ mi., from Hearts Desire Beach to Indian Beach.

Activities
Hiking: 6½ mi. of trails linking the beaches. Dogs not permitted on beaches and trails, or in nature areas.

Canoeing: No launching ramp. Hand-carried boats may be put in the water away from swimming areas.

Swimming: No lifeguards on duty.

Publications
Park map.

Nature trail guide, $0.50.

Headquarters
CA Dept. of Parks and Recreation, Star Rt., Inverness, CA 94937; (415) 669-1140.

Z O N E

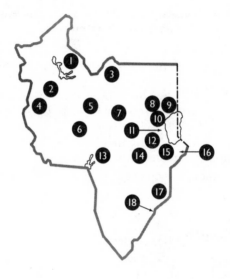

Z O N E

Includes these counties:

Butte	Sutter	El Dorado
Yuba	Placer	Amador
Sierra	Nevada	Calaveras

The zone includes a bit of the E portion of the Sacramento Valley, the foothills and W slope of the Sierra Nevada from near Yuba Pass to Bear Valley, and as much of the E slope as is in California. It includes the California side of Lake Tahoe. It is crossed by I-80, the main route from Sacramento to Reno, and US 50, from Sacramento to South Lake Tahoe.

By far the largest public sites are the National Forests that straddle the Sierra Nevada: Tahoe, Eldorado, and part of the Stanislaus. The Forests have many inholdings, chiefly along the principal roads, with summer and winter resorts. Proximity to major cities and easy access make this zone one of the state's most popular recreation areas. Many places are crowded in season, but we found quiet trails.

Many of those who saw Lake Tahoe pristine pronounced it the world's loveliest lake. Surely it should be a National Park. Early in the 20th century, legislation was introduced to achieve this. It failed to pass. Then, suddenly, it was too late. A National Park Service team sent there in the 1930s concluded the lake was a lost cause. Too much land had been sold, subdivided, and developed for resorts and summer homes along the lakeshore. Commercialism was far advanced. In the 1950s, roads were plowed during the winter, enabling year-round residence for the first time. Pollution became a serious problem. Finally, in 1968, the Tahoe Regional Planning Agency was established for the purpose of ensuring environmentally responsible development in the future. However, the area continued to deteriorate through the 1970s. Then stricter measures were taken.

From some vantage points the lake is still lovely. At Emerald Bay State Park, everyone reaches for cameras—it is the lake's most-photographed scene. Other State Parks on or near the lake are Burton Creek, D. L. Bliss, Sugar Pine Point. The Lake Tahoe Basin Management Unit (see entry) is a Forest Service effort to protect what remains of the undeveloped public lands near the lake.

The runoff from the W slope of the Sierra is precious, and many dams have been built to store the water for use in the dry season. Two of the largest impoundments, Lake Oroville and Folsom Lake, are State Recreation Areas. We have entries for them, but not for several other impoundments with developed shorelines.

In the Valley, two state Wildlife Areas, Gray Lodge and Spenceville, are of interest. Their function is much like that of the nearby Sacramento National Wildlife Refuges described in zone 3.

Burton Creek State Park and Natural Preserve

California Department of Parks and Recreation
2,000 acres.

2 mi. E of Tahoe City on Hwy 28.

Near, but not on the lake. Elevations from 6,270 to 7,170 ft. About 90% forested, second-growth Jeffrey, lodgepole, sugar pines. Also red and white firs. Understory includes manzanita, buck brush, squaw carpet. Some mountain meadows.

Activities

Hiking: About 13 mi. of old logging roads, one or two of which lead into the National Forest.

Ski touring: About 3–4 mi. of track set in the Park by the adjacent Nordic Ski Center.

Adjacent

National Forest land (see Lake Tahoe Basin Management Unit, this zone).

Tahoe State Recreation Area: 13 acres. Lakeside and hill camping, 39 sites (hill sites are for tents only). Reservations from Memorial

Day–Labor Day, (800) 444-7275. 100 yards of lakefront with pier. Swimming from rocky beach. Pier fishing.

Headquarters
CA Dept. of Parks and Recreation, Sierra District, P.O. Box 266, Tahoma, CA 96142; (916) 525-7232.

Calaveras Big Trees State Park
California Department of Parks and Recreation
6,500 acres.

From Angels Camp, NE on Hwy 4, about 4 mi. beyond Arnold. Hwy 4 is closed in winter at Lake Alpine, 25 mi. NE of the Park.

On both sides of the North Fork, Stanislaus River. Surrounded by Stanislaus National Forest (see entry zone 6). On the W slope of the Sierra Nevada; elevations from 3,400 to 5,500 ft. This is the only State Park with groves of the California big tree, the giant sequoia, largest of living things, the species seen in Sequoia National Park. (Coast redwoods are taller but less massive.)

Generally rugged terrain. 5 mi. of frontage on the Stanislaus River and Beaver Creek. The Stanislaus flows through a canyon, with rocky ledges, shallows with pebble beaches, a pool deep enough for swimming. Annual precipitation is about 51 in. The Park remains open all year. Usually, in winter, enough space has been plowed open to meet camping needs.

A scenic drive extends to 10 mi. from the Park entrance to Beaver Creek, passing campgrounds, overlooks, and trailheads. This drive is closed in winter beyond the North Grove area.

Plants: The giant sequoia was first discovered here at the height of the Gold Rush. Visitors came from everywhere, and this site continued to be the chief attraction for some years after other groves were found. About a quarter-million people per year now walk the easy 1-mi. trail through the North Grove, where the first discovery was made. The South Grove is much larger, more primeval. It takes a bit more walking, and fewer people see it. The Park is almost entirely forested. Giant sequoias grow in mixed stands with ponderosa and sugar pines, white fir, incense cedar, black and canyon live oaks. Understory species include Pacific dogwood, mountain alder, bigleaf maple, hazel. Flowering species include western azalea, monkeyflower, snow plant, lupine, yarrow.

Birds: Checklist of 90+ species available. Included: Steller's jay, robin, northern flicker, white-headed woodpecker, mountain chickadee, red-breasted nuthatch, goshawk, brown creeper, western tanager, black-headed and evening grosbeaks, dark-eyed junco.

Mammals: Include ground squirrels, chickaree, chipmunk, deer mouse, raccoon, coyote, black bear, mule deer. Present but seldom seen: mountain lion, bobcat, flying squirrel, gray fox.

Reptiles and amphibians: Include Sierra salamander, alligator lizard, Gilbert skink, garter snake, Pacific rattlesnake, rubber boa.

Interpretation

Visitor center: museum, herbarium, publications. Open daily in summer; weekends and holidays in winter.

Campfire programs and *guided hikes* in summer.

Three Senses Nature Trail through North Grove.

Activities

Camping: 2 campgrounds, 129 sites. All year; limited facilities off-season. Reservations May through Sept.; needed July–Aug.

Hiking: 40 mi. of trails.

Swimming: No supervision. Water can be cold, swift.

Ski touring, snowshoeing: 4 mi. of signed trail. Check before coming; snow is often wet.

Publications

Leaflet with hiking map, $1.00.

North and South Grove guides, $0.25 and $0.50, respectively.

Species checklists.

Winter activities information.

Campground information.

Headquarters

CA Dept. of Parks and Recreation, P.O. Box 120, Arnold, CA 95223; (209) 795-2334.

D. L. Bliss and Emerald Bay State Parks

California Department of Parks and Recreation
1,830 acres.

19 mi. S of Tahoe City on Hwy 89.

On Lake Tahoe. Emerald Bay is one of the most photographed points on the shoreline drive. The Emerald Bay Overlook is often crowded. The Parks, with 6 mi. of lake frontage, are among the few remaining natural areas on the lake. Much of the shoreline is rugged, with massive rock outcroppings. The land rises steeply from 6,229 ft. at the shore to 7,400 ft. Eagle Falls, an impressive cascade of several hundred feet, is at the head of Emerald Bay. Other features include Fanette Island, a balancing rock, and Vikingsholm, a reproduction of a Norse fortress. The two parks are contiguous, operate as a single unit, but have separate developed areas linked by trails.

Plants: 90% forested: Jeffrey, sugar, and lodgepole pines, red and white firs, incense cedar, western juniper, black cottonwood, aspen. Understory includes greenleaf manzanita, huckleberry oak, Sierra chinquapin, ceanothus. Flowering plants include red penstemon, snow plant, columbine, monkeyflower; peak blooming July–Aug.

Birds: No checklist. Reported: Canada goose (spring), common merganser, bald eagle (winter), goshawk, Cooper's hawk, Steller's jay, white-headed woodpecker, mountain chickadee, red-breasted nuthatch, dark-eyed junco.

Mammals: Include bats, California ground squirrel, chickaree, golden-mantled ground squirrel, chipmunk, white-footed mouse, beaver, coyote, raccoon, black bear.

Reptiles and amphibians: Reported: Pacific tree frog, yellow-legged frog, western fence lizard, garter snake.

Intepretation

Naturalist activities, including *campfire programs, guided hikes,* July–Labor Day. Notices posted.

Nature trail, 1 mi., around Balancing Rock.

Activities

Camping: 3 campgrounds, 288 sites. Open Memorial Day–Oct. 1st, depending on weather conditions. Reservations June–Labor Day. *Campground is constantly full July–Aug.* 22 primitive boat-in or hike-in sites on N shore of Emerald Bay.

Hiking: 10 mi. of trails. Rubicon Trail follows the shoreline from Vikingsholm to Calawee Cove, 4½ mi. Vikingsholm Trail descends from Emerald Bay Overlook; closed when icy.

Fishing: Rainbow, lake, brown trout; kokanee salmon.

Swimming: Lester Beach, at extreme N of site.

Boating: No ramp within the site. Mooring buoys at boat-in camp with 22 sites at Emerald Bay.

Adjacent

National Forest land (see Lake Tahoe Basin Management Unit, this zone). Nearby trails into Desolation Wilderness, in Eldorado National Forest (see entry this zone).

Publication

Leaflet with map, $0.50.

Headquarters

CA Dept. of Parks and Recreation, P.O. Box 266, Tahoma, CA 96142; (916) 525-7277.

Donner Memorial State Park

California Department of Parks and Recreation
353 acres.

From Truckee, 2 mi. W on Hwy 40, just off I-80.

As the name suggests, the Park's theme is historical. Donner Lake is almost 3 mi. long, most of the shoreline privately owned and developed. Elevation about 6,000 ft. Forested site. Lake and river frontage.

Activities

Camping: 154 sites, summer only. Reservations May 25–Sept. 3.

Fishing: Trout, kokanee.

Swimming: Cold water.

Boating: No ramp.

Headquarters

CA Dept. of Parks and Recreation, 12593 Donner Pass Rd., Truckee, CA 96161; (916) 582-7892.

Eldorado National Forest

U.S. Forest Service
695,904 acres; 786,994 acres within boundaries.

S and W of Lake Tahoe. US 50 crosses its center, Hwy 88 its S portion.

From the upper foothills to the Sierra Crest. Elevations from 2,000 to 10,000 ft. The portion E of the crest and nearest Lake Tahoe is now, for management purposes, part of the Lake Tahoe Basin Management Unit (see entry this zone). Although this portion is the most heavily impacted by visitors, the entire Forest is described in one of its publications as "a vast outdoor backyard for visitors from Sacramento, Stockton, and the San Francisco Bay Area."

As the acreage figures indicate, the Forest has many inholdings. From Lake Tahoe, a block about 20 mi. wide with relatively few inholdings extends SW to the Mokelumne River. The Forest land to the W and N is broken by many more inholdings, but the Forest map shows blocks where one can travel for 10 or 20 mi. without crossing private land. Furthermore, many of the inholdings are forested, and few owners of forested tracts have posted or marked their boundaries.

Annual precipitation varies from 40 to 75 in. The Forest has 660 mi. of fishing streams, 297 lakes and reservoirs. 14 lakes are over 1 mi. long. Most are surrounded by Forest land. In four cases, a major portion of the shoreline is privately owned. Forest campgrounds are beside most of these lakes.

Plants: The Forest is an important timber producer. Principal tree species are sugar pine, white and red firs, Douglas-fir, incense cedar, ponderosa and Jeffrey pines, interior live oak. A large part of the Forest is in the mixed conifer belt, where the understory includes deer brush, ceanothus, mountain whitethorn, mountain misery, greenleaf manzanita, thimbleberry, and Sierra currant. The belt includes numerous meadows with perennial grasses and forbs.

Above the mixed conifer belt, from 6,500–8,000 ft., is the true fir belt, characterized by red fir and by lodgepole, western white, and Jeffrey pines. Next above is the subalpine belt, with mountain hemlock, whitebark pine, alpine willow; here trees are scattered, and most vegetation is grasses, forbs, and shrubs.

An estimated 1,000 plant species occur in the Forest. Flowering species include Indian pink, wild rose, western azalea, snowberry, elderberry, little princes pine, snow plant, California harebell, false Solomon's seal, rattlesnake orchid, heartleaf arnica, larkspur, wild peony, eriogonums, waterleaf phacelia, lupines, fireweed, bear grass, columbine, violet, monkeyflower, penstemon.

Birds: Checklist available. Forest species include turkey vulture, goshawk, Cooper's, red-tailed, and Swainson's hawks, golden and bald eagles, blue grouse, mountain quail, band-tailed pigeon, great horned, pygmy, great gray, and saw-whet owls, pileated, Lewis's, hairy, downy, white-headed, acorn, and black-backed three-toed woodpeckers, yellow-bellied and Williamson's sapsuckers, Hammond's and olive-sided flycatchers, gray and Steller's jays, Clark's nutcracker, mountain and chestnut-backed chickadees, brown creeper, varied and Swainson's thrushes, western and mountain bluebirds, golden-crowned and ruby-crowned kinglets, solitary vireo. Warblers include Nashville, magnolia, yellow-rumped, Townsend's, hermit. Also western tanager, black-headed grosbeak, purple and Cassin's finches, pine siskin, rufous-crowned and chipping sparrows, dark-eyed junco.

Mammals: Include 3 species of shrew, 15 bat species, black bear, mule deer, marten, fisher, coyote, red and gray foxes, mountain lion, bobcat, mountain beaver, marmot, California, Belding, and golden-mantled ground squirrels, 5 species of chipmunk, gray squirrel, chickaree, northern flying squirrel, deer mouse, mountain vole, porcupine, pika, snowshoe hare.

Features

Desolation Wilderness: 63,475 acres. On both sides of the Sierra Nevada, just W of Lake Tahoe. One of the most N sections of glaciated High Sierra–type scenic lands. Elevations from 6,500–10,000 ft. Pyramid Peak, 9,983 ft., is one of a group of four summits on the S boundary. Many small streams. About 130 lakes, some as large as 900 acres. Because it is spectacularly lovely and readily accessible, the area attracted so many people that serious damage was occurring. In 1978, a rationing scheme was adopted: only 700 overnight visitors per day, June 15–Labor Day. Half the permits issued up to 90 days in advance, half on the date. We recommend avoiding this area. If you do visit, rangers will tell you which trails and destinations are least used.

Mokelumne Wilderness: 59,865 acres. Between Hwys 88 and 4, just W of the Sierra Crest. Mokelumne Peak, 9,332 ft., dominates the area. The Mokelumne River, flowing SW, has cut a canyon down to the 4,000-ft. elevation. Many small, scenic lakes in the shallow valleys N of the Peak. Wildflowers are abundant during the hiking season. The Pacific Crest Trail is near the E boundary. Permits are required, but rationing use has not yet been thought necessary. Rangers can advise which areas are least used.

The principal road-access recreation areas of the Forest are as follows. These areas attract the most people, in season:

Crystal Basin. From US 50 at Riverton, N on Ice House Rd. toward Cleveland Corral, information station, Ice House, Loon Lake, Union Valley and Hell Hole Reservoirs. This is a busy area with numerous campgrounds, a private resort, lakeside developments.

Silver and Caples Lakes area, along Hwy 88 W of Carson Pass, just N of the Mokelumne Wilderness. Water-based recreation, 5 private resorts, campgrounds, a major winter sports facility for downhill and cross-country skiing.

Highway 50 area. E of Riverton. Numerous streams flow into the South Fork of the American River beside the highway. Small lakes. Many recreation residences on private and Forest land. One down-hill ski area.

Bear River, S of Hwy 88. Lower Bear River Reservoir is one of the Forest's largest lakes. Two campgrounds; one private resort.

Interpretation

Information at ranger stations, Cleveland Corral information station.

Nature trail at Lake Edson Burn.

Campfire programs are infrequent. No guided hikes.

Activities

Camping: 48 campgrounds, 1,053 sites. Open May 1–July 1, close Sept. 15–Nov. 1 depending on weather. A reservation system in effect at larger campgrounds; inquire.

Hiking, backpacking: 350 mi. of trail, 72 mi. of 4-wheel-drive roads. The most popular trails are those in the two wilderness areas, but there are good trails and little-used logging roads in all parts of the Forest.

Hunting: Deer, bear, quail.

Fishing: 600 mi. of fishable streams. Nearly 12,000 acres of reservoirs and lakes; 11 of these account for 9,000 acres; the remainder are small lakes near the Crest. Rainbow, brown, and eastern brook trout.

Swimming: Especially in Crystal Basin.

Boating: Ramps on all major reservoirs.

Skiing: E of Riverton, 1 downhill area. Silver and Caples Lakes area has a major downhill and ski-tour area.

Ski touring: Kirkwood Meadows, Carson Pass, Echo Summit, Echo Lakes, Loon Lake.

Adjacent
Tahoe National Forest (see entry this zone), Stanislaus National Forest and Toiyabe National Forest (see entries zone 6).

Publications
Forest map, $3.25.

Desolation Wilderness map, $3.25.

Mokelumne Wilderness map, $.3.25.

Crystal Basin Recreation Area map.

Off-Road and Vehicle Travel Plan.

Headquarters
U.S. Forest Service, 100 Forni Rd., Placerville, CA 95667; (916) 622-5061; fax (916) 621-5297.

Ranger Districts
Amador R.D. 26820 Silver Dr., Hwy 88, Pioneer, CA 95666; (209) 295-4251; FTS (209) 295-5900. Georgetown R.D., 7600 Wentworth Springs Rd., Georgetown, CA 95634; (916) 333-4312; FTS (916) 333-5500. Pacific R.D., 7887 Hwy 50, Pollock Pines, CA 95726-9602; (916) 644-2349; FTS (916) 647-5400. Placerville, R.D., 4260 Eight Mile Rd., Camino, CA 95709; (916) 644-2324; FTS (916) 647-5300.

Information Centers
3070 Camino Heights Dr., Camino, CA 95709; (916) 644-6048. Placerville Nursery, 2375 Fruitridge Rd., Camino, CA 95709; (916) 622-9600; FTS (916) 642-5000. National Forest Genetic Electrophoresis Lab, 2375 Fruitridge Rd., Camino, CA 95709; (916) 642-5000.

Emerald Bay State Park

See D. L. Bliss State Park (this zone).

Folsom Lake State Recreation Area

California Department of Parks and Recreation
17,545 acres, including 11,500 acres of water.
From Folsom, take the Folsom-Auburn Rd.

25 mi. E of Sacramento. Called the most popular all-year, multiple-use State Park in California. Very heavy use on weekends and holidays, May–Sept. We visited on a fine weekend in March, and few people were there. The remote areas of the Park are attractive and uncrowded in spring and fall.

Folsom Lake, larger of two, has 120 mi. of shoreline at high water; Lake Natoma, 18 mi. Lakes are about 450 ft. above sea level. Reservoir is generally full in June, lowest in Nov.–Dec. In the Sierra foothills; rolling oak woodlands. Steep canyons up the N and S forks of the lake. Highest point is 1,200 ft. Annual precipitation about 18 in. Climate is hot and dry in summer. Fire hazard is sometimes extreme.

Plants: Oak and chaparral. Some of the finest examples of blue oak woodlands remaining in CA, in the Peninsula area. Poison oak and toyon prominent in understory. The many wildflowers include brodiaea, poppy, ceanothus, shooting star, vetch, camas, monkeyflower, Indian paintbrush, larkspur, lupine, fiddleneck, morning glory. Some areas of chaparral are impenetrable.

Birds: Some waterfowl, including Canada goose, winter here. Three large great blue heron rookeries. Species noted include northern flicker, acorn woodpecker, western kingbird, western wood pewee, Say's phoebe, common bushtit, kestrel, western meadowlark, Bewick's wren, western bluebird, Swainson's thrush, yellowthroat, western tanager, lesser goldfinch, savannah, chipping, fox, and white-crowned sparrows.

Mammals: Ground squirrels, raccoon, black-tailed jackrabbit, opossum, coyote, skunk, gray fox, bobcat.

Feature

Anderson Island Natural Preserve is site of heron rookery. Visitors not permitted ashore in nesting season.

Interpretation

Campfire programs and *guided hikes,* at campgrounds, by request.

Activities

Camping: 3 campgrounds, 150 sites. All year. Reservations May 25–Sept. 3.

Hiking, backpacking: 65 mi. of trails. Map available. Western State National Recreation Trail passes through the Park, to the mountains.

Horse riding: Popular. Horses allowed on most trails. Rentals nearby.

Fishing: Trout, bass, kokanee, catfish.

Swimming: Usually May–Sept.

Boating: Marina. No hp limit, but 5 mph within 200 ft. of shore. Dangerous in high winds. Hazards when lake is low.

Headquarters

CA Dept. of Parks and Recreation, 7806 Folsom-Auburn Rd., Folsom, CA 95630; (916) 988-0205.

Gray Lodge Wildlife Area

California Department of Fish and Game
8,400 acres.

8 mi. SW of Gridley. W on Colusa/Gridley Hwy to Pennington Rd., then S 4 mi. to entrance.

Gray Lodge Wildlife Area is an intensively managed habitat composed of permanent and seasonal wetlands as well as riparian and upland areas. Gray Lodge is most known for its wintering waterfowl.

Waterfowl populations build from an average of 20,000 in Aug. to 250,000 in mid-Oct. and peak in Dec. or Jan. The best time to see waterfowl is during the hunting season, generally from mid-Oct. through mid-Jan. Public hunting days are traditionally Wed., Sat., and Sun. A permit system limits the number of hunters. Reservations as well as first-come-first-served permits issued. A 3-mi. auto tour route stays open during hunting season as does a wheelchair accessible 0.3-mi. hiking route to a wildlife viewing platform complete with spotting scope. An additional 2-mi. trail also remains open during hunting season. Except during hunting season, visitors may hike on approximately 60 mi. of service roads closed to vehicles. There is a per-vehicle fee.

Birds: At peaks, more than 2 million waterfowl have been observed here. The most common ducks are pintail, mallard, wigeon, shoveler, gadwall, and green-winged teal. Of the geese, snows are most numerous, then white fronts. The marshlands support many other bird species—over 230 have been recorded.

Mammals: Include mule deer, black-tailed jackrabbit, cottontail, opossum, raccoon, striped skunk, muskrat, red and gray foxes.

Headquarters
CA Dept. of Fish and Game, P.O. Box 37, Gridley, CA 95948; (916) 846-3316; naturalist office, (916) 846-5176.

Lake Oroville State Recreation Area
California Department of Parks and Recreation
16,400 acres of water; 12,060 land acres. State property extends at least 300 ft. and as much as 1 mi. from the high-water line.
From Oroville, 7 mi. E on Hwy 162.

Lake Oroville is a Department of Water Resources project, built for water supply, flood control, and power generation. At full pool it has 167 mi. of shoreline, with four long arms. Although it is a popular recreation site, management reports capacity crowds only on major summer holidays. It is least crowded Sept.–May. The most popular recreation is water based. Even in summer, however, someone with a small boat can find quiet waters up the tributaries, where boat speed is restricted to 5 mph.

Most of the area is within the foothills of the Sierra Nevada. The dam is on the Feather River. Upstream the site adjoins the Feather Falls Scenic Area of the Plumas National Forest (see entry zone 2).

Lake elevation at maximum is 900 ft. Elevations within the site range from 140–1,300 ft. Annual precipitation ranges from 15–50 in.

Plants: From valley grasslands to chaparral. Principal trees are digger pine, valley, blue, live, and black oaks, madrone, cedar, ponderosa pine. Great variety of chaparral plants, including manzanita, buck brush, ceanothus, poison oak. Wildflowers include California poppy, mariposa lily, brodiaea, thistles, Indian paintbrush, buttercup, spring vetch, shooting star.

Birds: Checklist. Species include Canada and snow geese, western grebe, red-breasted merganser, coot, Arctic and common loons, double-crested cormorant, mallard, wood duck, Caspian tern, belted kingfisher, great blue heron, golden and bald eagles, osprey, red-tailed and Swainson's hawks, burrowing and pygmy owls, acorn and downy woodpeckers, mountain quail, cedar waxwing, rock wren, bushtit, plain titmouse, scrub jay, western bluebird, violet-green swallow.

Mammals: Species include coyote, raccoon, porcupine, black-tailed jackrabbit, California ground squirrel, ringtail, gray fox, black bear, beaver, mule deer, mountain lion.

Feature

Feather Falls—when the lake is high, one can boat to within ½ mi. of the 640-ft.-high fall, spectacular in spring runoff. No trail from the lake to the fall—and the way is difficult, requiring caution. There is a safe trail in the Plumas National Forest (see entry zone 2), where the waterfall is located, taking the hiker to a lookout above the fall.

Interpretation

Visitor center themes include natural and cultural history, as well as the dam.

Campfire programs Sat. and Sun., June–Labor Day.

Fishing clinics and other special activities June–Labor Day.

There is a *self-guided nature trail* at the visitor center, on chaparral fauna and flora.

Activities

Camping: 2 campgrounds, 212 sites. All year. Reservations April 1–Sept. 5. Also 73 primitive boat-in sites, with 2 group sites.

Hiking and horse riding: 20 mi. of horse and hiking trails, from downtown Oroville to the visitor center.

Hunting: Designated areas. Upland small game and waterfowl only.

Fishing: Rainbow and German brown trout, bass, silver salmon, kokanee.

Swimming: Unsupervised.

Boating: Marina, ramps. No hp limit but special zones. On-board boat camping in many areas if boat is properly equipped. Boat rentals at Lime Saddle Marina.

Adjacent or Nearby

Plumas National Forest (see entry zone 2).

Oroville Wildlife Area (see entry this zone).

Publications

Leaflet with map, $0.50.

Bird checklist, $0.50.

Chaparral Trail and Maidu Trail guides.

Boating information.

Lake Oroville Pro-Guide (fishing brochure), $3.50.

Headquarters

CA Dept. of Parks and Recreation, 400 Glen Dr., Oroville, CA 95966; (916) 538-2200.

Lake Tahoe Basin Management Unit

U.S. Forest Service
148,800 acres.

National Forest land near Lake Tahoe, in CA and NV.

Lake Tahoe is 21½ mi. long, 12 mi. at its widest, at an elevation of 6,225 ft. When pristine, it was called one of the world's loveliest sights. Development began early. Most of the shoreline is privately owned. In 1979 an official basin-wide assessment concluded what many environmentalists and local residents had said before: every element of the environment was deteriorating at an alarming rate.

Since then, the League to Save Lake Tahoe, other private groups, and various local, state, and federal agencies have achieved considerable progress. Stricter controls govern new construction. Road salting is out. Erosion control is improving.

Although only a few short sections of lakeshore are federally owned, parts of three National Forests are nearby, and these parts have had heavy visitor use. The Lake Tahoe Basin Management Unit was established by the Forest Service to bring these areas into the general scheme for protecting the lake and its environs.

Most of the acreage within the Unit is around the S half of the lake, extending almost as far S as Hwy 88. Forest Service land around the N half of the lake is patchwork. Other National Forest lands, of course, lie outside the Unit boundaries. Within the Unit are the trails, campgrounds, and other features visitors reach from the roads surrounding the lake.

Features

Angora Lookout is near the S end of Fallen Leaf Lake, reached by 3 mi. of mountain road. Views of the lakes and Desolation Wilderness.

Tahoe Rim Trail is a 150-mi. hiking and equestrian trail, begun in 1984, that follows the ridgetops of the Tahoe Basin, incorporating a portion of the Pacific Crest Trail. The remaining 20 mi. of the trail will be completed in 2001. Moderate difficulty, about 10% grade. Panoramic views.

Desolation Wilderness is described in the Eldorado National Forest entry (this zone). Wilderness permits (limited number) are required from June 15 to Labor Day. The most heavily used portion of the Wilderness is in the Management Unit.

Granite Chief Wilderness is W and NW of Tahoe City, a backcountry area within which all vehicles are banned. Steep, rugged ridges, peaks from 8,000–9,000 ft. Glacial valleys. Small lakes and streams.

Meiss Country is reached by a trailhead on Hwy 89, 4½ mi. S of the junction with US 50, S of South Lake Tahoe. Said to be one of the most beautiful hiking areas in the Basin, with more than 32 mi. of trails; a rugged alpine area, with alpine lakes, meadows, overlooks. The Forest Service says the Granite Chief and Meiss areas are similar to Desolation Wilderness but without its heavy use.

Interpretation

The Lake Tahoe *visitor center* is W of South Lake Tahoe on Hwy 89, just N of the turnoff for Fallen Leaf Lake. This is a good place to begin a tour. Includes stream profile chamber. *Guided walks, nature trails, and campfire programs.* Open daily in summer.

Activities

Camping: 19 campgrounds, over 2,000 sites. Summer months. Reservations. Pets allowed at some sites. Fees vary.

Hunting: Said to be generally poor in this area.

Fishing: Many lakes, streams. Fair to poor.

Swimming: Beaches and picnic areas situated at various locations around Lake Tahoe. Some fees may apply.

Boating: Public facilities on Lake Tahoe. Ramps on Fallen Leaf Lake, Echo Lake.

Horse riding: Outfitters offer horses, trail rides in summer.

Skiing: Concession-operated ski areas—downhill, cross-country, snowboarding.

Mountain biking: 80 mi. of trails, from easy to strenuous in difficulty.

Off-road vehicles: Restricted to designated roads and trails.

Publications

Maps and information sheets on biking, hiking, skiing, fishing, boating, birds, mammals, trees, and wildflowers.

Tahoe Rim Trail (brochure).

Lake of the Sky Journal.

Headquarters

U.S. Forest Service, 870 Emerald Bay Rd., Suite 1, S. Lake Tahoe, CA 96150; (916) 573-2600. Summer information station: (916) 573-2674. Tahoe Rim Trail Volunteer Hotline: (702) 588-0686.

Martis Creek Lake

U.S. Army Corps of Engineers
1,050-acre wildlife area; 770-acre lake (when full).

Off Hwy 267, about 6 mi. SE of Truckee.

The reservoir is usually kept near empty to provide space for floodwaters. The site is interesting because of the wildlife management area, where vehicles are excluded and land is kept in more or less natural condition.

Birds include red-tailed hawk, killdeer, mountain quail, Canada goose. Mammals include mule deer, coyote, golden-mantled ground squirrel, pocket mouse, chipmunk, raccoon.

Activities
Camping: 25 sites.

Hiking: 1-mi. trail around Lake.

Fishing: Catch and release program—anglers must use barbless hooks and artificial lures and all trout must be released back into the lake.

Publication
Leaflet.

Headquarters
U.S. Army Corps of Engineers, c/o Englebright Lake Park, P.O. Box 6, Smartville, CA 95977; (916) 639-2342.

Oroville Wildlife Area
California Department of Fish and Game
11,871 acres.

Just W of Oroville on Hwy 162, Oroville Dam Blvd. The Thermalito-Bay Unit is E of Hwy 99 and straddles Hwy 162.

An interesting demonstration of wetlands restoration. This site on the Feather River showed the effects of half a century of gold dredging: ridges of rock intermixed with sand and gravel tailings. During construction of Oroville Dam most of the rock piles were removed and land levels were lowered, creating wetlands and riparian habitat. Plantings and natural plant dispersal turned the area green, and wildlife moved in.

The site is about 9½ mi. long, extending S from Hwy 162. Improved dirt roads generally follow the river's course. Some may, at times, be closed to vehicles. The site includes over 350 acres of ponds and canals open to fishing.

Plants: Typical of valley riparian communities. Trees include Fremont cottonwood, willow, valley oak, western sycamore. Common ground-cover species include yellow sweet clover, western ragweed, annual grasses.

Birds: No checklist. 171 species recorded. Many species of waterfowl winter on the river and ponds. Common game birds include mourning dove, California quail, pheasant, band-tailed pigeon. Other species include northern harrier, green-backed heron, black-shouldered kite, osprey, merganser.

Mammals: Include muskrat, beaver, striped skunk, coyote, raccoon, black-tailed jackrabbit, gray fox, black-tailed deer.

Nearby
Lake Oroville State Recreation Area (see entry this zone).

Publication
Leaflet with map.

Headquarters
CA Dept. of Fish and Game, 945 Oro-Dam Blvd. W., Oroville, CA 95965; (916) 538-2236.

Plumas National Forest
U.S. Forest Service

87% of this Forest is in zone 2, where the entry appears. About 157,000 acres are in the N of zone 4. This includes the lower part of the Middle Fork, Feather River, and the Feather Falls Scenic Area above Lake Oroville. It adjoins the Tahoe National Forest at Canyon Creek.

South Yuba River Recreation Area
U.S. Bureau of Land Management
2,000 acres.

From Nevada City, 12 mi. N on Hwy 49; right on Tyler Foote Rd. to campground. Or, from Nevada City go ½ mi. N on Hwy 49 to Bloomfield Rd., right on Bloomfield Rd. to Edwards Crossing Trailhead. Or turn left on Purden Rd. to Purden Crossing Trailhead.

The South Yuba River, with a rugged canyon, cuts through the center of this irregularly shaped site. Terrain varies from rough and mountainous to gently sloping and flat. The far E of the site adjoins Malakoff Diggins State Park. On the S is a piece of the Tahoe National Forest. The setting is mostly forested with ponderosa pine, Douglas-fir, and oaks. Annual precipitation is about 55 in. Snowfall is usually light, and campgrounds can be used all year.

Activities

Camping: 16-unit campground at about 2,600-ft. elevation. 2 primitive sites along river. Camping restricted to designated sites.

Hiking: South Yuba Trail, a National Recreation Trail, was recently expanded to 10½ mi., linking it with trail systems of the State Park and National Forest. Above Edwards Crossing Trailhead is an undeveloped foot trail. Also 1½-mi. nature trail near campground.

Fishing: For trout.

Horse riding, mountain biking: 10 mi. of multiuse trails along and above the river.

Headquarters

Bureau of Land Management, Folsom Resource Area, 63 Natoma St., Folsom, CA 95630; (916) 985-4474.

Spenceville Wildlife Area

California Department of Fish and Game
11,213 acres.

From Smartville on Hwy 20, S on Smartville Rd.

The main body of the site is a narrow corridor for about 3 mi. along the Smartville Rd. S of Hammonton Rd. It then broadens, about 4 mi. to the E. The W boundary is the Beale Air Force Base, of which the site was once a part. The only permanent stream is, inappropriately, named Dry Creek. The creek has a waterfall. The site has 40 springs, several seasonal streams, three small reservoirs. Vegetation is predominantly blue oak, followed by live and valley oaks. Ground cover of annual grasses, filaree, bur clover. Cottonwood, willow, and alder along streams.

There is 1 site for camping, available from April 15–Sept. 1. *No drinking water.* No open fires—*fire hazard often high* May–Oct.

Birds: No checklist. Mentioned: quail, mourning dove, band-tailed pigeon, wild turkey. Great blue heron rookery.

Mammals: Cottontail, gray squirrel, coyote, bobcat, mule deer, gray fox, raccoon.

Publications

Leaflet with map.

Hunting and Other Public Uses on State and Federal Lands.

Headquarters

CA Dept. of Fish and Game, Spenceville Wildlife Area, 945 Oro-Dam Blvd. W., Oroville, CA 95965; (916) 538-2236.

Stanislaus National Forest

85,056 acres of this Forest are in Calaveras County of zone 4, adjoining the Eldorado National Forest. 9,097 acres of the Mokelumne Wilderness, described in the Eldorado entry this zone, are in the Stanislaus. But most of the Forest is in zone 6, and the entry appears there.

Sugar Pine Point State Park

California Department of Parks and Recreation
2,300 acres.

On Lake Tahoe 10 mi. S of Tahoe City.

See entry this zone for Lake Tahoe Basin Management Unit. This is a crowded resort area. Hwy 89, following the lakeshore, offers few glimpses of the lake until it reaches Emerald Bay. Park is heavily used from Memorial Day to Labor Day. It is nonetheless a most attractive area, a welcome contrast to the surrounding development.

On a gently sloping, forested promontory, with 1¾ mi. of lake frontage, including several small sandy beaches. The site extends 3½ mi. up the General Creek watershed, with trail access to the Desolation Wilderness (see entry, Eldorado National Forest). S of General Creek are the Ehrman Mansion, built in 1903, now part of the Park, and a pioneer-built historic structure. N of the creek is the *Edwin L. Z'berg Natural Preserve,* where the mature forest of the Tahoe Basin extends to the water's edge. The campground is on the inland side of the highway.

Plants: Most of the site is forested. Principal tree species are sugar and Jeffrey pines, red and white firs, incense cedar. Lodgepole pine, quaking aspen, black cottonwood, and mountain alder in moister areas. Understory includes manzanita, chinquapin, deer brush, willows, ferns. Flowering plants include lupine, Indian paintbrush, red columbine, penstemon, buckwheat.

Birds: No checklist. Reported: Steller's jay, American robin, flycatchers, woodpeckers, western tanager, belted kingfisher. Waterfowl on or near the lake.

Mammals: Include chickaree, chipmunk, California and golden-mantled ground squirrels, raccoon, deer, porcupine, coyote, weasel, black bear, beaver, pine marten, snowshoe hare.

Interpretation

Park ranger on site all year.

Campfire programs and *guided hikes* in summer.

Nature trail into the Natural Preserve.

Activities

Camping: 150 sites. All year. Reservations mid-June–Labor Day.

Hiking: 8 mi. of trail, including trail into the National Forest.

Swimming: Lake. Unsupervised.

Boating: No ramp. Boats may tie to pier in daylight. No overnight mooring.

Ski touring: 3 flagged trails: 1, 1½, and 4½ mi. Season usually late Nov.–late April.

Publication

Leaflet with map, $0.50.

Headquarters

CA Dept. of Parks and Recreation, P.O. Box 266, Tahoma, CA 96142; (916) 525-7982.

Tahoe National Forest

U.S. Forest Service
811,740 acres of Forest land; 1,208,993 acres within boundaries.
W and N of Lake Tahoe. Crossed by I-80 and Hwy 89.

In the central Sierra Nevada. Extends from the Sacramento Valley across the mountains to the Great Basin. Elevations rise gradually on the W to about 8,765 in the Sierra Buttes, then drop more steeply to about 6,000 ft. at Lake Tahoe. The area is scenic, diverse, with great contrasts in terrain and vegetation, many streams, rivers, and lakes.

A third of the land within the Forest boundaries is privately owned. The most extensive blocks of relatively solid Forest land are N of Truckee and N of the American River, Middle Fork. Because the area is attractive and accessible, it is heavily used for recreation all year. In the warm months, water is the chief attraction.

On the W side, annual precipitation is heavy, 50–80 in. per year. The E side, rain-shadowed, is drier, about 16 in. per year near Lake Tahoe. At the higher elevations, most precipitation falls as winter snow, and snow cover lasts from Oct. through April.

French Meadows Reservoir, on the upper reaches of the American River, Middle Fork, is nestled under the crest of the Sierra Nevada, at 5,200 ft. elevation. Almost entirely surrounded by Forest land, it provides a remote mountain environment that is very popular.

Jackson Meadow Reservoir, NW of Truckee on the Yuba River, lies over 6,000 ft. elevation. Much of the shore is privately owned.

The New Bullards Bar Reservoir, at the W end of the Forest near Camptonville, is a large lake at about 2,000 ft. elevation, at the edge of the Sacramento Valley. It is heavily used by boaters, campers, fishermen, and hikers.

The area near Lake Tahoe is within the Lake Tahoe Basin Management Unit (see entry this zone).

Plants: Largely forested, with many open areas. The lower western slopes and canyons (elevations 2,000–4,000 ft.) are gently rolling ridges, cut by steep, highly dissected canyons. Vegetation is mostly canyon and interior live oak, black oak, scattered conifers, mixed shrub species, and grasses. In wetter areas, world-class ferns may be seen.

The mixed conifer forest lies between 2,000 and 5,500 ft. Major species include ponderosa and sugar pines, incense cedar, Douglas-fir, and white fir. Some interspersed hardwoods are black oak, bigleaf maple, dogwood, interior live oak, California bay laurel, madrone, and tan oak. Understory includes deer brush, whitethorn, mountain misery, green- and whiteleaf manzanitas, grasses. Alders, willows, and other water-loving species occupy riparian habitat.

Between elevations of 5,500 and 9,500 ft. are the giant sequoias, lodgepole, western white, and Jeffrey pines, red and white firs. Mountain hemlock and whitebark pine occur in isolated colder pockets or on harsh ridgetops. Also bush chinquapin, snowbrush, huckleberry oak, bitter cherry, whitethorn, greenleaf manzanita, and wyethia. Numerous meadows and seeps, with alders, willows, quaking aspen, sedges, and forbs, occur throughout the community.

Below 6,500 ft. on drier sites on the E side of the Forest, tree species include Jeffrey pine, white fir, and western juniper. Lodgepole pine, cottonwood, quaking aspen, alders, willows, sedges, and forbs occur along drainages and wet depressions. Drier species include rabbitbrush, sagebrush, bitterbrush, wyethia, mountain mahogany, and perennial grasses.

Timber plantations occur at all levels, but are most prevalent in the mixed conifer and red fir forest communities. Ponderosa and sugar pines, white fir, and Douglas-fir are commonly planted below 5,500 ft., while Jeffrey, sugar, and western white pines, and red and white firs are commonly planted above 5,500 ft.

Birds: Checklist available. Eared grebe, goldeneye, and merganser common fall through spring. Golden eagle, goshawk, red-tailed and Cooper's hawks, kestrel, great horned owl. California and mountain quail, coot in marshes and lakeshores. Band-tailed pigeon, scrub and Steller's jays, pileated and acorn woodpeckers, Clark's nutcracker, northern flicker. Flycatchers in the lodgepole and ponderosa pine areas. Violet-green, tree, barn, and cliff swallows, brown creeper, Bewick's wren, mountain bluebird, varied thrush, ruby-crowned kinglet, warbling vireo, black-throated gray and Wilson's warblers, western meadowlark, Brewer's blackbird, northern oriole, black-headed grosbeak, purple and house finches, pine siskin, green-tailed and rufous-sided towhees, white-crowned, Brewer's, sage, and song sparrows.

Mammals: Mule deer, black bear, coyote, pine marten, mountain lion, bobcat, fisher, weasel, red fox, raccoon, ringtail, spotted skunk,

Belding and golden-mantled ground squirrels, gray squirrel, marmot, porcupine. No checklist.

Features

Scenic drives—several attractive routes. Hwy 89, N of Truckee, follows the Little Truckee River for some miles, later joins Hwy 49 and follows the Yuba River. South of Truckee, Hwy 89 follows the Truckee River in a steep-walled valley to Lake Tahoe. Many gravel roads in the Forest for backcountry travel, plus many roads requiring 4-wheel drive.

Activities

Camping: Approximately 84 campgrounds, varying in size and facilities. Main season is from Memorial Day–Labor Day.

Hiking, backpacking: 500 mi. of trails and unpaved roads. The Pacific Crest Trail extends for 97 mi. through the Forest. The PCT follows the ridges, thus limiting hiking to July–Oct.

Fishing: Lakes, streams, reservoirs. Rainbow, kamloop, cutthroat, and brown trout stocked.

Swimming: Lakes and streams. Unsupervised.

Boating: Boat docks and launch ramps on several smaller lakes.

Skiing: Many private downhill and Nordic ski areas throughout Forest.

Ski touring, snowmobiling: 30 mi. of marked trails, also unplowed roads and trails. 67 mi. marked for snowmobiles.

Adjacent

Plumas National Forest (see entry zone 2), Eldorado National Forest, and Lake Tahoe Basin Management Unit (see entries this zone).

Publications

Forest map, $3.25.

Birds of the Tahoe National Forest and Vicinity.

Tahoe National Forest: Camping and Picnicking, Trails and Fishing.

Winter Recreation.

Rock Creek Nature Trail (guided tour folder).

Off-Highway Vehicles.

Accessible Recreation Facilities for People with Disabilities.

Historic Points of Interest in the Tahoe National Forest

Discover Your National Treasure.

History of Big Bend.

Yuba-Donner Scenic Byway.

Tahoe National Forest Pacific Crest Trail (fact sheet).

Granite Chief Wilderness.

Headquarters
U.S. Forest Service, 631 Coyote St., Nevada City, CA 95959-6003; (916) 265-4531.

Ranger Districts
Downieville R.D., N. Yuba Ranger Station, 15924 Hwy 49, Camptonville, CA 95922-9707; (916) 288-3231. Foresthill R.D., 22830 Foresthill Rd., Foresthill, CA 95631; (916) 367-2224. Nevada City R.D., 631 Coyote St., Nevada City, CA 95959-6003; (916) 265-4538. Sierraville R.D., P.O. Box 95, Hwy 89, Sierraville, CA 96126; (916) 994-3401. Truckee R.D., 10342 Hwy 89 N., Truckee, CA 96161; (916) 587-3558.

Washoe Meadows State Park
California Department of Parks and Recreation
620 acres.

2.5 mi. E of South Lake Tahoe on Lake Tahoe Blvd.

Undeveloped area, meadows and forestlands. A nice quiet place. No facilities. Mainly used by locals for hiking in summer and cross-country skiing in winter.

Headquarters
(916) 525-7232.

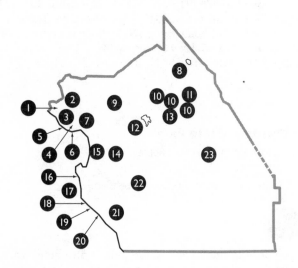

1 Big Basin Redwoods State Park

2 Castle Rock State Park

3 Fall Creek State Park

4 Henry Cowell Redwoods State Park

5 Wilder Ranch State Park

6 Natural Bridges State Park

7 Nisene Marks State Park (The Forest of)

8 Turlock Lake State Recreation Area

9 Henry W. Coe State Park

10 Central San Joaquin Valley National Wildlife Refuges

Merced Unit

Kesterson Unit

San Luis Unit

11 Great Valley Grasslands State Park

12 San Luis Reservoir State Recreation Area

13 Los Banos Wildlife Area

14 Fremont Peak State Park

15 Elkhorn Slough Reserve

16 Point Lobos State Reserve

17 California Sea Otter Game Refuge

18 Andrew Molera State Park

19 Pfeiffer Big Sur State Park

20 Julia Pfeiffer Burns State Park

21 Los Padres National Forest

22 Pinnacles National Monument

23 Mendota Wildlife Area

Z O N E

Includes these counties:

Santa Cruz	Monterey	Madera (W portion)
Santa Clara	San Benito	Fresno (W portion)
Stanislaus	Merced	Kings

This zone begins just S of the San Francisco Bay Area, extending almost to San Simeon. It includes the ocean coast, the Santa Cruz and Santa Lucia Mountains near the coast, the Salinas River Basin, the Diablo Range, and the W portion of the San Joaquin Valley.

The coastline is dramatically scenic. Hwy 1 hugs the coast, often on high ledges. Along the way are frequent overlooks. Looking down at the kelp beds, one often sees sea otters. There are many public beaches, several State Parks, and Los Padres National Forest. On a fine weekend in March, we found Hwy 1 busy though not congested. Many of the park and beach parking lots were full or nearly so. Along the highway were numerous places where cars had parked off the road, their occupants taking informal trails down the cliffs to isolated beaches. The beaches are popular, though not for swimming.

The largest public area in the zone is a 300,000-acre unit of Los Padres National Forest, lying on or near the coast in the Santa Lucia Mountains. A major portion of this unit is a wilderness area.

Several interesting areas are in the mountains and intermountain valleys, including Pinnacles National Monument, Big Basin Redwoods State Park, Henry Cowell Redwoods State Park, and Pfeiffer Big Sur State Park, also a redwoods park. Henry W. Coe State Park and Nisene Marks State Park are designed for hikers, with no roads beyond the developed areas.

The San Joaquin Valley is largely irrigated cropland. Before most of it was drained, natural ponds and marshes provided winter habitat for vast numbers of waterfowl. Wetlands are now preserved or restored in a number of federal and state refuges, all of them attractive to birds.

They include the Central San Joaquin Valley National Wildlife Refuges and Los Banos Wildlife Area Complex.

Andrew Molera State Park

California Department of Parks and Recreation
4,691 acres.

21 m. S of Carmel on Hwy 1.

On the Pacific Ocean. The E Big Sur River flows through the site. Elevations from sea level to 3,455 ft. at the top of the first coastal ridge. The Park provides wonderful opportunities for hiking, horse riding, picnicking, and tent camping. Trailers and motor homes are not permitted for overnight camping (numerous options are available for these types of vehicles in the immediate area). The unpaved parking area is next to the highway. All travel beyond is on foot. A path follows the river for about ¼ mi. to an open meadow where camping is permitted. The path then goes through a wooded area toward the sea. One can choose a route to the top of the bluffs, about 100 ft. above the sea, or turn left where the river has formed a wide flood plain. The park as 2½ mi. of ocean beach, mostly sandy, and about 2½ mi. of river frontage.

The area is usually not crowded except on major summer holidays.

Plants: About 25% forested. Scattered stands of old-growth Coast redwood along the river and in canyons. Also tan oak, California bay laurel, bigleaf maple, live oak, white alder, sycamore, cottonwood. Understory species include redwood sorrel, poison oak, blackberry, ceanothus, thimbleberry, coyote bush, ferns. Coastal grasses include wild oat, rattlesnake grass, little quaking grass, Italian rye, foxtail, ribgrass. Wildflowers include dune eriogonum, yellow verbena, silverweed, primrose.

Birds: Checklist. Reported are horned; eared, western, and pied-billed grebes, Brandt's cormorant, great blue and green herons, snowy and great egrets, surf scoter, black oystercatcher, black turnstone, willet, sanderling, northern phalarope, western, California, and mew gulls, turkey vulture, black-shouldered kite, red-tailed hawk, northern harrier, band-tailed pigeon, mourning dove, barn and great horned owls, dipper.

Mammals: Include sea otter, California and Steller sea lions, harbor seal, gray whale, gray squirrel, raccoon, coyote, bobcat, mule deer. Seldom seen but present: opossum, ringtail, weasel, brush rabbit.

Interpretation
Guided hikes, May–Sept. Notices posted.

Activities
Camping: Walk-in, ⅓ mi. About 50 sites. All year.

Hiking: 25 mi. of trails.

Fishing: Ocean fishing year-round. Stream fishing, winter only, according to Dept. of Fish and Game regulations.

Horse riding: Available May–Sept. by horse concessionaire operating within the Park.

Swimming is NOT recommended!

Headquarters
Big Sur State Park, Big Sur Station #1, Big Sur, CA 93920; (408) 667-2315.

Big Basin Redwoods State Park
California Department of Parks and Recreation
Over 18,000 acres.

From Santa Cruz, N 23 mi. on Hwy 9 and then Hwy 236.

Close to the San Francisco metropolitan area and thus heavily used in season. However, it's larger than most State Parks, and except on peak holiday weekends one can find uncrowded trails. Most visitors come to walk the short trail through the redwood grove and to picnic or camp.

The Park straddles the watershed of Waddell Creek and its tributaries. Although the main body of the Park is inland, a neck follows the creek to the sea. The Park has 6,336 ft. of ocean frontage. Elevations from sea level to 2,200 ft. The area is moderately humid, with 52 in. of precipitation yearly. The site has 4 waterfalls, of which Berry Creek Fall is 65 ft. and Sempervirens Fall 20 ft.

This is California's oldest State Park, established because of the old-growth redwoods, the largest 329 ft. tall. Several million visitors have walked the 0.6-mi. trail through the principal grove. Most of the site is forested: Coast redwood, Douglas-fir, tan oak, madrone. Flowering plants include hazel, coffeeberry, inside-out flower, honeysuckle, western azalea, iris, huckleberry.

Birds: Checklist. All-year residents include red-tailed and Cooper's hawks, horned, screech, and pygmy owls, northern flicker, downy, hairy, and acorn woodpeckers, California quail, Bewick's wren, purple finch, common bushtit, wrentit, Steller's jay, robin, chestnut-backed chickadee, Hutton's vireo, pine siskin, pygmy nuthatch, golden-crowned kinglet, dark-eyed junco, dipper.

Interpretation

Nature lodge with exhibits and publications.

Campfire programs and *guided hikes:* mid-June–Labor Day.

Activities

Camping: 4 campgrounds, 188 sites. Reservations May 1–Sept. 30.

Hiking, backpacking: 60 mi. of trails, including Skyline-to-the-Sea. Backpacking is by permit. The number of permits is limited. Reservations are recommended, all year; call HQ.

Horse riding: 14-mi. loop trail. No rentals. No camping.

Publications

Park map, $1.00.

Bird checklist, $0.10.

Headquarters

CA Dept. of Parks and Recreation, 21600 Big Basin Way, Boulder Creek, CA 95006; (408) 338-8860.

California Sea Otter Game Refuge

California Department of Fish and Game

Offshore, starts N of Pt. Lobos and continues S to Rosa Creek in San Luis Obispo County.

At the first overlook S of Pt. Lobos, we saw eight sea otters floating on their backs amid the kelp. We stopped at other overlooks on our way S and saw many more. Binoculars are useful.

Castle Rock State Park

California Department of Parks and Recreation
About 3,700 acres.

From Saratoga (SW of San Jose), Hwy 9 W to Saratoga Gap. S 2½ mi. on Skyline Blvd., Hwy 35.

This is a pedestrian and equestrian park. Castle Rock is linked to Big Basin State Park (see entry this zone) by the Skyline-to-the-Sea Trail. Terrain is steep, mountainous, with level areas only on ridgetops. Elevations from 800 ft. at the San Lorenzo River to 3,214 ft. The Park is a primitive wilderness, intended so to remain. Camping only in trail camps. No horse camping.

Plants: Site is about 75% forested, 25% chaparral, the later principally on the S slope of the ridge. Principal tree species are Douglas-fir, Coast redwood, knobcone pine, madrone, live, tan, and black oaks. Most of the redwoods are second growth, but a few virgin specimens remain. The black oak woodland has an exceptional wildflower display.

Birds: HQ has records. Species include red-tailed and Cooper's hawks, horned, screech, and pygmy owls, northern flicker, downy, hairy, and acorn woodpeckers, California quail, Bewick's wren, purple finch, common bushtit, wrentit, Steller's and scrub jays, robin, chestnut-backed chickadee, Hutton's vireo, pine siskin, pygmy nuthatch, golden-crowned kinglet, dark-eyed junco, dipper, fox sparrow.

Mammals: Include coyote, bobcat, gray fox, opossum, various bats, shrews, and moles, black-tailed jackrabbit, brush rabbit, cottontail, gray squirrel, raccoon, weasel, striped skunk, mule deer. Occasional mountain lion.

Reptiles and amphibians: Western fence and alligator lizards, western skink, rubber boa, ring-necked snake, racer, gopher snake, common kingsnake, mountain kingsnake, common garter snake, western rattlesnake.

Features

Several waterfalls notable during winter runoff. Castle Rock Falls drops 80 ft.

Goat Rock, 3,000-ft., 130-ft. S face, offers scenic views of Santa Cruz Mountains and Monterey Bay.

Skyline Blvd., which crosses the Park, is a scenic highway.

Large outcroppings of vaqueros sandstone are much used by *rock climbers. Sandstone caves.*

Interpretation
Guided hikes during summer months. Notices posted.

Activities
Hiking, backpacking, horse riding: About 20 mi. of trails within the Park, 30 mi. to the sea through Big Basin. Permits required for Skyline-to-the-Sea Trail. Ranger commented that trail camps have never been full, "but the time will come."

Since dogs are prohibited on all CA State Park trails, they are banned here altogether.
   Hazardous rocks; sheer cliffs. Stay on trails.
   High fire hazard sometimes closes Park in midsummer.

Publication
Park trails map, $0.50.

Headquarters
CA Dept. of Parks and Recreation, 15000 Skyline Blvd., Los Gatos, CA 95030; (408) 867-2952.

....

Central San Joaquin Valley National Wildlife Refuges
U.S. Fish and Wildlife Service
San Luis National Wildlife Refuge Complex: Merced: 4,572 acres.
Kesterson: 10,760 acres. San Luis: 15,332 acres.

Merced: From Merced, 8 mi. S on Hwy 59, 6 mi. W on Sandymush Rd.
Kesterson: From Merced, 39 mi. E on Hwy 140. *San Luis:* From Los Banos, N 8 mi. on N Mercy Springs Rd., then NE 2 mi. on Wolfsen Rd.

The San Joaquin Valley has historically been a vast wintering area for migratory waterfowl. However, up to 95% of the native wetlands have been drained and cultivated. State and federal refuges have been established both to support as many of these waterfowl as possible and to reduce the depredation of farm crops. Waterfowl concentrations of 500,000 or more are common in winter.

The *Merced National Wildlife Refuge* once looked like the irrigated cropland that surrounds it. Today, due to intense habitat management and restoration projects, the Refuge's wetlands and native grass uplands have been restored to provide traditional wintering grounds for many species of migrating waterfowl. In addition to wetland and upland habitat, cultivated fields provide an additional food source for wildlife. The wetlands are managed by pumping water from numerous deep wells and through irrigation canals. Seasonal wetlands are kept flooded from Sept. through May to attract wintering waterfowl and other wetland birds.

By spring, most of the waterfowl will have departed with the exception of a few thousand Ross's geese, a few hundred Canada and white-fronted geese, and sandhill cranes that stay as late as mid- to late spring. Nesting ducks, such as mallard, pintail, gadwall, cinnamon teal, ruddy, redhead, and wood, are present year-round in permanent marshes. The 5-mi. auto tour route in spring may provide views of white-crowned sparrow, pheasant, killdeer, red-winged blackbird, western meadowlark, red-tailed hawk, western tanager, nighthawk, burrowing owl, western kingbird, black-crowned night heron, great blue heron, black-necked stilt, avocet, shoveler, snowy egret, pintail, cinnamon teal, and geese. Interpretive information panels are located along the tour route for additional information about Refuge management practices. An observation platform with a high-powered scope is located near the entrance of the tour route for an overview of this small refuge.

The *Kesterson Unit* contains native grassland and wetlands, and during the winter and spring rains has vernal pools. Due to the intense development of the surrounding land for agriculture, grazing, and urbanization, this type of habitat has become unique and increasingly rare in CA. Kesterson is an important wintering ground for numerous species of migratory waterfowl and is home to several endangered species of animals. Hiking and bicycling are limited to the graveled footpaths in the open area at Hwy 140.

The *San Luis National Wildlife Refuge* is the largest of the units and provides the most recreational activities. Tree-lined Salt Slough is open to fishing and as a hiking trail for bird-watching and watching other wildlife. There are two hiking trails. One leads to the San Joaquin River and around a wetland while the other is fitted with an observation platform for a bird's-eye view of the Refuge. The Refuge is one of the largest remaining fragments of native grasslands, ponds, and marshes. Another highlight is the tule elk enclosure, which can contain as many as 50 elk. The Tule Elk Auto Tour Route follows a path around the elk pasture and includes a stop on the platform for close-up views of the elk. The Waterfowl Tour Route is a 10-mi. drive around the rest of the Refuge. Both routes include stops at interpretive information panels that describe the habitat, wildlife, and management practices of the Refuge.

Birds: Checklist available listing 209 species. Many species in all three Refuges. Sandhill cranes are seen Dec.–Jan. Many shorebirds pass through in spring and fall, among them Wilson's and red-necked phalaropes, yellowleg, dowitcher, sandpipers, and long-billed curlew. Recently, Merced has been the site for nesting Swainson's hawks, and San Luis hosted close to 50 tundra swans. Merlins have been seen occasionally in San Luis. Songbird and raptor populations are expected to increase due to riparian restoration efforts.

Mammals: Species reported include California ground squirrel, black-tailed jackrabbit, cottontail, badger, striped skunk, weasel, beaver, muskrat, coyote.

Reptiles and amphibians: Pond and softshell turtles, western spadefoot, western toad, Pacific tree frog, leopard frog, horned, fence, and side-blotched lizards, Gilbert's skink, tiger salamander, California legless lizard, gopher snake, several species of garter snake, western rattlesnake.

Activities

Hiking: Restricted to auto tour routes and walking trails in San Luis. Kesterson is open to foot traffic only. Due to the size of Merced, no hiking is allowed.

Hunting: Waterfowl hunting during the regular season is allowed on portions of Kesterson and Merced, and waterfowl and pheasant hunting is allowed in portions of San Luis. Hunt days in Kesterson and San Luis are Wed., Sat., and Sun. Hunt days in Merced are Wed. and Sat.

Fishing: Salt Slough in San Luis is open to fishing during daylight hours.

Parking is limited to designated parking areas.

Publications

Central San Joaquin National Wildlife Refuges brochure.

Maps of the three units.

Bird checklist.

Headquarters
U.S. Fish and Wildlife Service, 947 W. Pacheco Blvd., Suite C, Los
Banos, CA 93635; (209) 826-3508. Mailing address: San Luis Refuge
NWR Complex, P.O. Box 2176, Los Banos, CA 93635.

Elkhorn Slough Reserve
California Department of Fish and Game
2,500 acres.

US 101 to Hwy 156W to Elkhorn Rd., N to the visitor center entrance.

This is one of California's few remaining coastal wetlands that has
escaped development. It's home to more than 400 invertebrate
species, 200 bird species, and more than 80 kinds of fish. The slough is
also home to six rare or endangered species, including sea otter, clapper rail, brown pelican, least tern, and peregrine falcon.

Birds: Waterfowl frequently seen include Canada goose, mallard, cinnamon teal, ring-necked duck, and bufflehead. Shorebirds include
snowy plover, killdeer, western sandpiper, and red phalarope. Owls,
hummingbirds, acorn woodpecker, great blue heron, pelican, cormorants, loons, and wood warbler are also spotted here.

Mammals: Sea otter, harbor seal, a small herd of deer, gray fox, skunk,
bobcat, opossum, raccoon, weasel, coyote, bats.

Invertebrates: Bat ray, leopard shark, and smoothhound shark (which
bears live young).

Interpretation
The Elkhorn Slough Foundation sponsors *monthly educational activities,* such as *kayaking trips* and *nature walks* off the Reserve. Call (408)
728-5939.

Activities
Hiking: Trails lead through eucalyptus groves, a marsh restoration project, a dairy site, and 5 fingers of Parson's Slough.

Publication
Brochure with map.

Headquarters
CA Dept. of Fish and Game, 1700 Elkhorn Rd., Watsonville, CA 95076; (408) 728-2822.

Fall Creek State Park
California Department of Parks and Recreation
2,335 acres.
From Santa Cruz, N on Hwy 9 to Felton. Left ½ mi. on Felton Empire Rd. Parking on N side.
Open: Daylight hours.

A subunit of nearby *Henry Cowell Redwoods State Park (see entry)*. Roadless. A hiker's park. On Ben Lomond Mountain. Elevations from 360 to 1,920 ft. Steep-sided creek canyons, heavily forested. From the parking area, trails to N and S forks of Fall Creek. Small falls.

Mostly forested, second-growth Coast redwood, Douglas-fir, with tan oak, madrone, California bay laurel, live oak. Some small upper areas are covered with chaparral.

Hiking: 17 mi. of trails.

Publication
Information page with map.

Headquarters
CA Dept. of Parks and Recreation, c/o Henry Cowell Redwoods State Park, 101 N. Big Trees Park Rd., Felton, CA 95018; (408) 335-4598.

Fremont Peak State Park
California Department of Parks and Recreation
190 acres.
E of Salinas. From US 101, S on Hwy 156 to San Juan Bautista, then S 11 mi. on San Juan Canyon Rd.

A small, long, narrow Park, somewhat isolated, in the Gabilan Mountains at the end of a moderately steep, winding road. Elevation 2,750 ft. Rolling hills with oaks, madrone, and Coulter pine (with the heaviest of all pine cones).

Activities

Camping: 25 primitive sites, 2 group sites.

Hiking: 4 mi. of trails go all around the Park and to summit of Fremont Peak.

Astronomical observatory: Open to public on selected Sat. evenings. For information call (408) 623-2465.

Headquarters

CA Dept. of Parks and Recreation, P. O. Box 787, San Juan Bautista, CA 95045; (408) 623-4255.

Great Valley Grasslands State Park

California Department of Parks and Recreation
2,826 acres.

6 mi. NE of Gustine on Hwy 140.

One of the few remaining grasslands in the Central Valley, this unbroken prairie is located between the San Joaquin River and Salt Slough. The boundaries now include Fremont Ford State Recreation Area. 5 mi. of river frontage, vernal pools, drainages, mounds, and swales have escaped intensive modern farming methods. Among the rare grassland communities found here are valley wild rye grassland, cottonwood riparian forest, and claypan vernal pool. Freshwater marsh communities are permanently inundated and support bulrush, cattail, sedges, and a variety of grasses. Nonnative grasslands and wildflowers are also found throughout the region. Rare plant species include Delta button celery, Delta coyote thistle, and bearded allocarya.

Headquarters

CA Dept. of Parks and Recreation, 4394 Kelly Rd., Hilmar, CA 95324; (209) 632-1852.

Henry Cowell Redwoods State Park

California Department of Parks and Recreation
1,737 acres.

From Santa Cruz, N on Hwy 9. For campground: from Santa Cruz, N on
Graham Hill Rd.

Almost 7 mi. of the San Lorenzo River are within the Park, the land
dropping from 1,100 ft. to 80. The Park is best known for its Coast
redwoods. Most of the area is second growth, but a large grove of virgin redwoods remains, at the N end of the site, near the day-use
entrance. The largest tree is 285 ft. tall. The largest area of the Park,
accessible only on foot or horseback, is mostly forested, redwood with
tan oak, madrone, Douglas-fir, California bay laurel, live oak, knobcone pine; huckleberry, ceanothus, manzanita in understory with lots
of poison oak. There is also a ponderosa pine forest, unusual at this
elevation and nearness to the coast. Wildflowers include trillium,
oxalis, wild ginger.

Birds: Checklist. Noted: mallard, kestrel, great horned owl, Cooper's
and red-shouldered hawks, California quail, band-tailed pigeon,
belted kingfisher, northern flicker, acorn woodpecker, Steller's and
scrub jays, golden-crowned kinglet, yellow-rumped warbler, dark-
eyed junco.

Mammals: Include gray fox, ground squirrels, cottontail, opossum,
raccoon, mule deer. Seldom seen but present: coyote, bobcat, ringtail.

Features

Redwood grove, with self-guiding nature path.

Garden of Eden, scenic swimming area on the river.

Observation deck, on water tower. View of Monterey Bay.

Interpretation

Campfire programs and *guided hikes* in summer; other seasons on
request.

Activities

Camping: 113 sites. Closed Dec. and Jan. Reservations Mar. 3–Oct. 1.
Needed in summer.

Hiking: 20 mi. of trails. (Also see Fall Creek State Park, this zone).

Horse riding: 10 mi. of trails.

Swimming: River. Unsupervised.

Fishing: Steelhead and salmon, Nov. 16–Feb. 28 (dates may change yearly). Limit 2. Only on Sat., Sun., legal holidays, and opening and closing days.

Publications

Leaflet with map.

Nature trail guide.

Bird checklist.

Headquarters

CA Dept. of Parks and Recreation, P.O. Box P-1, Felton, CA 95018; (408) 335-4598.

Henry W. Coe State Park

California Department of Parks and Recreation
79,527 acres.

From Morgan Hill on US 101, 13 mi. E on E. Dunne Ave. Road is paved but steep, narrow, winding.

This, the largest State Park in Northern CA, includes a 22,000-acre designated wilderness. The rugged and varied terrain includes deep canyons, forested ridges, and wooded slopes. Located in the Mount Hamilton Range (a section of the Diablo Range) E of Santa Clara Valley. Elevations range from 710 to 3,560 ft. HQ is at the end of the paved road and includes a visitor center, parking areas, and a 20-unit campground. Travel beyond this point is on foot, mountain bike, or horseback.

The Coe family owned the ranch that became the original 12,500-acre Park and operated it from the late 19th century to the early 1950s. Coe's daughter donated the ranch to Santa Clara County in 1953, and 5 years later the county sold it to the state for $10.00.

S- and W-facing slopes are mostly grassland and chaparral; oak and mixed woodlands dominate N- and E-facing slopes. Canyons are steep sided below gently rounded ridgetops. Annual precipitation is 25½ in.; summers are hot and dry. The Park straddles three major watersheds: Coyote Creek, Pacheco Creek, and Orestimba Creek.

Plants: The area is about 60% wooded. Mostly oak woodlands: blue, valley, black, coast live, canyon live, and interior live oaks with intermixed gray pine, laurel, madrone, and buckeye. Ridges in the W are topped with ponderosa pine, at the edge of its range. At Manzanita Point, Middle Ridge, and other areas, there are exceptionally large manzanitas, tree-size with large crowns. April and May are the peak months for wildflower displays. Over 600 flowering species, including milkmaids, hounds tongue, buttercups, Indian warrior, shooting stars, violets, larkspur, sanicles, lupine, poppy, owl's clover, globe lily, mariposa lily, and California fuchsia.

Birds: Checklist includes 137 species plus accidentals. Typical of the area: scrub and Steller's jays, California quail, red-tailed hawk, golden eagle, acorn woodpecker, mourning dove, white-breasted nuthatch, western bluebird, western meadowlark, brown and rufous-sided towhees, dark-eyed junco.

Mammals: Include California ground squirrel, mule deer, black-tailed jackrabbit, raccoon, coyote, gray fox, bobcat. Mountain lion and badger are present but rarely seen.

Reptiles and amphibians: Include western fence lizard, California newt, Pacific tree frog, western pond turtle, aquatic garter snake, western rattlesnake, gopher snake, ringneck snake, and common kingsnake. California mountain kingsnake is present but seldom seen. In late summer/early fall, male tarantulas leave their burrows in search of mates. It's possible to see 6–8 a day, though usually fewer are visible. Don't disturb them.

Features

Pine Ridge offers *fine views* of the Santa Cruz Mountains to the W, the Santa Lucia Range to the S, and on exceptionally clear days, 140 miles E to the Sierra Nevada crest. *Blue Ridge* also has fine viewpoints, especially on 3,216 ft. Mount Sizer.

China Hole, reached by a 5.1-mi. hike, is a pool in Coyote Creek big enough for a swim.

Mississippi, Coit, and *Kelly Lakes* are three popular reservoirs in the center of the Park, which are a minimum 11-mi. hike from HQ.

Orestimba Wilderness is a 22,000-acre state-designated wilderness area reached by a minimum one-day hike. Few backpackers visit this remote area.

Interpretation

Visitor center and *museum* with ranch history and natural history exhibits. Small museum store sells books, maps, T-shirts, water bottles, and interpretive items. Free literature available.

Evening programs on Sat. nights, mid-March through Memorial Day. *Guided hikes* on Sat. and Sun. in spring. Schedules available.

The *Pine Ridge Association* sponsors the volunteer program for the Park. Volunteers *lead hikes* and staff special events, the visitor center, and the museum.

Activities

Camping: 20 primitive drive-in sites with drinking water, fire rings, picnic tables. Also 10 hike-in group camping sites at Manzanita Point.

Hiking, backpacking: 250 mi. of fire roads and trails. Permits required for backcountry camping. Space available for 60 parties (maximum 8 per party). Spring is the busy season; summers are quieter due to heat and dryness. *No fires allowed,* stoves only. *Dogs and firearms also not allowed.* All-day hikers must register and pay parking fees before departure. *Carry water.*

Swimming: China Hole and a few other pools in Coyote Creek, until early fall when levels diminish. All of the reservoirs in the Park are open for swimming, but expect muddy shorelines and pondweed.

Horse riding: 240 mi. of roads and trails open to horses, all shared by other users. No local rentals.

Mountain biking: 200 mi. of roads and trails. Some single-track trails on Pine Ridge are closed to bikes. All trails closed after rain.

The Park may be closed at times of extreme fire danger (though that rarely happens). Summer hikers should be prepared for sun, heat, and scarce water. Heavy winter rains may make some areas inaccessible due to impassable creeks.

Publications

Trail and camping map, $1.00 ($2.00 by mail, postpaid).

General information folder.

Fishing at Henry W. Coe State Park, $1.39.

Scrubs of Henry W. Coe State Park, $6.00.

Vascular Plants of Henry W. Coe State Park $2.78.

Bird checklist, $0.25.

Animal Tracks and Using the Track Tracer, $0.92.

Bike and horse information.

Mimeo info pages on natural history.

Headquarters
CA Dept. of Parks and Recreation, P.O. Box 846, Morgan Hill, CA 95038; (408) 779-2728; sector office, (408) 848-4006.

Julia Pfeiffer Burns State Park
California Department of Parks and Recreation
2,405 acres and 1,680 acres of underwater park.

From Carmel, S 37 mi. on Hwy 1.

Ocean access is at Partington Canyon, 2 mi. N of McWay Canyon. On the Big Sur coastline. Day-use area. Parking and picnic areas are in a redwood grove on the inland side of the highway. From here a trail follows McWay Canyon up toward the ridge, to about 1,500 ft. elevation. The Coast redwood is here near the S limit of its range and thrives only on cool, N-facing slopes of deep canyons with sufficient all-year moisture. With the redwoods: tan oak, madrone, California bay laurel, various ferns; flowering species include trillium, oxalis, baby blue eyes, columbine. Beyond the redwood grove is chaparral.

From the parking area, a path leads under the highway to the edge of a bluff about 100 ft. above the sea, offering a sweeping view. The water of McWay Creek drops 70 ft. from the cliff directly into the sea. A trail about 1,600 ft. long leads to an overlook. There are additional trails in the area above Partington Point. Ocean access is at Partington Canyon, 2 mi. N of McWay Canyon.

The area offshore became an underwater park in 1970. Access is limited to experienced diving groups, by permit. McWay Cove is closed to entry due to safety and resource protection.

Publication
Leaflet with map.

Headquarters

CA Dept. of Parks and Recreation, Rt. 1, Big Sur, CA 93920; (408) 667-2315.

Kesterson National Wildlife Refuge

See Central San Joaquin Valley National Wildlife Refuges (this zone).

Los Banos Wildlife Area

California Department of Fish and Game
5,586 acres.

From Hwy 165 N of Los Banos, E 0.8 mi. on Henry Miller Ave.

We visited several of the federal and state Wildlife Refuges in the San Joaquin Valley and enjoyed this one most. One reason is that camping is permitted. We parked our RV by a lake one April evening and, apparently, had the place to ourselves until next morning. Another reason is the natural appearances of the ponds and marshes, unlike the rectilinear flooded fields we saw elsewhere.

The area was, historically, an important waterfowl wintering area. Draining and cultivation of wetlands reduced habitat, and severe droughts in the late 1920s drastically reduced waterfowl populations. A number of Refuges in the area now are managed to support maximum numbers of waterfowl and, incidentally, to minimize their depredation on farm crops.

An auto tour route extends from the HQ area almost to the N boundary, about 5 mi. away. Other roads are open to car and foot travel. Along the way are lakes, shallow ponds, marshes, ditches, and some upland. Trees and shrubs grow beside the lakes. Many places are available to park beside water, and a car makes a good blind.

Birds: Checklist of 203 species available. Seasonally common species include eared, western, and pied-billed grebes, great blue heron, great and snowy egrets, black-crowned night heron, American bittern, white-faced ibis, cackling Canada, white-fronted, and lesser snow geese, mallard, gadwall, pintail, green-winged and cinnamon teals, wigeon, shoveler, ruddy duck, coot, turkey vulture, black-shouldered kite, red-tailed hawk, northern harrier, kestrel, pheasant, sandhill crane, Virginia rail, common gallinule, common snipe, long-billed curlew, killdeer, greater yellowlegs, least sandpiper, long-billed dowitcher, American avocet, black-necked stilt, northern flicker, western kingbird, black phoebe, horned lark, tree, barn, and cliff swallows, yellow-billed magpie, marsh wren, mockingbird, water pipit, loggerhead shrike, yellow-rumped warbler, western meadowlark, yellow-headed, red-winged, and tricolored blackbirds, Brewer's blackbird, house finch, savannah, white-crowned, house, and song sparrows.

Mammals: Include coyote, gray fox, beaver, muskrat, mink, badger, raccoon, weasel, black-tailed jackrabbit, cottontail, spotted and striped skunks, opossum.

Satellite Units

Several other state Wildlife Areas are satellites of Los Banos. Information about them can be obtained here. We were advised that, for the ordinary visitor, Los Banos is the most interesting and accessible.

Volta Wildlife Area: 2,200 acres. About 5 mi. NW of Los Banos on Ingomar Grade Rd. Except in waterfowl season, foot access only. The Volta Wasteway, a large canal, crosses the site. Of interest chiefly to fishermen and hunters.

Cottonwood Creek Wildlife Area: 6,000 acres. On the San Luis Reservoir N of Hwy 152. Foot access only.

Mud Slough Unit: approximately 545 acres. 5 mi. E of Los Banos on the N side of Hwy 152 between Patton and Delta Rds.

The following areas are managed for big game, upland game, and waterfowl nesting habitat to mitigate losses occasioned by construction of San Luis Reservoir, which flooded over 15,000 acres.

Little Panoche Reservoir Wildlife Area: 780 acres. Further S, about 5 mi. W of I-5 on Little Panoche Rd. Foot access only.

O'Neill Forebay Wildlife Area: 700 acres. On Hwy 33. Foot access only.

San Luis Reservoir Wildlife Area: 900 acres. On Dinosaur Point Rd., off Hwy 152. Foot access only.

Activities

Camping: Between the end of the waterfowl season and Sept. 15. Los Banos only, not in satellites. No campground, but numerous suitable areas. Water available at HQ. Latrines in parking lots. Campers must register at HQ.

Hunting: Must have valid hunting or trapping license. Seasonal. Dates change yearly, so call for exact dates.

Fishing: Between the end of the waterfowl season and Sept. 15.

Bird-watching: Between the end of the waterfowl season and Sept. 15. Los Banos only: birding area in sanctuary zone on Sat., Sun., and Wed. during waterfowl season.

There is a $2.50 per person entry fee for persons older than 16 who do not have a valid hunting, trapping, or fishing license or an annual CA Wildlands Pass.

Nearby
Central San Joaquin Valley National Wildlife Refuges (see entry this zone).

Publications
Leaflet with map.

Hunting and Other Public Uses on State and Federal Areas.

Wing Beat News.

Bird checklist.

Headquarters
CA Dept. of Fish and Game, 18110 W. Henry Miller Ave., Los Banos, CA 93635; (209) 826-0463.

Los Padres National Forest
U.S. Forest Service, Monterey Ranger District

See entry in zone 8. 304,023 acres of this 1,750,857-acre Forest are in zone 5. This area, a unit somewhat separated from the main body of the Forest, is in the Santa Lucia Mountains. From Big Sur to just beyond Lucia on Hwy 1, the Forest boundary is 1–2 mi. inland, although there are two small bits on the coast near Big Sur. From there S to the Monterey County line, the Forest is on the coast, although there are a number of inholdings.

A large part of this Forest unit is in the Ventana and Silver Peak Wildernesses.

Mendota Wildlife Area

California Department of Fish and Game
12,425 acres.

From Mendota (W of Fresno), 3 mi. SE on Santa Fe Grade. E on Hwy 180 to entrance.

In the central San Joaquin Valley. Like other Refuges in the Valley, this was once an extensive wetland habitat for wintering waterfowl. Now managed to support optimum populations and to reduce crop predation on neighboring farmlands. Management objectives now include fostering upland species.

From a point near the entrance, Fresno Slough cuts across the site to the SE. Unpaved all-weather roads provide access to most parts of the area. About 8,470 acres have been converted into marsh and mudflats attractive to waterfowl and shorebirds. Water level is manipulated to check the natural change of marshland into dense tule-cattail stands. About 3,105 acres are good upland habitat.

In recent years management has encouraged general recreational use of the area, outside of hunting season: fishing, sightseeing, nature study, picnicking, swimming, boating, and—the leaflet notes—an occasional baptism!

No species checklists are available, but common birds and mammals are much the same as at the Central San Joaquin Valley National Wildlife Refuges and Los Banos Wildlife Area (see entries this zone).

Activities

Hiking: On roads and levees.

Fishing: Open to fishing 24 hrs. a day, but only boat fishing is allowed in waterfowl hunting season.

Hunting: Dates change yearly, vary for different species. Call for information.

Boating: On the Slough. Ramp near entrance.

Nearby

San Joaquin Valley National Wildlife Refuges and Los Banos Wildlife Area (see entries this zone).

Publication

Leaflet with map.

Headquarters

CA Dept. of Fish and Game, P.O. Box 37, Mendota, CA 93640; (209) 655-4645.

Merced National Wildlife Refuge

See Central San Joaquin Valley National Wildlife Refuge (this zone).

Natural Bridges State Beach

California Department of Parks and Recreation
65 acres.

From Hwy 1 take Swift St. to West Cliff Dr. to park entrance.

A winter home to as many as 150,000 monarch butterflies, this small oceanfront park is also a good spot to see shorebirds, marine mammals, and tide pool creatures. Three connected arches hewn from a sandstone cliff make this one of the coast's most popular photographic landmarks. First occupied by Ohlone Indians, the region was later visited by Spanish settlers and occupied by Mexican citizens. After being used by a dairy, and being converted into a South Seas movie set, the site became a state beach and, finally, a State Park.

Monarch butterflies wintering here are a popular attraction. A boardwalk leads to the eucalyptus grove where they rest. The mild coastal climate protects the butterflies from inland frost. A milkweed patch provides food for the caterpillars. The tide pools are best visited at low tide. Hermit crabs, crabs, and snails may be picked up as long as they are returned. Don't touch sea stars, sea urchins, limpets, chitons, anemones, and mussels attached to the rocks. *Always watch out for waves.*

Interpretation

Visitor center with bookstore open daily 10–4 in monarch season, Oct.–early March. Check for spring and fall hours.

Interpretive trails lace the park and butterfly preserve.

Butterfly tours offered Oct.–Feb.

Tide pool tours are conducted when the tide is 1 ft. or lower.

Nature walks offered.

In addition to docent-led tours here, guided tours of the nearby Long Marine Laboratory of the University of California at Santa Cruz are also available; call (408) 459-4308.

There's no camping at the park, but public and private campgrounds are available nearby.

Publication
Brochure with maps.

Headquarters
Ca Dept. of Parks and Recreation, 2431 W. Cliff Dr., Santa Cruz, CA 95060; (408) 423-4609.

Nisene Marks State Park (The Forest of)

California Department of Parks and Recreation
9,917 acres.
From Hwy 1 E of Santa Cruz, Aptos-Seacliff exit. N on Aptos Creek Rd.

As the single symbol indicates, this is a hiker's park, although cars can be driven on a dirt road to the picnic areas. Steep coastal mountains, deeply carved by 6 creeks that originate within the Park. Elevations from 190 to 2,600 ft. Maple Falls, 35 ft., flows all year. Aptos Creek has cascades between the 1,200-ft. and 600-ft. elevations. The Park was a gift from two brothers and a sister in honor of their mother; their wish was that it remain undeveloped.

Plants: 90% forested. Chiefly second-growth Coast redwoods with tan oak, madrone. The area was logged between 1870 and 1925. 20 old-growth redwoods remain. Riparian vegetation in drainages. Chaparral on ridges above 1,800 ft. Two freshwater sag ponds. Flowering species include redwood sorrel, trillium, starflower, toothwort, red clintonia, false Solomon's seal, fetid adder's tongue.

Birds: No checklist, but record cards at HQ. Noted: great horned owl, Steller's and scrub jays, California quail, band-tailed pigeon, brown creeper, golden-crowned kinglet, dark-eyed junco.

Mammals: Noted: opossum, black-tailed jackrabbit, cottontail, coyote, mule deer, bobcat, feral pig.

Interpretation

Guided hikes in summer, occasionally; notices posted.

Hiking, backpacking: 32 mi. of trails. Longest named trail is 7 mi. One trail camp with 6 sites. Reservations required, from HQ.

Park may be closed in midsummer if fire hazard is extreme.

Publication
Leaflet with map.

Headquarters
CA Dept. of Parks and Recreation, c/o Henry Cowell State Park, P.O. Box P-1, Hwy 9, Felton, CA 95018; (408) 335-4598.

Pfeiffer Big Sur State Park

California Department of Parks and Recreation
821 acres.

From Carmel, S 26 mi. on Hwy 1.

In a valley on both sides of the Big Sur River, within the Santa Lucia Mountains. A short distance from the coast. Elevations from 215 to 3,000 ft. Southernmost of the redwood parks. The Park is highly developed, with lodge, cabins, store. Heavily used in season. It adjoins the Ventana Wilderness of Los Padres National Forest (see entry zone 8); access is at a ranger station 1 mi. S of the Ventana Wilderness.

Pfeiffer Falls, within the Park, is in a fern-lined canyon. Pfeiffer Beach, a detached bit of the National Forest, on the coast, is nearby. (The ocean is not for swimming.)

Summers have warm days, cool, foggy evenings. Winters are mild; snow is rarely seen. Fall and spring have the best climate. Annual precipitation is about 40 in.

Plants: In the moister areas, Coast redwood with sycamore, black cottonwood, bigleaf maple, alder, willow. Dry, S-facing slopes are covered with chaparral: live oak, tan oak, California bay laurel, chamise, ceanothus, buckeye, toyon, coffeeberry, cascara, manzanita, yucca.

Birds: No checklist, but checklist for Los Padres National Forest is applicable. Species here include Steller's jay, quail, canyon wren, dark-eyed junco, chestnut-backed chickadee, band-tailed pigeon, turkey vulture, red-tailed hawk, dipper, belted kingfisher.

Mammals: Include opossum, gray squirrel, raccoon, wild pig, mule deer.

Interpretation

Campfire programs and *nature walks* in summer. Also walks at nearby Julia Pfeiffer Burns State Park (see entry this zone).

Exhibits at the lodge.

Nature trail, 1 mi.

Activities

Camping: 218 sites. All year. Reservations year-round.

Hiking: Trails to overlooks, other points of interest. Extensive trails in the National Forest. Trailhead is 1 mi. S.

Nearby

Andrew Molera State Park (see entry this zone).

Publication

Leaflet with map, $0.50 (with self-addressed stamped envelope).

Headquarters

CA Dept. of Parks and Recreation, Big Sur Station #1, Big Sur, CA 93920; (408) 667-2315.

....

Pinnacles National Monument

U.S. National Park Service
16,251 acres.

From Hollister, 34 mi. S on Hwy 25, right turn onto Hwy 146, then S to entrance. A second entrance, on the W, is reached from Soledad via Hwy 146; this road is not recommended for large trailers and campers; it leads to the Chaparral ranger station and campground. One cannot drive through the Monument.

Noted for its many spirelike rock formations, 500–1,200 ft. high, with caves and other volcanic features. These are the last remains of an ancient volcano, eroded by rain, wind, heat, and frost. The spires rise from smoothly rolling hills. The site is on the W side of the San Andreas Fault, has moved N 195 mi. in 23.5 million years. Highest point is North Chalone Peak, 3,304 ft., in the SW corner of the Monument, reached by trail.

Precipitation is about 16 in. per year, mostly in winter and early spring, followed by a hot, dry summer and fall. Spring is the best time for a visit, when vegetation is green and many flowers bloom. Vegetation is chaparral, mostly chamise mixed with manzanita, buck brush, hollyleaf cherry, and toyon.

The area is used almost entirely by day visitors. The only campground inside the Monument is small and on the W. A commercial campground is just outside the E entrance. The trail system is extensive.

Birds often seen include acorn woodpecker, brown towhee, California quail, turkey vulture, scrub jay. Mammals include raccoon, mule deer, as well as the less commonly seen gray fox and bobcat.

Features

High Peaks Trail, 5.4 mi., from Chalone Creek picnic area to Bear Gulch parking, a 1,650-ft. climb. Views of the entire park.

Condor Gulch Trail, 1.7 mi., ascends 1,100 ft., linking the visitor center and High Peaks Trail.

Chalone Peak Trail, 5½ mi. each way, is the longest in the park, with a 2,150-ft. rise.

Old Pinnacles Trail, 2 mi., from Chalone Creek picnic area over fairly level terrain to *Balconies Caves.*

Balconies Caves can also be reached by a 1.2-mi. trail from the Chaparral ranger station.

Juniper Canyon Trail, 1.2 mi., links the Chaparral ranger station with the High Peaks Trail.

Bench Trail, 1.2 mi., Pinnacle Campground to Bear Gulch Trail and visitor center.

Interpretation

Bear Gulch *visitor center,* 3 mi. inside E entrance, and Chaparral ranger station, 2 mi. inside W entrance. Naturalist, exhibits, publications. *Evening programs* on weekends at E campground.

4 nature trails: Moses Spring, to Bear Gulch Caves. *Geology hike,* up the Condor Gulch Trail. *Bear Gulch. Balconies Trail.* These are self-guiding. Leaflets on sale.

Camping: 19 tent sites. All year except Presidents' Day weekend to Memorial Day weekend. Camping only Mon.–Thurs. night—*no weekend camping.*

Publications

Leaflet with map.

Guide to Plants of the Pinnacles, $0.75.

Pinnacles Guide, $5.95.

Pinnacles topographic map, $2.25.

Pinnacles Geological Trail, $1.00.

Nature trail guides, $0.25–$1.00.

Checklist of birds, mammals, reptiles, amphibians, $0.50 each.

Headquarters

National Park Service, 5000 Hwy 146, Paicines, CA 95043; (408) 389-4485.

Point Lobos State Reserve

California Department of Parks and Recreation
1,276 acres.

From Carmel, S 3 mi. on Hwy 1.

Open: 9 A.M.–7 P.M. in summer; otherwise 9–5.

Maintained as a pristine site, a unique area scenically. Includes the first underwater reserve. All the tide and submerged land surrounding the Reserve, 775 acres, are the *Point Lobos Ecological Reserve,* managed by the CA Dept. of Parks and Recreation in cooperation with the CA Dept. of Fish and Game. The adjoining tide and submerged lands in Carmel Bay are the *Carmel Bay Ecological Reserve,* 1,642 acres, also managed cooperatively. This Reserve also includes the Pinnacles, a cluster of offshore rocks.

Point Lobos is a rugged peninsula of red-brown rock. Highest point is 260 ft. The site has 6 mi. of coastline in an irregular configuration. Strict rules protect the site: visitors must stay on trails; nothing may be collected from land or sea; scuba and skin diving require a permit; fishing is prohibited.

Plants: Monterey and Gowen cypress occur naturally only here and in a small nearby area. (The Gowen cypress specimens are in a part of the site not open to visitors.) Also here are fine specimens of Monterey pine, a species gradually becoming extinct for natural causes in its native habitat, but one that is extensively planted commercially in South America, New Zealand, and Australia. Other plant species include coastal sagebrush, coyote brush, poison oak, bluff lettuce on cliffs, lace lichen on trees.

Over 350 species of plants occur here. Some species are in bloom in almost every season, but spring is the peak. Species include sun-cups, poppy, lizard-tail yarrow, iris, seaside painted cup, sea pink, zigadene lily, Johnny-jump-up, cream-cup, ceanothus, brodiaea, blackberry, aster, lupine, blue-eyed grass.

Birds: Over 250 species recorded. Common residents include western gull, Brandt's cormorant, black phoebe, great blue heron, killdeer, black oystercatcher, great horned owl, hairy woodpecker, Steller's and scrub jays, wrentit, Bewick's wren, song sparrow, chestnut-backed chickadee, pygmy nuthatch, bushtit. Gulls and cormorants nest on offshore rocks. Brown pelicans are summer visitors to the offshore. Common migrants include loons, grebes, scaup, surf scoter, red-breasted merganser, black turnstone.

Mammals: Good opportunities to see marine mammals. Sea otter, California and Steller sea lions, harbor seal are permanent residents. Gray whales pass in winter and early spring. Occasional killer whale. Dusky-footed woodrats build homes 3 ft. high in much of the Reserve. Other terrestrial species: California ground squirrel, gray squirrel, California meadow mouse, gray fox, bobcat, raccoon. Occasional sightings of mountain lion, opossum, striped skunk.

Interpretation

Naturalist programs daily in summer, weekends otherwise.

Nature trail.

Headquarters

Point Lobos State Reserve, Rt. 1, Box 62, Carmel, CA 93923; (408) 624-4909.

Ranger District
Monterey R.D., 2211 Garden Rd., Monterey, CA 93940; (408) 649-2839.

San Joaquin Valley National Wildlife Refuges
See Central San Joaquin Valley National Wildlife Refuges (this zone).

San Luis National Wildlife Refuge
See Central San Joaquin Valley National Wildlife Refuges (this zone).

San Luis Reservoir State Recreation Area
California Department of Parks and Recreation
2,311 land acres; 15,800 water acres (at full pool) in two impoundments.
6 mi. W of I-5 on Hwy 152.

The Reservoir, part of the Central Valley Project, is formed by a dam 3½ mi. long. It is an element in a complex of aqueducts, canals, forebays, pumping stations, and reservoirs. The region is dry, with about 8 in. of rain yearly, mostly in the winter months. The Reservoir is surrounded by rolling hills, with some steep canyons. Slopes are sparsely vegetated, mostly grass. The site is heavily used for camping and water-based recreation.

On the N, on both sides of Hwy 152, are the San Luis Reservoir Wildlife Area and Cottonwood Creek Wildlife Area (see Los Banos Wildlife Area entry). These are managed to develop winter waterfowl habitat in partial mitigation of the habitat loss caused by the dam.

Camping: 3 campgrounds: *Basalt,* with 79 developed sites on a reservation system; *San Luis Creek,* with 53 developed sites with water and electricity; and *Medeiros,* where up to 400 campers can use the undeveloped area.

Publication
Leaflet with map.

Headquarters
CA Parks and Recreation, Four Rivers District, 31426 Gonzaga Rd., Gustine, CA 95322; (209) 826-1196.

Turlock Lake State Recreation Area

California Department of Parks and Recreation
228 acres.

21 mi. E of Modesto, off Hwy 132.

In foothill country, the Park is bounded on the S by Turlock Lake and on the N by the Tuolumne River. It provides an ideal setting for water-oriented outdoor recreation. Elevation is 250 ft.

The Tuolumne River flows past the campground, treating the visitor to an excellent riparian habitat much like what once characterized all the rivers of the San Joaquin Valley. Recent increases in water releases from Don Pedro Reservoir make this portion of the Tuolumne River an excellent area for flatwater float trips. Several locations upstream, as well as the Park itself, allow public river access for launching and delaunching canoes and rafts.

Over 190 plant species have been identified at the Park as well as 115 bird species. Warm summers, mild winters. Spring and fall camping are especially enjoyable.

Camping: 66 sites, all developed but without hookups. Reservations may be made all year, but are absolutely necessary for weekends and holidays. April–Labor Day.

Publications
Park folder.
Bird checklist.

Headquarters
CA Dept. of Parks and Recreation, 22600 Lake Rd., La Grange, CA 95329; (209) 874-2008 or (209) 874-2056.

Wilder Ranch State Park

California Department of Parks and Recreation
4,000 acres.

2 mi. N of Santa Cruz, off Hwy 1.

The Park is an attractive place with 5 mi. of scenic coastline, fine forest and grassland, deep creek canyons. Several historic outbuildings once belonging to the Wilder family are preserved. 34 mi. of hiking, biking, and horse trails. Weekend tours.

Interpretation

Weekend and group tours.

Historic buildings *and* exhibits.

Visitor center.

Nature trails.

Headquarters

CA Dept. of Parks and Recreation, 1401 Coast Rd., Santa Cruz, CA 95060; (408) 426-0505.

Z O N E

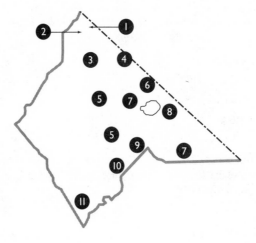

Z O N E

Includes these counties:

Alpine Mono Madera (E portion)
Tuolumne Mariposa

Due E of San Francisco, on the Nevada border, this zone straddles the Sierra Nevada, encompassing over 3.5 million acres of National Forest and National Park land. Yosemite National Park is at its center, surrounded by National Forests.

The Sierra, a gigantic fault block, rises gradually from chaparral-covered foothills to the crest, a line of peaks, some over 13,000 ft. Snowfall is heavy in the high country, and the spring runoff brings to life countless waterfalls and cataracts, many of which dwindle or go dry in summer. The high country has many small lakes in glacial basins, deep canyons, flower-carpeted mountain meadows.

Few roads cross the Sierra, and all but one in this zone are closed in winter. Strangers to the West are often surprised to discover that "winter" here is a season that may extend to the Fourth of July. Much of the high country is closed by snow to foot or automobile travel until June or later.

The W slope is relatively near San Francisco and other CA cities. It sometimes seems that their entire populations head for the mountains on summer weekends. Resorts are crowded, as are most of the more accessible Park and Forest campgrounds. Quotas are in effect at most trailheads giving access to wilderness areas. But these areas are vast. Park and forest rangers will be happy to direct you to lightly traveled trails and little-used destinations.

The High Sierra is unquestionably magnificent, but the snow-free season there is short. For those who do not choose to spend the other 10 months indoors, opportunities are great. We found Yosemite Valley uncrowded and at its best in April. Some hikers scorn the chaparral, but we were delighted by the hillsides and canyon trails we hiked in springtime, sunny and warm, alive with birds, brilliant with flowers. We met other hikers perhaps twice in a day.

Crossing the mountains from the W is difficult for those in the San Francisco area. From the Los Angeles area, it's a straight run up US 395 to the Owens Valley. The E side of the Sierra is steep, somewhat drier than the W but with enough snow to support a few ski areas. Here, too, are popular resorts, notably at Mammoth Lakes. Wilderness areas are more readily reached from the W side. In many cases, paved roads come to parking areas at or very near their boundaries. Here, too, trailhead quotas have become necessary to limit environmental damage in the more popular places. But here, too, the hiker who seeks isolation can find it.

Although the Sierra is the main attraction, the other side of the valley is well worth exploring. The White Mountains, for example, in the Inyo National Forest, have much of interest. So do parts of the Toiyabe National Forest on the NV border.

Bodie Hills

U.S. Bureau of Land Management
85,000 acres.

From US 395, E on Hwy 270, "Bodie Rd."

Rounded, pinyon-covered hills surround the ghost town of Bodie, now a State Historical Park. Most of the land between US 395 and the NV border, N of Mono Lake, is managed by the BLM, although there are scattered privately owned tracts. To the N is the Toiyabe National Forest. Terrain varies from rolling to steep. Hilltop elevations from 7,500 ft. to Potato Mountain and Bodie Peak, both over 10,000 ft. Lower slopes have sagebrush, mixed shrubs, annual grasses. Pinyon pine and juniper on higher slopes. Quaking aspen in drainages, turning bright yellow and gold in the fall. The area has many enclosed canyons, interior valleys, several springs.

Several features indicate past volcanic activity. Beauty Peak, NE of Bodie, is a volcanic cone. Alkali Meadows hot springs are N of Clearwater Canyon. The Alkali Meadows bowl is thought to be an old caldera.

Several roads, mostly unpaved, enter the Bodie Hills through narrow canyons such as Aurora, Clearwater, Cottonwood, and Bridgeport, climbing to points with fine views of Mono Lake and the Sierra.

Wildlife includes deer, rabbit, coyote, sage grouse, a small population of pronghorn.

Headquarters
Bureau of Land Management, Bishop Resource Area, 785 N. Main St., Suite E, Bishop, CA 93514; (619) 872-4881.

Calaveras Big Trees State Park

See Stanislaus National Forest (this zone).

Devils Postpile National Monument

U.S. National Park Service
800 acres.

Near Mammoth Lakes Village, off US 395 39 mi. NW of junction with US 6.

Closed in winter; season determined by snow.

Within the Inyo National Forest; one of the attractions of the popular Mammoth Lakes resort area (see Inyo National Forest entry, zone 7). The Monument is about 7 mi. from the resort area. Congestion in the Reds Meadow–Devils Postpile area has become so great that a shuttle bus (fee) is required for day-use visitors to the National Monument and backpackers going beyond it. The shuttle runs during peak season daytime hours, 9 A.M.–6 P.M. Visitors staying in the campground can use cars.

The Monument is at 7,600 ft. elevation on the W slope of the Sierra Nevada, on the Middle Fork of the San Joaquin River. Its central feature is an impressive columnar basalt formation, individual columns 60 ft. high. Glacial action has sheared and polished the tops of the polygonal columns so that they resemble a tiled floor. At Rainbow Falls, the Middle Fork drops 101 ft. The area is within the Sierra lodgepole pine–red fir zone.

Activities
Camping: 23 sites. Approximate season: June 20–Oct. 1.

Hiking: Trails to top of the basalt cliffs, Rainbow Falls. Trails into the surrounding National Forest.

Publication
Leaflet with map.

Headquarters
National Park Service, c/o Sequoia and Kings Canyon National Parks, Three Rivers, CA 93271; (209) 565-3341.

Grover Hot Springs State Park
California Department of Parks and Recreation
650 acres.

From Markleeville on Hwy 89, W 4 mi. on Hot Springs Rd.

The hot springs once made this a health resort. Today it's a scenic camping and hiking base, a park surrounded by the Toiyabe National Forest. Elevation is about 5,800 ft. Terrain is gently sloping. About half of the Park is high mountain meadow, surrounded by forest, with 10,000-ft. mountains rising abruptly on three sides. Water flows from springs at 148°F and is regulated to about 102° in a small concrete pool. Most of those using the pool today seem more entertained by the phenomenon than persuaded that the water has curative powers. Normal summer temperatures here range between 50°F at night and 80° by day, although June frosts are not uncommon. Autumn frost brings a blaze of colors. Annual precipitation is about 25 in. The Park is open all year.

Plants: About 50% forested: Jeffrey pine, white fir, ponderosa pine. California sage and bitterbrush in the understory. Meadow grasslands. Flowering species include asters, lilies.

Birds: Checklist. Over 75 species spotted including great blue and green backed herons, Canada goose, bald and golden eagles, hawks, prairie falcon, merlin, blue and sage grouse, mountain quail, killdeer, spotted sandpiper, owls, calliope and rufous hummingbirds, wood-peckers, Williamson's and yellow-bellied sapsuckers, swallows, nuthatches, house and marsh wrens, various warblers, hermit and varied thrushes, golden-crowned and ruby-crowned kinglets, gros-beaks, finches, sparrows, buntings.

Mammals: Often seen: coyote, squirrels, deer, chipmunks, raccoon, black bear, cottontail. Present, seldom seen: bobcat, weasel.

Reptiles and amphibians: Species reported include western fence and alligator lizards, garter snake, western rattlesnake. Less often seen: rubber boa, western racer.

Interpretation

Campfire programs and *guided hikes.* July–Aug. *Ranger-naturalist* present all year.

Self-guiding *nature trail,* 1 mi.

Activities

Camping: 76 sites. All year, depending on snow. Reservations Fri. before Memorial Day–Labor Day weekend.

Hiking: Trails into the National Forest. One popular trail rises 2,000 ft. in less than 4 mi., on the way to Burnside Lake.

Fishing: Cutthroat and rainbow trout.

Ski touring: 3-mi. trail section of a longer trail within the Park. Trails into the Forest.

Publications

Leaflet with map.

Nature trail guide.

Headquarters

CA Dept. of Parks and Recreation, P.O. Box 188, Markleeville, CA 96120; Park (916) 694-2248; pool (916) 694-2249.

Hidden Dam and Hensley Lake

U.S. Army Corps of Engineers
500 acres.

From Madera on Hwy 99, N on Yosemite Ave. (Hwy 145) and Rd. 400. Dam is 17 mi. from Madera.

The 500 acres is a wildlife area at the head of this lake built for irrigation and flood control. The wildlife area is open to foot access only. The lake is about 4 mi. long at full pool, the dam over a mile long. In the gently rolling foothills of the Sierra Nevada. Like most such lakes, it is heavily used for water-based recreation. Site boundaries are generally less than ½ mi. from the lakeshore. Natural vegetation is reclaiming the shoreline.

Interpretation

Visitor center at HQ. The site has a monument to Major James D. Savage, the white discoverer of Yosemite Valley, and the center presents somewhat sanitized information about his colorful activities.

Campfire programs in summer.

Camping: 51 sites. Al year.

Publication

Leaflet with map.

Headquarters

U.S. Army Corps of Engineers, P.O. Box 85, Raymond, CA 93653; (209) 673-5151.

Indian Creek Recreation Area

U.S. Bureau of Land Management
7,008 acres.

From Markleeville, 2½ mi. N on Hwy 89 and follow signs.

On the E slope of the Sierra Nevada. A small reservoir, 160 acres. In the N half of the area, land in the W and central portions is rolling, elevations 4,900 to 5,400 ft., several small peaks toward the center rising to over 5,600 ft. E portion is rough to mountainous, land rising from 5,400 to 6,000 ft. steeply. In the S half of the area, elevations are from 5,600 to 6,000 ft. in the W and central portions, rising to 7,600 ft. near the E boundary. The site is crossed by the E and W forks of the Carson River. Indian Creek rises on the site. Several other streams. Moderate flow all year. Annual precipitation is about 21 in. Winter storms are often severe. The camping season is normally May–Oct.

Plants: Principal tree species are ponderosa, Jeffrey, and pinyon pines, white fir, incense cedar, Utah juniper, aspen, willow. On the lower slopes, big sagebrush, bitterbrush, rabbitbrush, low sagebrush, manzanita, snowberry, mountain mahogany, squaw carpet. Small marshy areas with cattail, sedges, rushes. Wildflowers include Sierra thistle, paintbrush, lupine, poppy.

Birds: Species reported include Canada goose, mallard, pintail, cinnamon teal, ruddy duck, coot, California gull, golden and bald eagles, mourning dove, California quail, common nighthawk, kestrel, white-headed woodpecker, Williamson's sapsucker, Steller's jay, cliff swallow, magpie, mountain chickadee, brown creeper, dipper.

Mammals: Include black-tailed jackrabbit, cottontail, ground squirrels, chipmunk, kangaroo rat, porcupine, coyote, striped skunk, mule deer.

Interpretation
Curtz Lake Environmental Study Area is on Airport Rd., midway between Woodfords and Markleeville. It features 3 *nature trails*, each with a different theme, with trail markers. A full tour requires about 1 hr.

Activities
Camping: 19 sites, plus a nearby tenting area with 10 sites.

Hiking: Trails into the Toiyabe National Forest.

Fishing: Mountain whitefish, brown, cutthroat, rainbow, and eastern brook trout, Lahontan redside, brown bullhead.

Adjacent
Toiyabe National Forest (see entry this zone).

Publications
Leaflet with map.

Curtz Lake Environmental Study Area (leaflet).

Headquarters
Bureau of Land Management, Carson City District, 1050 E. William St., Carson City, NV 89820; (702) 882-1631.

Inyo National Forest
U.S. Forest Service

Of this 1,900,000-acre National Forest, about 52% lies in zone 7, 45% in zone 6, the remainder in NV. However, we feel that the Forest is best described as a whole so the principal entry is in zone 7.

The zone 6 portion begins with Yosemite National Park and Mono Lake and extends S to the Inyo County line just N of Bishop. Some of the Forest's principal features are located in zone 6, including the Hoover Wilderness, the Tioga Lakes area, the Ansel Adams Wilderness, the Mammoth Lakes area, the John Muir Wilderness, the White Mountain area, and the Ancient Bristlecone Pine Forest. Also included: Devils Postpile National Monument (see entry this zone).

Mono Lake
U.S. Forest Service and California Department of Parks and Recreation
About 100 sq. mi.

E of US 395 at Lee Vining, E of Yosemite on Hwy 120.

The lake, remnant of an ancient inland sea, has no natural outlet. The deep blue water and islands are highlighted by the mountain backdrop. In 1984, Mono Lake became the first congressionally designated Scenic Area in the National Forest system. Surface evaporation is 4 ft. per year. The water is saline and alkaline. In 1941, Los Angeles began diverting water from the creeks feeding the lake. Since then the lake has dropped 42 ft.

The lake produces vast quantities of brine shrimp and alkali flies, food for the gulls, grebes, and phalaropes that gather here in great numbers in migrations. The food web within the lake is very simple. Bacteria nourish algae that are consumed by alkali flies and brine shrimp, which then feed the birds. One damaged link could cause the whole system to collapse. The nesting gull population is the largest in CA. The lowered lake level opened a land bridge to black Negit Island, the principal gull nesting area, allowing predators to cross.

The receding water has also uncovered pinnacle-shaped tufa towers, formed at the lake bottom from the interaction of springs and lake water. A large grove of these tufa towers is on the S shore, a short walk from a Forest Service parking area on a dirt road N of Hwy 120. The "beaches" around the lake are eroded pumice. Panum Crater, near the SW shore, is a northern extension of nearby Mono Craters.

Most of the land surrounding the lake is managed by the U.S. Forest Service and the CA Department of Parks and Recreation. Some is owned by the City of Los Angeles. A few tracts are privately owned. A 1984 comprehensive Forest Service management plan recommended keeping the lake high enough to protect nesting habitat on Negit Island and to preserve scenic views of the lake and the tufa formations. But within 5 years the lake level had dropped far below this plan's recommended level, and windblown alkali dust was affecting air quality. In 1994, after 16 years of court fights, study, and hearings, the State Water Resources Control Board ordered a 17-ft. rise in the lake's elevation over the next 20 to 30 years. The Los Angeles Department of Water and Power, the Mono Lake Committee, Mono Lake Tufa State Reserve, and the Forest Service are now working together to restore the Mono Basin's creeks and wetlands.

Plants: Around the lake, desert scrub, dominated by rabbitbrush and blazing stars. Farther away, sparse stands of Jeffrey pine.

Birds: 800,000 eared grebes during fall migration, Aug.–Oct.; 50,000 nesting California gulls (about 90% of the CA population are born here); 400 snowy plovers (about 10% of the CA population). Wilson's and red-necked phalaropes are also dependent on the brine shrimp and flies. Many other birds stop at the lake during their fall migrations. Pintail, mallard, cinnamon and green-winged teals, Canada geese, and tundra swans remain into the winter. The area is kept neat and tidy by scavengers such as magpies and ravens, as well as the gulls. Also hawks, golden eagle, great-horned owl.

Mammals: Include mice, squirrels, skunks, porcupine, weasel, bobcat.

Interpretation

Visitor center with interpretive exhibits, film. Ranger-led *canoe tours*. In Lee Vining, *Mono Lake Committee store* with slide show, books and other interpretive materials, activities list.

Activities

Camping: Is allowed on Paoha or the exposed lakebed by a camping agreement form from the scenic area visitor center or the ranger station.

Canoeing, kayaking: Best launch site is at Navy Beach on the S shore. Keep boats close to shore if even a slight breeze is blowing—winds can intensify very suddenly. Morning is usually the calmest time.

Boating: Motor boats are allowed, but there are no developed launch ramps.

Swimming, snorkeling: Water is delightfully buoyant but may irritate eyes. Bring your own fresh water for a rinse; showers are only available in Lee Vining.

Publications

Leaflet with map of area.

General information sheets.

Headquarters

U.S. Forest Service, P.O. Box 429, Lee Vining, CA 93541; (619) 647-3044.

Sierra National Forest

U.S. Forest Service
1,303,120 acres.

Between Yosemite and Kings Canyon National Parks. Hwy 168 from Fresno penetrates the Forest. Hwy 41 crosses the NW portion en route to Yosemite's South Entrance Station.

The Forest lies W of the Sierra Crest, where it adjoins the Inyo National Forest and Kings Canyon National Park (see entries, zone 7). The Sequoia National Forest is on its S boundary (see entry, zone 7). Road entry to the Forest is somewhat limited. No paved roads enter from the E or S. Hwy 41, from the N, crosses only a neck of Forest land. The Forest has 1,970 mi. of roads in its internal system, most unpaved, many maintained only as Forest operations require.

Elevations range from 900 ft. to 13,986-ft. Mount Humphreys. In the western portion, at low elevations, steeply rolling chaparral and grass- and woodland-covered foothills. Midelevations have steep-walled river canyons as well as moderately sloping, heavily forested areas and steep-walled basins. In the basins below the peaks are more than 1,000 lakes and ponds, most of them in the John Muir Wilderness. Above are knife-edged ridges and sharp peaks, barren wind-swept crags along the Sierra Crest.

Annual precipitation ranges from 20 in. at lower elevations to over 80 in. in the high country, where most of it falls as snow. Summers are dry, but thunderstorms are common in the higher elevations. Highest summer temperatures range from 100°F below 4,000 ft. to 80° at 7,000 ft. and above. Most of the recreational areas are above 4,000 ft. and snow-covered from late Oct. to late May. In most years, travel above 8,000 ft. is hazardous before June 1. Many high passes and streams are unsafe to cross with horses before July 1. Most Forest visitors come in July and Aug.

Runoff gathers in more than 1,200 mi. of streams that flow to rivers, including the San Joaquin, Merced, and Kings. Ten reservoirs in the Forest store water for irrigation and power generation. The reservoirs are used for boating, swimming, and fishing.

The Forest records more than 4 million visitor-days per year. The most heavily used areas are those along the better roads, especially the recreation areas beside the larger lakes. These are often crowded in summer, the lakeside campgrounds full. Some of the wilderness trails have become so popular that quotas have been applied to limit environmental damage. However, the Forest area is vast, and the hiker who wants solitude can find it. Ask at any ranger station for information on lightly traveled areas.

More than one-quarter of the Forest is classed as wilderness, and other roadless areas have been proposed for additions to the wilderness system.

Plants: The several vegetation zones begin at low elevations with valley grassland, foothill woodland, and chaparral. The ponderosa pine forest extends from about 2,000–6,500 ft. elevation; other tree species here include sugar pine, Douglas-fir, white fir, incense cedar, black cottonwood, black oak, bigleaf maple, California dogwood. Understory includes greenleaf manzanita, buck brush, deer brush, mountain mahogany, bitter cherry, serviceberry, kit-kit-dizze.

Somewhat higher, from about 6,500–9,000 ft., is the lodgepole pine–red fir forest, including such tree species as silver and Jeffrey pines, Sierra juniper, and aspen; understory with bush chinquapin, whitethorn, huckleberry oak, greenleaf manzanita. Higher, somewhat overlapping, from about 7,500–10,000 ft., is the subalpine belt, where stands are sparse rather than dense, and include whitebark, foxtail, and lodgepole pines, mountain hemlock, and red and white heathers. Above timberline are low-growing plants: grasses, sedges, various wildflowers, among them alpine buttercup, shooting star, elephant's head, rosy stonecrop, alpine paintbrush, alpine aster, alpine goldenrod.

The Forest has two notable groves of giant sequoias. Nelder Grove is in the NW sector, E of Hwy 41. The McKinley Grove is in the SE sector W of Wishon Reservoir.

Birds: Checklist available. Waterfowl are not numerous, but water-associated species are seen at the many lakes. Common species of the Forest include red-tailed hawk, California and mountain quail, great horned owl, white-throated swift, hummingbirds, Bullock's oriole, western tanager, black-headed and evening grosbeaks, lazuli bunting, finches, goldfinches, towhees, wrens, California thrasher, hermit thrush, western and mountain bluebirds, Townsend's solitaire, vireos, warblers, northern flicker, woodpeckers, red-breasted sapsucker, flycatchers, swallows, jays, raven, Clark's nutcracker, mountain chickadee, plain titmouse, nuthatches, brown creeper, wrentit, dipper.

Mammals: Include mice, shrews, bats, black bear, ringtail, coyote, gray fox, bobcat, raccoon, mountain beaver, beaver, marmot, ground squirrels, chickaree, flying squirrels, chipmunks, kangaroo rat, wood rats, pika, cottontail, brush rabbit, mule deer.

Features

John Muir Wilderness: 620,000 acres. About 55% in the Sierra National Forest, the rest in the Inyo National Forest. Extends along the Sierra Crest from the Mammoth Lakes area to near Mount Whitney. The wilderness is more readily accessible from the Inyo National Forest, where auto roads lead to trailheads at or close to the boundary. Most visitors enter from the E side, and quotas are in effect at principal trailheads on both sides. Sectors reached by trails from the Sierra

National Forest are less heavily used. This is California's largest wilderness, a region of high snow-capped peaks, steep slopes, knife-edge ridges, countless streams, several hundred lakes and ponds, dense forests.

Ansel Adams Wilderness: 155,800 acres. About 45% in the Sierra National Forest, the rest in the Inyo National Forest. Straddles the Sierra Crest on the SE border of Yosemite National Park. Elevations from 7,000 to 14,000 ft. Sharp, rugged peaks. Remnants of glaciers are on several of the high mountains. The Minarets, thought to resemble mosque towers, are on the central portion of the divide, in the Ritter Range. This range divides the area and severely restricts travel from E to W. As in the case of the John Muir Wilderness, the E portion is more accessible and more heavily used. However, several trailheads in the Sierra National Forest, on the SW boundary of the wilderness, can be reached by car with little difficulty. Most of this area is above timberline.

Kaiser Wilderness: 22,500 acres. Just N of Huntington Lake, with trailheads reached by Hwy 168. The area is divided by the E–W Kaiser Ridge, on which the highest point is 10,320-ft. Kaiser Peak. The S part rises from the Huntington Lake resort area. The N part, considered the more attractive, contains all but 2 of the 20 small lakes, the largest about 40 acres. Travel into the N sector is usually over Potter Pass. Upper Twin Lake is the most popular, so overused that camping is now banned within 100 ft. of the lakeshore. Most lakes are reached by off-trail, cross-country hiking. Snow remains until early June.

South Fork, Merced River, area. On the S boundary of Yosemite National Park, in the Mariposa Ranger District. Reached by Mount Raymond Rd. and Sky Ranch Rd. from Hwy 41. Elevations from 5,000 ft. at the river to 9,165 ft. atop Iron Mountain. All below timberline. About 30 mi. of foot and horse trails lead to several attractive lakes, streams, and the river canyon. Several pleasant campsites are within easy hiking distance of trailheads. The area has a number of roads requiring 4-wheel-drive vehicles.

Bass Lake area. At 3,400 ft. elevation, E of Hwy 41 at Oakhurst. The lake, 4 mi. long, ½ mi. wide, is a popular resort, with some inholdings along the shore. It is accessible all year. Forest Service campgrounds are likely to be crowded Memorial Day weekend and July–Aug. Ten backcountry campgrounds, most of them on quiet fishing streams, are reached by unpaved roads. Trails lead through the South Fork, Merced River area into Yosemite NP. Points of interest in the area include the Nelder Grove of giant sequoias; the Yosemite Mountain

Railroad, now operated by a concessioner; Fresno Dome, a viewpoint; Goat Mountain Lookout; Mile High Vista. Water level is usually maintained near full pool in summer, drops rapidly in the fall, fills in spring.

Huntington Lake area. At 7,000 ft. elevation, on Hwy 168. Also a popular resort. The lake is 4 mi. long, ½ mi. wide. The usual season is Memorial Day–Labor Day, but some Forest Service campgrounds remain open until closed by snow in late Oct. Summer daytime temperatures range from 60° to 85°F, dropping to 40° or below at night. The Kaiser Wilderness is a short distance N. The chairlift at the China Peak Ski Area operates in summer, taking visitors to the top. Black Point offers fine views to those climbing the steep ½-mi. trail from trailhead. Many unpaved Forest roads, some suitable for cars, others requiring 4-wheel drive, penetrate the lightly used backcountry. The road from the Eastwood visitor station toward Florence Lake leads to 9 High Sierra campgrounds at about 7,500 ft. elevation; lakes, streams, fine views.

Dinkey Lakes area is S of Huntington Lake. A large area at 8,000 ft. elevation reached only on foot or horse, or by 4-wheel-drive vehicle on primitive roads. Forest, meadow, many small lakes. No developed sites. Camp anywhere—but 100 ft. from the nearest lake or stream bank.

Redinger Lake area is near the W boundary, reached by road N from Hwy 168 through Auberry. At 1,400 ft. elevation in a steep, narrow valley of the San Joaquin River, hills rising 1,000 ft. on either side. The lake is 3 mi. long, ¼ mi. wide. Because of extreme fire hazard in this chaparral area, camping is restricted to designated sites and campfire permits are required.

Shaver Lake area, at 5,600 ft. elevation, on Hwy 168. Most of the land on and near the lake is privately owned. The Forest Service has one campground within walking distance of a swimming area.

Pine Flat Reservoir is at the SW corner of the Forest, on the Kings River, N of Hwy 180. National Forest land is on the N shore. Forest campgrounds here and on the N shore of the river, upstream. Trails and Forest roads N to primitive campsites on Big Creek and NE toward Dinkey Creek.

Other lakes, less developed, accessible by Forest roads, include Mammoth Pool, Lake Thomas A. Edison, Florence Lake, Courtright Reservoir, Wishon Reservoir. Edison and Florence Lakes have commercial ferry service to reach trailheads into the John Muir Wilderness, usually early June–Sept.

Interpretation

Visitor information and *ranger stations* are located on most of the principal routes to recreation areas.

Campfire programs are offered from mid-June to Labor Day in the larger camping areas. Schedules available at information and ranger stations and campground bulletin boards.

Nature trails include those at Nelder Grove and McKinley Grove. *Way-of-the-Mono Trail* is on County Road 222 near Bass Lake.

Activities

Camping: 61 campgrounds, 1,357 sites. A few are open all year. Most are closed in winter, open beginning mid-April–mid-June. Closings from Sept. 10 to mid-Nov. Bass Lake campgrounds require reservations by BIOSPHERICS (800) 280-CAMP (2267) in summer.

Hiking, backpacking: 1,100 mi. of trails, ranging from short, easy day hikes to strenuous wilderness journeys. Permits required for wilderness areas; campfire permits required except in campgrounds. The John Muir Trail is a segment of the Pacific Crest Trail and is one of the most heavily used wilderness trails. High-country trails can often be hiked by mid-June, but some passes and stream crossings may be difficult or hazardous into July.

Hunting: Deer, black bear, rabbit, dove, pigeon, quail.

Fishing: The 1,200 mi. of streams and over 1,000 lakes have more than 30 fish species, including rainbow, brown, golden, and brook trout, kokanee salmon, large- and smallmouth bass, bluegill, crappie, sunfish, catfish.

Swimming: Swimming areas at the resort lakes. Elsewhere as you choose.

Boating: Ramps on the larger lakes reachable by car. Sailing is popular on Huntington Lake, water skiing on Shaver and Bass Lakes. Speed limits and zones apply on some lakes.

Rafting: On the Merced and Kings Rivers. Canoeing and kayaking are also popular.

Horse riding: Packers at the principal resort areas and other main access points. HQ will supply a list.

Skiing: China Peak Ski Area.

Ski touring, snowshoeing: Favorite areas are Tamarack Ridge near Shaver Lake, Fish Camp area along Hwy 41. However, many trails and unplowed roads above 5,000 ft. offer good opportunities.

Snowmobiling: Whisky Trail (9 mi.); Tamarack Ridge Trail (3 mi.); Red Mountain Trail (9 mi.). Snowmobiles prohibited in Wilderness Areas.

Publications

Forest map, $3.25.

Ansel Adams Wilderness map, $3.25.

Recreation Guide.

Leaflets for John Muir, Ansel Adams, Kaiser Wildernesses. Recreation guides for Huntington, Bass, Redinger, Shaver Lakes. Trail guide for the South Fork, Merced River.

Whisky Snowmobile Trail (leaflet).

Checklists of birds, mammals.

Off-Road Travel Plan.

Headquarters

U.S. Forest Service, 1600 Tollhouse Rd., Clovis, CA 93611-4809; (209) 297-0706, ext. 4925.

Ranger Districts

Kings River R.D., Trimmer Rt., Sanger, CA 93657; (209) 855-8321. Mariposa R.S., Oakhurst, CA 93644; (209) 683-4665. Mariposa R.S., Mariposa, CA 95338; (209) 966-3638. Ansel Adams R.D., North Fork, CA 93643; (209) 877-2218. Pineridge R.D., Prather, CA 93651; (209) 855-5360.

Stanislaus National Forest

U.S. Forest Service
899,894 acres of Forest land; 1,089,967 acres within boundaries.

Bounded by Eldorado National Forest on the N, Toiyabe National Forest and Yosemite National Park on the E, Sierra National Forest on the S. Crossed by Hwys 4, 108, 120. Hwy 140 and the Merced River are the boundary with the Sierra National Forest.

On the W slopes of the Sierra Nevada, a rugged, mountainous region deeply cut by the canyons of the Merced, Tuolumne, Stanislaus, and Mokelumne Rivers. Elevations from 1,100 ft. to 11,570 ft. at Leavitt Peak. The Forest is the nearest high country to San Francisco. This, together with the crossing roads, makes it one of the most heavily used National Forests. The heaviest use occurs in summer, in recreation areas on and near these paved roads.

The most heavily used area is at Pinecrest and Strawberry, communities within the Forest on Hwy 108. Several resorts are here. The Forest Service has two campgrounds with a total of 300 sites. A lake about 1 mi. long offers swimming and boating. Winter sports centers are nearby. Hwy 108 E of here is closed in winter.

A somewhat similar development is at Lake Alpine on Hwy 4: a lake about 1 mi. long, Forest campgrounds, resorts, winter sports areas.

Cherry Lake, about 4 mi. long, largest in the Forest, has much less development. Boats can be launched at the S end. A Forest campground has 48 sites. Most of the lakeshore is roadless.

The Sierra Crest includes a succession of peaks over 9,000 ft. elevation, several of them over 11,000 ft. The slopes are drained by 810 mi. of streams. Many small lakes are in glacial bowls above 8,000 ft. From Sonora Pass S to Cherry Lake, the Crest is the boundary of the Emigrant Wilderness. The largest concentration of small lakes is in the Emigrant Basin area.

N of Sonora Pass, the NE sector of the Forest is mountainous and largely roadless. The area has fewer lakes, but hikers can find a number of attractive ones, notably the Highland Lakes cluster. Good trails follow several stream valleys. Hikers should be aware that several of these are open to trail bikes.

Annual precipitation ranges from 30 in. in the foothills to 50 in. in the high country. Most of the latter falls as snow. Summers are dry. Although summer thunderstorms are common in the high country, the alpine zone receives little or no moisture in the summer months.

Plants: Vegetation ranges from valley oak woodland to the alpine zone. Forested areas are mostly between 3,000–8,000 ft. Principal tree species are ponderosa, Jeffrey, lodgepole, and sugar pines, red and white firs, incense cedar. Broadleaf species include black oak and canyon live oak in suitable habitats. Streamside species include bigleaf maple, white alder, willows, mountain dogwood, black cottonwood. Understory includes greenleaf manzanita, deer brush, buck brush, bear clover, mountain mahogany, gooseberry, ceanothus, snowberry.

Wildflowers include striped coralroot, orchid, false Solomon's seal, prince's pine, rattlesnake orchid, harebell, heartleaf arnica, Indian pink, wild peony, eriogonums, waterleaf phacelia, fireweed, bear grass.

Wildflowers of the mountain meadows include monkeyflower, shooting star, geraniums, penstemons, sneezeweed, camas, lupine, elephant's head, starworts, marsh marigold, blue-eyed Mary, aster. Plant growth in the alpine zone is limited not only by harsh winter conditions but by lack of moisture in summer. Species adapted to such severe conditions include alpine fescue, alpine paintbrush, Sierra primrose, mountain sorrel, phlox, draba, alpine lupine, alpine columbine, dwarf daisy.

Birds: Checklist available. Common or abundant species include turkey vulture, sharp-shinned, red-tailed, and Cooper's hawks, kestrel, California and mountain quail, band-tailed pigeon, white-throated swift, hummingbirds, belted kingfisher, woodpeckers, black phoebe, western wood pewee, swallows, Clark's nutcracker, mountain chickadee, plain titmouse, common bushtit, nuthatches, dipper, varied and hermit thrushes, western bluebird, Townsend's solitaire, ruby-crowned kinglet, warblers, finches, pine siskin, sparrows, western tanager.

Mammals: Checklist available. Common species include various shrews and bats, pika, jackrabbits, cottontail, marmot, ground squirrels, chipmunks, gray squirrel, chickaree, northern flying squirrel, mice, kangaroo rat, wood rats, porcupine, gray fox, coyote, black bear, raccoon, weasel, striped skunk, bobcat, mule deer.

Reptiles and amphibians: Checklist available. Common and abundant species include California newt, ensatina, California slender and arboreal salamanders, western toad, Pacific tree frog, bullfrog, lizards, garter snakes, western ringnecked snake, racer, gopher snake, common and California mountain kingsnakes, western rattlesnake.

Features

Emigrant Wilderness: 112,191 acres. Trailheads near Hwy 108 on the N, Cherry Lake on the S, various Forest roads on the W. Elevations from 5,200 ft. at Cherry Creek to 11,570-ft. Leavitt Peak. Most trails are closed by snow until July. Winter snows often begin in Oct. A scenic area: rocky domes, deep granite-walled canyons, many high lakes, miles of rushing streams. Deer Lake, Wood Lake, and Emigrant Lake are popular destinations, heavily used. Less heavily used are trails from the Hells Mountain–Bourland Mountain area N of Cherry Lake to destinations such as Chain of Lakes in the SW sector. Wilderness permits are required for all-day or overnight trips.

Mokelumne Wilderness: 49,561 acres, of which 9,097 acres are in the Stanislaus, the larger part in the Eldorado National Forest. N of Hwy 4. Trails N from Lake Alpine and other points. The area is dominated by 9,332-ft. Mokelumne Peak and is bisected by the canyon of the SW-flowing Mokelumne River. Many small lakes are in the shallow valleys N of the peak. Area use is light to moderate, heaviest on trails from Lake Alpine and at such destinations as Camp Irene and Fourth of July Lake. Portable stove needed. Stock feed must be carried in. Wilderness permit required for all-day or overnight hikes.

Carson-Iceberg Wilderness: 182,000 acres in the Stanislaus and Toiyabe National Forests. In the NE sector, between Hwys 4 and 108, straddling the Sierra Crest. Topography ranges from flat streams to steep, jagged cliffs. Elevations from about 6,000 to over 12,000 ft. At least 12 peaks over 12,000 ft. Steep ridges, narrow valleys, granite peaks and boulders. Striking volcanic formations. The East Fork of the Carson River, Clark Fork of the Stanislaus, and the Mokelumne River have their headwaters here. Carson Falls, with an 80-ft. drop, is a landmark. Long valleys with meadows are found in several places. Mixed conifer forest up to the timber line. About one-fourth of the area is alpine, with little vegetation. Portions of this area, at 6,000–7,000 ft., become snow-free sooner than trails in the Emigrant Wilderness, permitting access as early as May 15.

The Tuolumne River is part of the Wild and Scenic Rivers System. The river flows form Yosemite National Park, entering the Stanislaus National Forest just N of the road to the Hetch Hetchy Reservoir. It flows generally westward through the Forest, exiting between the towns of Tuolumne and Groveland. Two Forest campgrounds, Lumsden and Lumsden Bridge, are on the river, on a steep unimproved road.

Calaveras Big Trees State Park: 6,500 acres. A fine grove of giant sequoias, within the Stanislaus National Forest (see entry zone 4). Many visitors stop at the State Park, especially when the road beyond is wet and muddy.

Dardanelles Cone and *Columns of the Giants* are impressive volcanic formations seen from Hwy 108.

Interpretation

Interpretive programs are limited to the Summit Ranger District, crossed by Hwy 108.

Campfire programs are offered July 2–Sept. 6, Mon., Wed., and Fri., at the Pinecrest amphitheater. Programs are offered on Tues. and Sat. evenings at the Sand Flat amphitheater.

Guided tours are offered in the same season, daily except Sun., departing mornings from the Summit ranger station.

Nature trails are at 7 locations in the district: Beardsley Lake, Eagle Meadow Rd., Donnell Vista, Pinecrest School, Pigeon Flat Campground, Herring Creek, and Pinecrest ranger station.

Activities

Camping: 27 campgrounds, 943 sites. Earliest season opening: April 1. Latest: July 1. Most close Oct. 1 or 15; latest closing: Nov. 15. Pinecrest, with 200 sites, requires reservations by DESTINET May 24–Sept. 10.

Hiking, backpacking: 750 mi. of trails. Linked with the trail systems of Eldorado, Toiyabe, and Sierra National Forests, Yosemite National Park.

Hunting: Bear, deer, grouse, quail, rabbit.

Fishing: Golden, rainbow, brook trout in many high lakes. Rivers and lakes stocked with Kamloops rainbow, kokanee, brown trout. Some lakes and streams lightly fished.

Swimming: Supervised only at Pinecrest. Elsewhere as you choose.

Boating: Ramps on Lake Alpine, Beardsley Reservoir, Pinecrest, Cherry Lake. 20-mph limit at Pinecrest and Alpine. Rentals at Pinecrest.

Canoeing, kayaking: White water on Stanislaus and Tuolumne Rivers. Rapids to class IV and V seasonally. Get information.

Horse riding: Forest HQ will supply list of packers. Many trails are suitable for horse travel. In some areas it is necessary to carry feed.

Skiing: Ski areas at Dodge Ridge, near Pinecrest, and Mount Reba, near Lake Alpine.

Ski touring: Winter sports areas near Pinecrest. Ski touring and snowshoeing on many trails. Map available.

Snowmobiling: Map of trails available.

Publications

Forest map, $1.00.

Checklists of birds, fish, mammals.

Leaflets for Emigrant and Mokelumne Wildernesses.

Lake Alpine Recreation Area (leaflet).

Off-Road Vehicle Plan.

Snow Mobile and Ski Trails map.

Headquarters
U.S. Forest Service, 19777 Greenley Rd., Sonora, CA 95370; (209) 532-3671.

Ranger Districts
Calaveras R.D., P.O. Box 500, Hathaway Pines, CA 95232; (209) 795-1381. Groveland R.D., P.O. Box 709, Groveland, CA 95321; (209) 962-7825. Mi-Wok R.D., P.O. Box 100, Mi-Wuk Village, CA 95346; (209) 586-3234. Summit R.D., Star Rt., Box 1295, Sonora, CA 95370; (209) 965-3434.

Toiyabe National Forest; Sierra Front Division
U.S. Forest Service

Approximately 1.4 million acres, including acreage administered by Lake Tahoe Basin Unit.

On the CA-NV border between Reno and Mono Lake. Crossed by I-80, US 395, US 50, various CA and NV routes.

Largest National Forest in the lower 48, the Toiyabe is one of the most scattered and diverse. In CA, a small block N of Lake Tahoe is described in the entry for Tahoe National Forest. This entry describes a block lying between Lake Tahoe and Mono Lake, most of the acreage in CA but with significant pieces in NV on the E side of Lake Tahoe and farther S.

The Sierra Front is the E slope of the Sierra Nevada, which drops abruptly about 4,000 ft. from the crest to the floor of the Great Basin. Along the crest, this division is bounded on the W by the Eldorado, Stanislaus, and Tahoe National Forests. It is bounded on the S by Yosemite National Park and the Inyo National Forest.

US 395 is the main travel route, roughly paralleling the base of the Sierra for 420 mi., from the Walker Pass turnoff near Freeman Junction N to Susanville. From US 395 the motorist has spectacular views of snow-capped peaks. About 165 mi. of the route are within this portion of the Toiyabe National Forest. From US 395 are routes to the seven historic mountain passes into California. Five of these routes are within the Toiyabe: Donner Summit (I-80), Lake Tahoe–Echo Summit (US 50), Carson Pass (Hwy 88), Ebbetts Pass (Hwy 4), and Sonora Pass (Hwy 108).

The area just N of Donner Summit, extending to Beckwourth Pass, is known locally as the Dog Valley area. South of I-80, the Carson Range forms the barrier containing Lake Tahoe. Mount Rose is the only peak higher than 10,000 ft. The Mount Rose Hwy (NV 27) is a short, winding, cross-mountain road providing access to two ski areas and spectacular views.

Moving S, the next 70 mi. of the Sierra Front are in CA, about half in Alpine County, half in Mono County, extending to Yosemite NP. Toiyabe National Forest land extends E of US 395 into NV around the Sweetwater Mountains, which have several peaks over 11,000 ft.

The Sierra Front is a popular recreation area. It has 30 peaks over 10,000 ft., 4 of them over 11,000 ft. The peaks are separated by deep canyons and valleys, sometimes green and lush, sometimes barren and rocky, nearly always with perennial streams. In the course of a planning study, the Forest Service rated the scenic qualities of various settings. An exceptional number here received the highest (A) rating. Included were all the wilderness areas described in this section. Also the areas around Ebbetts Pass, the Raymond-Reynolds Peak, the Markleeville-Hawkins Peak high country, the lake country at the head of Pleasant Valley, and the crest from the Nipple N to the Freel-Jobs Peak complex. The A rank was also given to a number of valleys and canyons: the E and W forks of the Carson River; Silver King, Wolf, Pleasant Valley, Sawmill, Hot Springs, and Red Lake Creeks; and Horsethief Canyon.

Annual precipitation varies from less than 10 in. at low elevations to as high as 70 in. in the upper regions, where about 80% falls as snow. Hwys 4 and 108 are closed by snow each winter.

Although few roads cross the crest, dead-end roads penetrate at least partway into a number of the canyons, and recreation sites are clustered along these.

Plants: As in many other parts of the Sierra, the high alpine meadows and sparsely vegetated rocky areas are the least altered. Most of the timbered land was logged by 1900. Many areas have burned. Heavy grazing checked the regrowth of trees. Areas of sagebrush and chaparral expanded. Under Forest Service management, trees have reestablished.

Vegetation zones are exceptionally well marked on the Sierra Front, starting from sagebrush and grasses dominating the foothills, pinyon pine and juniper in the montane zone. Above this zone are ponderosa, Jeffrey, and lodgepole pines, Douglas-fir, incense cedar, mountain hemlock, red fir, some western white pine. Shrubs include waxberry, pinemat manzanita, mountain big sagebrush, antelope bitterbrush. Alpine vegetation occurs above 10,000 ft.

Birds: Information was available here associating bird species with habitats. Examples: *Riparian:* common nighthawk, yellow-bellied sapsucker, hairy woodpecker, belted kingfisher, violet-green swallow, western wood pewee, Swainson's thrush, dipper, vireos, warblers. *Rock and cliff:* golden eagle, red-tailed hawk, cliff swallow, rock wren, rosy finch. *Mountain meadow:* western bluebird, alder flycatcher, American goldfinch, western meadowlark, poor-will, spotted sandpiper, yellow-throated warbler, Lincoln's sparrow. *Alpine meadow:* mountain bluebird, rosy finch, dark-eyed junco, horned lark, Clark's nutcracker, golden-crowned sparrow, rock wren. *Mountain chaparral:* red-tailed hawk, mountain quail, calliope hummingbird, dark-eyed junco, rufous-sided towhee, western bluebird, lazuli bunting, MacGillivray's warbler, fox and lark sparrows. *Jeffrey pine–white fir:* golden eagle, mountain quail, Williamson's sapsucker, woodpeckers, northern flicker, flycatchers, Townsend's solitaire, pine siskin, western tanager, nuthatches, mountain chickadee, dark-eyed junco, kinglets, grosbeaks, warblers, fox sparrow.

Mammals: Include mice, dusky shrew, pocket gophers, ground squirrels, marmot, raccoon, beaver, muskrat, pine marten, pika, spotted skunk, short-tailed weasel, porcupine, black bear, coyote, bobcat, mountain lion, mule deer.

Features

Carson-Iceberg Wilderness: 182,000 acres in the Toiyabe and Stanislaus National Forests. Elevations from 6,000 to over 12,000 ft. Steep ridges, narrow valleys, granite peaks and boulders, jagged cliffs. Striking volcanic formations. The East Fork of the Carson River has its headwaters here. Carson Falls, 80-ft. drop, is a landmark. Seven small lakes. Springs of carbonated, mineralized water in the Silver King drainage and lower reaches of Poison Creek. Heavy use by backpackers, horse-packers, and fishermen in summer, concentrated along streams, especially Silver King and Wolf Creeks. 45 mi. of the Pacific Crest Trail. Hwy 4 is the N boundary.

The *Carson River* is protected under the National Wild and Scenic Rivers Act. The West Fork flows into NV past Woodfords, the East Fork past Markleeville. Canoeing and rafting on the East Fork are popular.

Hoover Wilderness: 100,000 acres, including 9,000 acres within the Inyo National Forest. The Hoover is on the N boundary of Yosemite NP, and many who enter it from the N and E cross into Yosemite's high country. The wilderness is a narrow border for the Park, nowhere more than 5 mi. wide, not much over 1 mi. at its narrowest point. Elevations range from 7,700 to 12,596 ft. The Sawtooth Ridge forms a portion of the E boundary. Prominent peaks include Matterhorn, Twin, Crown Point, Eagle, Dunderberg, Excelsior, Hawksbeak, and Black. The Matterhorn area has five remnant glaciers. The area is characterized by U-shaped canyons. Canyon bottoms commonly have extensive flats with shallow streams and grassy meadows. The six major drainages are Little Walker River, Molybdenite Creek, Buckeye Creek, Robinson Creek, Green Creek, and Virginia Creek. The area has nearly 60 lakes.

Trails generally cross the wilderness, rather than running its length. More extensive hiking is available along the W Walker River and several canyons. Trailheads and pack stations are mostly on the E side, at Twin and Virginia Lakes, Green Creek, and Leavitt Meadows.

Vegetation zones are similar to those of the NW sector, but most of the Hoover Wilderness is high country, much above timberline. Scattered stands of timber grow on little more than 10% of the area. Mixed conifers with Jeffrey pine and white fir predominate in the lower elevations. Higher up: lodgepole pine with red fir, limber pine, western hemlock, western white pine, western juniper. Small subalpine meadows are associated with some lakes and larger streams. Unfortunately, these are attractive to visitors as campsites and are also extremely fragile.

Average annual precipitation is 25–30 in., most of it as snow. Some high country trails are closed by snow into June or early July. The recreation season is usually June 15–Oct. 1.

Many visitors camp at one of the several campgrounds just outside the wilderness boundary, entering only for day hikes. Of those who stay overnight, backpackers outnumber horsepackers 20 to 1. Heavy use has become a matter of concern.

Part of the *Mokelumne Wilderness,* 16,500 acres, is also located within Toiyabe. (The remaining 38,500 is administered by the Eldorado National Forest, see entry zone 4.) This section includes 45 mi. of trails, through canyon and stream bottoms, to alpine ridgetops. It is rugged and spectacular mountain country. Wildlife includes mule deer, black bear, coyote, bobcat, mountain lion, and beaver. Birds include blue grouse, mountain quail, red-tailed hawk. The lakes hold rainbow, cutthroat, golden brown, and brook trout.

Lake Tahoe area. The Forest map shows a few scattered bits of land on and near the E side of Lake Tahoe, in NV. The map of Lake Tahoe Nevada State Park, which adjoins Forest land, shows additional tracts.

Several tracts are on or near NV 431, which crosses the Carson Range, from the NE edge of Lake Tahoe to Mount Rose Junction on US 395. Mount Rose, 10,778 ft., is the highest point. A number of ski areas are on this route. The 24-site Mount Rose campground opens about June 15. There are hiking trails on the mountain.

US 50 turns inland from the lake at Glenbrook, crossing a block of Forest land. Kings Canyon Rd., SW from Carson City, also enters this area. The Clear Creek campground has 14 units, opens about June 1.

Nevada Beach is a small fragment of Forest land on the lakeshore about 1 mi. N of the CA line. ½-mi. beach. 60-site campground.

Excelsior Mountains. On the CA-NV border, crossed by NV 359. This irregularly shaped area is about 25 mi. N-S, 18 mi. W-E, adjoining a block of Inyo National Forest land in CA. Almost all of the area S and E of NV 359, plus adjoining Inyo National Forest land, is a 160,000-acre roadless wilderness area. Elevations from about 6,000 ft. to several peaks over 9,000 ft. Annual precipitation is less than 12 in. Thunderstorms often cause flash floods. Rugged hills, including the SW portion of the Excelsior Mountains. Steep cliffs, ridges, slopes, canyons, dry lakebeds. Vegetation is mostly pinyon-juniper; sagebrush-bitterbrush flats. Scattered dry and wet meadows, the latter dependent on springs. Wildlife includes sage grouse, mule deer, pronghorn, wild horse.

Portions of the area are much used for ORV activity. All motorized equipment is excluded from the wilderness area, which has been lightly used.

Activities

Camping: 20 campgrounds, 549 sites. Most are open May–Oct., several not open until June.

Hiking, backpacking: Extensive trail system. Wilderness permits required for Hoover Wilderness.

Hunting: Deer, upland game birds.

Fishing: Prior to settlement, the lakes were barren, and Lahontan cutthroat trout inhabited some streams. Extensive and varied stocking has since occurred, with mixed results. Several trout species are now common. Some lakes are overfished, a few underfished.

Boating: Twin Lakes, Trumbull Lake.

Canoeing, rafting: East Fork, Carson River.

Skiing: Two developed ski areas: Mount Rose, Heavenly Valley.

Ski touring: No groomed trails, but some naturally fine areas.

Publications

Hoover Wilderness map, $3.25.

Carson Ranger District map, $3.25.

Carson-Iceberg Wilderness map, $3.25.

Bridgeport Ranger District map, $3.25.

Headquarters

U.S. Forest Service, 1200 Franklin Way, Sparks, NV 89431; (702) 331-6444.

Ranger Districts

Bridgeport R.D., P.O. Box 595, Bridgeport, CA 93517; (619) 932-7070.
Carson R.D., 1536 S. Carson, Carson City, NV 89701; (702) 882-2766.

Yosemite National Park

U.S. National Park Service
760,917 acres.

From San Francisco and points N, Hwy 120. From the S, Hwy 41. Only access from the E is Hwy 120 over Tioga Pass, a steep, winding, 2-lane road, closed in winter.

One of the first and greatest U.S. National Parks, Yosemite has also been one of the first to experience the problems of overcrowding. The acute problems have been in Yosemite Valley. For many visitors, especially those from outside CA, the valley is Yosemite, although it occupies only 7 of the Park's 1,200 sq. mi. Over the years, far too much development was permitted in the valley: more than 1,000 buildings, 30 mi. of roads, large parking areas, a golf course. In summer, over 1,500 employees live in the valley, most of them employees of concessioners. More than a million vehicles a year travel on the valley roads.

The situation became intolerable: traffic jams, campgrounds termed "outdoor slums," damage to vegetation, visitor misbehavior. Several years of study and public hearings yielded plans for change: 90% of the Park's area to become wilderness, free from development; removal of most staff housing, warehouses, offices, etc., from the valley; more public transportation to limit use of private cars in the valley; abandoning the golf course and some other facilities; eliminating some parking lots. Commercial interests objected to some proposals. Conservationists argued for stronger measures. Successive versions of the plan have been modified, and the present outlook is uncertain. Some changes have been made. A reservation system eliminated long waiting lines at campgrounds. A few roads have been closed to autos, others make one-way.

To enjoy the valley, don't come on summer weekends or holidays. We last visited in April and thought it the best time of year. Campgrounds were less than a quarter full. Waterfalls were at their best; many go dry in summer. Wildflowers were dazzling. Some trails had numerous hikers, but we found others untraveled. But April is not the time for the high country. The backpacking season often begins in June but in some years the trails are not snow-free until early or mid-July.

Yosemite as a whole is a land of scenic wonders. On the gentle western slope of the Sierra Nevada, the average grade is only 2.5%. Terrain is mountainous, with peaks, domes, and deep, glacier-carved canyons. Elevations range from 2,127 to over 13,000 ft. Annual precipitation ranges from 36 in. in the valley to about 50 in. at Snow Flat, elevation 8,700 ft. Summers are hot and dry, winters moist and cool.

The Park is entirely surrounded by National Forests: the Stanislaus, Toiyabe, Inyo, and Sierra. It is crossed by a single road, Hwy 120, from the Big Oak Flat entrance on the W to the Tioga Pass entrance on the E. Tioga Pass is closed in winter—a season that here can extend beyond June. Outside the valley the only other roads are Hwy 41, entering from the S; a spur from Hwy 41 to Glacier Point, closed in winter beyond Summit Meadow; Hwy 140, entering on the W by way of Merced and Mariposa; and a spur road from Hwy 120 to the Hetch Hetchy Reservoir. Construction of the Hetch Hetchy Dam was bitterly opposed by conservationists in a fight they lost in 1913. The defeat did much to promote establishment of the National Park Service and the principle that National Parks should be inviolate—a principle once again being challenged.

Most of the high country is roadless. An area of 704,624 acres, 94.45% of the Park, has been given wilderness status. This backcountry is accessible only by foot or horse in summer, by ski or snowshoe in winter. Overnight use is regulated by permit, and the number of permits is subject to tailhead quotas.

Plants: Plant communities include chaparral, mixed conifer, giant sequoia, red fir, lodgepole pine–subalpine, and alpine. Chaparral covers less than 20,000 acres at the lowest elevations. The mixed conifer community extends to about 6,500 ft., covering about one-fifth of the Park. Prominent tree species of this zone are ponderosa and sugar pine, incense cedar, Douglas-fir, and white fir. At three locations are groves of giant sequoias, notably the Mariposa Grove near the S entrance. From about 6,500–8,000 ft. is the red fir community, covering almost one-quarter of the Park. Pure stands of red fir are common, but most of this forest includes Jeffrey pine and lodgepole pine.

By far the largest plant community, covering two-fifths of the Park, is the lodgepole pine–subalpine association. Here, below timberline, are western white pine, western juniper, whitebark pine, mountain hemlock, with some pure lodgepole stands.

What makes the Yosemite forests so unique and impressive is their pristine quality. Almost none of the Park acreage has ever been logged, but a few areas do show marks of recent severe fires.

Between 7,000–10,000 ft. are mountain meadows with countless wildflowers. Spring in the high country comes in July and lasts only 7 to 9 weeks. During this time, many species bloom simultaneously. Lemmon's paintbrush appears in vivid magenta patches in Tuolumne Meadows. Buttercup and bright pink shooting stars are early bloomers. In the higher meadows, large blue lupine, lavender asters, forget-me-nots, and yellow wallflowers are prominent. About 1,500 plant species have been identified.

Birds: 223 species have been identified. Checklist available. Seasonally common or abundant species include band-tailed pigeon, black and white-throated swifts, northern flicker, acorn woodpecker, Hammond's, dusky, and olive-sided flycatchers; violet-green swallow, Steller's jay, western wood pewee, Clark's nutcracker, mountain chickadee, red-breasted nuthatch, brown creeper, golden-crowned kinglet. Orange-crowned, Nashville, yellow-rumped, black-throated gray, and hermit warblers. Also western tanager, black-headed grosbeak, Cassin's finch, pine grosbeak, gray-crowned rosy finch, dark-eyed junco, chipping, white-crowned, fox, Lincoln's, and song sparrows.

Mammals: No checklist available. 80 species recorded. Species often seen include raccoon, mule deer, black bear, marmot, gray squirrel, Belding ground squirrel, coyote. Present but seldom seen: mountain lion, wolverine, fisher, pika.

Reptiles and amphibians: No checklist available. About 12 amphibians, 16 reptiles recorded.

Features

Yosemite Valley is so well known and publicized that description of its features would be redundant. They include Yosemite Falls, Bridalveil Fall, El Capitan, Half Dome, Sentinel Rock, Cathedral Rocks, Mirror Lake, The Three Brothers, Washington Column, the Merced River. The Happy Isles Trail Center, served by free shuttle bus, is a high country trailhead and provides trail information.

Glacier Point overlooks the valley. The road from Summit Meadow is closed in winter. There is hikers' bus service daily from late spring through autumn. Fee.

Tuolumne Meadows, at 8,600 ft., is the largest subalpine meadow in the High Sierra, bordering the Tioga Road, Hwy 120. The campground here is the one nearest to Tioga Pass. A popular base for day hikes and backcountry travel. There is hikers' bus service daily to Tuolumne Meadows from the valley, late June through Labor Day. Fee. Also free shuttle bus service from Tioga Pass to Tenaya Lake.

High Sierra Camps spaced a day apart in the high country offer spectacular views, beds, and meals. Space is on a lottery system; contact the Park for fees and information.

Tuolumne Grove, one of the three groves of giant sequoias, is near the Big Oak Flat entrance, on Hwy 120 W. *The Grand Canyon of the Tuolumne River* is a mile-deep gorge. Waterwheel Falls, near the head of the canyon, is most spectacular in the days just after the hiking season opens. The falls and canyon are about a 6-mi. hike from the nearest trailhead on Hwy 120. The trail in the canyon is suitable for foot or horse travel.

The *Hetch Hetchy Valley* was spectacular before the dam was built. A road leads to the O'Shaughnessy Dam parking area, a good trailhead for backpacking into Yosemite's N country.

North of the Tuolumne River is some of the Park's most rugged, least traveled backcountry, almost a third of the Park's area. Terrain ranges from subalpine to alpine. Timberline is at about 9,500 ft. Above that, hikers find stark granite peaks, dwarfed vegetation, shallow meadows. Climatic extremes. Drainages are generally NE–SW, with such streams as Falls, Rancheria, and Return Creeks. Upstream are numerous canyons: Jack Main, Stubblefield, Thompson, Kerrick, Matterhorn, Virginia. Most trails follow stream courses. The region has many small lakes. On its boundaries are the Stanislaus and Toiyabe National Forests, with trail links.

South of the Merced River the landscape is softened by giant sequoias, many species of broadleaf trees, shrubs, and flowered meadows, forms and colors changing with the seasons. Several of the most popular backcountry routes are in this area. One from the Happy Isles Trail Center in the valley follows the Merced River to Merced and Washburn Lakes, then loops S and SW to Wawona. Popular day hikes from Wawona include Chilnualna Falls and Wawona Point.

The *Wawona basin,* 4,012 ft., a few miles beyond the South Entrance and Mariposa Grove, is a developed area with store, campground, and other facilities. Trails to Crescent Lake and backcountry points.

Interpretation

We know of no park with a more complex and comprehensive interpretive program. On entering, obtain the latest issue of *Yosemite Guide,* a newspaper-style bulletin issued seasonally, which lists all current programs and describes new and changed facilities.

Three visitor centers and *four museums* have information, publications, exhibits, slide shows. Information is also available at entrance stations and ranger stations.

Bus and tram tours are offered daily. Valley, all year; Mariposa Grove, 6 months; Glacier Point from the valley, 5 months.

Park naturalists are present all year, currently 30 of them in summer, 14 in winter.

Campfire programs are offered daily, at several locations in summer, in the valley in winter. Notices posted throughout the Park.

Guided hikes are also offered daily, with notices posted. Some are brief and easy, others all day. Many have special themes: camera walks, snowshoe walks in winter.

Nature trails are at numerous locations, including Mariposa Grove, Cooks Meadow, Tuolumne Grove, Olmstead Point.

Many special programs are offered, including programs for the handicapped. Look for announcements.

The Yosemite Institute (P.O. Box 487, Yosemite, CA 95389) offers a variety of courses, seminars, and workshops, including weekend outdoor workshops on such subjects as winter ecology, winter survival, wildflowers, waterfalls, outdoor skills.

The Yosemite Natural History Association (P.O. Box 545, Yosemite, CA 95389) publishes literature and maps.

Activities

Camping: 15 campgrounds, 1,840 sites. All year in Wawona, the valley, and Hodgdon Meadow, summer and early fall elsewhere. Reservations required for the valley year-round, and for Hodgdon Meadow, Crane Flat, and half of Tuolumne Meadows from summer through fall. Other campgrounds on first-come, first-served basis. Reservations can be made through DESTINET (800) 436-7275. Reservations can be made 4 months in advance, on the 15th of the month. Campsites are in heavy demand from May–Sept. From May 1–Sept. 15 camping in the valley is limited to 7 days, as is camping in Wawona, elsewhere limited to 14 days.

Hiking, backpacking: More than 840 mi. of trails. Many short, easy trails for day hikes. Others, some strenuous, into the backcountry. Wilderness permits required for overnight trips. Good trail guides are available for the principal trails.

Fishing: State regulations, plus special Park regulations. Trout are established in 880 mi. of permanent streams. Lakes have been stocked in the past, introducing species exotic to the area; the practice has been discontinued.

Swimming: Streams, unsupervised. Some backcountry lakes.

Canoeing, kayaking: Merced River, in the valley. Tenaya Lake on Tioga Rd.

Horse riding: 635 mi. of suitable trails. 4 stables in the Park, 8 pack stations adjacent to the Park boundary. List of packers available.

Skiing: Ski area at Badger Pass. Usual season: Dec.–April 15.

Ski touring: 500 mi. of trails. Season Dec.–May. Trees and limbs removed from trails; no snow grooming.

Snowmobiling is prohibited.

Pets must be restrained at all times. No pets in backcountry.

Publications

Leaflet with map.

Yosemite Guide (issued seasonally).

Bird checklist.

Hiking in Yosemite.

Fishing Regulations (mimeo).

List of packers (mimeo).

Welcome to the Yosemite Backcountry (leaflet).

Headquarters

National Park Service, P.O. Box 577, Yosemite, CA 95389; (209) 372-0265.

For Recorded Information on Road Conditions, Weather, Camping

(209) 372-0200.

ZONE 7

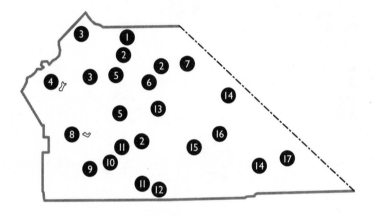

Z O N E

Includes these counties:

Fresno (E portion)   Inyo   Tulare

This zone includes well over a third of the Sierra Nevada Crest. It includes the W foothills and slopes, the E escarpment, Owens Valley, the Inyo Mountains, and, in Death Valley National Park, the Panamint and Margosa Ranges.

Kings Canyon and Sequoia National Parks are its centerpiece, almost entirely surrounded by the Sierra, Sequoia, and Inyo National Forests. Death Valley, with over 2 million acres, is by far the largest site.

Along the crest, Mount Whitney, highest peak in the Lower 48, is within this zone. Many points along the crest are over 12,000 ft., an impressive number of them over 13,000 and 14,000 ft. In this zone, no all-year road crosses the Sierra Nevada. Most of the roads penetrating the Parks and Forests are closed by snow in winter above 7,000 ft. The hiking season in the high country usually begins in June, but sometimes not until July.

Most of the area within the National Parks is roadless and wilderness. Large areas of wilderness are also within the National Forests.

No section of the Sierra Nevada is more heavily impacted by visitors. The W slope is within easy driving distance of San Francisco, Sacramento, Stockton, and other cities. It is almost as easy for residents of the Los Angeles area to drive N into the Owens Valley on the E side of the great mountains. Many trails show signs of overuse, and vegetation around the edges of some mountain lakes has been trampled to death. Quotas are now in effect at many wilderness trailheads, and backpackers must now camp at least 100 ft. away from lakeshores.

Mount Whitney is the highest mountain. Giant Forest in Sequoia NP has the biggest trees. The John Muir Trail may well be the most scenic trail in the state. Badwater, in Death Valley, is 282 ft. below sea level. Such features attract people, and one who follows the crowds can't expect to find solitude. Nonetheless, solitude is easily attained. We found many quiet places no less lovely than the famous ones and never spent a night in a crowded campground.

E of the Sierra, much of the zone is arid or semiarid. The brown tones used to show this area on many maps suggest a region of unrelieved heat and dryness. The landscapes beside many roads across the desert can seem monotonous and forbidding. But increasing numbers of visitors are becoming desert enthusiasts, finding here new kinds of variety in flora, fauna, and personal experience.

Alabama Hills Recreation Lands

U.S. Bureau of Land Management
30,000 acres.

W of US 395 at Lone Pine.

Millions of people have seen this area, the setting for many motion pictures and TV shows. Needless to say, it's scenic. The road from Lone Pine to Whitney Portal, trailhead for Mount Whitney, passes through the area, which lies between the Owens Valley and the Inyo National Forest boundary.

The Alabama Hills are granitic, rounded, highly eroded, resembling giant boulder piles in old southwestern colors. Their appearance contrasts with the sculptured Sierra peaks, and they were once thought to be much older, although they were formed in the same period.

Vegetation is sparse, mostly scattered sagebrush and other desert shrubs. Lone Pine and Tuttle Creeks are perennial water sources. Wildlife includes small game and raptors. Deer and a herd of tule elk inhabit the valley areas.

Movie Flat is about 1 mi. N of the Whitney Portal road. Several graded dirt roads lead to colorful rock formations moviegoers may find familiar. A BLM campground with 85 sites is in the Tuttle Creek area SW of Lone Pine.

Publication

Leaflet.

Headquarters
Bureau of Land Management, Bishop Research Area, 785 N. Main St., Suite E, Bishop, CA 93514; (619) 872-4881.

Chimney Peak Recreation Area; Owens Peak Area

U.S. Bureau of Land Management

This area adjoins the Dome Land Wilderness of Sequoia National Forest. It lies generally N of Walker Pass on Hwy 178. Most of the area is in zone 8, and the entry appears there.

Darwin Falls and Canyon

U.S. Bureau of Land Management
22,400 acres.

From Olancha on US 395, 27 mi. E on Hwy 190. Area is S of Hwy 190, near the town of Darwin, extending to boundary of the Naval Weapons Center.

Waterfalls in the desert always seem dramatic, and this one stops many travelers driving to or from Death Valley. The stream flows all year, supporting thick green vegetation in striking contrast to the surrounding sparse desert shrubs.

There is more to the area than the falls. The Argus Range forms a long, narrow chain E of the area, rising to 8,839 ft. from the valley floor at 2,200 ft. W of the range, the Darwin Plateau is at about 4,000 ft. The plateau is cut by deep chasms, exposing volcanic rock faces. Spring-fed creeks within the canyons create cool, moist, shaded canyon floors. Darwin Falls and China Garden Spring are scenic places where falls and shaded pools are framed by mosses, ferns, and other riparian vegetation. The habitat is highly attractive to wildlife.

Headquarters
Bureau of Land Management, CA Desert District Office, 1695 Spruce St., Riverside, CA 92507; (909) 697-5200.

Death Valley National Park

U.S. National Park Service
3,336,000 acres.

On the NV border, W of Las Vegas. Principal E–W route is Hwy 190.
Hwy 178 from the S joins Hwy 190, as does Hwy 374 from Beatty, NV,
in the NE.

A common concept of Death Valley is that it is a huge waterless
desert, below sea level, baking in the sun, where a flat tire or broken
fan belt can become a fatal accident. The concept is partly right. People have died here, and it is not a place to become careless, especially
off the main roads. But it is also a place of surprising variety and singular beauty.

Two places W of Badwater are 282 ft. below sea level, the lowest
dry-land points in the U.S. The sand dunes near Stovepipe Wells cover
14 sq. mi., the salt flat farther S more than 200 sq. mi. Death Valley
itself is a relatively minor portion of the National Park, a narrow N–S
strip along the dry course of the Amargosa River, 6 mi. across at its
widest point. To the E, the land rises steeply in the Amargosa Range,
with several peaks over 1 mi. high. On the W, the Panamint Range is
even higher, Telescope Peak reaching 11,049 ft. Enough snow and
rain fall on the upper mountain slopes to support forests with juniper,
mountain mahogany, pinyon and other pines. Snow accumulates on
the high peaks, at times in deep drifts, and roads over high passes are
sometimes closed.

The highest temperature of record was 134°F at Furnace Creek. The
average July maximum at this point is 116°. At this same point the
lowest recorded winter temperature on the valley floor was 15° in January. The average minimum for that month is 39°. Small wonder
most visitors to the Park come in winter!

It's cooler upstairs, and the native Indians took to the mountains
in summer. Normally temperatures decline by 3½° to 5° for each 1,000
ft. of elevation. It's cooler at night, too, and many desert wildlife
species remain underground by day, emerging only after the surface
soil radiates away much of its store of daytime heat.

The Park offers many opportunities for hiking and backpacking,
but its size and the long distances between points of interest mean

that most travel is by automobile. The Park has several hundred miles of roads, including unpaved roads suitable for ordinary cars and about 100 mi. of jeep tracks. The first-time visitor should stay on the main routes. There's plenty to see and do along these routes. Backcountry touring is for those who understand the desert and their vehicles and know what to do when things go wrong. Even on the main routes precautions are essential. Gasoline is available at only three places in the Park. Although any decent person will stop to aid a motorist in trouble, it could be hours before a summoned tow truck appears.

The principal centers are around Scotty's Castle, Furnace Creek, and Stovepipe Wells. A typical auto tour of the most popular features covers about 200 mi., plus side trips and the entering and departing mileages. Some of these miles are on steep, winding roads where vehicles over 25 ft. long are not recommended.

Winter temperatures in the valley are pleasant, usually in the 60s or 70s by day, the 40s or 50s at night. Rainfall in the valley is so slight that monthly averages have little meaning. The annual average is less than 2 in. The wettest year of record had about 4½ in. Even so, as in other desert regions, flash floods are a hazard. A summer cloudburst can dump a sudden load of rain in a small area, most of which may run off through a single drainage, sending a wall of water down a dry channel to places where no rain has been seen or suspected. It's wise to be alert whenever a road dips down into such a dry channel.

Plants: With a range of elevations to more than 11,000 ft., the Park has numerous plant communities. Botanists have identified some 20 plant species here that grow nowhere else. The salt flats are nearly barren. One would have to look closely to find any of the primitive, inconspicuous algae and fungi that live marginal existences here. On the perimeter, pickleweed and saltgrass grow, plants with a peculiar adaptation: they require much moisture, but they are salt tolerant.

Beyond the salt flats are zones of desert plants: creosote, mesquite, shadscale, arrowweed, rabbitbrush, sagebrush, burrobrush, desert tea, and various cacti, notably beavertail, cholla, and cottontop. On the mountain slopes are pinyon pine and juniper. Species occurring in scattered locations include Joshua tree and tamarisk.

The desert wildflower display is unpredictable. It may occur between Nov. and March, most often after early Jan. Temperature and moisture conditions must be just right for seeds to germinate. On one of our visits, conditions seemed right but the display was thin; botanists told us that conditions had been optimum for several previous years and the seeds required resting time. Even this thin display was rewarding, however, and in peak years great carpets of blooms, over 100 species, cover the desert floor.

Birds: Death Valley would not be our first choice for a birding expedition, but there are birds here. Indeed, the checklist has an astonishing 258 species, plus 74 others considered casual or accidental. The list even includes an assortment of waterfowl and shorebirds. Most birds are seen in spring and fall, many fewer in summer and winter.

Mammals: Checklist includes an array of species that have learned to take shelter from daytime heat, as well as species limited to the cooler upper slopes. They include various bats, ringtail, spotted skunk, badger, kit fox, coyote, bobcat, mountain lion, pronghorn, and round-tailed ground squirrels, pocket gophers, kangaroo rats, various mice and rats, porcupine, black-tailed jackrabbit, cottontail, mule deer, and bighorn sheep. Two unwanted species are the wild (feral) horse and burro. The burros, especially, have caused much environmental damage, threatening the existence of other species, but efforts to remove them have aroused controversy.

Reptiles and amphibians: Include red spotted toad, Pacific tree frog, bullfrog, desert tortoise, desert banded gecko, iguana, chuckwalla, other lizard species, western blind snake, desert rosy boa, striped whipsnake, gopher snake, California kingsnake, Panamint rattlesnake, Mojave Desert sidewinder.

Features

Ubehebe Crater near Grapevine, is about 500 ft. deep, ½ mi. in diameter. Smaller craters are nearby. Cinders from past steam and gas explosions cover the surrounding area.

Scotty's Castle is the valley's most publicized feature, site of many legends. Near Grapevine.

Sand dunes, E of Stovepipe Wells, are a popular site for day hikes.

Mosaic Canyon also near Stovepipe Wells, has water-polished marble walls in white, gray, and black.

Telescope Peak, S from Stovepipe Wells, is the highest point in the Park, a stiff hike from trailhead. Ascending the peak in winter requires snow equipment and experience.

Golden Canyon is about 3 mi. S of Furnace Creek. A 1½ mi. nature trail, with guide pamphlet, explains Death Valley geology. Nearby is *Zabriskie Point,* a viewpoint, and a loop dirt road through *Twenty Mule Team Canyon.*

Artists Drive is another loop, on a somewhat better road, through colorful badlands and canyon country.

Badwater, a bit farther S, was once thought to be the lowest point in the U.S. Then a nearby spot was found to be 2 ft. lower.

The *backcountry* offers at least as great variety, with many fewer people. Although some of the unpaved roads can be traveled by an ordinary car, one can visit more areas with greater security in a pickup truck or 4-wheel-drive vehicle. Some of the most fascinating trips are up canyons. The *Phinney Canyon* road tops out at 7,500 ft. *Off-road vehicular travel is banned.*

Additional areas are listed separately because of multiple management; these include: *Darwin Falls, Greenwater Range* and *Valley, Panamint Mountains* and *Valley,* and *Saline Valley,* all also in zone 7.

Interpretation

A *Visitor center, Death Valley Museum,* and *Borax Museum* are at Furnace Creek.

Guided walks are offered daily in winter. Schedules are posted.

Evening programs are presented daily in winter. Schedules are posted.

Walking tours are conducted regularly at Scotty's Castle.

Nature trails are at Salt Creek and Golden Canyon.

Activities

Camping: 9 campgrounds, 1,601 sites. (The largest, Sunset, has 1,000 sites!) Several operate all year. Others, at low elevations, Nov.–April, those at high elevations April–Oct. Campgrounds are crowded on any 3-day winter weekend, the 2nd weekend of Nov., Thanksgiving weekend, Christmas–New Year's week, Easter week.

Hiking, backpacking: Park guides describe many short hikes, plus longer trips. Backcountry travel is fascinating for those who know what they're doing. That means careful choice of season and routes, checking with rangers before departure, knowing how to use map and compass—and having both, carrying sufficient water, having the right gear, and knowing what to do if something goes wrong. The Park has almost 3 million acres of backcountry, some accessible by 4-wheel-drive vehicle, most only to those who travel on foot.

Publications

Leaflet with map.

Checklists of birds, mammals, reptiles.

Mimeo info pages: on the burro problem, road grades, endemic plants, average temperatures and precipitation, hiking Telescope Peak, Mesquite Spring, Ubehebe Crater, ghost towns.

Cacti of Death Valley.

Picture-Taking in Death Valley.

How to Survive Your Summer Trip.

Dirt Road Travel and Backcountry Camping.

Headquarters

National Park Service, Death Valley, CA 92328; (619) 786-2331. Visitor center (619) 786-3244.

Greenwater Range and Valley

U.S. National Park Service

187,900 acres.

Bounded by Hwys 190, 127, 170.

One of the few very large, relatively pristine valleys in the desert region. Most of the area is in natural condition. The valley lies between the Greenwater Range to the E and the Black Mountains, within Death Valley NP, to the W. The Greenwater Range extends about 30 mi. NW–SE, its highest point 5,148 ft. The mountains are rough and irregular, with an eroded break at Deadman Pass, 3,263 ft., where a road once crossed. At Greenwater Canyon, waters have carved a narrow, steep-sided, twisting passage through volcanic rock.

The valley also slopes NW–SE, dropping from about 4,500 to 2,500 ft., much higher than the below-sea-level Death Valley. Valleys and canyons are well vegetated, hillsides sparsely. Creosote is the dominant plant species, with sagebrush, desert holly, prickly pear, bunch grasses, annuals. Quail and chukar populations are good. The range is an important corridor for bighorn sheep. Hiking is cross-country.

Headquarters

National Park Service, Death Valley National Park, Death Valley, CA 92328; (619) 786-2331.

Inyo National Forest

U.S. Forest Service
1,798,638 acres in CA; 60,576 acres in NV.
Lies both E and W of US 395 for over 175 mi. S of Mono Lake.

The Toiyabe National Forest lies to the N. The W boundary adjoins Yosemite NP, Sierra National Forest, Kings Canyon and Sequoia National Parks, and Sequoia National Forest. This boundary is the crest of the Sierra Nevada. In the entire 165-mi. distance N to S, only one road crosses the Sierra: Hwy 120, through Yosemite. It is closed in winter.

Between Mono Lake and Lake Crowley, the Forest includes 11,123-ft. Glass Mountain and the Banner Ridge. A separate, roughly parallel section of the Forest E of US 6 and 395, along the NV border, includes the White Mountains and part of the Inyo Mountains. The Forest sections are divided by the Owens Valley.

W of the valley, the mountains rise in a steep, dominating escarpment up to 2 mi. above the valley floor, a continuous ridge with many peaks over 13,000 ft. Further N, toward Mono Lake, the peaks are not quite as high, and the valley floor is higher than to the S. The pattern of the mountains is more complex, spur ranges extending E.

Mount Whitney, 14,495 ft., is the highest peak in the Lower 48. It is on the boundary of Sequoia National Park, and the last bit of the trail from Whitney Portal is inside the Park.

Winter and summer, this is one of the most heavily used National Forests. US 395 leads directly here from Los Angeles. Backpacking became not only popular but fashionable. So many boots trampled fragile vegetation that a wilderness permit system had to be adopted, with access to certain trails and destinations rationed. The Pacific Crest Trail passes through the area. Best-known locally is the John Muir Trail, longest mountain wilderness trail in the Lower 48, 200 mi. without crossing a paved road. The Forest has 1,150 mi. of trails, as well as many areas where off-trail hiking is feasible. Anyone who wants isolation can find it, especially with help from maps, trail guides, and a ranger. Hikers should bear in mind that they will often

be at elevations of 10,000 ft. or higher and plan progress appropri-
ately. If altitude sickness is suspected, descend immediately to a lower
level.

Much of the moisture blown in from the sea drops on the W side
of the crest. Most of the annual precipitation falls in winter as snow in
the higher altitudes, as much as 40 ft. of snow in some locations.
Between 5,000 and 6,000 ft., annual precipitation is about 12 in. On
the W-facing slopes in the E portion of the Forest, the average is 6–12
in. per year. But sudden, drenching thunderstorms may occur at any
time of the year.

This is enough moisture to supply some 500 lakes in the Forest,
and to feed about 100 streams. S of the Mono Basin, these streams
join in the Owens River, and this water made the Owens Valley attractive to farmers. No longer. The water supply was acquired by the Los
Angeles Department of Water and Power. The flow of the Owens River
has been diverted into concrete ditches. Desert plants now grow on
land that once was farmed.

To visit the Forest, one has little choice other than to take US 395.
Along the way are many side roads, to E and W, some paved, some all-
weather gravel roads, some that—at least at times—require 4-wheel
drive. These side roads lead to busy resorts, lakes, canyon campgrounds, viewpoints, wilderness trailheads.

One effect of the steep escarpment is the quick transition visitors
can make from one climate and life zone to another. In early June
they can stand in snow beside a frozen lake and only a few minutes
later feel the blasting heat of summer sun in the valley below. In so
doing, they will leave the zone of alpine vegetation, where flowers
will soon poke through melting snow, descend through several forest
zones, and arrive in sagebrush desert. The ski areas are usually still
operating at the end of May, sometimes even a month later. Long
before then many trails at lower elevations are snow-free.

Most of the land around Mono Lake and along US 6 N of Bishop is
public domain, administered by the Bureau of Land Management.
The land surrounding Lake Crowley is BLM or Los Angeles land. The
Owens Valley S of Bishop is also part BLM, part Los Angeles land. The
BLM has a large recreation area W of Lone Pine (see Alabama Hills
entry this zone).

Plants: A typical transect down from the High Sierra would pass
through the alpine zone and subalpine forest, across mountain meadows, then down through forests of lodgepole pine, red fir, mixed
conifers, and pinyon woodland to desert shrubs.

Common trees of the E slope of the Sierra include Jeffrey pine, white and red firs, western white pine, lodgepole pine, western juniper. In moister areas: quaking aspen, cottonwood. Because of the wide range of life zones, hundreds of species of flowering plants occur here. Among them: tiger lily, western wall flower, cinquefoil, corn lily, thistle, poppy, evening primrose, pyrola, mariposa lily, monkeyflower, red columbine, mullein, Indian paintbrush, scarlet gilia, shooting star, larkspur, lupine, gentian, fireweed, red and white heathers, rein orchid. The W slopes of the White and Inyo Mountains, across the valley, are dry, with juniper, pinyon, limber, and bristlecone pines, and areas of safebrush-bitterbrush.

Birds: No checklist, but HQ states that 242 species have been recorded. Reported: golden eagle, sharp-shinned hawk, goshawk, pygmy, great horned, great gray, and saw-whet owls, Williamson's and yellow-bellied sapsuckers, pileated and white-headed woodpeckers, blue and sage grouse, pinyon, gray, and Steller's jays, raven, Clark's nutcracker, hermit thrush, mountain bluebird, olive-sided flycatcher, western wood pewee, pine siskin, pygmy nuthatch, brown creeper, mountain chickadee, hermit warbler, dark-eyed junco, fox sparrow.

Mono Lake still supports large numbers of gulls, phalaropes, avocet, plover, sandpipers, and waterfowl. Species of the sagebrush and pinyon-juniper areas include loggerhead shrike, horned lark, western kingbird, nighthawk, black-billed magpie, rufous-sided towhee, kestrel.

Mammals: Species differ from habitat to habitat: white-tailed antelope squirrel and black-tailed jackrabbit in the desert zone, pica on high talus slope, alpine chipmunk near timberline. Species of the area include California and golden-mantled ground squirrels, kangaroo rat, white-tailed jackrabbit, chipmunks, chickaree, cottontail, weasel, marmot, beaver, badger, coyote, black bear, bobcat, mountain lion, mule deer, California and desert bighorn sheep. Tule elk range from Sequoia-Kings Canyon National Park to Owens Valley.

Features

Hoover Wilderness: 48,601 acres, in the extreme N of the Forest, W of Mono Lake, bordering Yosemite NP. About 9,500 acres are in the Inyo National Forest; the larger part is in the Toiyabe. Extremely rugged terrain. Elevations from 8,000 to 13,000 ft. Alpine zone, with little timber. Numerous lakes bordered by meadows. An occasional small stand of aspen or lodgepole pine. Recommended travel period is July–Aug., possibly Sept., but heavy rain, blizzards, extreme cold, and high winds are possible even then. Good trout fishing. The S part, access from the Inyo National Forest, is heavily used, the N part less so, except for the Pacific Crest Trail.

Ansel Adams Wilderness: 107,380 acres, on the border of Yosemite N.P. just S of Hwy 120, about 55% in the Inyo National Forest, the remainder in Sierra National Forest. High country E of the Sierra Crest. Elevations from 7,000–14,000 ft. The Minarets are on the central portion of the divide, W of Mammoth Lakes, in the Ritter Range. The area has many lakes, the largest of them, in the central portion, over a mile long. Crossed by the John Muir and Pacific Crest Trails. Because of its proximity to Mammoth Lakes, this area is heavily used, and quotas are in effect at principal trailheads.

John Muir Wilderness: 499,675 acres, is California's largest wilderness, about 45% in the Inyo National Forest, the larger part in the Sierra National Forest. Extends from the Mammoth Lakes area S along the Sierra Crest, bordering Kings Canyon and Sequoia National Parks, to a point near Mount Whitney. Snow-capped mountains, many lakes and streams. Its general shape is long and narrow, in places only 2 mi. wide. Areas accessible on an overnight trip are heavily used. Quotas in effect at many trailheads.

Golden Trout Wilderness: 302,800 acres, about 55% in Inyo National Forest, the remainder in Sequoia National Forest. Adjoins the S boundary of John Muir Wilderness. On the SE boundary of Sequoia National Park. W portion is a large drainage basin surrounded by high, rugged mountains. E part is an extension of the Kern Plateau. Many mountain streams, flowing into the Kern River. Pacific Crest Trail crosses. Not as heavily used as the other wilderness areas. Quota for entry into the National Park.

Mammoth Lakes is a resort, the most popular place in the Forest. The village in on Hwy 203, at the gateway to much of the Forest's most scenic backcountry. Mammoth Mountain is a popular ski area. A commercial gondola gives summer visitors views of the high country. Nearby are the Devils Postpile National Monument (see entry zone 6), Rainbow Falls, Minaret Vista, trails into the John Muir Wilderness. Above the village is 1 mi.-wide lakes basin. Many Forest campgrounds are nearby. These campgrounds begin opening in late April or early May, some remaining open after Labor Day until closed by snow.

Mount Whitney is not the place to seek solitude. Because it is the highest point in the Lower 48 and has a trail to the top, many people make the trip. Trailhead is Whitney Portal. From there it's 10½ mi., with a 6,000-ft. rise. Some physically fit hikers make the trip in 1 day, but 2 days is recommended. Altitude sickness affects many. Trail use is now limited to 50 people per day, by reservation. Permits are required for overnight stays.

Big Pine Canyon is another popular resort area, on a road W from Big Pine and US 395. The developed area has a lodge, campgrounds, trailheads for the John Muir Wilderness. Pack trains depart from here. *Palisade Glacier* is 7 mi. from the road's end. It is the most S glacier in the U.S. N and S fork trails provide spectacular scenery.

Rock Creek Canyon also has commercial resort facilities and Forest campgrounds. The road S from Toms Place on US 395 is in a corridor penetrating several miles into the John Muir Wilderness. Near its end, at Mosquito Flat, the road reaches an elevation of 10,250 ft., highest road point in the Sierra. The canyon area is popular for ski touring in winter.

Bishop Creek, still another resort area, is on a road 9 mi. SW from Bishop. The road divides, the N branch ending at Sabrina Lake, the S at South Lake, both on the John Muir Wilderness boundary. Popular hiking area.

The *White Mountain area* is on the drier E side of the Forest. A circuit auto tour begins at Big Pine, proceeds NW on Hwy 168, N on Hwys 266 and 264, W and S on US 6, returning to US 395 at Bishop. The 160-mi. loop passes Deep Springs Valley, Fish Lake Valley, viewpoints at Montgomery Pass, and other points of interest.

Ancient Bristlecone Pine Forest: 28,000 acres. Reached by taking Hwy 168 from Big Pine, turning N at Cedar Flat S of Westgard Pass. These bristlecone pines are the world's oldest living things, older, even, than the giant sequoias. High on the rocky slopes of the White Mountains, elevations over 10,000 ft. Many wildflowers. Trails through the groves. No water, gas, or commercial facilities available beyond the town of Big Pine.

Interpretation

Visitor center at Mammoth. *Entrance/information stations* at Bishop Creek, Rock Creek, and Ancient Bristlecone Pine Forest.

Evening programs at the Mammoth Visitor Center and at Schulman Grove in the Bristlecone Pine Forest. Occasionally elsewhere.

Activities

Camping: 82 campgrounds, 2,191 sites. Most are closed in winter, Nov.–May. Some at lower elevations remain open. Reservations required for some campgrounds.

Hiking, backpacking: 1,150 mi. of trails. Permit required to enter any wilderness area, even for a day hike. Quotas in effect at many trailheads. Reservations are taken at ranger stations for wilderness areas. John Muir Trail, Pacific Crest Trail, Mount Whitney Trail, and others are popular. Trail guides and ranger advice can identify lightly traveled areas.

Hunting: Chiefly mule deer, black bear, sage hen, grouse, quail, chukar.

Fishing: Hundreds of lakes and streams, many of them stocked. Rainbow, brook, brown, golden trout.

Swimming: At lakeside campgrounds, or wherever you find suitable water.

Boating: Ramps at larger road-access lakes. Rentals at several resorts.

Horse riding: Outfitters and liveries at several resorts.

Skiing: Mammoth and June Mountains have downhill ski areas. Mammoth's is the largest in CA.

Ski touring: Several popular areas, including trails at Mammoth and June Mountain resorts.

Snowmobiling: Prohibited in wilderness areas. Restrictions apply elsewhere; inquire.

Publications

John Muir Wilderness map (includes 3 maps), $6.00.

Inyo National Forest map, $3.25.

Mammoth trails map, $3.25.

Ancient Bristlecone Pine Forest Guide (in preparation).

Forest Service leaflets for individual hiking or camping areas.

Headquarters

U.S. Forest Service, 873 N. Main St., Bishop, CA 93514; (619) 873-2400.

Ranger Districts

Mammoth R.D., P.O. Box 148, Mammoth Lakes, CA 93546; (619) 924-5500. Mono Lake R.D., P.O. Box 429, Lee Vining, CA 93541; (619) 647-3000. Mount Whitney R.D., P.O. Box 8, Lone Pine, CA 93545; (619) 876-6200. White Mountains R.D., 798 N. Main St., Bishop, CA 93514; (619) 873-2500. Wilderness reservations: (619) 938-1136; (888) 374-3773.

Kings Canyon National Park

See Sequoia and Kings Canyon National Parks (this zone).

Lake Kaweah

U.S. Army Corps of Engineers
1,945 acres of water.

From Visalia, 20 mi. E on Hwy 198.

A flood control project on the Kaweah River. The lake is 5 mi. long and much used for water-based recreation. In the foothills area, chaparral-covered slopes on both sides of the inundated valley. The N side of the lake appears to be roadless. However, the government-owned land is only a narrow strip around the lakeshore. Hwy 198 is a loop route passing through Sequoia National Park and meeting the Kings Canyon National Park access road.

Camping: 80 sites. All year.

Publication
Leaflet.

Headquarters
U.S. Army Corps of Engineers, P.O. Box 44270, Lemoncove, CA 93244; (209) 597-2301.

Mountain Home Demonstration State Forest

California Department of Forestry and Fire Protection
4,807 acres.

From Porterville, NE on CR 137.

A State Forest within the Sequoia National Forest, on the boundary of and a trailhead for the Golden Trout Wilderness. The site has many old-growth giant sequoias, including one specimen 31½ ft. in diameter, 247 ft. tall. Elevations from 5,100–7,200 ft. Annual precipitation about 45 in. A curiosity of the site is its "Indian bathtubs," depressions in granite outcrops 3–5 ft. across, 2–5 ft. deep, their origin unexplained.

Plants: Although the sequoias are protected, this is a working forest: Other species are harvested and planted. Generally a mixed conifer forest with a mixture of black oak. Understory of manzanitas, whitethorn, deer brush, Pacific dogwood, wild gooseberry, blue elderberry, western raspberry.

Birds: No checklist; use checklist for Sequoia National Forest. Mentioned by local staff: blue jay, red-tailed hawk, band-tailed pigeon, woodpeckers, nuthatches, raven, dark-eyed junco, warblers.

Mammals: Generally those found in Sequoia National Forest. Black bears have been a campground nuisance at times.

Interpretation

The *Forest Information Trail* is a *self-guiding nature trail* jointly maintained by CA Dept. of Forestry and Tulare County Parks Dept.

Visitor center at Balch Park.

Self-guided archaeological trail at Sunset Point leads to "Indian bathtubs."

Activities

Camping: 6 campgrounds, 90 sites. May 15–Oct. 15.

Hiking, backpacking: Trailhead for Golden Trout Wilderness.

Hunting: Mule deer, black bear, tree squirrel.

Fishing: Wishon Fork of the Tule River is the largest of several streams. Rainbow and brown trout. 3 ponds stocked with rainbow trout.

Horse riding: Balch Park Pack Station, on the site, has horses for local or wilderness travel.

Ski touring: No maintained trails. Usual season Jan.–April.

Snowmobiling: On roads only. Not in the wilderness area.

Publications

Leaflet with map.

Nature trail guide.

Headquarters
CA Dept. of Forestry and Fire Protection, P.O. Box 517, Springville, CA 93265; summer: (209) 539-2321; winter: (209) 539-2855.

Owens Valley
U.S. Bureau of Land Management and others
On US 395 from Owens Lake N to Bishop.

The valley runs between the Sierra Nevada on the W and the Inyo Mountains on the E. In the past, the Owens River flowed through the valley. Now, from Mono Lake S, part of the water is in an aqueduct, and the City of Los Angeles, which takes the water, owns a corridor of land 1–8 mi. wide down the center of the valley. Diversion of the water has caused disappearance of the green riparian vegetation along the riverbanks, as well as of the associated wildlife. N of Bishop, however, the river environment remains healthy, and recreational opportunities, including fishing, are plentiful.

The Inyo National Forest occupies the E slope of the Sierra, as well as the Inyo Mountains N from a point about 10 mi. N of Lone Pine. Between the Forest boundaries on each side and the Los Angeles land at the Valley's center are two strips of BLM-managed public land.

Some of the BLM lands have been designated Wilderness Study Areas (WSA). Because roads and structures are disqualifying for such study, these study areas are really a number of tracts separated by developments. Often an important factor favoring their designation has been that they adjoin a portion of the Inyo National Forest already designated or potentially designated wilderness. These areas include Independence Creek WSA, NW of Lone Pine on the Forest boundary, part of the broad, alluvial apron of the Sierra Nevada with dense stands of big sage and other shrubs. Also included are Symmes Creek WSA and Crater Mountain WSA. The latter is an interesting volcanic cinder cone landscape, offering hiking and nature study. (The recreation planners at the BLM told us, "We don't want them *just* to read about it. Tell them to come and visit us!")

Headquarters
Bureau of Land Management, Bishop Resource Area, 785 N. Main St., Suite E, Bishop, CA 93514; (619) 872-4881.

Panamint Mountains and Valley

U.S. Bureau of Land Management and U.S. National Park Service
210,000 acres.

On the W side of Death Valley National Park, N and S of Hwy 190.

The lower portion of the Panamints and Panamint Valley, S of Hwy 190, is BLM-managed. The rest of the area is within Death Valley National Park.

Several good roads make this area more accessible than the lands described in the Saline Valley entry. We've included four wilderness areas, two in the Park, and two managed by BLM.

Hunter Mountain: 23,844 acres, 7,454 ft. tall at the junction of the Panamint, Saline, and Death Valleys. The road, unpaved, hazardous in inclement weather, originates at Hwy 190, crosses into the Death Valley NP, and continues N to Ubehebe Crater and Grapevine.

Terrain varies from the flat valley floor to bajada, with sheer smooth walls, jagged rock outcrops, deeply eroded canyons and valleys, plateaus, and coarse mountaintops. Grapevine Canyon, paralleling the Hunter Mountain road, has an abundance of water, supplied by springs high up the slopes. The riparian habitat continues to a thick stand of pinyon pine and juniper on the high slopes. Valley vegetation is mainly creosote and low desert shrubs. Wildlife includes bighorn sheep, mule deer, various small mammals. Birding is said to be good in the N portion. The mountain offers fine views of Mount Whitney and the complete Death Valley area.

Wildrose Canyon Area: 38,900 acres. Just to the S, across Hwy 190, with Panamint Valley Rd. on the W, Wildrose Canyon Rd. on the S. Elevations range from 1,600 ft. on the Panamint Valley floor to 6,200 ft. in the Panamint Mountains. The mountains are cut by deep canyons with gently sloping alluvial fans. In the SE, broken and eroded hills have a badlands appearance. The W half consists of low rolling hills. Creosote and desert holly are the principal vegetation on the fans. Creosote in the canyons is sparse but tall. The slopes have a thin cover of low shrubs.

Panamint Dunes: 93,220 acres, within Death Valley NP. The area includes the N portion of Panamint Valley, elevations ranging from 1,500 ft. at the valley floor to 6,000 ft. in the Panamint Mountains.

The S includes a flat, dry lakebed. Land slopes upward toward the N, where a dune system is developing. The dunes, covering about 6 sq. mi., are isolated, peaked sand hills known as "star dunes," rising as much as 250 ft. above the floor. *Rainbow Canyon,* on the W side of the valley, N of Panamint Springs on Hwy 190, is a steep-sided, bright, colorful area.

Surprise Canyon, an exceptionally scenic 54,400 acres within the Death Valley NP, is designated an Area of Critical Environmental Concern.

The highest point of the Panamint Range is *Telescope Peak,* 11,045 ft. Terrain is mostly rugged mountains and deep canyons, with small, steep alluvial fans emerging from the canyons. A small badlands area is in the NW.

From the county road, a number of stub roads penetrate the canyons, reflecting the history of mining here. At least four of the canyons have flowing springs. The springs maintain riparian vegetation, including several unusual species, among them the Panamint daisy. Birding is good. The alluvial fans have bright seasonal flower displays.

Camping: 3 small campgrounds, 50 sites. Sites begin at Wildrose ranger station and continue to go up the canyon to Mahogany Flat.

A pickup truck or 4-wheel-drive vehicle is needed on the canyon roads.

Headquarters
National Park Service, Death Valley National Park, Death Valley, CA 92328; (619) 786-2331.

Pine Flat Lake
U.S. Army Corps of Engineers
4,000 acres of water (average recreation pool).

From Fresno, about 26 mi. E on Belmont Rd., which turns into Trimmer Springs Rd.

Flood control project on the Kings River. The Kings River canyon is the boundary between the Sierra and Sequoia National Forests, which surround two-thirds of the project area. The lake, much used for water-based recreation, is 20 mi. long, irregular in shape. Boat camping is popular. There is a full-service Marina.

Camping: Island Campground, 112 sites. All year. Deer Creek Campground for groups, May 1–Sept. 30.

Publication
Leaflet.

Headquarters
U.S. Army Corps of Engineers, P.O. Box 117, Piedra, CA 93649; (209) 787-2589.

Saline Valley Area

U.S. National Park Service
700,000 acres.
NV border is the E boundary, Hwy 168 the N. Extends W to the Inyo National Forest. Access by unpaved roads: Eureka Valley Rd., Cucamonga Rd., Saline Valley Rd., Death Valley Rd.

This area is not one to be explored on a Sunday drive. One needs a 4-wheel-drive vehicle, good maps, water, and emergency supplies. Even on one of the named roads, it might be more than a day or two before another vehicle appears. The large central part of the area is roadless. Because the area has wilderness status, ORVs are banned except on roads.

The area has great diversity and many attractive features. Its valleys are ¼ mi. higher than the below-sea-level Death Valley. It includes portions of several mountain ranges, with several peaks over 8,000 ft. With advice and a topo map, a hiker can find his or her way to a canyon with a flowing spring and lush vegetation, and solitude.

Terrain varies from flat to rolling in the N and NE, sloping to the SE toward playas near the Eureka Sand Dunes. The remainder of the area is rolling to steep and mountainous. Elevations range from 1,150 ft. in the SW to 8,674 ft. atop Dry Mountain near the boundary with Death Valley NP. Land forms include flat, white, dry lake; heavily vegetated salt marsh; low rolling hills; sand dunes; rugged mountain ranges; colorful badlands.

This is desert country, where availability of water creates oases with rich plant and animal life. Springs flow in several canyons, notably 8 springs in the canyon separating Eureka and Saline Valleys. The Saline Valley also has 3 mineral hot springs, 2 of them popular recreation sites.

Plants: Vegetation includes Joshua tree–creosote–burrobrush scrub at low elevations to pinyon-juniper woodlands on upper slopes. The Eureka Valley Joshua tree forest is the northernmost large stand of this species. Riparian vegetation, sometimes lush, occurs in canyons. In the marsh, tall cattails and other reedy plants, and a dense growth of catclaw. Spring wildflower displays are often colorful in both Saline and Eureka Valleys.

Birds: Include large numbers of migratory waterfowl. Resident bird species range from those found in Death Valley to those of the Inyo Mountains. Foraging range for golden eagle and prairie falcon, with several eyries.

Mammals: Much of the area is used by bighorn sheep. Large mule deer population. Among the rare species in the valley is the pale kangaroo mouse.

Features

Eureka Sand Dunes Natural Area can be reached by Eureka Valley Rd., which runs S from Hwy 168, about 32 mi. NE of Big Pine on US 395. The area has the largest dunes in CA. The system is about 3 mi. long, 1 mi. wide, rising to 680 ft. The Eureka Valley lies between the White Mountains and the Last Chance Range, at about 3,000 ft. The area has had considerable scientific study, and a number of rare plants have been identified. ORV use of the area has been heavy in recent years, with severe impact on dune vegetation. *The National Park Service now strictly enforces ORV closures.*

Last Chance Mountains: 38,000 acres. Just S of Sylvania Mountains area, between Eureka Valley Rd. and NV border. Mountainous, elevations to 8,456 ft. Many deep canyons. A few springs. An extremely scenic area. Eroding rock formations in Cucamonga Canyon expose strata with bands in many shades of red, yellow, blue, purple. Seasonal range for desert bighorn. Cucamonga Canyon attracts the most visitors.

Little Sand Springs: 33,500 acres. On Death Valley Rd. Contains the W foothills of the Gold Mountain Range, sloping gradually to Death Valley. The foothills are rounded, with many canyons draining to the valley. Big Sand Springs and Little Sand Springs are in the valley. The BLM rates the scenic values "medium."

Waucoba Wash: 11,700 acres. W of the Saline Valley, adjoining a part of the Inyo National Forest. Flat to rolling in the E; rough and mountainous in the W, with deeply cut canyons. Elevations to 7,600 ft. Numerous springs and intermittent streams.

Saline Dunes: 5,800 acres. In the heart of the Saline Valley, surrounded by dirt roads, including Saline Valley Rd., and by relatively flat land. Groundwater and run-off from the Inyo Mountains support dense vegetation, in sharp contrast to the surrounding area. Tall stands of catclaw. Also arrowweed, mesquite, and marsh grasses.

Adjacent BLM Areas

Sylvania Mountains: 15,450 acres. Between Eureka Valley Rd. and the NV border, S of Sylvania Canyon Rd. Rugged mountains dissected by several large washes. Elevations to 7,998 ft. Vegetation mostly shadscale and blackbrush types, with Joshua tree; pinyon-juniper at higher elevations. Canyons have colorful strata.

Piper Mountain: 72,930 acres. W of Eureka Valley Rd. Includes the N end of Eureka Valley and the surrounding mountains, the Inyo Mountains to the N and W. Terrain in SE portion rolling to gently sloping, the remainder rough and mountainous. Highest point is 9,792 ft. Joshua tree woodland near the base of the Inyos. Cottonwood and willow in the canyons. Brush on the valley floor.

Desert bighorn range. Also mule deer, pale kangaroo mouse, western pipistrel bat.

Inyo Mountains: 87,945 acres. On the W side of Saline Valley, between Saline Valley Rd. and the Inyo National Forest. From the S, the Saline Valley Rd. drops sharply through Grapevine Canyon to the valley floor at about 1,000 ft. Beyond the valley, the Inyos rise to about 9,000 ft. Vegetation on the valley floor is chiefly creosote, catclaw, annual grasses, low desert shrubs. Above are dense stands of pinyon and juniper. Grapevine Canyon is fed by numerous springs on the side of Hunter Mountain, forming a stream with lush riparian vegetation. On the high slopes of the Inyos is a stand of bristlecone pine. Very scenic area. Abundant wildlife.

Headquarters

National Park Service, Death Valley National Park, Death Valley, CA 92328; (619) 786-2331. Visitor center (619) 786-3244.

Sequoia and Kings Canyon National Parks

U.S. National Park Service
402,108 acres and 459,995 acres.

To Kings Canyon: Hwy 180 E from Fresno. For Sequoia, turn S from Hwy 180 in Grant Grove area onto Generals Hwy. Or Hwy 198 E from Visalia.

These adjoining Parks are part of the enormous area of public land that encompasses most of the Sierra Nevada. They are almost completely surrounded by National Forests: the Sierra on the W and N, Inyo on the E, Sequoia on the W and S. Within the Parks is a great range of elevations, from about 1,500 ft. to Mount Whitney, at 14,495 ft. the highest peak in the Lower 48. Here is some of the most magnificent scenery of the Sierra: towering granite mountains, sharp ridges, deep canyons, waterfalls and cascades, high mountain lakes, forests of great trees, including the greatest of all, the giant sequoia.

Most of the area is roadless and undisturbed, with many stands of virgin timber. No road crosses the Sierra here. Roads enter the Parks only from the W.

For visitors who see the Parks from their cars, the primary route is Hwy 180 to Grant Grove, a detached bit of Kings Canyon National Park, then by the Generals Hwy through the Giant Forest area of Sequoia NP, continuing SW to Hwy 198.

A single road penetrates the main portion of Kings Canyon National Park: Hwy 180, N and W from Grant Grove to a developed area at Cedar Grove. This road is open in summer only. Generals Hwy from Grant Grove through Sequoia NP, is often closed by snow in winter. From Hwy 198, two roads enter the S part of Sequoia NP: the Mineral King road, open in summer only, and a road along the South Fork of the Kaweah River that ends just inside the Park boundary.

Thus, except in summer the motorist visitor is limited to Grant Grove and the Giant Forest. In April, we found great masses of wildflowers blooming at about 3,500 ft. Patches of snow were just above. From Park HQ at Ash Mountain, near the entrance, the road rises 5,700 ft. in 16 mi., with 230 curves and 24 major switchbacks. The views are splendid, and the road has many turnouts.

Above 5,000 ft. we were in snow. At the Lodgepole visitor center, the elevation is 6,720 ft. Here the snow had been cleared only from the road, a few parking places, and a few walkways. One could camp only by pitching a tent in the snow.

We were not disappointed. Photographs can't portray the awesome size of the great sequoias, and hundreds of them are near the road. The ponderosa and Jeffrey pines are also magnificent here. Rangers told us the backpacking season usually begins in June. We asked about hiking at lower elevations and were told few people do it. We camped at a campground just above 2,000 ft. and hiked all the next day, usually near a rushing stream, on chaparral hillsides, bright with sun and flowers. The Marble Falls Trail climbed 2,000 ft. in the first 3½ mi.

At Ash Mountain, 1,700 ft., winter temperatures range between 32° and 57°F, rarely dropping below 25°. At 6,400 ft., the winter average range is 21°–40°F, with extreme lows below 10°. In the high country, summer days are generally mild and sunny, but afternoon thundershowers are common and night temperatures below freezing are not unusual.

Many visitors never stray far from their cars. From the developed areas, many trails offer opportunities for short or all-day hikes or one-night backcountry trips. Most of the Park area, however, is beyond this range. The long-distance hiker, unlike the motorist, can enter the Park from the N, E, or S. Many do enter from the Inyo National Forest, along the John Muir Trail and by other routes. The Park has a dozen backcountry ranger stations operated mid-June to Labor Day.

Sequoia became a National Park in 1890, the same year as Yosemite. General Grant National Park was also established that year, a small area around Grant Grove. In 1940, Kings Canyon National Park was established, incorporating General Grant NP.

Plants: At elevations below 4,000 ft., chaparral on the lower slopes, blue oak and California buckeye in the valleys and on the higher slopes. In this zone: manzanita, ceanothus, mountain mahogany, live oak, poison oak. Flowering species include lupine, yucca, monkeyflower, bush poppy, blazing star, paintbrush, fiddleneck, popcorn flower, brodiaea, poppy, iris, fiesta flower, baby blue eyes.

From 4,000–9,000 ft., forests of red and white firs, sugar, Jeffrey, and ponderosa pines, incense cedar, and the giant sequoias. Understory species include rabbitbrush, kit-kit-dizze, bitter cherry, mountain mahogany, greenleaf manzanita, serviceberry, wallflower. The giant sequoia occurs only on the W slopes of the Sierra, in scattered sites or groves. The 75 groves each contain from fewer than a dozen to many thousands of individual trees. 80% of the sequoia lands are in public ownership, more than 28% in National Parks. The largest specimen, the General Sherman tree, is in Sequoia NP. It is 2,300–2,700 years old, 275 ft. tall, 36½ ft. in diameter.

Above 9,000 ft. is the high country, an area of lakes and meadows, some open forest, and bare rock. Trees of this zone include whitebark and lodgepole pines, mountain hemlock, foxtail pine. Wildflowers of the mountain meadows include gentians, geraniums, buttercups, shooting star, blue-eyed Mary, elephant's head, alpine aster, camas, penstemons, paintbrushes, lupines, heathers.

Birds: Checklist published by Sequoia Natural History Association. Species in the foothills include California quail, scrub jay, lesser goldfinch, Bewick's wren, wrentit, woodpeckers, brown towhee, ash-throated and dusky flycatchers, Say's phoebe, California thrasher, western bluebird, sparrows. In the forest zone: great horned, flammulated, and spotted owls, goshawk, Cooper's and red-shouldered hawks, northern flicker, woodpeckers, yellow-bellied sapsucker, flycatchers, wood pewee, raven, white-breasted and red-breasted nuthatches, winter wren, hermit thrush, Townsend's solitaire, golden-crowned kinglet, warbling and solitary vireos. Many warblers. Also western tanager, black-headed and evening grosbeaks, purple and Cassin's finches, dark-eyed junco, chipping and Lincoln's sparrows, mountain quail, blue grouse.

Mammals: Species frequently seen include cottontail, ground squirrels, gray squirrel, marmot, black bear, mule deer. Also resident: mountain beaver, mountain lion, bobcat, coyote, chipmunks, pocket gophers, beaver, pika, jackrabbits, porcupine, shrews, bats, ringtail, raccoon, marten, fisher, weasel, wolverine, spotted and striped skunks. A few mountain bighorn in high country.

Reptiles and amphibians: Include California newt, ensatina, slender salamanders, western and Yosemite toads, Pacific tree frog, yellow-legged frogs, western fence and sagebrush lizards, western whiptail, alligator lizards, rubber boa, ring-necked snake, sharp-tailed snake, racers, gopher snake, common and California mountain kingsnakes, garter snakes, western rattlesnakes.

Features

The backcountry is high, with many peaks over 12,000 ft., several over 14,000 ft. Trails often cross high passes, some higher than 12,000 ft. The region has about 1,000 lakes, none large, and many mountain streams. Some of the less difficult trails follow stream valleys. Trailheads are on and at the ends of all access roads. Cedar Grove is a principal trail center. However, many hikers enter the Parks on foot from adjacent National Forests.

Cedar Grove is the center of summer activity in Kings Canyon NP. The access road follows the canyon, on the South Fork of the Kings River. Several campgrounds are on the S side of the canyon. A motor nature trail is on the N side. Hiking trails and overlooks are along the canyon rim. Features such as Zumwalt Meadow and Roaring River Falls are easily reached on foot. The Mist Falls trail is a strenuous all-day hike.

Grant Grove is on Hwy 180, about 40 road mi. W of the main body of the Park. Several famous trees are here, the Centennial Stump, and the basin where giant trees were cut in the early logging era. Several short trails offer easy day hikes. Somewhat longer is the 10-mi. loop to Redwood Canyon, site of one of the finest sequoia groves.

Giant Forest/Lodgepole is the activity center in Sequoia NP. The largest of all the trees is here, but so are many other giants. The area has one campground, a variety of visitor facilities, many trailheads. Many day-hiking opportunities include such features as Moro Rock, a viewpoint, Crescent Meadow, and Sunset Rock, another viewpoint. Conducted tours to *Crystal Cave* in season.

Mineral King was added to Sequoia NP in 1978. It is reached by a narrow, winding road that climbs close to 5,000 ft. in 25 mi. The road, open summer only, has almost 700 curves. Trailers are prohibited. Ranger station is operated Memorial Day–Labor Day. Campgrounds. Many backcountry hikes begin or end here.

Interpretation

Visitor centers are at Grant Grove, Ash Mountain, Foothills, and Lodgepole. Information, exhibits, publications.

Summer evening programs are offered at Lodgepole, Grant Grove, Dorst, Mineral King, and Cedar Grove. Notices posted.

Guided walks are scheduled all year in the big-tree areas, and in summer also at Mineral King and Cedar Grove. *Only weekend snowshoe walks in winter.*

Nature trails *are at several points in the main activity areas.*

Activities

Camping: 14 campgrounds, 1,375 sites. Most are open from Memorial Day until closed by snow in Oct. Potwisha (near the Ash Mountain entrance to Sequoia), Lodgepole, and Azalea campgrounds are open all year. Reservations at Lodgepole only, by Destinet, Memorial Day–Labor Day. Group sites available, summer only, at Dorst Campground.

Hiking, backpacking: About 900 mi. of trails. Wilderness permits required for backcountry travel. Backpackers should have topographic maps, gear suitable for the variety of weather that maybe encountered. Trailhead quotas Memorial Day–Labor Day.

Fishing: Many lakes and streams have brook, brown, rainbow, and golden trout.

Horse riding: Saddle horses and pack animals at Giant Forest, Grant Grove, Cedar Grove, Mineral King. Many pack trips originate on the E side, in the Owens Valley, from the Inyo National Forest.

Ski touring: Marked trails connect the Giant Forest, Wolverton, and Lodgepole areas with scenic points. Trail guide available. Wolverton has a ski touring center with instructors, rentals. Backcountry touring is increasingly popular; check with park rangers before departure. Permit required for overnight trips.

Publications

Leaflet with map.

Checklists of birds, mammals, reptiles, amphibians.

Mimeo info pages: the giant sequoia and the coast redwood, brief history of Sequoia and Kings Canyon National Parks, brief geology, suggested hikes, Bearpaw Meadow Sierra camp and spur trips, trails of Redwood Canyon, Crystal Cave.

Headquarters

National Park Service, Three Rivers, CA 93271; (209) 565-3341. For recorded weather and road information, (209) 565-3351. For backpacking information, (209) 565-3708.

Sequoia National Forest

U.S. Forest Service
1,138,095 acres.

E of the San Joaquin Valley between Visalia and Bakersfield. Access routes include Hwy 190 E from Porterville, Hwy 155 E from Delano, Hwy 178 NE from Bakersfield, Hwy 180 E from Fresno.

At the S end of the Sierra Nevada. From the Kings River on the N to the Kern River and Piute Mountains, near its S boundary. Elevations from 1,000 to 12,000 ft.

The Forest land is in several large units. In the N, a unit adjoins the Sierra National Forest, the Kings River serving as boundary; this unit adjoins Kings Canyon National Park on the E and S.

The largest unit extends from the S boundary of Sequoia National Park beyond Lake Isabella almost to Bakersfield. Its SW corner is crossed by the Kern River. Two smaller units, the Piute and Scodic Mountains, are S and E of Lake Isabella. Together the three almost completely surround the lake. The Forest has lake frontage.

This region is drier than the mountains to the N. Most of the San Joaquin Valley receives less than 8 in. of precipitation annually; Bakersfield has less than 6 in. More moisture is received at higher elevations, but most of the mountain slopes receive no more than 40 in., and desert to semiarid conditions prevail in the Domeland Wilderness on the E side of the Forest, even at relatively high elevations. High roads and trails are blocked by snow in winter, but the hiking season begins a few weeks earlier here than in the Sierra to the N. Several of the Forest campgrounds at low elevations are open all year, and most others open in April or May.

This is the part of the Sierra nearest to the Los Angeles area, and heavy public use is concentrated in the several resort areas, among them Hume Lake and Kern Canyon. The largest of the Forest campgrounds, on good roads in attractive settings, are in demand. Some of the trails, including wilderness trails, show the marks of too many boots. But one can find quiet trails, and rangers can point the way. The choice is more limited, of course, on holiday weekends, greatest out of season.

The Forest is best known for its giant sequoias. Of the 30-odd groves, some have 100 trees or fewer, but several have thousands of them. The Boole Tree on Converse Mountain, NW of Hume Lake, is the largest tree in any National Forest, 90 ft. around at the base, 269 ft. tall.

The Forest has over 700 mi. of fishing streams, some of them with fine cascades and waterfalls. Some three dozen small lakes are in the high country. 87-acre Hume Lake is the largest wholly within the Forest. Pine Flat Lake (see entry this zone) is partly within the N sector, but the shoreline and recreation facilities are managed by the U.S. Army Corps of Engineers.

Only the wilderness areas are closed to all motorized vehicles. In certain other zones, ORVs may use roads and trails but may not travel cross-country. A majority of the Forest area, however, is open to ORVs on or off trail, except in special locations.

Many visitors come for sightseeing by car. One popular scenic route is Hwy 180 E from Fresno, which passes the General Grant Grove, continues through the Forest, and enters Kings Canyon National Park along the South Fork of the Kings River. Another is Hwy 190 E from Porterville. On a long loop, one can turn S, follow the Kern River to Lake Isabella, then drive to Bakersfield on Hwy 178. Or, with a Forest map, one can explore the several hundred miles of Forest roads.

Outstanding waterfalls include Grizzly Falls, N of Hwy 180 in Kings Canyon; Salmon Creek Falls, E of Sierra Way (Fairview Campground in Kern Canyon); South Creek Falls, W of the Kern River on Forest Hwy, from the end of Sierra Way in Kern Canyon.

Plants: More than two-thirds of the Forest is conifer forest. Below 4,000 ft., chaparral and oak woodland. Chaparral species include chamise, whiteleaf manzanita, redbud, buck brush, chaparral white-thorn, silk-tassel, flannel bush. Areas of annual grasses with blue oak. The ponderosa and Jeffrey pine forests are between 4,000 and 7,500 ft., though predominant between 4,500 and 6,500 ft. Tree species include ponderosa, Jeffrey, and sugar pines, white fir, incense cedar, black oak. Somewhat higher is the fir forest, to 8,500 ft., with red and white firs, lodgepole pine, chinquapin. Lodgepole pine and numerous mountain meadows are just below the subalpine forest, where the principal tree species include foxtail pine, related to the bristlecones, and limber and whitebark pines. Understory species above 5,000 ft. include bitter cherry, bear clover, whitethorn, Sierra gooseberry, squaw currant, greenleaf manzanita, willows, chinquapin.

The Forest is the most southern habitat for the giant sequoia and foxtail pine. Numerous old-growth stands of these and red fir. Virgin stands of all of the principal conifers can be observed.

No plant checklist is available, but over 2,500 species are known to occur in the southern Sierra. Principal display species here include buckeye, redbud, quaking aspen, flannel bush, ceanothus, dogwood, many wildflowers. Best flowering season is usually Mar.–April in the foothills, May–June from 4,500–6,500 ft., July in the next higher region, to 8,500 ft., Aug. in the subalpine zone.

Birds: Checklist available. Seasonally common and abundant species include turkey vulture, sharp-shinned, Cooper's, and red-tailed hawks, kestrel, blue grouse, band-tailed pigeon, great horned owl, poor-will, common nighthawk, white-throated swift, hummingbirds, northern flicker, woodpeckers, ash-throated flycatcher, western wood pewee, horned lark, violet-green swallow, jays, crow, Clark's nut-cracker, mountain chickadee, plain titmouse, common bushtit, nuthatches, wrentit, dipper, wrens, mockingbird, hermit thrush, western and mountain bluebirds, golden-crowned and ruby-crowned kinglets, warbling vireo. Many warblers. Also western meadowlark, northern oriole, western tanager, blackheaded grosbeak, finches, pine siskin, lesser goldfinch, green-tailed towhee, dark-eyed junco, sparrows. Around water: pied-billed grebe, great blue heron, mallard, pintail, redhead, ring-necked duck, ruddy duck, coot.

Mammals: Regional checklist available. Species include opossum, various bats, shrews, mice, white-tailed jackrabbit, cottontail, ground squirrels, pika, gray squirrel, northern flying squirrel, porcupine, striped and spotted skunks, raccoon, ringtail, black bear, badger, coyote, bobcat, mountain lion, mule deer. Present but seldom seen: wolverine, fisher, marten, red fox.

Reptiles and amphibians: Include California newt, ensatina, California slender and Sierra Nevada salamanders, western toad, Pacific tree frog, mountain yellow-legged frog, western fence and sagebrush lizards, southern and northern alligator lizards, western whiptail lizard, rubber boa, striped racer, gopher snake, California mountain kingsnake, garter snakes, western rattlesnake.

Features

Golden Trout Wilderness: 303,290 acres, 36% in the Sequoia National Forest. Adjoins the S boundary of the John Muir Wilderness. Further W, the wilderness adjoins the S boundary of Sequoia National Park. W part is a large drainage basin surrounded by high, rugged mountains, E part is an extension of the Kern Plateau. Elevations from 4,800 ft. at the Forks of Kern to 12,432 ft. at Mount Florence, at the borderline of the Mineral King area, and 12,900 ft. at Cirque Peak in the Inyo National Forest, at the John Muir Wilderness boundary. Many mountain streams, flowing to the Kern River and its South Fork. Portions of the area are above timberline. The Pacific Crest Trail crosses. For season and trail information, consult the Tule River or Cannell Meadow Ranger District or the Mount Whitney Ranger District in Inyo National Forest. Wilderness and campfire permits required.

Domeland Wilderness: 130,995 acres. The southernmost wilderness area in the Sierra. At the S end of the Kern Plateau, the area is on the E boundary of the Forest, N of Hwy 178. The Forest map shows no trail entering from the S. Trailheads are at Big Meadow and Taylor Meadow on the W, both accessible from Kernville via the Sierra Hwy and Cherry Hill Rd., and at Long Canyon in the E. Elevations from 3,000 to 9,730 ft. Climate is desert to semiarid, but several perennial streams flow through the area. Vegetation is mostly mixed conifer and pinyon. The name derives from the many granite domes in the area. Campfire permit required.

Note that Owens Peak and Chimney Peak Recreation Areas (BLM) are adjacent (see entry in zone 8).

Monarch Wilderness: 45,000 acres (23,000 acres within the Sequoia National Forest, 21,000 acres extending into the adjacent Sierra National Forest). At the NE corner of the northern unit of the Forest, just N of the Kings River, with the Kings Canyon National Park backcountry on its N and E boundaries. The area is dramatically scenic, rising from 2,000 ft. at the river to 11,077 ft. at Hogback Peak. Terrain is so steep and rugged that trail access is limited. From Hwy 180, the Deer Cove Trail climbs over 3,000 ft. in 4 mi., on a S-facing slope. This trail gives access to Wildman Meadow, Grizzly Lakes, and the National Park. The lakes are small, shallow, have no fish. Grizzly Creek and Silver Creek are the principal drainages. There are many streams in the area as well as the South and Middle Forks of the Kings River. Water is available from these streams, but must be treated before drinking. Fishing and hunting (in season) are permitted with permits. This is the only area in the Forest where whitebark pines grow. Campfire permit and trail information at Hume Lake Ranger District (see following description).

Kern Canyon is a popular resort area. Hwy 178 from Bakersfield follows the Kern River to Lake Isabella. Three Forest campgrounds are on this part of the river, as well as private resorts. Lake Isabella has 9 campgrounds around it. N of the lake, the Sierra Hwy follows the canyon. The Kern Canyon information station is 2 mi. N of Kernville, at the entrance of the Upper Kern Canyon Recreation Area, which includes 15 Forest campgrounds as well as private resorts. *Lake Isabella.* The South Fork Wildlife Area at the lake is identified as a watchable wildlife site. Osprey are present. Bald eagle winter in the area as do some other uncommon species of birds and wildlife.

Jennie Lakes Wilderness: 10,500 acres. A mixture of lakes, forest, streams, and meadows. Elevations range from 7,000 to 10,365 ft. at the summit of Mitchell Peak. Tree species include red fir, lodgepole pine. Wildflowers are plentiful in the spring. 26 mi. of hiking trails within the area. 2- or 3-day loop hikes to Jennie and Weaver Lakes. Contact Hume Lake Ranger District for road and trail conditions and campfire permits.

South Sierra Wilderness: Borders Golden Trout Wilderness on its N boundary and Domeland Wilderness on the S, except for the Kennedy Meadows Rd. corridor. All of this area is within the South Fork of the Kern River watershed. It's a fragile land of meadows, between forested ridges, rolling hills, and steep craggy peaks. The relatively gentle terrain in the Forest is ideally suited for family-oriented recreation. Fishing and hunting (in season), with licenses. 30 mi. of trails, for horses and hikers, including the Pacific Crest Trail.

The Hume Lake area is also popular, accessible all year. The access road, Hwy 180, passes through the Grant Grove section of Kings Canyon National Park. The lake, only 87 acres in size, is the center of an area with numerous attractions, notably the giant sequoias. Kings Canyon is more than 7,000 ft. deep at its deepest point. Buck Rock Lookout offers splendid views. Hwy 180 continues into the main portion of Kings Canyon NP. At Grant Grove, Generals Hwy turns S into Sequoia NP. Includes Mountain Home Demonstration State Forest (see entry this zone).

Dome Rock, 7,221 ft. high, is 4 mi. S of Quaking Aspen. The rock is a massive granite monolith. Splendid vistas from the top.

Kiavah Wilderness: See Scodie Mountains (zone 8).

Activities

Camping: 50 campgrounds, 1,900 sites. Several open all year; others open April or May. Reservations may be made.

Hiking, backpacking: Over 1,300 mi. of trails, in all parts of the Forest. The Forest map shows numbered and maintained trails, but it is advisable to consult Ranger Districts for current conditions, routes, destinations. The Pacific Crest Trail crosses the Forest for about 78 mi. Summit, a National Recreation Trail, is about 12 mi. long. It crosses Hwy 190 about ½ mi. W of Quaking Aspen Campground. Cornell Meadow, a 9-mi. trail, begins on Sierra Way 1 mi. N of Kernville. Jackass Creek Trail, 3 mi., begins 1 mi. N of Fish Creek Campground. The latter two are also National Recreation Trails.

Hunting: Deer, black bear, small game.

Fishing: Most streams and lakes. Golden trout in some high-country streams.

Kayaking, rafting: Commercial raft trips on Kings River begin 3½ mi. above Mill Flat Campground. This section considered suitable for kayaks, not open canoes. Rafting above this stretch should not be attempted. Whitewater trips also available on most of the Kern River.

Horse riding: Packers and stables at several points adjoining the Forest. HQ and Ranger Districts can provide current list.

Skiing: Ski area at Shirley Meadow. Dec.–March, weekends and holidays only, if snow is sufficient.

Ski touring: Stony Creek–Big Meadows and Quaking Aspen areas.

Publications

Forest map, $3.25.

Checklists of birds, mammals, reptiles, amphibians.

Mimeo info pages: Domeland, Golden Trout, Jennie Lakes, Kiavah, Monarch, and South Sierra Wildernesses, also on Kern Canyon and Hume Lake areas. Off-road vehicle map.

Headquarters

U.S. Forest Service, 900 W. Grand Ave., Porterville, CA 93257; (209) 784-1500.

Ranger Districts

Cannell Meadow R.D., 105 Whitney Rd., Kernville, CA 93238; (619) 376-3781 (voice/ext. 202 TDD). Hume Lake R.D., 35860 E. Kings Canyon Rd., Dunlap, CA 93621; (209) 338-2251. Kings River R.D., Trimmer Rt., Sanger, CA 93657; (209) 855-8321. Lake Isabella Visitor Center, 4875 Ponderosa Dr., Lake Isabella, CA 93240; (619) 379-5646 (voice/TDD). Mount Whitney R.D., P.O. Box 8, Lone Pine, CA 93545; (619) 876-6200/5542 (TDD). Sierra National Forest, 1600 Tollhouse Rd., Clovis, CA 93612; (209) 487-5155. Tule River R.D., 32588 Hwy 190, Porterville, CA 93257; (209) 539-2607.

Sierra National Forest

U.S. Forest Service
See entry zone 6.

Success Lake

U.S. Army Corps of Engineers
2,450 water acres.

From Hwy 99 at Tipton, E 5 mi. beyond Porterville on Hwy 190.

A flood control project on the Tule River, about 7 mi. W of Sequoia National Forest. In the foothills of the Sierra Nevada, with fine views of the mountains. Elevation is about 650 ft. Low hills covered with annual grasses, shrubs, many wildflowers surround the lake. The lake is 3½ mi. long, has 30 mi. of shoreline. The site is heavily used for camping and water-based recreation. However, around two arms of the lake in the NW, the Corps has set aside 1,400 acres as a roadless wildlife management area.

Camping: 2 campgrounds, 104 sites. All year.

Headquarters
U.S. Army Corps of Engineers, Porterville, CA 93257; (209) 784-0215.

Volcanic Tableland

U.S. Bureau of Land Management
36,000 acres.

Take US 6 N from Bishop. Then Five Bridges Rd. to the Tableland.

From about 3 mi. N of Bishop to Mono Lake, most of the area between the E and W portions of the Inyo National Forest is BLM land. This entry concerns the S portion. An improved road along the Owens River is part of the S boundary. An unpaved road from Bishop NW to Casa Diablo Mountain crosses the area.

A series of pyroclastic lava flows built the tablelands above the valley floor. It appears as a wall standing N of Bishop, the river at its base. The road to Casa Diablo Mountain has a series of drops over the edges of terraces, then climbs over the lip of the next terrace. Numerous canyons and drainages dissect the E portion.

The land becomes steeper and more rugged in the NW, rising to 7,912-ft. Casa Diablo Mountain, just across the National Forest boundary.

Fish Slough has a perennial water source. It is noted for its populations of Owens Valley pupfish, an endangered species. Other features include Chidago and Red Rock Canyons. A road passes through Red Rock Canyon, a narrow cut with some nearly vertical walls, often colorful.

Vegetation is sparse: low shrubs, cholla, and annual plants at the lower elevations, some juniper on higher slopes. The open terrain provides splendid, sweeping views of the Sierra Nevada to the W and the White Mountains to the E. Striking visual effects are provided by the low sun angle morning and evening.

Headquarters

Bureau of Land Management, Bishop Resource Area, 785 N. Main St., Suite E, Bishop, CA 93514; (619) 872-4881.

Z O N E 8

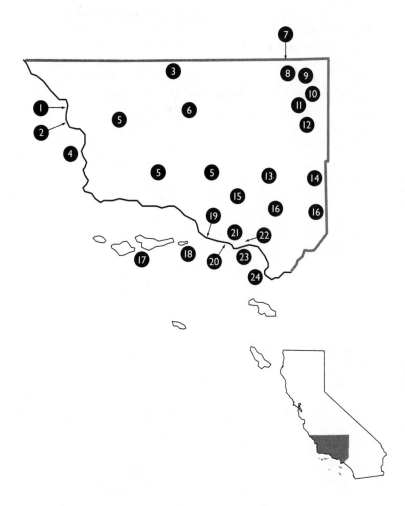

Z O  N E

Includes these counties:

San Luis Obispo	Santa Barbara	Los Angeles
Kern	Ventura	

Zone 8 extends from the ocean to the Mojave Desert, from San Simeon to Long Beach. An enormous urban population lives within its bounds, and the pressure on most outdoor recreation sites is intense.

The S end of the Sierra Nevada is in the NE corner of the zone. Several large blocks of the Sequoia National Forest surround Lake Isabella; because most of this Forest is in zone 7, the entry appears there.

The largest public land areas in the zone are Los Padres and Angeles National Forests. Both are heavily used, but one need not follow the crowds. Each has extensive backcountry. Backpacking is popular, but with a bit of advice from the rangers one can find times and places to enjoy the hills without too much company.

US 101 and Hwy 1 take turns serving as the Coast Highway, although in several places neither is near the beach. Weekend and holiday traffic is likely to be heavy, and beaches near LA are crowded whenever the sun shines. We have not written entries for beach sites as such. It is enough to say that on weekdays, out of season, driving the Coast Hwy can be pleasant, and one may have a choice of beaches for easy hiking. We have included several coastal sites that extend back into the hills.

S and E of the Sierra Nevada is desert. Although the largest areas of CA desert are in zones 7 and 9, a number of interesting sites are here. Many motion pictures have been made in the colorful Red Rock Canyon area. At Saddleback Butte, one can see many Joshua trees and, perhaps, a desert tortoise.

Abalone Cove Ecological Reserve

California Department of Fish and Game
124 acres.

Rancho Palos Verdes Coast, 20 mi. S of Los Angeles. Seaward of Palos Verdes Dr. S, E of Sea Cove Dr.

Managed cooperatively with Los Angeles County. Concentration of geological, biological, historical, and archeological resources unique to this peninsula. Beach and offshore area set aside for preservation and public observation of natural marine environment. The cove, protected from most storms, had the last naturally occurring giant kelp (the species is now restored). Tide pools; whale watching during migratory seasons.

Anacapa Island Ecological Reserve

California Department of Fish and Game
9,114 acres.

Ocean waters adjacent to Anacapa Island, 10.6 nautical mi. SW of Port Hueneme.

See entry this zone for Channel Islands National Park, where the Reserve is described. These waters were part of the Park until a U.S. Supreme Court decision held that submerged lands and waters within 1 nautical mi. of an island are state property.

Angeles National Forest

U.S. Forest Service
652,704 acres of Forest land; 693,452 acres within boundaries.

Northern Los Angeles County. Numerous access routes, including roads N from Foothill Blvd. and I-210.

Two large blocks. The Saugus Unit is N of Saugus, W of Palmdale. The Main Unit includes the San Gabriel Mountains from the San Fernando Valley E to San Bernardino County and the San Bernardino National Forest. Mountainous. The highest point is 10,064-ft. Mount Baldy. The Forest adjoins a huge metropolitan area and receives over 15 million visitors a year, yet it includes roadless areas, secluded canyons, peaks reached only by energetic hikers. The Forest includes the watersheds of four rivers: Los Angeles, San Gabriel, Santa Clara, and Mojave. It has 189 mi. of fishing streams and 8 lakes, 4 of them natural.

Two-fifths of the many visitors have just come for the ride, sightseeing along one of the Forest's scenic drives. Second in popularity is picnicking, while third, somewhat surprisingly, is winter sports. The Forest has 9 winter sports areas. Hikers and backpackers from the Los Angeles area are attracted because the Forest is nearby and many trails are open in the spring, when the high country of the Sierra Nevada is still deep in snow.

Annual precipitation ranges from more than 30 in. on the high ridges to less than 15 in. on the lower N slopes. Summers are hot and dry. The fire season usually begins about May 1. Fire permits are required year-round for any type of fire outside a developed recreation site (campground or picnic area). Permits are free and may be obtained at any Forest Service office. In extreme circumstances, parts of the Forest may be closed.

Plants: Diverse terrain, together with a range of soil and moisture conditions, produces a variety of plant communities, marked changes occurring as one rounds a bluff or crosses a ridgeline. In general, the lower slopes, including most of the Forest acreage, have thickets of chaparral: chamise, toyon, scrub oak, mountain mahogany, yucca, ceanothus, manzanita. Higher, generally above 5,500 ft., slopes are forested, tree species including incense cedar, Douglas-fir, ponderosa, sugar, Jeffrey, and limber pines, white fir, golden cup oak, interior live oak, white alder. Understory includes yerba santa, yucca, coffeeberry, rabbitbrush, willow, elderberry, ironwood, mountain mahogany, bush penstemon, manzanita, poison oak. The numerous wildflowers include California goldenrod, blue-eyed grass, Indian paintbrush, prickly phlox, prickly poppy, penstemons, snakeweed, scarlet bugler, snow plant, Indian tobacco.

Ancient limber pines, some over 2,000 years old, occur near timberline, above 8,000 ft., on Mount Baden-Powell to Mount Burnham and Throop Peak.

Birds: Checklist available. Around lakes and reservoirs: great blue heron, mallard, green-winged teal, canvasback, ring-necked duck, merganser, coot, killdeer, spotted sandpiper, black phoebe. Common species of forested and brush areas include Cooper's, red-tailed, and sharp-shinned hawks, mountain and California quail, band-tailed pigeon, screech and great horned owls, poor-will, white-throated swift, hummingbirds, northern flicker, woodpeckers, flycatchers, wood pewee, swallows, jays, mountain chickadee, plain titmouse, bushtit, wrentit, Bewick's and canyon wrens, mockingbird, California thrasher, western bluebird, yellow warbler, Bullock's oriole, western tanager, black-headed grosbeak, lesser and Lawrence's goldfinches, towhees, dark-eyed junco, sparrows.

Mammals: Include ground squirrels, gray squirrel, cottontail, raccoon, striped skunk, coyote, bobcat, gray fox, black bear, mule deer.

Reptiles and amphibians: Include California newt, alligator and whip-tailed lizards, horned toad, coral kingsnake, gopher snake, Pacific rattlesnake.

Features

San Gabriel Wilderness: 36,118 acres. On S slope of San Gabriel Mountains, from the Angeles Crest down to the West Fork of the San Gabriel River, between Hwys 2 and 39. Scenic, rugged terrain; elevations from 1,600 to 8,200 ft. Much of the area is covered with chaparral, often in dense thickets. Mixed pine and fir along the ridgetops. Several trails, moderate to strenuous, lead to the interior, where off-trail hiking is feasible in some places. Fishing is said to be good in several streams.

Sheep Mountain Wilderness: 30,100 acres. E of the San Gabriel Wilderness, separated from it by the Crystal Lake Recreation Area. Includes Mount Baldy, 10,064 ft., and Mount Baden-Powell, 9,399 ft. Numerous streams, including the East Fork, San Gabriel River. Chaparral, montane forest, and southern mixed evergreen forest. Stands of ancient limber pine. Wildlife includes a herd of Nelson bighorn sheep.

Fish Canyon Roadless Area: 32,900 acres. In the N central portion of the Saugus Unit. Wilderness status proposed. Rugged. Steep-walled canyons. Dense chaparral thickets. Large stand of black oak. According to Forest map dated 1977, this is part of a larger area open to ORV travel. Several roads penetrate the area to campgrounds; these corridors are excluded from the wilderness proposal.

Cucamonga Wilderness: 4,400 acres. Adjacent to San Bernardino National Forest (see entry zone 9). It lies immediately E of Mount Baldy, S of Thunder Mountain.

Pyramid Lake, about 3 mi. long, lies between the W boundary of the Saugus Unit and Los Padres National Forest, beside I-5. It is heavily used for boating, fishing, and swimming. Boats must conform to a one-way traffic pattern. Day use only.

Crystal Lake is the principal center in the Main Unit, on Hwy 39. The "lake" is only a pond. The main campground has 233 sites and others are nearby. The complex includes a ranger station, store, visitor center, nature trails, amphitheater, hiking trails. The area lies between the San Gabriel and Sheep Mountain Wildernesses; trials into both.

Charlton-Chilao Recreation Area is just W of the San Gabriel Wilderness, on Hwy 2. It has a large campground, ranger station, amphitheater, trails.

The Angeles Crest Highway, Hwy 2, is the principal scenic route in the Forest, and a designated Scenic Byway, from La Canada on I-210 NE to Big Pines. The Angeles Forest Hwy, N-3, branches off to the N 9 mi. from La Canada.

Interpretation

Visitor centers located at Chilao, Vista de Lago (Pyramid Lake), Mount Baldy Village, Grassy Hollow, and Crystal Lake. *Information stations* at Clear Creek and at San Gabriel Canyon entrance station on Hwy 39.

Naturalist programs, in summer at the major recreation centers, include *campfire programs, guided walks.*

Nature trails are at several recreation areas.

Interpretive signs along Hwys 2 and 39.

Activities

Camping: 110 campgrounds, 1,173 sites. Most open all year.

Hiking, backpacking: 556 mi. of trails. 28-mi. Gabrielino Trail links 7 campgrounds, crosses diverse habitats from canyon bottoms to forested ridgetops. Pacific Crest Trail from the N runs close to N boundary of Saugus Unit, enters Main Unit, continues into San Bernardino National Forest.

Hunting: Deer, quail. Discharge of firearms prohibited near roads, recreation areas, etc.

Fishing: Lakes and streams. Some water stocked with rainbow trout.

Swimming: Facilities at three lakes. Usual season May 1–Oct. 1.

Boating: Pyramid Lake and Castaic Lake. On Elizabeth Lake, motors of 10 hp or less.

Horse riding: On most trails.

Skiing: 9 winter sports areas.

Ski touring: Trails and unplowed Forest roads.

Smoking is prohibited except in camp and picnic areas, other approved locations.

Roads are sometimes closed by snow, rainstorm, mudslides.

Adjacent

Los Padres (see entry this zone) and San Bernardino (see entry zone 9) National Forests.

Publications

Forest map, $3.25.

Forest Facts.

Trees of the Angeles National Forest.

Bird checklist.

Flora-Fauna of Crystal Lake.

Pyramid Lake (leaflet).

Recreation Area Information—Saugus Ranger District.

Self-Guided Hiking Tour of Historic Mount Lowe.

Headquarters

U.S. Forest Service, 701 N. Santa Anita Ave., Arcadia, CA 91006; (818) 574-5200/1613.

Ranger Districts

Arroyo Seco R.D., Oak Grove Park, Flintridge, CA 91011; (213) 790-1151. Mount Baldy R.D., 110 N. Wabash Ave., Glendora, CA 91740; (213) 335-1251. Saugus R.D., 30800 Bouquet Canyon Rd., Saugus, CA 91350; (805) 296-9710. Tujunga R.D., 12391 Little Tujunga Cyn Rd., San Fernando, CA 91342;(213) 365-9107. Valyermo R.D., 29835 Valyermo Rd., Valyermo, CA 93563; (805) 944-2187.

Antelope Valley California Poppy Preserve

California Department of Parks and Recreation
1,630 acres.

From Lancaster on Hwy 14 (N of Pasadena), 15 mi. W on Ave. I.

An extraordinary floral display, poppies and other species, in mid-spring. Small, rolling hills; area of disturbed grassland. 8 mi. of trails. Alternative-energy interpretive center open March–mid-May, (805) 942-0662.

Channel Islands National Park

U.S. National Park Service
1,120 land acres.

By commercial boat from Ventura or private boat.

Of the 8 Channel Islands off the southern CA coast, 5 are included in the National Park. *San Miguel,* the one farthest W of Ventura, is owned by the U.S. Navy, but administered by the Park Service. Landing only by special permit. Some of the surrounding waters are part of an ecological reserve and are closed to boats.

   Anacapa is a chain of three islands, about 5 mi. long, S of Ventura. West Anacapa, the largest, rises abruptly from the sea to two peaks; the higher one is 930 ft. East and Middle Anacapa have rolling plateaus almost entirely surrounded by cliffs 90–300 ft. high. Travel from one island to another is by boat only. The commercial boat lands only at East Anacapa and Frenchy's Cove on West Anacapa. A nature trail and campground are on East Anacapa.

Island vegetation is short and scrubby, appearing brown and lifeless until the winter rains come. Past farming, grazing, and burning almost eliminated most native plant species, but there is now a slow recovery.

The boat from Ventura, weather permitting, allows day visitors 2½–3 hrs. ashore. This is ample time to explore East Anacapa, because there are only 2 mi. of trails and visitors must stay on trails. The islands have no beaches, and the cliffs at East Anacapa prevent any approach to the shore by land except at the landing. A nature trail covers most of the island, noting points of interest, from the giant kelp in Cathedral Cove to the giant coreopsis, or tree sunflower, which grows only here and in isolated stands along the mainland coast.

The islands are rookeries for seabirds, including a large brown pelican nesting site. Sea lions and harbor seals are often seen around Anacapa, although they are more abundant around Santa Barbara Island. In Dec.–March the annual gray whale migration passes close to Anacapa.

Visitors who come by private boat can anchor at Frenchy's Cove on Middle Anacapa, picnic ashore, and enjoy the nearby tide pools. Scuba diving off West Anacapa is popular. Several caves can be explored by skiff when waters are calm.

Camping is permitted on East Anacapa, in a small campground limited to 30 people. Everything, including water, must be carried up 152 steps and ⅜ mi. uphill by trail. Extra food should be brought in the event that weather delays the boat. Gear should be adequate for strong winds, wet fog, unshaded sun. A free camping permit must be obtained from HQ in advance of visit.

Santa Barbara Island, about 640 acres, is SW of Los Angeles. There is no regularly scheduled boat service. Groups often arrange charter trips, and individuals can often arrange to join one. Like Anacapa, Santa Barbara is almost entirely surrounded by cliffs, some more than 500 ft. high. The island has two hills, the highest 635 ft. Caves, coves, offshore pillars, blowholes.

Here, too, native plants were almost eliminated by past abuse. Introduced species, notably grasses and ice plant, are prominent. The giant coreopsis is here in small stands. Native vegetation is slowly recovering.

Sea mammals are abundant, mostly California sea lions and harbor seals. A few elephant seals appear in late summer and fall. Whales are often seen during migration. Western gulls nest in large numbers. Birds include brown pelican, burrowing owl, horned lark, scoter, oystercatcher. Early summer is the best birding season.

Santa Barbara has about 5 mi. of trails, and visitors must stay on them. Access to the shore is at the landing cove only, and swimming from shore is possible only here; the beach is stony. Some tide pools can be explored from the land side.

A primitive campground is available, occupancy limited to 30. Everything, including water, must be carried in up a steep trail. A free camping permit must be obtained from HQ in advance of visit.

Santa Rosa Island, the second-largest Park island, is nearly 15 mi. long and 10 mi. wide. High mountains, deep canyons, and gently rolling hills. Grasslands cover about 85% of the island, but columnar volcanic formations and highly colored hill slopes are visible. Beneath the grasslands are the remains of a rich cultural heritage. More than 180 archeological sites have been mapped.

Native plants include tree poppy, island manzanita, an endemic sage. Two groves of Torrey pine are visible near Bechers Bay.

Birds include large populations of European starling, horned lark, meadowlark, house finch, song sparrow. Other creatures seen on the island include tree frogs, slender salamanders, gopher snake, deer mouse, two species of lizard. Harbor seals breed on the sandy beaches.

Santa Cruz Island, the largest and most diverse island, is 24 mi. long, covering about 96 square mi. The highest of the Channel Island mountains, at 2,400 ft., is found here. Varied coastline, steep cliffs, gigantic sea caves and coves, sandy beaches. More than 600 plant species and 140 land and bird species are found here. Since the Island is privately owned, a permit is needed to land.

Interpretation

Visitor center is on the mainland, at Ventura. Information, exhibits, publications, interpretive slide program, and films are available.

Park rangers are stationed on all 5 islands. *Campfire programs* when enough people are camping and weather permits. *Guided hikes* are regularly given.

Activities

Camping: See preceding descriptions.

Fishing: From boats. The surrounding waters are a state ecological reserve, and special regulations govern fishing and diving for invertebrates. Inquire.

Swimming: Chiefly from boats. Popular scuba area.

Boating: Visiting the islands by private boat should be undertaken only by people with experience in these waters. Islands have anchorages but no docks. Skiff needed to go ashore.

Pets are not permitted.

Publications

Leaflet.

Mimeo info pages: camping, excursions.

Headquarters

National Park Service, 1901 Spinnaker Dr., Ventura, CA 93001; (805) 658-5730.

Excursion Information

Boat: Island Packers, 1867 Spinnaker Dr., Ventura, CA 93001; (805) 642-1393/3370. *Air:* Channel Islands Aviation, Camarillo (805) 987-1301.

Chimney Peak Recreation Area; Owens Peak Area

U.S. Bureau of Land Management
Approximately 125,000 acres.

About 12½ mi. N of Inyokern on US 395, take Nine Mile Canyon Rd. W ¼ mi. beyond the BLM work station and follow signs.

Bounded on the S by Hwy 178 and on the N by Nine Mile Canyon Rd., this area straddles the Sierra Crest, the Chimney Peak area being W of the crest. Elevations range from about 3,000 ft. to the highest point, Owens Peak, at 8,453 ft. Chimney Peak, in the N part of the area, is 7,994 ft. Several other peaks along this section of the crest are above 7,500 ft. The Pacific Crest Trail follows the crest through much of this area.

Climate is semiarid. Winters are cold, and snow covers the upper parts of the area, but not for long. Snow is neither as deep nor as long-lived as in more northern parts of the Sierra. Summer daytime temperatures are in the 80s, summer nights cool.

Owens Peak is one of the three new wilderness areas designated in the California Desert Protection Act of 1994. The others are Dome-land (additions) and Chimney Peak. Owens Peak is about 8 mi. N of Walker Pass. The BLM campgrounds and parking areas serve as bases for hikers and equestrians entering the wilderness.

Plants: The desert side has creosote and associated desert shrubs with scattered yucca in the valleys and bajadas. Lower elevations, near Hwy 178, contain desert scrub with rabbitbrush, chollas, Joshua tree, yucca, horsebrush, and encelia. Much of the higher elevations of the Chimney Peak area consists mainly of the pinyon woodland community with sagebrush openings. Some ponderosa pine occurs on N slopes at high elevations. Common shrubs include big sage, Mormon tea, silk tassel, flannel bush, Wetter areas support willow, coyote bush, alder, and cottonwood. Joshua tree woodland near Walker Pass.

Birds: Include California and mountain quail, sharp-shinned hawk, kestrel, roadrunner, northern flicker.

Mammals: Include deer, black bear, bobcat, mountain lion, raccoon, coyote, black-tailed jackrabbit.

Activities

Camping: 3 BLM campgrounds, over 50 sites. Potable water available mid-April–Oct. at Walker Pass Campground, nonpotable water at other sites.

Hiking, backpacking: One can take the Pacific Crest Trail through the area and on into the Sequoia National Forest. Campfire permit required, but not a wilderness permit. In the Owens Peak area, the PCT has great views of the desert. Off-trail hiking is feasible in a number of the valleys and canyons.

Hunting: Deer, quail, dove, rabbit.

Publication
Chimney Peak Recreation Area (leaflet).

Headquarters
Bureau of Land Management, Caliente Resource Area, 3801 Pegasus Dr., Bakersfield, CA 93308-6837; (805) 391-6000.

Desert Tortoise Natural Area

U.S. Bureau of Land Management
25,000 acres.

From Mojave, NE 4 mi. on Hwy 14, E 10 mi. on California City Blvd., NE
5½ mi. on Randsburg-Mojave Rd.

In the NW Mojave Desert on the W edge of the Rand Mountains. Elevations from 2,100 to 3,100 ft. A unique habitat with the densest known population of the desert tortoise, a burrowing species that often digs long tunnels, winters in a communal den. Parts of the area have more than 200 tortoises per sq. mi. Because of threats to the species, the BLM closed the public land to vehicles in 1973. A protective fence was erected in 1977 to exclude livestock. The Desert Tortoise Preserve Committee has assisted by raising money to buy private land and by providing guided tours to school and conservation groups. The BLM has designated this area as an "Area of Critical Environmental Concern."

Plants: Tortoises feed on annual wildflowers and grasses in the spring and sometimes again in the fall; summers and winters are generally spent underground. Wildflowers are a major attraction of the area. Species include Bigelow coreopsis, goldfields, desert dandelion, Mojave aster, blazing star, phacelia, forget-me-not, creosote, lupine, primrose, desert candle, desert trumpet, gilia.

Birds: Species include turkey vulture, red-tailed hawk, golden eagle, prairie falcon, kestrel, chukar, roadrunner, burrowing owl, less nighthawk, ash-throated flycatcher, Say's phoebe, horned lark, sage sparrow, cactus wren, ladder-backed woodpecker.

Mammals: Include endangered Mojave ground squirrel. Also, black-tailed jackrabbit, cottontail, antelope ground squirrel, desert wood rat, kit fox, coyote, badger, bobcat.

Reptiles: In addition to the tortoise: desert iguana, chuckwalla, zebra-tailed, leopard, side-blotched, and desert horned lizards, western whiptail, gopher snake, red racer, glossy snake, sidewinder, Mojave rattlesnake. The tortoises are best seen mid-March to mid-June, morning and late afternoon.

Interpretation

Interpretive center is near entrance. Signs, exhibits, species checklists. *Guided tours* in the spring months.

Visitors should stay on marked trails. Tortoises must not be touched or approached closely. Pets must be leashed, and not taken beyond the parking lot. Bring water; none is available.

Publication
Leaflet.

Headquarters
Bureau of Land Management, Ridgecrest Resource Area, 300 S. Richmond Rd., Ridgecrest, CA 93555; (619) 384-5400.

El Paso Mountains

U.S. Bureau of Land Management
23,780 acres.

2 mi. E of Hwy 14, along Red Rock–Inyokern Rd.

From 2,000 ft. elevation on the S boundary in Fremont Valley, terrain rises sharply. Numerous reddish-colored buttes and dark, uplifted volcanic mesas. At times the intervening slopes appear golden because of masses of annuals. Highest point is 5,244-ft. Black Mountain. Ridges are generally SW–NE. The terrain descends more gradually in the N to a broad wash at about 3,000 ft. Slopes are dissected by narrow canyons, creating a badlands appearance. Last Chance Canyon, originating near Saltdale, is deep and winding, with an intermittent stream draining from Black Mountain. Scenic value of area is high.

Vegetation is mostly creosote bush scrub, with a notable array of conspicuous flowering annuals.

The *El Paso Mountain Wilderness* surrounds Black Mountain. According to BLM, the most spectacular attribute is the abundance of cultural sites. The S portion of the wilderness is included in the Last Chance Archeological District and is listed on the National Register of Historic Places.

Activities

Hiking: No designated trails, but cross-country trails lead to Black Mountain.

Hunting: For dove, quail, chukar, and rabbit.

No vehicles allowed in the wilderness area.

Headquarters

Bureau of Land Management, Ridgecrest Resource Area, 300 S. Richmond Rd., Ridgecrest, CA 93555; (619) 384-5400.

Guadalupe–Nipomo Dunes Preserve

The Nature Conservancy
3,417 acres.

From Hwy 1 in Guadalupe, take Oso Flaco Lake Rd. W 3 mi.

Roughly 18,000 years ago wind-borne sand began shaping this central coast region. Originally home to the Chumash, who first lived here more than 8,000 years ago, the area was later visited by Spanish explorers and settled by Mexican ranchers. In the 19th century Americans began farming the area. This scenic spot also attracted half a dozen film producers, including Cecil B. DeMille. A visionary group called the Dunites were the last to live here before environmentalists from The Nature Conservancy began working to preserve it as open space.

Plants: Among the 18 rare plant species found in the coastal dune scrub are the Graciosa thistle, surf thistle, beach spectacle pod, and crisp dune mint.

Birds: More than 200 bird species live here or migrate through the region. S of the Santa Maria River is one of the few remaining nesting colonies of the least tern. Other endangered species include brown pelican and snowy plover.

Headquarters

The Nature Conservancy, P.O. Box 15810, San Luis Obispo, CA 93406; (805) 545-9925.

Kern National Wildlife Refuge

U.S. Fish and Wildlife Service
10,618 acres.
From Delano on Hwy 99, 19 mi. W on Garces Hwy.
Open: Daylight hours.

Much of the lower San Joaquin Valley was once a large, shallow lake and marsh. When it was drained in the late 1800s, millions of waterfowl and other fauna lost their habitat. The Kern and other federal and state Refuges in the valley were established to restore a small fraction of that habitat. However, the region is dry, receiving only about 7 in. of precipitation yearly, and the Refuge has no claim on the water brought to the region for irrigation. The Refuge is dependent upon federally mandated water sources, which fluctuate from year to year depending on precipitation. Thus the number of waterfowl remaining to nest on the Refuge depends on moisture conditions that change from year to year.

Much of the Refuge is flat alkali grassland; about 4,500 acres is marsh at present, but is expected to increase to about 7,000 acres by the year 2002. A Research Natural Area set aside for study of the grassland community is closed to the public.

The best time to visit the Refuge is Oct.–March. Summers are hot, dry, and dusty, and in many years summer birding is not impressive. In winter many waterfowl, shorebirds, and upland species are present.

Birds: Checklist of 211 species available. Seasonally common and abundant species include eared and pied-billed grebes, great blue heron, snowy egret, black-crowned night heron, American bittern, mallard, gadwall, pintail, green-winged and cinnamon teals, wigeon, northern shoveler, ruddy duck, red-tailed and Swainson's hawks, kestrel, northern harrier, ring-necked pheasant, Virginia rail, sora, common gallinule, coot, killdeer, common snipe, long-billed curlew, greater and lesser yellowlegs, sandpipers, dowitcher, avocet, black-necked stilt, California and ring-billed gulls, mourning dove, roadrunner, barn, burrowing, and short-eared owls, horned lark, rough-winged, barn, and cliff swallows, raven, crow, long-billed marsh wren, loggerhead shrike, yellow-rumped warbler, western meadowlark, yellow-headed, red-winged, and tri-colored blackbirds, western tanager, vesper, lark, whitecrowned, and song sparrows.

Hunting: Ducks, geese, coots. Special regulations posted.

Nearby

Pixley National Wildlife Refuge, 6,192 acres, managed by Kern, is about 20 mi. N. Similar habitat. Inquire at Kern about open hours.

Publications

Site map.

Bird checklist.

Headquarters

U.S. Fish and Wildlife Service, P.O. Box 219, Delano, CA 93216; (805) 725-2767.

....

Leo Carillo State Beach

California Department of Parks and Recreation
1,578 acres.

On Hwy 1, 28 mi. W of Santa Monica.

Rocky Sequit Point divides 1¼ mi. of broad sand beach. Close to Los Angeles, the beach is often crowded with swimmers, surfers, and windsurfers, and the campground across Hwy 1 is often at capacity. Mulholland Hwy, running inland from Hwy 1, divides the camping area from the largest section of the beach, undeveloped except for a trail. At the foot of the Santa Monica Mountains, this is about 1,000 acres of upland, elevations to 1,500 ft., heavily wooded with Coast live oak, CA sycamore, willow, sumac, poison oak. Wildlife includes gray fox, coyote, mule deer, raccoon, skunk, bobcat, various rodents.

Camping: 138 sites. All year. Reservations May 18–Oct. 1.

Publication

Leaflet.

Headquarters

CA Dept. of Parks and Recreation, Angeles District Office, 1925 Las Virgenes Rd., Calabasas, CA 91302; (818) 880-0350.

Los Padres National Forest

U.S. Forest Service
1,751,698 acres; 1,963,249 acres within boundaries.

Mountains of the central CA coast. The smaller of two sections is on or near the coast and Hwy 1 between Point Sur and San Simeon (see entry zone 5). The larger section is N and E of Santa Barbara, crossed by Hwys 166, 33, and 154.

Most of the mountainous land near the central coast of CA is within this National Forest. The smaller unit includes the Santa Lucia Mountains. The larger includes La Panza, and the Santa Ynez, San Rafael, and Sierra Madre Mountains. Elevations from sea level to 8,831-ft. Mount Pinos. On the E, the Forest adjoins the Angeles National Forest. Close to the LA area, the Forest receives great numbers of visitors.

Although about one-third of the area is forested, this is not a timber-producing forest. Trees are cut only to maintain or improve the stand. Steep slopes, thin soils, and a generally dry climate are unfavorable for tree growth. The Forest's chief economic value is as a supplier of water to the towns and cities of the coast and valleys. The Big Sur, Carmel, Salinas, Santa Maria, Santa Ynez, Santa Clara, and Ventura Rivers originate in the Forest. 35 lakes and reservoirs larger than 5 acres are on or adjacent to Forest land.

This Forest is highly vulnerable to fire. Seldom does a summer pass without a fire in this region making news across the country. Firefighting is highly organized and effective.

Generally, smoking is only allowed in a cleared area, say, a roadway, with at least 3 ft. of clearance. However, when Fire Restrictions are in effect, smoking is only allowed in an enclosed vehicle or building, a developed recreation site, or an area so designated by signs. California campfire permits (CCP) are required in Ventura and Santa Barbara Counties year-round. They are required in San Luis, Monterey, and Kern Counties from May 1 until the fire hazard has abated for the year. Portable lanterns and stoves using gas or liquid fuel also require CCP. Permits are not required at developed recreation sites.

Pleasure driving is the chief recreation use of the Forest. The Coast Hwy (Hwy 1) is along the spectacular Big Sur Coast. Nearly 10 million people visit each year. But the Forest also has 1,611 mi. of roads in its internal system, and it is not difficult to escape traffic.

On fine weekends and holidays, the larger campgrounds, picnic areas, and other developed sites are overloaded. Sites by water are especially in demand. A car camper may be able to find an isolated spot that's uncrowded, but only if he or she knows the Forest well or takes time for some back-road exploring. It's not quite so bad on foot. Backcountry visitors are less numerous than car campers. Rangers can advise where trail use is lightest.

Climate varies greatly with elevation and terrain. At and near the coast, annual precipitation is about 16 in. per year. On only a very few days a year does the temperature dip below 32°F, and it is equally unusual for it to rise above 90°. Along the ridges, precipitation is as high as 120 in. per year, and several feet of snow may remain on N-facing slopes in the winter months. The dry season is May–Oct. Across the ridges, in the E part of the Forest, semiarid conditions prevail. Many of the campgrounds are open and accessible all year.

Plants: Only about 30% of the area is forested. Lower slopes are generally chaparral, with such shrubs as scrub oak, poison oak, chamise, and manzanita. Flowering species include paintbrush, owl's clover, monkeyflower, many more. Coast redwoods are commonly found along the coast, except in the extreme S of the Forest. Southern slopes and poorer soils normally support stands of annual grasses, chamise, and sagebrush. Mixed coniferous forests occur at the higher elevations. These stands are described as "esthetic" rather than "commercially productive." Species include Monterey, sugar, Coulter, and ponderosa pines, and white fir. The area has great botanical diversity. Plants identified in the Monterey Ranger District represent more than three-quarters of the vascular plant families found in the entire state. The bristlecone fir, rarest and most unusual North American fir, was discovered on Cone Peak. The Cuesta Ridge Botanical Area, located N of San Luis Obispo, contains one of the larger groves of the Gowan cypress.

Birds: Two condor sanctuaries have been established within the Forest. Captive-bred condors are being returned to the wild in remote areas of the Forest.

Species of the grassland and chaparral include black-shouldered kite, sharp-shinned, Cooper's, red-tailed, and Swainson's hawks, golden eagle, mountain quail, killdeer, poor-will, white-throated swift, hummingbirds, northern flicker, dusky flycatcher, scrub jay, house and Bewick's wrens, cedar waxwing, loggerhead shrike, Hutton's and solitary vireos, warblers, finches, sparrows. Coniferous forest species include band-tailed pigeon, great horned owl, calliope hummingbird,

Lewis's, hairy, downy, and white-headed woodpeckers, western and olive-sided flycatchers, western wood pewee, Steller's jay, mountain and chestnut-backed chickadees, nuthatches, varied and hermit thrushes, warblers, finches, dark-eyed junco, chipping sparrow. Many seabirds can be seen on the bays and ocean.

Mammals: Include numerous bat species, mice, opossum, various shrews and moles, ground squirrels, chipmunk, pocket gopher, black-tailed jackrabbit, brush rabbit, raccoon, ringtail, badger, coyote, gray fox, wild pig, spotted skunk, black bear, bobcat, mountain lion, mule and black-tailed deer. Several species escaped from the Hearst Ranch are occasionally seen, including Rocky Mountain elk, tahr, Barbary sheep.

Reptiles and amphibians: Include salamanders, California toad, California tree frog, Great Basin, northwestern fence, and blunt-nosed leopard lizards, western skink, alligator lizards, red racer, coast patch-nosed snake, gopher snakes, California and Coast mountain king-snakes, garter snakes, Pacific rattlesnake.

Features

Ventana Wilderness: 216,500 acres. In Monterey County and the Monterey Ranger District, straddles the Santa Lucia Range. Hot in summer, cool and wet in winter. Famous for its scenic vistas.

Silver Peak Wilderness: 14,500 acres. In SW portion of the Monterey R.D., along the famous Big Sur Coast. Dramatic scenery, steep terrain, coastal redwood groves. Wildlife abounds in the more remote areas. Access to parts of the backcountry is by dirt road, subject to weather conditions.

Machesna Mountain Wilderness: 20,000 acres. 25 mi. from San Luis Obispo. High peaks, chaparral, oak woodland, conifer forest. Prairie falcon and tule elk here. Camping, hiking, hunting. One developed recreation site, Pine Springs. 1,500-acre Natural Research Area devoted to studying a unique strain of Coulter pine.

Chumash Wilderness: 38,200 acres. In the Mount Pinos R.D., near the town of Frazier Park. Contains Mount Pinos, religious site for the local Chumash. Pine forests in the N, badlands and chaparral in the S. Hiking and camping. Snow provides opportunities for winter recreation.

Matilija Wilderness: 29,600 acres. In the Ojai R.D., 12 mi. from town of Ojai. Chaparral setting. Hiking, camping at large, along two different trails, fishing at certain times of the year.

Sespe Wilderness: 219,700 acres. In both the Ojai and Mount Pinos R.D.s. Best known for hot springs near Lioncamp. Chaparral; rock cliffs in various sites. Includes the Sespe Condor Sanctuary, closed to the public.

Garcia Wilderness: 14,100 acres. In the Santa Lucia R.D., between Santa Lucia and Machesna Wilderness Areas. Offers panoramic views, solitude, lush wildflowers in spring. Ranges from chaparral-covered mountains to grassland; abundant creekside vegetation. Several trails lead into the area; hiking is through remote territory, may pass near private property. Two designated recreation areas. Hunting and fishing permitted.

Santa Lucia Wilderness: 21,704 acres. Also in the Santa Lucia R.D., behind Arroyo Grande and San Luis Obispo. Remote and beautiful; offers spring wildflowers, solitude year-round. Many trails for hiking, hunting, fishing. Morro Rock and Seven Sisters may be visible.

Dick Smith Wilderness: 68,000 acres. In Santa Lucia and Santa Barbara R.D.s. Remote and very rugged. Abundant wildlife, tree species, indigenous vegetation. Hiking, fishing, hunting are primary uses. Contains part of the historic Chumash Indian Trail, 12 mi. N of Santa Barbara (the trail was once a major trade route between the coast and the central valley).

San Rafael Wilderness: 197,570 acres. In Santa Lucia and Santa Barbara R.D.s. Elevations from 1,600 to 6,800 ft. Winter and summer recreation and camping. In the "Hurricane Deck" area, winds have carved rock into interesting shapes. 1,200 acres are a restricted santuary designed to further the return of the California condor to the wild. Whole area under restriction during fire season; often inaccessible in wet weather.

Pfeiffer Beach and Sand Dollar Beach are the two principal ocean recreation areas. Swimming is unsafe. Sand Dollar is a popular day-use area. Pfeiffer is a fragment of Forest land near Pfeiffer Big Sur State Park (see entry zone 5).

Santa Ynez River, 6 mi. N of Santa Barbara, E of Hwy 154. The Paradise–Santa Ynez road follows the river for 5 mi. River hiking trails.

Big and *Little Caliente Hot Springs,* by dirt road, 25 mi. N of Santa Barbara, off East Camino Cielo Rd. Hot springs are 2½ mi. from Pendola Station. Water as hot as 118°F.

East and *West Camino Cielo Scenic Drive,* 14 mi. N of Santa Barbara. Views of the ocean and front country on one side, backcountry on the other.

Interpretation

According to Forest HQ, "Present programs have been confined to information displays, nature trails, vista points, wildlife observation stations." Best advice is to check at Ranger Districts, campground bulletin boards.

Activities

Camping: 88 campgrounds, 986 sites. Many all year, others May 13–Oct. 31. The largest campground has 68 sites. Many have 5 or fewer.

Hiking, backpacking: 1,762 mi. of trails. 265 trail camps, the only backcountry places where chemical fuel stoves can be used, or fires built, only in the provided stoves.

Hunting: Deer, outside the fire closure area. Some black bear. Chiefly rabbit, turkey, quail, pigeon, dove, wild pig.

Fishing: 485 mi. of streams. Some native trout, some stocked. Many streams have water only in the wet season.

Swimming: About 14 of the campgrounds have swimming opportunities. Elsewhere, find a pool large enough, swim at your own risk. The ocean is not safe.

Horse riding: Although most visitors hike, some use pack and saddle stock in the wilderness areas. A visitor permit is required.

Ski touring: Mount Pinos is the most popular area for snow play. A 6-mi. flagged Nordic ski trail begins at the top parking lot. The Mount Pinos road is sometimes closed, either because new snow has not yet been plowed or because the area is full. People are often turned away on weekends.

Snowmobiling: Prohibited in wilderness areas. Snowmobiles are restricted to unplowed roads.

Motorized vehicles and mountain bikes are prohibited in wilderness areas.

Publications

2 Forest maps, $3.25 each.

Recreation information, maps, and publications for each Ranger District. Campground information for each Ranger District.

Headquarters

U.S. Forest Service, Forest Supervisor's Office, 6144 Calle Real, Goleta, CA 93117; (805) 683-6711.

Ranger Districts
Monterey R.D., 406 S. Mildred, King City, CA 93930; (408) 385-5434.
Mount Pinos R.D., HC1, Box 400, 34580 Lockwood Valley Rd., Frazier
Park, CA 93225; (805) 245-3731. Ojai R.D., 1190 E. Ojai Ave., Ojai, CA
93023; (805) 646-4348. Santa Barbara R.D., Star Rt., Los Prietos, Santa
Barbara, CA 93105; (805) 967-3481. Santa Lucia R.D., 1616 Carlotti
Dr., Santa Maria, CA 93454; (805) 925-9538.

Malibu Creek State Park
California Department of Parks and Recreation
6,600 acres.

From US 101 about 14 mi. W of I-405, S 4 mi. on Las Virgenes/Malibu
Canyon Rd.

Rugged, mainly virgin land in the middle of the Santa Monica Mountains. Mulholland Hwy crosses the site, and internal roads, open to
hikers, but closed to vehicles, follow Malibu Creek, which meanders
W to E, dropping from 700 to 500 ft. Numerous small streams join the
creek in winter and spring. The creek was dammed years ago to form
Century Lake, now about 4 acres. Rainfall averages 20–25 in. a year,
most of it in winter. No trails reach the highest and most rugged sector, in the S, with peaks over 2,000 ft.

Plants: From the creek to the N border, mostly sloping grassland with
scattered valley oak; some chaparral-covered slopes. Patches of Coast
live oak include some over 6 ft. in diameter, with poison oak and some
bay laurel trees. Other vegetation includes coffeeberry, ceanothus,
currant, snowberry, ferns. Along the creek: willow, sycamore, leatherleaf ash, cottonwood. Some more remote canyons have bigleaf maple.
Blackberry, wild rose, and mugwort are also common. Several fine
wildflower areas. Late March to early May: poppy, violets, lupines,
goldfields, larkspur, Chinese houses, creamcups, golden currant, gooseberry. Mid-may through June: clarkia, golden yarrow, penstemon,
mariposa lily, Humboldt lily, yucca, ceanothus, bush monkeyflower.

Birds: Include some ducks, coot, and great blue heron along the creek
and at the lake. Cooper's, red-shouldered, and red-tailed hawks, occa-

sional golden eagle, scrub jay, acorn woodpecker, violet-green swallow, roadrunner. Golden eagles nest in the Park. Many migratory species.

Mammals: Include ground squirrels, brush rabbit, coyote, gray fox, mule deer, bobcat, raccoon, skunk, occasional mountain lion.

Interpretation
Interpretive walks. Check at the Park.

Activities
Camping: 60 developed sits.

Hiking: 15 mi. of trails. No overnighting.

Horse riding: Combination trails.

Fishing: Creek and lake.

Mountain biking: On fire roads.

Publication
Map.

Headquarters
CA Dept. of Parks and Recreation, 1925 Las Virgenes Rd., Calabasas, CA 91302; (818) 880-0350.

Montana de Oro State Park
California Department of Parks and Recreation
Over 8,000 acres.

From San Luis Obispo, 12 mi. NW on Los Osos Valley Rd. to Los Osos, then S 3 mi. on Pecho Rd.

On the ocean, 5 mi. of coastline, most of the upland area undeveloped. The coast has coves, sand beaches, bluffs, tidepools, scenic rock formations. From primary dunes the land rises to flat marine terraces, from which the coastal hills rise to almost 1,700 ft. Between the ridges are wooded valleys, some with streams. A sand spit extending 3 mi. N along the coast is maintained as a natural preserve.

The access road enters from the N, runs above and parallel to the beach, with numerous parking areas, from which trails lead down to the shore. This is the only internal road. From several parking areas trails go back into the hills, the longest about 4½ mi. to 1,649-ft. Alan Peak. Trails along Hazard Canyon, Coon Creek, and Islay Creek; Islay has a small waterfall.

Plants: Steep hills are covered primarily with chaparral intermixed with grassland. Few trees, except along creeks: black cottonwood, box elder, creek dogwood, wax myrtle. A few California live oak, interior live oak. In the S, a stand of Bishop pine, unusual in this region. Riparian community includes hemlock, monkeyflower, watercress, horsetail. Chaparral includes black sage, lotus, chamise, California sage.

Some 260 species of flowering plants have been identified, among them poppy, fiddleneck, mustards, paintbrush, morning glory, brass buttons, red maids, tidy tips, mariposa lily, farewell to spring, hummingbird sage.

Beach plants on the sand spit include sea rocket, sand verbena, beach primrose, silver beach weed, sea fig, hottentot fig, yarrow, beach lupine, and sea thrift.

Birds: Checklist available. Include double-crested, Brandt's, and pelagic cormorants, brown pelican, oystercatcher, surfbird, western, eared, and horned grebes, plovers, curlew, whimbrel, willet, black turnstone, black-necked stilt, avocet, pigeon guillemot. Upland species include barn, screech, and great horned owls, Anna's, Allen's, and rufous hummingbirds, kestrel, merlin, northern flicker, acorn woodpecker, western kingbird, plain titmouse, wrentit, wrens, barn and bank swallows, yellow-rumped warbler, white-crowned sparrow.

Mammals: California and Steller sea lion, harbor seal, and sea otter often seen. On land: badger, striped skunk, bobcat, mule deer, opossum, mole, black-tailed jackrabbit, pocket gopher, Morrow Bay kangaroo rat, coyote, weasel, gray fox. Mountain lion has been seen.

Features

Los Osos Oaks State Reserve: 90 acres. SE of Morro Bay on Los Osos Valley Rd. Acquired to preserve an old oak forest, one of the few remaining stands of Coast oak in this area. The old oaks, Coast live oak, scrub oak, and hybrids, have grown into bizarre, gnarled shapes. Understory is mostly poison oak. Parking lot. Self-guided trails.

Valencia Peak, 1,345 ft., offers a view of 90 mi. of coastline.

Corallina Cove has fine tide pools.

Interpretation
Campfire programs in summer. Schedule posted.

Guided hikes offered occasionally all year, depending on interest. Ask at HQ.

Visitor center open weekends all year, daily in summer.

Junior Ranger program daily in summer.

Activities
Camping: 50 primitive sites. All year. Reservations Memorial Day weekend to Labor Day weekend.

Hiking: 50 mi. of trails.

Fishing: Surf. Perch, rockfish.

Swimming: Unsupervised.

Horse riding: Horses are allowed on some hiking trails. A horse camp is available on request. No rentals available in Park.

Nearby
Morrow Bay Area (see entry this zone).

Publication
Leaflet with map.

Headquarters
CA Dept. of Parks and Recreation, San Luis Obispo Coast District, 3220 S. Higuera St., Suite 311, San Luis Obispo, CA 93401; (805) 549-3312.

Morro Bay Area
California Department of Parks and Recreation
About 3,500 acres.

On and near Morro Bay, N of San Luis Obispo, off Hwy 1.

Morro Bay is enclosed by a long sand spit, part of Montana de Oro State Park (see entry this zone).

Morro Bay State Park: A beautiful wooded region with dunes and ocean views. Excellent beach hiking.

Morro Rock Ecological Reserve: 30 acres. N of harbor entrance. The rock was once about 1,000 ft. offshore, then linked with the mainland by an embankment. It is an important nesting area for marine and pelagic birds. Peregrine falcons nest annually. A parking lot adjoins the site. Some of the best birding is on the causeway.

Morro Strand State Beach: 109 acres. Sandy beach. Several miles of beach are accessible for hiking.

Birds: Checklist available from Morro Coast Audubon Society. As many as 173 species have been seen in the area on a single day, over 250 recorded. Included are pelagic species, waterfowl, wading and shore birds, upland species.

Interpretation

Evening campfire and *Junior Ranger* programs in summer. *Nature hikes,* scheduled monthly.

Morro Bay State Park *Museum of Natural History,* open 10–5 daily (except New Year's, Thanksgiving, and Christmas). Located within the Park near the golf course and campground.

Camping: 145 sites at Morro Bay State Park. Reservations all year. 104 sites at Morro Strand; reservations Memorial Day–Labor Day.

Publication
Leaflet.

Headquarters
CA Dept. of Parks and Recreation, San Luis Obispo Coast District, 3220 S. Higuera St., Suite 311, San Luis Obispo, CA 93401; (805) 549-3312.

Placerita Canyon Nature Center
Los Angeles County Parks and Recreation Department
350 acres.

I-5 N to Hwy 14 E to Placerita Canyon Rd., then E 1.5 miles.

This shady, oak-filled canyon is a nature education center for all ages. Birding, nature hikes, and star walks are all popular. Set at the junction of the San Gabriel Mountains and the Antelope Valley's desert terrain, the Nature Center exhibits displays on ecology, geology, flora, and fauna. Spring wildflowers, interpretive trails, and animal shows are also popular.

The Park has a short *self-guiding nature trail,* as well as easy *Heritage Trail,* the *Hillside Trail* to a rocky point overlook, and ½-mi. *Ecology Trail.*

Plants: More than 400 species. The canyon is home to chaparral, coastal sage scrub, and oak woodlands. Also chamise, flowering ash, buckwheats, toyon, holly-leaved cherry, and white sage. The riparian environment includes bigleaf maple, big-cone spruce, white alder, canyon oak, cottonwood, and sycamore.

Birds: Include yellow-rumped warbler, brown towhee, Canada goose, Allen's hummingbird, red-breasted nuthatch, golden-crowned kinglet, belted kingfisher. Also seen are great blue heron, brown creeper, road-runner, western screech owl.

Mammals: Opossum, mole, coyote, gray fox, raccoon, badger, striped skunk, mountain lion, bobcat, black bear, agile kangaroo rat, desert wood rat, black-tailed jackrabbit, mule deer, and CA leaf-nosed bat.

No camping here, but Walker Ranch Campground is located 6 mi. E in Placerita Canyon County Park.

Publications

Park leaflet.

Trail guides.

Bird checklist.

Headquarters
Los Angeles County Parks and Recreation Dept., 19152 W. Placerita Canyon Rd., Newhall, CA 91321; (805) 259-7721.

....

Point Mugu State Park
California Department of Parks and Recreation
13,300 acres.

From Oxnard, S 15 mi. on Hwy 1.

The Park has 3½ mi. of ocean beach, extending SW from Point Mugu. The Coast Hwy is just back of the beach, and the two campgrounds are just off the highway. In summer, the beach is often crowded, the campgrounds full. Most visitors are unaware that the Park extends more than 6 mi. inland, a large area open to foot and horse travel only.

The beach is generally broad and sandy, offering good swimming, body surfing, fishing, and skin diving. It has one exceptionally large dune, several rocky bluffs.

The site is at the W end of the Santa Monica Mountains, a rugged, hilly area. Near Point Mugu, the land rises steeply to the top of Mugu Peak, 1,266 ft., in less than ½ mi. The campgrounds are at the mouths of La Jolla and Big Sycamore Canyons, each with trails leading into the hills. Highest point is Tri-Peaks, 3,010 ft.

Plants: Most open slopes are covered with chaparral, prominent species including black and California sage, chamise, toyon, ceanothus, coffeeberry. The steep, irregular contours and interior springs combine to create cool, damp areas along stream valleys, with tall oaks, sycamore, cottonwood, ferns in the understory, grassy areas on the adjoining slopes.

Birds: No checklist.

Mammals: Species reported include mule deer, ground squirrels, gray fox, striped and spotted skunks, badger, coyote, bobcat. Mountain lions have been seen. Seal and sea lion visit the coast. Gray whale seen offshore in migration.

Interpretation
Guided hikes are offered in summer. Notices posted.

Activities
Camping: 2 campgrounds, 85 primitive sites and 55 developed sites. All year. Reservations March 1–Oct. 1.

Hiking, backpacking: More than 70 mi. of trails, through the several backcountry habitats. Overlook Trail has viewpoints. One hike-in campground 2 mi. from La Jolla trailhead. Register at the family campgrounds.

Swimming: Supervised areas in summer.

Publications
Leaflet with map.

Headquarters
CA Dept. of Parks and Recreation, Angeles District, 1925 Las Virgenes Rd., Calabasas, CA 91302; (818) 880-0350.

Red Rock Canyon State Park
California Department of Parks and Recreation
26,000 acres.
25 mi. NE of Mojave on Hwy 14.

The canyon is a long-established travel route between the E edge of the El Paso Mountains and the S tip of the Sierra Nevada. The canyon and surrounding desert mountains are colorfully scenic, each tributary canyon distinctive, sedimentary layers showing color contrasts from white to vivid reds and chocolate brown. The site and surrounding area have been used as locations in many films. Much of the surrounding area is BLM land, crossed by primitive roads, some parts much used by ORVs.

Hwy 14 traverses the canyon, crossing the site. On the W is the *Hagen Canyon Natural Preserve,* on the E the *Red Cliffs Natural Preserve,* both open to foot travel only. Terrain is generally hilly, with cliffs, palisades, rimrock. Highest point is 3,780 ft. The Park includes natural springs and seeps.

Climate is arid. Spring is the best time for a visit. Winters are cool, summers hot and dry.

Plants: Desert vegetation. Joshua tree, creosote, desert holly. Several rare species occur. The area is known for spectacular spring wildflower displays when winter rain has been sufficient.

Birds: Checklist can be seen at ranger station. Reported: hawks, vultures, owls, cactus wren, Say's phoebe, roadrunner, raven, horned lark, Le Conte's and crissal thrashers, loggerhead shrike, quail, chukar, canyon and rock wrens, mourning dove.

Mammals: Checklist can be seen at ranger station. Mentioned: bats, mice, rabbits, squirrels, occasional coyote, kit fox.

Activities

Camping: 50 primitive sites. All year.

Hiking: No formal trails, but none are needed. Several primitive roads cross the area, open to ORVs.

Publication
Leaflet with map.

Headquarters
CA Dept. of Parks and Recreation, Red Rock Canyon Box 26, Cantil, CA 93519. Or CA Dept. of Parks and Recreation, Mojave Desert Sector Office, 1051 W. Ave. M, Suite 201, Lancaster, CA 93535; (805) 942-0662.

Saddleback Butte State Park

California Department of Parks and Recreation
2,875 acres.

17 mi. E of Lancaster on Ave. J E.

In the Antelope Valley on the W edge of the Mojave Desert. A desert park near the Los Angeles metropolitan area. The acreage is a bit misleading because the surrounding landscape has much the same appearance as the Park. Elevation is 2,600 ft. at the campground. To the E, the land rises steeply to Saddleback Butte Peak, 3,651 ft., a jagged mound of granite above the alluvial bottomland.

The Park and surrounding area have numerous Joshua trees. Spring and fall are the best times to visit because the weather is mild and flowering plants may be in bloom. When we visited in early April, there were masses of coreopsis. Few animals will be seen by day, except perhaps a desert tortoise. The best time to view wildlife is in the evening and morning hours.

Camping: 50 sites. All year.

Nature trail: ½ mi., self-guided.

Publication
Leaflet with map.

Headquarters

CA Dept. of Parks and Recreation, Mojave Desert Sector Office, 1051 W. Ave. M, Suite 201, Lancaster, CA 93535; (805) 942-0662; fax (805) 940-7327.

Santa Monica Mountains National Recreation Area

U.S. National Park Service
150,000 acres.

In the Santa Monica Mountains, between US 101 and Hwy 1, includes beaches between Point Mugu and Santa Monica.

Over 70,000 acres of city, county, state, and federal park lands are located along the coast and in the mountains within the 150,000 acres lying inside the authorized boundary. Local, state, and federal agencies have been working since 1978 to coordinate planning, acquisition, and recreation programs. To date the National Park Service has acquired an additional 22,000 acres to preserve coastal uplands, stream drainage basins, and beaches; connect existing parks; protect the Mulholland scenic corridor; and develop historic sites, hiking and riding trails, scenic overlooks, and visitor facilities.

The Santa Monica Mountains National Recreation Area, a botanical island, includes chaparral, coastal sage, oak grasslands, oak woodlands, southern coastal salt- and freshwater marshes, and tidepools. Much native wildlife still survives in the mountains, including a small population of mountain lion and golden eagle.

Interpretation

An *information center* at HQ provides trip planning advice and information on weather and trail conditions throughout the system.

Ranger-led tours of the National Park area.

Activities

Camping: 6 campgrounds, 384 sites.

Hiking, horse riding: 580 mi. of public trails. Completing the Backbone Trail is a top priority. This 70-mi. trail spans the ridgeline of the mountains, from Will Rogers State Historic Park in Los Angeles County to Point Mugu State Park in Ventura County.

Swimming: At coastal beaches, also Malibu Creek.

Publications

Quarterly events calendar.

Outdoors.

Headquarters

National Park Service, 30401 Agoura Rd., Suite 100, Agoura Hill, CA 91301; (818) 597-9192, ext. 201.

....

Scodie Mountains; Kiavah Wilderness

U.S. Bureau of Land Management
About 48,000 acres; 44,000 acres U.S. Forest Service.

From Mojave, take Hwy 14 55 mi. N to Hwy 178. Continue W 10 mi. to Walker Pass. Area includes isolated portion of Sequoia National Forest as well as BLM lands.

This area includes lands between Hwy 178 on the N, Bird Springs Pass on the S, Kelso Valley on the W, and the CA Desert on the E. The Scodie Mountains are part of the southern Sierra Nevada. Mountain ridges flank deep, winding canyons. Notable are Cow Heaven, Sage, Horse, and Bird Spring Canyons, each of which contains an unimproved road to or beyond the Sequoia National Forest boundary.

This is a transition zone from mountain to desert. Elevation on the desert floor is about 3,400 ft. The long, deep, winding canyons climb to about 5,000 ft. Ridge elevations are about 6,800 ft. within the Forest. The Pacific Crest Trail crosses the area from Bird Springs Pass to Walker Pass. Most of the Forest Service lands and much of the BLM lands were designated as the *Kiavah Wilderness* by the CA Desert Protection Act of 1994. Several vehicle routes on the SE side were excluded from the wilderness designation.

Plants: Desert plants such as creosote, burrobrush, and shadscale grow in proximity to such mountain species as pinyon pine, juniper, canyon oak, and gray pine. The lower canyon floors have Joshua tree, cacti, and low desert shrubs. Riparian communities along springs and intermittent stream. W slopes have Joshua tree, ephedra, horsebrush, buckwheats, rabbitbrush, cholla. There are attractive spring wildflower displays.

Birds: Include sharp-shinned and red-tailed hawks, prairie falcon, California and mountain quail, roadrunner, great-horned and burrowing owls, ladderback woodpecker, northern flicker, mourning dove. The canyons are critical habitat for neotropic migrating birds.

Mammals: Include pronghorn, ground squirrels, wood rat, black-tailed jackrabbit, desert cottontail, coyote, mule deer.

Reptiles and amphibians: Mix of desert and mountain species. Western toad, striped racer have dispersed E through the canyons, while desert night lizard, banded gecko, and other desert fauna have dispersed W.

Activities
Camping: Walker Pass Campground includes 9 walk-in and 2 vehicle-access sites. Water available mid-April–Oct.

Hiking: The Pacific Crest Trail runs through Walker Pass.

Headquarters
W: Bureau of Land Management, Caliente Resource Area, 3801 Pegasus Dr., Bakersfield, CA 93308-6837; (805) 391-6000. Center: U.S. Forest Service, Cannell Meadow R.D., 105 Whitney Rd., P.O. Box 6, Kernville, CA 93238;(619) 376-3781. E: Bureau of Land Management, Ridgecrest Resource Area, 300 S. Richmond Rd., Ridgecrest, CA 93555; (619) 384-5400.

Sequoia National Forest
U.S. Forest Service

288,380 acres of this Forest are in zone 8, with several large blocks of Forest land almost surrounding Lake Isabella, although the Forest has no lake frontage and the boundary is generally 3 or more mi. from the lakeshore. Most of the Forest is in zone 7, and the entry appears there.

Sheephole Mountains and Valley; Cadiz Valley

U.S. Bureau of Land Management
See entry for Joshua Tree National Park (zone 9).

Topanga State Park

California Department of Parks and Recreation
11,000 acres.

From Santa Monica, Hwy 1 W to Topanga Canyon Blvd., N to Entrada
Rd., then every left turn to Park. From Woodland Hills, S on Topanga
Canyon Blvd. to Entrada.

Topanga is one of the world's largest wilderness parks within a major
metropolitan area (Los Angeles), offering more than 35 mi. of trails
and fire roads for hiking and horseback riding. Elevations range from
200 to 1,500 ft. The Park's canyons and ridges are covered with dense
chaparral. Canyon creek drainages host rich riparian habitats. Tippet
Ranch, the Park's headquarters and main entrance, is set in an oak
woodland community.

Interpretation

Small *visitor center,* open Sun, 12–4.

Mountain bikes restricted to fire roads.

Nearby

State beaches between Malibu and Santa Monica. Malibu Creek State
Park.

Headquarters

CA Dept. of Parks and Recreation, 20825 Entrada Rd., Topanga, CA
90290; (310) 455-2465.

Tule Elk State Reserve

California Department of Parks and Recreation
956 acres.

17 mi. W of Bakersfield. 3 mi. W and S of Stockdale Rd. interchange on I-5, via Stockdale Rd. and Morris Rd.

A 5-acre viewing area is the only part of the Reserve open to the public.

Tule elk were numerous in CA until the Gold Rush. By 1863, numbers were greatly depleted, and the last remaining range was fast disappearing. Since then, public and private efforts have been made to preserve the species and reestablish adequate herds. The chief difficulty has been to secure suitable habitat. The Dept. of Parks and Recreation continues to look for "spacious and appealing natural environment for the elk." In 1996, they had found locations for 22 herds. The largest herd is at La Ponza, with over 700 elk.

The Reserve is mostly flat, open grassland with a few seasonally flooded ponds and flood channels. Annual precipitation is less than 5 in. The viewing area is sometimes crowded on major holidays.

Interpretation
Visitor center open 10–4 in season, closed Mon. and Fri. Also closed in winter months.

Publications
Tule Elk (leaflet), $0.50.

Checklists for birds, mammals, $0.50 each.

Headquarters
CA Dept. of Parks and Recreation, 8653 Station Rd., Buttonwillow, CA 93206; (805) 765-5004.

Upper Newport Bay Ecological Reserve and Regional Park

Orange County Environmental Management Agency and California Department of Fish and Game
892 acres.

Jamboree Rd. exit off I-405 to Back Bay Dr. Turn right and drive ¼ mi. to the Reserve.

This estuary is a popular wildlife refuge that is home to several hundred bird species including half a dozen rare and endangered species. Open water, tidal flats, salt marsh, freshwater marsh, and upland environments make this refuge, in the midst of a busy urban area, a popular retreat. Hiking, bird watching, canoeing, and kayaking are all popular here.

Plants: Upper Newport Bay is home to streamside willows and acacia, California buckwheat, cattail, bulrush, and bull tule. A variety of cacti and succulents grow here along with pickleweed and cord grass near the water's edge. Also poison hemlock, poppy, salt heliotrope, and dragon sagewort. Watercress grows in the freshwater streams.

Birds: From late summer to early spring, tens of thousands of birds reside here. Mallard, green-winged teal, brown pelican, great blue heron, cormorants, bushtit, hawks, spotted sandpiper, hummingbirds, mockingbird, orange-crowned warbler, western meadowlark. Among the rare and endangered species are the least tern, Belding's (savannah) sparrow, clapper and black rail, peregrine falcon.

Headquarters
Orange County Environmental Management Agency, 600 Shellmaker, Newport Beach, CA 92660; (714) 640-1751.

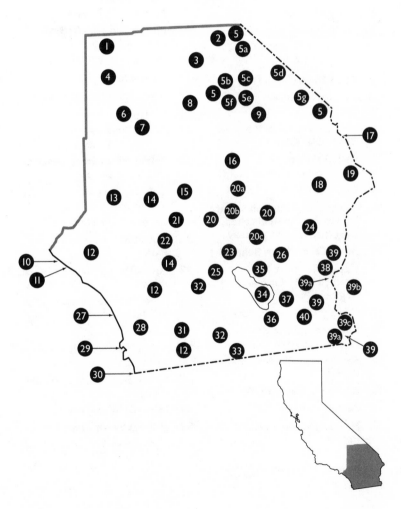

1 Trona Pinnacles Natural Area

2 Kingston Range/Amargosa Canyon–Dumont Dunes Natural Area

3 Avawatz Mountains

4 Golden Valley Wilderness

5 Mojave National Preserve

5a Clark Mountains

5b Cinder Cones

5c Cima Dome

5d New York Mountains

5e Kelso Mountains

5f Kelso Dunes

5g Fort Piute/Piute Creek/Piute Gorge

6 Harper Dry Lake; Rainbow Basin–Owl Canyon

7 California Desert Information Center

8 Cronese Lakes

9 Providence Mountains State Recreation Area; Mitchell Caverns Natural Preserve

10 Bolsa Chica State Beach

11 Upper Newport Bay Ecological Reserve and Regional Park

12 Cleveland National Forest

13 Silverwood Lake State Recreation Area

14 San Bernardino National Forest

15 Bighorn Mountains

16 Amboy Crater

17 Havasu National Wildlife Refuge

18 Turtle Mountains

19 Whipple Mountains Wilderness

20 Joshua Tree National Park

20a Coxcomb Mountains/Sheephole Mountains–Cadiz Valley

20b Pinto Mountains

20c Eagle Mountains

21 Morongo-Whitewater

22 Mount San Jacinto State Park and State Wilderness

23 Mecca Hills Wilderness

24 Palen-McCoy Wilderness

25 Santa Rosa Mountains

26 Chuckwalla Mountains

27 Buena Vista Lagoon Ecological Reserve

28 Torrey Pines State Reserve and State Beach

29 Cabrillo National Monument

30 Border Field State Park

31 Cuyamaca Rancho State Park

32 Anza-Borrego Desert State Park

33 In-Ko-Pah Mountain Wilderness

34 Salton Sea

35 Salton Sea State Recreation Area

36 Salton Sea National Wildlife Refuge

37 Imperial Wildlife Area

38 Milpitas Wash - Palo Verde Mountains

Z O N E

Includes these counties:

San Bernardino	Orange	Imperial
Riverside	San Diego	

This is our largest CA zone and the only one that extends across the state from the ocean to the E boundary. At the coast, its boundary passes between Los Angeles and Anaheim. Their populations have a heavy impact on many of the natural areas.

Few of the public beaches along the coast met our selection criteria. Planned for recreation, they serve that purpose well, and we have enjoyed them on uncrowded days. Several coastal sites are attractive natural areas, notably Torrey Pines State Reserve and Beach.

The mountains E and SE of Los Angeles are largely occupied by the San Bernardino and Cleveland National Forests. Both are heavily used, but both have many attractions and some quiet areas. One can avoid the crowds.

The largest part of the zone, across the mountains, is desert. The CA Desert, a region of more than 25 million acres, includes a great variety of landforms: valleys, bajadas, pediments, alluvial fans, mountain ranges, washes, sand dunes, dry lakebeds. Almost half of the area, over 12 million acres, is public domain. The area also includes Anza-Borrego Desert State Park, Joshua Tree National Park, and Death Valley National Park, several large military installations, and a number of smaller state and federal sites.

In 1976, Congress directed the BLM to take the lead in developing a comprehensive, long-range land-use plan for the California Desert Conservation Area. As with earlier plans for National Forests, the theme was to be sustained yield: use of resources without environmental damage. It was a monumental task, requiring acre-by-acre analysis of everything from geothermal potential and native American artifacts to flora and fauna. Completed in 1980, the plan identified wilderness areas and other sites that required protection because of their special natural qualities.

The California Desert Protection Act was passed by Congress in 1994. This important legislation designated nearly 4 million acres of desert land in Death Valley National Park, in Joshua Tree National Park, and in the newly created Mojave National Preserve as wilderness. In addition, it conferred wilderness status on 69 individual BLM areas containing 3.6 million acres of desert land.

For strangers who wish to understand and appreciate the desert, a good place to begin is the BLM's California Desert Information Center (see entry). The Center is within what the BLM calls the High Desert, an area that includes a number of our entries. A leaflet available there describes the area.

Anza-Borrego Desert State Park and Joshua Tree National Park also have splendid visitor centers and interpretive programs. (So does Death Valley National Park, zone 7). A few hours in one of these centers makes a visit to the CA Desert more fascinating.

The desert sites offer great diversity. No two are quite alike, and some are unique. Some are beside good roads and can be explored in an easy walk. Many are roadless areas, with opportunities for day hikes up attractive canyons. Some are vast and rugged, to be explored only by those who understand the requirements of desert survival.

Water in the desert is always dramatic, creating a palm oasis, a strip of green riparian vegetation, a waterfowl marsh, even a waterfall. We mention streams and springs, where they exist, but one should not assume that all are easily found, or that the water is necessarily safe for drinking.

Canoeing in the desert? Indeed yes, on the Colorado River. The entry for the Colorado River National Wildlife Refuges and Wilderness Areas describes this opportunity.

Algodones Dunes

U.S. Bureau of Land Management
See Sand Hills (this zone).

Amargosa Canyon–Dumont Dunes Natural Area

U.S. Bureau of Land Management
See Kingston Range (this zone).

Amboy Crater

U.S. Bureau of Land Management
3,200 acres.

From Ludlow on I-40, 27 mi. SE to Amboy on Old National Trail Hwy.
Crater is just W of Amboy.

Located about 10 mi. S of the Mojave National Preserve, this 250-ft.-high crater is about 6,000 years old and is one of the best examples of a volcanic cinder cone in the Mojave Desert. It is steep-sided, black, surrounded by extensive lava flows. Unlike most other cinder cones in the desert it has not been mined and is a National Natural Landmark. A footpath leads to the top of the cone where there are great views of the surrounding area. The hike to the Crater and back will take 2–3 hr. Late January through March are good times to see wildflowers.

Headquarters

Bureau of Land Management, Barstow Resource Center, 150 Coolwater Lane, Barstow, CA 92311; (619) 255-8760.

Anza-Borrego Desert State Park

California Department of Parks and Recreation
Over 600,000 acres.

85 mi. NE of San Diego via I-8, Hwy 79 or 78.

A huge, unique desert Park with great diversity of topography, flora, and fauna. A National Natural Landmark, containing some of the best examples of the various desert biotic communities in the CA Desert and excellent examples of desert geological phenomena. Three principal roads, all scenic, cross the area: S-2, from NW to SE; Hwy 78, W to E, near the midpoint; and S-22, W to E across the N portion, through Borrego Springs. The Park also has several hundred miles of backcountry roads, many requiring 4-wheel drive, as well as hiking trails.

Although it has conventional campgrounds, primitive campsites (with latrines but no water) are also scattered throughout the Park. You are also welcome to camp anywhere along designated travel routes. "For many people," says the Park leaflet, "this is the *only* way to camp in the desert."

The Salton Sea, a few mi. E of the Park, is 232 ft. below sea level. S-22, the Borrego Salton Seaway, climbs gradually through sloping, heavily eroded terrain, to an elevation of 580 ft. at Borrego Springs, a town within the Park, site of Park HQ. Continuing W, this route now climbs steeply, with splendid views, topping the mountain ridge at 4,006 ft., the Park boundary.

The western and northeastern parts of the Park are mountainous. Highest point is Combs Peak, 6,193 ft., in the NW corner. Each of the mountainous areas has peaks over 5,000 ft. Several higher peaks are on adjoining BLM and Forest Service land. The central part of the Park is a basin surrounded by higher elevations.

Rainfall averages 6.86 in. a year at Borrego Springs. Large areas of the Park receive much less, the heights of the Santa Rosa Mountains and the Peninsular Ranges somewhat more. Winter rains, when they occur, are likely to be moderate and steady, summer thunderstorms heavy and brief. But desert rainfall is erratic and unpredictable.

Most visitors come in winter and spring, when the climate is most pleasant. Winter temperatures generally range between 43° and 75°F. If rainfall has been sufficient and the temperature is right, wildflowers begin blooming at lower elevations in Feb., as late as May and June in the mountains.

Numerous springs in the Park support distinctive plant life as well as both resident and migratory animals. Coyote Creek, in the NW, rises from the ground, flows 2 mi., and vanishes, creating a unique strip of riparian vegetation.

What brings people back here again and again is the infinite variety. This desert is not an endless waste of shifting sands. A few yards off a main road, the dirt track may descend into a dry wash, giving an immediate sense of isolation, and that isolation can be quite real until you find your way back to a paved road again. The landscape includes many dry washes, steep-walled canyons, badlands, dry lakes, bizarre sandstone formations, cliffs several hundred feet high, oases, waterfalls that flow after a rain.

Don't go into the backcountry unprepared. Even experienced desert travelers can encounter problems, but they know what to do and have the equipment they need.

Plants: Trees are scarce in the desert. A few stands of Coulter and Jeffrey pines occur at high elevations. Pinyon, juniper, mountain mahogany, and desert scrub oak on some slopes below 6,000 ft., with manzanita, Parry nolina, desert agave, buckwheats. Usually somewhat lower, but above 3,000 ft., chaparral community, common species including chamise, scrub oak, manzanita, sumac, Mojave yucca.

The lower slopes and valleys have generally sparse but conspicuous vegetation. One prominent species is the ocotillo, up to 20 ft. tall, which produces small green leaves quickly after rain, drops them in dry weather. Other members of this community include barrel cactus, creosote, indigo, cholla. Desert washes vary greatly in plant species and density, some of the more common species including smoke tree, ironwood, palo verde, desert willow, mesquite, bunch grass, desert lavender, loco weed, mistletoe.

The Park boasts 600 species of flowering plants, among them trumpet flower, desert aster, bladderpod, desert lily, verbena, dune primrose, lupine, desert mariposa, blazing star, phacelia, penstemon.

Birds: Checklist available. 206 species recorded, including golden eagle, prairie falcon, mountain quail, scrub jay, raven, red-tailed hawk, roadrunner, prairie falcon, Say's phoebe, loggerhead shrike, poor-will, black-throated sparrow, canyon, cactus, and rock wrens, mockingbird, California thrasher, Bell's vireo.

Mammals: Include California ground squirrel, pinyon mouse, desert wood rat, antelope ground squirrel, kangaroo rat, coyote, black-tailed jackrabbit, cottontail, kit fox, gray fox, mule deer, bighorn sheep. Ringtail and mountain lion reported, seldom seen.

Reptiles and amphibians: Include western fence, flat-tailed horned, collared, zebra-tailed, and banded rock lizards, chuckwalla, desert iguana, Sonoran gopher snake, red racer, rosy boa, sidewinder, red diamond rattlesnake, shovel-nosed snake, and glossy snake.

Features

The Park leaflet mentions a number of points of interest, among them:

Coyote Canyon, site of a year-round flowing stream. Good birding.

Yaqui Well, a seep that attracts migratory birds.

Split Mountain, high canyon walls, a gorge that carries torrential flash floods after a downpour. Geological interest.

Elephant Trees, a botanical oddity near Split Mountain, with nature trail.

17 Palm Oasis, a dry desert seep. 29 palms now growing.

Calcite Canyon Scenic Area, bizarre sandstone formations.

Palm Spring, another oasis with native palms, good birding.

Some of the following can be reached only with 4-wheel-drive vehicles.

Font's Point, viewpoint in the Borrego Badlands, uplifted by faulting action hundreds of feet. Some say it's the Park's grandest viewpoint. Ancient river sediments nearby recently yielded a million-year-old mammoth skeleton. Check road conditions; 4-wheel drive sometimes required.

Borrego Palm Canyon, several mi. long. Year-round water, hundreds of native palms. Desert bighorn sheep, migratory birds. Hiking trail into canyon mouth.

These publicized features attract many visitors. By all means see them, but this is only a beginning. Backcountry roads and trails lead to many areas no less fascinating.

Anza-Borrego Desert State Wilderness: 46,000 acres. In NW sector, SW of Coyote Canyon. Sheep Canyon and Borrego Palm Canyon penetrate the area. Rugged and remote. Water and palms in most canyons. Some 150 bighorn sheep are in the area. Three of the canyons have heavy backpacking use on weekends and holidays, Oct.–May. Horse camp in Coyote Canyon.

Santa Rosa Mountains State Wilderness: 87,000 acres. Occupies the mountainous NE sector, E of Coyote Canyon. The highest and least traveled portion of the Park. It adjoins the BLM's Santa Rosa Mountains Wilderness (see entry for Santa Rosa Mountains, this zone). Very rugged. Almost no water. Stronghold for peninsular bighorn sheep.

Bow Willow Canyon. A marked road turns W off S-2 about 8 mi. from the SW Park boundary, to Bow Willow Campground and ranger station. Nearby is *Mountain Palm Springs,* a palm oasis. Ask about trails in Bow Willow Canyon. Palm groves in secluded side canyons. With directions from the ranger, one can hike across the boundary into the BLM's Bow Willow Palms area, an isolated fan palm grove.

Bow Willow Palms: 720 acres. At edge of Park in San Diego County. An isolated, undisturbed area of California fan palms, at 2,000 ft. Part of McCain Valley national cooperative land and wildlife management area. Walk in from Park.

Interpretation

The *visitor center* is unique, a million-dollar project built with much local support. A fine audiovisual presentation, exhibits, publications, information.

Campfire programs. Notices posted in campgrounds and local newspaper.

Guided hikes. Notices posted.

Nature trails: Narrows Earth Trail, Bow Willow Nature Trail, Borrego Palm Canyon, and Elephant Trees Discovery Trail. Leaflets.

Self-guided auto tours, with leaflets: Erosion Rd. and Southern Emigrant Trail.

Activities

Camping: 3 developed campgrounds, 142 sites. Reservations Sept. 28–June 4. 10 primitive campgrounds. Camp anywhere on designated travel routes, subject to Park rules. Water only at developed campgrounds.

Hiking, backpacking: Many miles of hiking trails, but one can also hike on backcountry dirt roads and, in many places, cross-country. The Pacific Crest Trail crosses the NW corner of the Park, runs generally W of the boundary.

Horse riding: About 80 mi. of trails. No rentals or nearby outfitters. A horse camp in the NW sector can be reserved.

Adjacent or Nearby

Cleveland National Forest (see entry this zone).

Cuyamaca Rancho State Park (see entry this zone).

Santa Rosa Mountains (see entry this zone).

Publications

Leaflet with map.

Nature and auto trail guides.

Checklists of birds, mammals, reptiles, amphibians.

Headquarters

CA Dept. of Parks and Recreation, 200 Palm Canyon Dr., Borrego Springs, CA 92004; (619) 767-5311.

Avawatz Mountains

U.S. Bureau of Land Management
96,600 acres.

At the SE corner of Death Valley National Park, on Hwy 127 and the unpaved road that leaves Hwy 127 5 mi. E of the Park.

From the dry bed of Silurian Lake on Hwy 127, at about 500 ft. elevation, the land slopes gradually upward toward the SW to about the 2,500-ft. contour, then steeply to 6,154 ft. The large mass of the Avawatz Mountains, extending about 10 mi. NW–SE, has many colorful, eroded slopes, rugged ridges, and narrow, steep-walled canyons. From numerous viewpoints, one looks N into Death Valley National Park.

Vegetation is mostly desert scrub. An extremely dense stand of Joshua trees adjoins the mountains. Nine springs provide water for wildlife, including a resident herd of bighorn sheep.

The low area along Hwy 127 has had considerable ORV use, but the canyons are generally undisturbed.

Headquarters

Bureau of Land Management, Barstow Resource Center, 150 Coolwater Lane, Barstow, CA 92311; (619) 255-8760.

Bighorn Mountains

U.S. Bureau of Land Management
58,500 acres.

From Barstow, take Hwy 247 S 30 mi. to Lucerne, then Hwy 247E for 25 mi. to Pipes Canyon Rd. (gravel road) W for 15 mi. to Big Bear Lake.

This area adjoins the Granite Peak Roadless Area of the San Bernardino National Forest (see entry this zone). Terrain rises from N to S, from about 3,000 ft. in the valley to 6,000 ft. at the Forest boundary, the highest point 6,265 ft. One of the more scenic portions is Rattlesnake

Canyon, a broad canyon in the S part of the area. Landforms include craggy peaks, granitic boulder piles, interior valleys, broad desert bajadas.

Typical desert vegetation at lower elevations: creosote bush scrub, blackbrush scrub, sagebrush scrub, with yucca and cacti. Moving up the slopes, this gives way to pinyon-juniper and some ponderosa pine forest. The Granite Peak area of the Forest has many Joshua trees, including the world's largest specimen, and this BLM area also has many exceptionally large specimens, in the Mound Springs area of the SW corner.

The *Big Bear Lake* resort area of the Forest is also in the NE sector, and for much of the year traffic on Forest roads in this sector is heavy. Hikers and backpackers may well prefer to hike into the Granite Peaks area through the BLM lands. Primitive access ways are in some of the canyons, maintained only by the passage of vehicles and subject to occasional obliteration by washouts. Sites on the perimeter of the area are accessible by automobile and have some recreational use: camping, rockhounding, hunting, and ORVs. No developed campgrounds.

Headquarters
Bureau of Land Management, California Desert District, 6221 Box Springs Blvd., Riverside, CA 92507; (909) 697-5200.

Bolsa Chica State Beach

California Department of Parks and Recreation
84 acres.

3 mi. NW of Huntington Beach on Hwy 1.

This small, heavily used beach in the metropolitan area is an entry because it adjoins the 530-acre *Bolsa Chica Ecological Reserve*. There the CA Dept. of Fish and Game has undertaken to restore a salt marsh from an altered and abused tidal marsh ecosystem. The area was acquired from an oil-refining company in 1973. Numerous bird species now nest and visit. The beach is wheelchair accessible and has a bike trail. The Reserve is across Hwy 1 from the beach, on the inland side.

Camping: 50 sites for self-contained vehicles only. Fire ring, dressing rooms, cold showers.

Headquarters
CA Dept. of Parks and Recreation, Orange Coast District Office, 18331 Enterprise Lane, Huntington Beach, CA 92648; (714) 848-1566.

Border Field State Park
California Department of Parks and Recreation
680 acres.

15 mi. S of San Diego via I-5 and Monument Rd.

Over 1 mi. of ocean front. The most southerly CA State Park, on the Mexican border. The salt marsh at the mouth of the Tia Juana River is an outstanding natural area, with good birding all year. Facilities include nature, hiking, and equestrian trails.

Headquarters
CA Dept. of Parks and Recreation, Frontera District Office, 3990 Old Town Ave., Suite 300-C, San Diego, CA 92110; (619) 237-6768.

Buena Vista Lagoon Ecological Reserve
California Department of Fish and Game
192 acres.

On the coast between Carlsbad and Oceanside.

A coastal lagoon and freshwater marsh. A young Carlsbad resident initiated the move to make this a bird sanctuary in 1939. By the early 1950s the Buena Vista Lagoon Association had acquired 85 acres of submerged land. Other bits were acquired to bring the Reserve to its present size. Over 200 bird species and 50 plant species have been identified. Viewing opportunities from outside are good.

Cabrillo National Monument

U.S. National Park Service
144 acres.

In San Diego, S on Hwy 209, Catalina Blvd. Through Navy gates to the tip of Point Loma.

Open: 9–5:15, 7 days a week. Extended hours during summer.

A small site, and except for the walkways and overlooks, in a natural condition. The peninsula has rocky coastal cliffs, overlooking San Diego Harbor and the CA and Mexican coast. The 19th-century lighthouse has been restored. Upland areas have desert and chaparral vegetation. Highest point is 420 ft. On the ocean side are tide pools, best observed at low tides Oct.–April. Over 375 bird species identified here. The whale-watching station is a good place to observe gray whales in the Dec.–March migration. 2-mi. Bayside Trail.

Interpretation
Visitor center has films and exhibits.

Publication
Leaflet with map.

Headquarters
National Park Service, P.O. Box 6670, San Diego, CA 92166-0670; (619) 557-5450.

California Desert Information Center

U.S. Bureau of Land Management

From I-15, Barstow Rd. exit. One block N to 831 Barstow Rd.

Open: Daily. Mon.–Sun. 9–5. Closed Christmas and New Year's Day.

The BLM's *visitor center* for the CA Desert, a region about the size of the state of Ohio. The Center has exhibits, displays, information, literature. Themes include desert ecology, wildflowers, wildlife, desert safety, ORV areas, camping.

Publication
High Desert Recreation Resources Guide.

Headquarters
Bureau of Land Management, 831 Barstow Rd., Barstow, CA 92311; (619) 255-8760.

....

Carrizo Plain Natural Area

U.S. Bureau of Land Management
200,000 acres.

From Hwy 99 exit on Hwy 166 W 25 mi. to Maricopa, then N on Hwy 33 20 mi. to McKittrick. Continue W on Hwy 58 15 mi. to Elkhorn Rd. S into the Natural Area.

A gentle reminder of what the CA scene looked like 3 centuries ago, the Carrizo Plain is the largest of the remaining San Joaquin Valley grasslands.

The plain is an internal drainage basin with all water flowing to Soda Lake. This lake evaporates into a white, salt-encrusted basin during the dry months. The plain stretches roughly 50 mi. N to S. Caliente Mountain, the highest peak in San Luis Obispo County, stands 5,106 ft. high, while the Temblors reach a height of 4,332 ft. at McKittrick Summit. The San Andreas Fault runs through the area and is clearly seen at Wallace Creek. The plain is one of the sunniest places in CA and summer temperatures often exceed 100°F. On winter nights, temperatures dip below freezing. Dirt roads are sometimes impassable or closed when wet.

Chumash, Yokut, and other native Americans hunted and traded in this region. Painted Rock, probably used for religious ceremonies, is a fascinating example of native American rock art. The Painted Rock area is open all year, except from March 1–July 15 when access is only by guided tour. Dryland grain farming and ranching began in the late 19th century. Today, most people come to Carrizo for recreation— birding, hiking, photography, camping, hunting, and just to relax. The Carrizo Plain Natural Area is jointly administered by the BLM, The Nature Conservancy, and the CA Dept. of Fish and Game. Area is managed for the benefit of rare and endangered plants and animals and for restoration of native ecosystems.

Plants: Plant communities range from iodine bush scrub and salt-bush scrub to valley grasslands and juniper woodland. Spring is wonderful here thanks to blooming perennials.

Birds: Winter brings sandhill cranes to Soda Lake. Many different raptors can also be found throughout the area, including red-tailed hawks, golden eagles, black-shouldered kites, northern harrier, owls. The CA condor has been reintroduced nearby.

Mammals: Endangered animals living on the plain include the blunt-nosed leopard lizard, the San Joaquin kit fox, the giant kangaroo rat, and the San Joaquin antelope ground squirrel. Tule elk and pronghorn antelope have been reintroduced into the area.

Interpretation
Goodwin Education Center (visitor center), information, campfire permits, spring wildflower and Painted Rock tour reservations. Open Jan.–May, Thur.–Sun. P.O. Box 3087, California Valley, CA 93453; (805) 475-2131.

Publication
Carrizo Plain leaflet.

Headquarters
Bureau of Land Management, Caliente Resource Area, 3801 Pegasus Dr., Bakersfield, CA 93308-6837; (805) 391-6000.

Chemehuevi Mountains
U.S. Bureau of Land Management
See Havasu National Wildlife Refuge (this zone).

Chino Hills State Park
California Department of Parks and Recreation
13,000 acres.

Hwy 71 S from I-10 to Pomona-Rincon Rd. Continue N to Soquel Canyon Pkwy. Turn left (W) to Elinvar Rd. and turn left (S) to Park entrance.

With its beautiful rolling grassland hills, oak woodlands, and several creeks, this Park is a fine retreat. Hiking, biking, and riding are all popular. Abundant spring wildflowers and wildlife.

Activities

Camping: 8 primitive sites.

Hiking: Popular backcountry hiking trails include Water Canyon and Hills for Everyone. Trails range from ¼ to 5 mi.

Horse riding: Allowed on all roads.

Biking: Allowed on wide dirt roads. 15 mph speed limit applies.

Publication
Park leaflet with map.

Headquarters
CA Dept. of Parks and Recreation, 1879 Jackson St., Riverside, CA 92504; (714) 780-6222.

Chuckwalla Mountains
U.S. Bureau of Land Management
140,100 acres.

10 mi. S of Desert Center on I-10. Bounded by I-10, Graham Pass Rd. on E, Chocolate Mountains Aerial Gunnery Range, and Bradshaw Mountain Rd.

From about 500 ft. elevation along I-10 in the Chuckwalla Valley to the NE, the bajada rises gradually to the mountain base at about 1,500 ft. The valley to the SW, between the Chuckwalla and Chocolate Mountains, is about 1,000 ft. higher. The Chuckwalla Mountains are a range of colorful rock ridges, boulders, and hills, rising to several peaks over 3,000 ft., the highest 4,504-ft. Black Butte. Numerous canyons wind into the interior, penetrating the mountain mass, notably Corn Springs Wash from the NE and Ship Creek from the E. Wide-open spaces and large interior valleys give a feeling of spaciousness, while rugged, narrow canyons and jumbles of rocky spires and ridges give a sense of isolation. Water is relatively abundant: many springs, but quality is untested. Bighorn sheep, burros, deer, raptors, and coyotes choose these mountains as their home.

The Chuckwalla Bench in the S is a transition zone between the Colorado and Mojave Deserts. It is crucial habitat for the desert tortoise and sustains an unusual assemblage of plant species: clusters of ocotillo, cholla cactus gardens, yucca, thick stands of creosote, barrel cactus, nolina. The Munz cholla, largest cholla in the CA Desert, is found only here and in the Chocolate Mountains. Several other rare plant species occur. In 1994, 80,770 acres of the Chuckwallas were designated as wilderness. Not included in the wilderness designation was the Corn Springs area, in a canyon deep in the mountains. The spring supports a rich riparian vegetation including about 20 fan palms, a dense thicket of gnarled mesquite, catclaw, desert willow, and smoke tree. The oasis attracts wildlife, including many migratory birds. It is one of the few CA sites where the elf owl is known to have bred. The area has petroglyphs and other artifacts. It has been designated an Area of Critical Environmental Concern. The canyon has attracted many visitors, and the BLM closely manages vehicle traffic in an effort to control further damage.

The route from Corn Springs to the Red Cloud mine is said to be scenic and provide access to good rockhounding sites. St. Augustine Pass is also mentioned as scenic.

Camping: 10 tent sites at Corn Springs. 8 mi. E of Desert Center via I-10, then follow signs.

Headquarters
Bureau of Land Management, California Desert District, 6221 Box Springs Blvd., Riverside, CA 92507; (909) 697-5200. Also, Bureau of Land Management, Palm Springs–S. Coast Resource Area, 63-500 Garnet Ave., P.O. Box 2000, N. Palm Springs, CA 92258; (614) 251-4800.

Cibola National Wildlife Refuge
U.S. Fish and Wildlife Service
See Colorado River National Wildlife Refuges and Wilderness Areas (this zone).

Cima Dome
U.S. National Park Service
See Mojave National Preserve (this zone).

Cinder Cones

U.S. National Park Service
See Mojave National Preserve (this zone).

Clark Mountains

U.S. National Park Service
See Mojave National Preserve (this zone).

Cleveland National Forest

U.S. Forest Service
419,841 acres of National Forest land; 566,781 acres within boundaries.

Three separated parts. (1) SE of Anaheim; S of Hwy 91; W of Hwy 71; crossed by Hwy 74. (2) At Palomar Mountain. S and W of Hwy 79; crossed by Hwy 76. (3) About 50 mi. E of San Diego, crossed by I-8.

Planning a visit to the Cleveland requires a bit of study. Its three parts (four, counting a slightly detached part of the Palomar District) have irregular shapes and each contains many inholdings. All three include mountains that lie between the desert and the sea, but are not a continuous ridge, nor are the mountains very high. The northern part, the Trabuco Ranger District, covers the Santa Ana Mountains, in which the highest peak is 5,687 ft. Palomar Ranger District, the central part, includes Palomar Mountain, 6,140 ft., and neighboring hills. Descanso Ranger District, the southern part, includes the Laguna Mountains and the highest point in the Forest, 6,271 ft.; most of that range is considerably lower. Terrain is complex, with many canyons and interior valleys. On the E side, it drops off sharply into desert.

Climate is Mediterranean, though with much local variation. On the W side at low elevations, rainfall is as little as 10 in. annually, though generally a bit over 15 in. On the highest slopes it may exceed 30 in., with a marked seasonal pattern and sharp year-to-year differences. Most streams are seasonal. Several reservoirs are near or within the Forest boundaries, but most of the land around them is private, and they are subject to marked seasonal drawdowns. Snowfall on the high slopes is sometimes sufficient for ski touring and snow play. However, most of the Forest, close to several large cities, is available for hiking when the High Sierra is closed by snow. One reason for the popularity of these Forest campgrounds in summer is that most are at high elevations, several at 6,000 ft., many over 4,000 ft., where it is cooler than in the valleys below.

In the Trabuco Ranger District, much of the visitor recreation use is on or near Hwy 74, which runs through San Juan Canyon. However, the Forest map suggests that many visitors, familiar with the area, enter by various unpaved roads and foot trails around the perimeter and proceed up small canyons.

Palomar Mountain is the site of one of the world's largest optical telescopes. This Ranger District is irregular in shape, about 40 mi. long, from 2–8 mi. wide, with many inholdings. A detached portion is across Hwy 79; this portion includes about 5 mi. of the Pacific Crest Trail. There are concentrations of recreation facilities, including state and county parks and commercial resorts. The NW corner of the area is the *Agua Tibia Wilderness*.

The Descanso R.D. is the largest of the three, 30 mi. from N to S, 24 from E to W, but irregular in shape and with more inholdings than the others. Visitation is greatest in the E sector, the highest country and the coolest in summer. Here 11 campgrounds, including 2 with over 100 units each, are at or above 5,600 ft. The Pacific Crest Trail runs through this sector, connected by a temporary section between the Pioneer Mail trailhead, at the N end of the District, and the town of Warner Springs.

The Laguna Mountain area, so named because of the small seasonal lakes in the high country, receives more snow than other parts of the Forest. Traffic jams are common on winter weekends when the snow is good, and the Sunrise Hwy, S-1, is occasionally closed because all roadside parking is full.

Plants: Most of the hillsides are covered with chaparral. Species include mountain mahogany, buckwheats, several manzanita species, scrub oak, Coast and interior live oaks, white sage, chamise, toyon, coastal sagebrush, willow, sycamore, wild rose, holly-leaved cherry. Valley woodlands include cottonwood, live oak, sycamore, willow, with poison oak and wild rose in the understory. On the higher slopes, conifer forest, with Jeffrey pine, Douglas-fir, black oak, white fir, incense cedar, Coulter pine. Throughout the Forest there are interesting riparian zones, oak woodlands, and meadows. Flowering plants include ceanothus, slender sunflower, monkeyflower, wild hyacinth, Humboldt lily, penstemons, lupines, wild sweet pea, virgin's bower, yerba buena, yucca.

Fire in chaparral burns fiercely and spreads quickly in dry weather. In Sept. 1979, the Laguna fire burned 180,000 acres. Now the E sector of the Descanso R.D., together with adjoining private and public lands, is a demonstration area, testing ways to manage chaparral areas.

Birds: Checklist available. Over 200 residents and migrants, including common loon, pied-billed and horned grebes, white pelican, double-crested cormorant, great and snowy egrets, Canada, greater white-fronted, and snow geese, Swainson's hawk, kestrel, merlin, prairie falcon, California and mountain quail, Wilson's and red-necked phalarope, barn, flammulated, and western screech owl, black-chinned, Anna's, and calliope hummingbirds, belted kingfisher, acorn, Nuttal's, and hairy woodpecker, southwestern willow flycatcher, horned lark, swallows, jays, plain titmouse, white-breasted and red-breasted nuthatches, mockingbird, California and sage thrasher, warblers, warbling and Hutton's vireos, sparrows.

Mammals: Include black-tailed jackrabbit, brush and pigmy rabbits, mule deer, badger, gray fox, raccoon, bobcat, coyote, weasel, skunks, opossum, mole, rodents, mountain lion, and desert kit fox.

Reptiles and amphibians: Include tiger salamander, small-scaled tree lizard, western toad, California and canyon tree frogs, gopher snake, mountain kingsnake, western diamondback, rattlesnake.

Features

Agua Tibia Wilderness: 15,934 acres. NW corner of Palomar R.D. Often closed in fire season, beginning July 1. Elevations from 1,400 ft. in canyon bottoms to 5,400 ft. at the crest. Most of the area is chaparral—but with a difference, for this area has had no major fire in the past century. Dense vegetation with plants of exceptional size: treelike manzanitas with 3-ft. trunks, red-shank chamise with 25-ft. spreads. Some shrubs 14–16 ft. high. Conifer forest at the crest. Best travel time is winter and spring. No overnight use of horses. Water is scarce.

San Mateo Canyon Wilderness: 39,500 acres. Springs and intermittent streams feed the San Mateo River, which has cut a winding canyon through the Trabuco R.D. Its crooked course flows through about 10 sq. mi. of the Forest before it becomes a perennial stream near the S edge.

Side walls clad with oaks and sycamore slope up to rounded hills. Chaparral in the drier spots. Many wildflowers, birds, and mammals.

The road leading NE from the coast near San Clemente ends at the Forest boundary. Some miles upstream and outside the wilderness area, another road comes in from the E and follows the canyon N. Fisherman's Campground, located at the point where that road enters the canyon, was burned in 1980 and will not be rebuilt. It will remain an access point, possibly a trailhead.

Pine Creek Wilderness: 13,100 acres. SW portion of the Descanso R.D. Area drained by Pine Creek and its numerous tributaries, all intermittent. Relatively gentle slopes, from 2,000 ft. in the S to slightly over 4,000 ft. in the N. The area has no notable peaks. Plant cover is chaparral, reestablishing after the 1970 fire. Riparian vegetation along Pine Creek.

Hauser Wilderness: 8,000 acres. In the most S portion of the Descanso R.D. Large rock outcrops and granite boulders are common features of this area. Elevations range from 1,600 ft. at Barrett Reservoir to 3,700 ft. near Bronco Flats.

Interpretation

Campfire programs, weekends at Laguna and Burnt Rancheria Campgrounds. Summer season. Occasional campfire programs at Oak Grove Campground, fall, winter, and spring. Monthly summer campfire programs at Observatory Campground.

Guided hikes.

Nature trails in each District. At Trabuco, the El Cariso Trail. At Palomar, Inaja Nature Trail, through chaparral. Also the Observatory Trail, a 2¼ mi. hike, in conifer forest. In the Laguna Mountain area, four trails, each with a theme.

Ask about *star parties, Junior Ranger* programs, and other interpretive activities.

Activities

Camping: 26 campgrounds, 591 campsites, including group, equestrian, and family sites. These may change from year to year, so inquire.

Hiking, backpacking: Portions of Pacific Crest Trail and the 10-mi.-long Noble Canyon Trail. Other trails include the Dripping Springs Trail and Inaja Nature Trail. Ask rangers about other trails.

Hunting: Turkey, quail, mourning dove, ducks, geese, rabbits, mule deer.

Horse riding: Miles of excellent trails offer easy backcountry access.

Also, *Sunrise National Scenic Byway,* 24 mi. long.

3 *ORV areas* in the Descanso R.D. include designated 4-wheel-drive routes, cycle trails, and open ORV area.

Adjacent
Anza-Borrego Desert State Park and Cuyamaca Rancho State Park (see entries this zone).

Publications
Forest map, $3.25.

Visitor guide for each R.D.

Remote area camping leaflets for each R.D.

ORV maps and regulations for each R.D.

Nature trail guides.

Mammals of the Cleveland National Forest.

Headquarters
U.S. Forest Service, 10845 Rancho Bernardo Rd., #200, San Diego, CA 92127-2107; (619) 674-2901, fax (619) 673-6192, TTY (619) 445-6235. Palomar R.D., 1634 Black Canyon Rd., Ramona, CA 92065; (619) 788-0250. Trabuco R.D., 1147 E. 6th St., Corona, CA 91719; (909) 736-1811.

....

Colorado River National Wildlife Refuges and Wilderness Areas

U.S. Fish and Wildlife Service
Cibola: 1,255 acres in CA; 8,208 in AZ. Imperial: 7,958 in CA; 17,806 in AZ. Picacho State Recreation Area (CA Dept. of Parks and Recreation): 7,000 acres. Adjacent wilderness areas (BLM): 178,633 acres.

Along the Colorado River from Blythe to point near Mexican border. W to Hwy 78 and S-34.

The two National Wildlife Refuges extend for about 50 mi. along the Lower Colorado River, are narrow strips of land on both sides. The Picacho State Recreation Area is on the river at about the midpoint of Imperial Refuge. The extensive BLM desert lands are generally adjacent on the W.

Cibola National Wildlife Refuge, at the N end of the area, is about 20 mi. long. It includes the river, a lake, marshes, river bottomland, and a small fringe of desert ridges and washes. A dredged and diked channel was created before the site became a National Refuge. The old channel is canoeable. The Refuge was established to mitigate wildlife losses caused by 50 mi. of stream channelization. Unlike Imperial and a third National Wildlife Refuge, Havasu, 100 mi. N, Cibola does not have extensive wetlands. However, it does have 2,000 acres of cropland where wildlife feed is cultivated.

Entrance to Cibola on the CA side is from Hwy 78, 3 mi. S of Palo Verde. Visitors may drive on the dikes on both sides of the dredged channel. A bridge just N of the access road crosses to the AZ side. However, the best way to see the area is by boat. Power boats operate on the river. They can be launched nearby, not in the Refuge. Traveling by canoe is even better. This section of river has no white water. If one has the time, launch at Blythe and make the 60-mi. run to take-out at the S end of Imperial National Wildlife Refuge. Camping is not permitted within the Refuges, but one can camp between them and at Picacho State Recreation Area.

The Refuge's mission is to maintain Canada geese and field-feeding ducks such as pintail and mallard in the winter season. It is habitat for the endangered Yuma clapper rail. Species of interest include snow and white-fronted geese and sandhill crane, and such occasional visitors as brown pelican, wood stork, and roseate spoonbill.

Most visitors come in summer, for fishing and boating. Best period for visiting is Dec.–June. Management warns that traffic is light and roads unimproved, with low and sandy places. No road service is nearby.

Imperial National Wildlife Refuge, S of Cibola, includes 30 mi. of the river with adjacent backwater lakes. For most of its length, its width is about a mile, becoming broader at the S end. Elevation at the river is about 185 ft. The highest point within the boundaries is about 1,000 ft. Road access is on the AZ side. The map shows no roads to or within the Refuge on the CA side. A road N from Winterhaven leads to Picacho SRA. Boats can be launched there, and much of the adjacent area can be explored on foot.

Like Cibola, most of Imperial is river bottomland. Vegetation is largely mesquite, willow, arrowweed, screwbean, and salt cedar. In the marshes, cattail, bulrush, marsh cane. On the desert hills: ironwood, palo verde, mesquite, smoke tree, creosote, bear-sage, lycium, various cacti.

A marina is on the AZ side, 4 mi. S of the Refuge. Boats can be launched and rented there. For birding, Dec.–June is the best period. Summer visitors are usually interested in fishing and boating.

Picacho State Recreation Area is reached by driving 24 mi. N from Winterhaven over a steep, winding, unsurfaced road. The site has about 8 mi. of frontage on the river. Terrain is much the same as in Imperial: river bottomlands, rising to sparsely vegetated hills and the colorful Chocolate Mountains. The HQ campground has 59 sites, piped water. Reservations available Sept. 29–June 18, indicating that this is the popular season. Summer temperatures average over 100°F. The site has two boat-in camp areas, 4 and 8 mi. upstream.

Adjacent BLM desert wilderness areas: Most of the land to the W of the Refuges is public domain, although part of the area is checkerboarded with private holdings. Four roadless sections are designated wilderness.

W of Cibola is the *Palo Verde Mountains Wilderness,* in which the highest point is 1,795 ft. Rolling hills and steep, jagged, colorful volcanic peaks. Small, narrow canyons lead into enclosed basins and small, isolated valleys.

Vegetation is generally sparse. Large stands of ironwood in Milpitas Wash. A small palm oasis at Clapp Spring. Bighorn sheep have a transient range here. This is also desert tortoise habitat. Deer, quail, chukar, prairie falcon are present. The area is of interest to rockhounds.

The Indian Pass Wilderness: has Hwy 78 and S-34 as its W boundary, Indian Pass Rd. on the S. Highest point is 2,177-ft. Quartz Peak. Most of the area is flat to rolling, cut by washes, some wide and deep. Scattered, rugged low mountains and canyons. River bottomland vegetation extends up many of the washes: creosote, mesquite, smoke tree, catclaw. The S portion of the area is the most scenic, with jagged buttes, spires, lava-capped mesas, in rich colors.

Bighorn sheep use the area. Deer, quail, and rabbit are primary game species.

Adjoining BLM land is used for ORV activity. Rockhounding and camping are also popular activities.

The *Picacho Peak Wilderness* is adjacent, across Indian Pass Rd. Peak's elevation is 1,947 ft. This area adjoins the State Recreation

Area. Terrain is varied, including vegetated washes, deep canyons, volcanic rock, rolling hills, flat desert, mountains.

The *Little Picacho Peak Wilderness* lies immediately S of the State Recreation Area, bordering Imperial National Wildlife Refuge. Within its 260 sq. mi. are flat, meadowlike areas, low rolling hills, table-top mountains, rough and jagged peaks, deep canyons, and washes. Vegetation is varied near the river and lakes.

Birds: From the National Wildlife Refuge checklists: seasonally common or abundant species include eared and pied-billed grebes, white pelican, double-crested cormorant, great blue heron, great and snowy egrets, Canada goose, mallard, gadwall, pintail, green-winged and cinnamon teals, wigeon, northern shoveler, redhead, lesser scaup, bufflehead, ruddy duck, common merganser, turkey vulture, Cooper's and red-tailed hawks, Gambel's quail, sora, common gallinule, coot, killdeer, sandpipers, long-billed dowitcher, black-necked stilt, Wilson's phalarope, ring-billed gull, Forster's and black terns, mourning and white-winged doves, roadrunner, screech, great horned, and burrowing owls, lesser nighthawk, Costa's hummingbird, northern flicker, Gila and ladder-backed woodpeckers, western kingbird, flycatchers, phoebes, swallows, verdin, wrens, mockingbird, crissal thrasher, black-tailed gnatcatcher, ruby-crowned kinglet, water pipit, phainopepla, loggerhead shrike, warbling vireo, warblers, western meadowlark, yellow-headed and red-winged blackbirds, brownheaded cowbird, western tanager, black-headed and blue grosbeaks, house finch, towhee, sparrows.

Mammals: Include leafnose, Mexican freetail, and pallid bats, western pipistrel, black-tailed jackrabbit, cottontail, antelope squirrels, roundtail ground squirrel, pocket mice, Merriam kangaroo rat, beaver, hispid cotton rat, desert wood rat, muskrat, coyote, kit fox, gray fox, ringtail, raccoon, striped skunk, bobcat, burro, wild horse, mule deer, bighorn sheep.

Amphibians and reptiles: Include zebra-tailed, collared, leopard, desert spiny, side-blotched, long-tailed brush, ornate tree, and desert horned lizards, western whiptail, banded gecko, desert iguana, chuckwalla, Great Plains, red-spotted, and Woodhouse's toads, bullfrog, leopard frog, spiny softshell turtle, western blind snake, coachwhip, western patch-nosed snake, glossy snake, gopher snake, kingsnake, long-nose snake, checkered garter snake, western ground snake, western shovel-nosed snake, spotted night snake, western diamondback rattlesnake, sidewinder, Mojave rattlesnake.

Activities

Camping: Prohibited in the National Wildlife Refuges. 59 primitive sites at Picacho State Recreation Area. Camping also at any suitable place on BLM land. (Wilderness status closes certain areas to vehicles.)

Hiking, backpacking: Few trails, but much opportunity for cross-country hiking, with possible campsites in isolated basins and valleys.

Hunting: Deer, quail, rabbit.

Fishing: River. Largemouth bass, crappie, catfish.

Swimming: No supervised areas.

Boating: Commercial facilities N and S of the Refuges.

Canoeing: Entire section of river; rentals at Walters Camp, P.O. Box 31, Palo Verde, CA 92266. Float trips usually originate at Walters Camp (near Blythe). Usual float trip is 1 day to Picacho SRA, next day to Martinez Lake or Imperial Dam.

Publications

Leaflets for Refuges.

Public use regulations, with map.

Checklists of birds, mammals, reptiles, amphibians.

Hunting map and regulations (for Imperial).

Headquarters

Cibola: U.S. Fish and Wildlife Service, P.O. Box AP, Blythe, CA 92225; (714) 922-2129. Imperial: U.S. Fish and Wildlife Service, P.O. Box 2217, Martinez Lake, AZ 85364; (602) 783-3400. Picacho: CA Dept. of Parks and Recreation, P.O. Box 1207, Winterhaven, CA 92283; (619) 339-5110. Bureau of Land Management: CA Desert District, 6221 Spruce St., Riverside, CA 92507-0714; (909) 697-5200. El Centro Research Area, 1661 S. 4th St., El Centro, CA 92243-4561; (619) 337-4400.

Coxcomb Mountains

U.S. Bureau of Land Management
See Joshua Tree National Park (this zone).

Cronese Lakes

U.S. Bureau of Land Management
N of I-15, about 16 mi. SW of Baker.

These two intermittent lakes, East and West, shown on many high-way maps, are at the foot of the Soda Mountains, just off I-15. East Cronese often contains water and provides habitat for wintering and migratory waterfowl and shorebirds, attracting raptors. The Yuma clapper rail has been seen here.

Headquarters

Bureau of Land Management, Barstow Resource Center, 150 Coolwater Lane, Barstow, CA 92311; (619) 255-8760.

Cuyamaca Rancho State Park

California Department of Parks and Recreation
24,677 acres.

9 mi. N of I-8 on Hwy 79.

High in the Peninsular Range, about 40 mi. E of San Diego. It adjoins the Descanso Ranger District—more specifically the Laguna Mountain Recreation Area of that District—of the Cleveland National Forest and is a short distance W of Anza-Borrego Desert State Park (see entries this zone).

Terrain is rugged, mountainous, from an elevation of about 3,400 ft. in the S end to 6,512-ft. Cuyamaca Peak near the midpoint of the W border. Hwy 79, the only auto road through the Park, follows a stream valley from Cuyamaca Lake, just outside the N end of the Park, at about 4,600 ft., leaving the Park at the 3,800-ft. contour at the S end. Several peaks are over 1 mi. high.

Especially if one has just come from the desert area just E of Cuyamaca, it is surprising to find a richly forested area here. On Hwy 79, much of the vegetation is mature forest, exceptionally large black and canyon live oaks, willow, alder, and sycamore along the stream, dense stands of tall incense cedar, white fir, and pines: Coulter, Jeffrey, sugar, and ponderosa. Hwy 79 is the approximate boundary between plant zones: woodland areas on the W, chaparral on the E.

Most developments are along Hwy 79: campgrounds, picnic areas, an interpretive center, history museums, Park HQ, and trailheads. Fire roads lead back into the hills, but they are closed to private vehicles, open to foot and horse travel.

April through Sept. is the big visitor season here, although campgrounds and other facilities are open all year. Occasionally winter snow provides enough depth for ski touring and snow play.

Plants: About one-third of the site is forested. Tree species include California live oak, Kellogg oak, Jeffrey, Coulter, sugar, and ponderosa pines, incense cedar, white fir, California sycamore, white alder, Fremont cottonwood, leatherleaf ash, interior live oak, arroyo willow. Somewhat more than one-third is covered with chaparral: typical species include chamise, manzanita, sumac, buckwheats, buckthorn, ceanothus, coffeeberry. Most of the balance is grassland, although there are scattered pockets of desert vegetation: cacti and agave.

Birds: Birding is outstanding, with nearly 300 species observed in the Park. Although the streams are seasonal and the Park has no year-around wetlands, the checklist includes such species as wigeon, bufflehead, canvasback, common goldeneye, mallard, pintail, redhead, ring-necked duck, ruddy duck, shoveler, blue-winged and cinnamon teals, great and snowy egrets, Canada goose, eared and least grebes, great blue heron. Other species include Cooper's, red-shouldered, red-tailed, sharp-shinned, and Swainson's hawks, northern harrier, golden and bald eagles, osprey, barn, great horned, pygmy, and screech owls, California and mountain quail, band-tailed pigeon, red-breasted and yellow-bellied sapsuckers, Nuttall's, white-headed, acorn, downy, hairy, and ladder-backed woodpeckers, violet-green, cliff, tree, and barn swallows, California thrasher, hermit and varied thrushes, ash-throated and olive-sided flycatchers, common bushtit, lesser and Lawrence's goldfinches, roadrunner, horned lark, pygmy nuthatch, gray and Hutton's vireos. Warblers include orange-crowned, hermit, yellow-rumped, black-and-white, black-throated green, Wilson's, Townsend's. Also pine siskin, chipping, golden-crowned, lark, sage, savannah, song, and white-crowned sparrows.

Mammals: Include big brown, evening, and long-eared bats, Merriam chipmunk, nimble kangaroo rat, deer mouse, desert and dusky-footed wood rats, pocket gopher, broad-footed mole, opossum, cottontail, black-tailed jackrabbit, raccoon, ground squirrels, gray squirrel, weasel, ringtail, spotted and striped skunks, coyote, bobcat, mountain lion, mule deer.

Reptiles and amphibians: Include alligator, sagebrush, side-blotched, western fence, and western whiptail lizards, granite spiny lizard, western toad, Pacific and canyon tree frogs, ensatina, western skink, racer, ringneck snake, gopher snake, common and mountain kingsnakes, red diamond, speckled and western rattlesnakes.

Feature
Cuyamaca Peak, reached by a 3½-mi. trail, offers vistas of the Pacific Ocean, Mexico, Salton Sea, and desert.

Interpretation
Interpretive center has exhibits on native flora and fauna.

History museum, near HQ, depicts lives of early residents.

Campfire programs and *guided hikes* in summer. Notices posted.

Two *nature trails,* self-guiding.

Exhibit at *Stonewall mine,* large gold mine closed in 1892.

Activities
Camping: 3 campgrounds, 182 sites. All year. Reservations April 6–Oct. 1.

Hiking, backpacking: 130 mi. of trails. Trails into Cleveland National Forest and Anza-Borrego Desert State Park. Two trail camps, 6 and 7 mi. from trailheads; registration required before departure. No trailside camping.

Horse riding: 90 mi. of trails. Riders may use trail camps, registering in advance. Special campground for auto campers with horses.

Ski touring: When snow is sufficient; not every year.

Adjacent or Nearby
Cleveland National Forest and Anza-Borrego Desert State Park (see entries this zone).

Publications
Leaflet with map.

Information on use of trail camps.

Checklists of plants, birds, mammals, reptiles and amphibians.

Headquarters
CA Dept. of Parks and Recreation, Rt. 1, Box 2700, Descanso, CA 92016; (619) 765-0755. District Office, (619) 767-5311.

Eagle Mountains

U.S. Bureau of Land Management
See Joshua Tree National Park (this zone).

Fort Piute/Piute Creek/Piute Gorge

U.S. National Park Service
See Mojave National Preserve (this zone).

Golden Valley Wilderness

U.S. Bureau of Land Management
37,300 acres, including other federal and state lands.

10 mi. SE of Ridgecrest via Hwy 395 to the Red Mountain–Trona Rd. 1 mi. N of Red Mountain to Steam Well Rd. on the S or Savoy Rd. on the N.

The BLM ranked this area high on its scenic values. The Golden Valley, for which the area is named, is surrounded by two distinct mountain ranges, the Lava and the Almond Mountains. The Lava Mountains, in the NW section of the wilderness, rise about 1,700 ft. from the desert floor to a high point at Dome Mountain of almost 5,000 ft. Canyons in the mountains have walls with spectacular, multicolored sedimentary layers. The Almond Mountains enclose the valley on the SE, rising to an elevation of 4,500 ft.

The E boundary is China Lake Naval Weapons Center. Beware, *do not enter*. Roads and boundaries are well marked.

Vegetation is typical of the Mojave Desert, mostly creosote bush scrub with Joshua trees and numerous annuals. The valley is known for its spectacular spring wildflower displays.

The area offers great nesting and foraging habitat for raptors, also habitat for the desert tortoise and Mojave ground squirrel.

Because this is wilderness, cars are not allowed.

Headquarters
Bureau of Land Management, Ridgecrest Resource Area, 300 S. Richmond Rd., Ridgecrest, CA 93555; (619) 384-5400.

Harper Dry Lake; Rainbow Basin–Owl Canyon

U.S. Bureau of Land Management
About 4,000 acres.

Rainbow Basin–Owl Canyon is 5 mi. N of Barstow via Camp Irwin Rd., then 5 mi. W on Fossil Beds Rd. Harper Dry Lake, shown on most highway maps, is several miles farther W, crossed by a local road.

Rainbow Basin was so named because of its spectacular display of colorful sedimentary rocks. The area is also a rich source of Miocene vertebrate fossils, including fossilized camel tracks. Fossil Canyon is nearby. There is a road loop through the area. The campground is in Owl Canyon.

Harper Dry Lake is no longer dry because of irrigation on neighboring farmlands. Usually there is some standing water, and a good marsh has developed, attracting waterfowl and shorebirds. Species reported include the endangered Yuma clapper rail and bald eagle. The BLM is cooperating with the CA Dept. of Fish and Game to develop a habitat management plan.

Camping: 31 tent sites.

Headquarters
Bureau of Land Management, Barstow Resource Center, 150 Coolwater Lane, Barstow, CA 92311; (619) 255-8760.

Havasu National Wildlife Refuge

U.S. Fish and Wildlife Service
7,747 acres in CA; 35,323 acres in AZ.

Along the Colorado River between Needles, CA, and Lake Havasu City, AZ. Crossed by I-40.

The Refuge was established in 1941 to compensate for wildlife habitat flooded by Parker Dam. Somewhat to the dismay of wildlife managers, portions of the Refuge and adjacent areas have become popular with motorboating enthusiasts. On the whole, birds and boaters coexist, using different parts of the Refuge and at different times. Bird populations are greatest in winter and during migrations; the boaters come mostly in summer. Waterbirds favor the shallows and marshes; boaters choose the scenic river canyon.

The Refuge has two units. *Topock Marsh* lies between Needles and Topock, AZ, where I-40 crosses the river. The channelized river is its W boundary, as well as the CA–AZ boundary. The E side of the marsh is a 4,000-acre lake. The marsh is cut by a network of channels and ponds.

In floating the river, one can choose the river or the marsh, the latter requiring a couple of short portages. To visit the marsh by boat, one can launch at North Dike, Five Mile Landing or Catfish Paradise. The marsh has numerous stubs and snags, menacing to propellers.

The route through the marsh is about 13 mi., assuming no detours. Camping is prohibited, so one must plan to be at Five Mile Landing, about the midpoint, before dark. Portions of the marsh are closed seasonally; the main route is open. Those who choose the river route have only a 10-mi. run to Park Moabi, a county park, 1 mi. N of the Topock Bridge, where camping is available.

Topock Gorge extends S from the Topock Bridge to Lake Havasu, a 16-mi. trip. Some enthusiasts call this the most scenic section of the Lower Colorado. Others limit this superlative to the 7 mi. of colorful rock cliffs in Mojave Canyon. The 16 mi. can be made by canoe in a day, if one starts early. There is little choice, because camping is prohibited in the gorge, and sundown is no excuse. Take-out is at Castle Rock, on the AZ side, unless one is continuing on through Lake Havasu, inadvisable in windy weather. Beyond the buoys marking the end of the gorge, camping is allowed on the AZ side, except at Mesquite Bay.

At one time the Refuge included Lake Havasu. It now includes only a bit of the upper end, to a point about 3 mi. S of the gorge boundary. On the AZ side of the gorge, the Refuge includes part of the Mojave Mountains. The Needles are a series of pinnacle-shaped volcanic plugs. Highest point is Powell Peak, just over 2,200 ft. Most of this upland area in AZ is now the 19,000-acre Havasu Wilderness.

The CA side of the gorge is the E edge of the Chemehuevi Mountains. The strip of desert upland on the W side of the river, generally less than 1 mi. wide, is the only land area of the Refuge in CA. Most of this area is now the 2,800-acre Havasu Wilderness in CA.

The Colorado River is unchannelized through the gorge. The dam has created a number of backwater bays that are good wildlife habitats. Motors are allowed on the river, but the land area of this unit is closed to all motor vehicles. All Refuge backwaters for 15 mi. S of I-40 are closed to personal watercraft such as jetskis.

Plants: Extensive areas of bulrush and cattail. Desert plant communities include creosote, ocotillo, brittlebush, palo verde, white bur-sage, desert lavender, desert holly. Cacti include saguaro, cholla, jumping cholla, barrel, beavertail, hedgehog. Wildflowers include phacelia, evening primrose, desert trumpet, snapdragon, globe mallow, golden aster, poppy, lupine, milk vetch, desert lily, sand verbena.

Birds: Of the 292 species recorded, only 82 are known to nest on the Refuge. Most are seasonal visitors. Best period to see waterfowl is Oct. to mid-March. Wintering snow and Canada geese usually arrive early Nov. An observation tower near the levee road in the Topock Marsh unit offers a view of geese grazing on the Refuge fields. Migrating bald eagles are sometimes seen at the marsh during winter and early spring. Active rookeries of great blue heron and double-crested cormorant can be seen between Feb. and May. Western grebe colonies are best seen in the backbays of the gorge in summer. The Refuge is a major nesting area for the endangered Yuma clapper rail, but these solitary, secretive birds are seldom seen.

Checklist available. Seasonally common or abundant species include eared, western, and pied-billed grebes, white pelican, green-backed heron, great and snowy egrets, black-crowned night heron, least bittern, mallard, gadwall, pintail, green-winged and cinnamon teals, wigeon, shoveler, redhead, ring-necked duck, lesser scaup, bufflehead, ruddy duck, common and red-breasted mergansers. Also sora, common gallinule, coot, snowy plover, sandpipers, willet, greater yellowlegs, long-billed dowitcher, marbled godwit, avocet, black-necked stilt, Wilson's and northern phalaropes. Raptors include Cooper's, sharp-shinned, and red-tailed hawks, northern harrier, kestrel. Upland species include Gambel's quail, white-winged, mourning, and Inca doves, roadrunner, lesser nighthawk, white-throated swift, Costa's hummingbird, northern flicker, Gila and ladderbacked woodpeckers, western kingbird, flycatchers, western wood pewee, swallows, raven, verdin, wrens, black-tailed gnatcatcher, ruby-crowned kinglet, phainopepla, loggerhead shrike, warbling vireo, warblers. Also western meadowlark, yellow-headed and red-winged blackbirds, hooded and northern orioles, western tanager, black-headed and blue grosbeaks, house finch, Abert's towhee, sparrows.

Mammals: Include bats, black-tailed jackrabbit, cottontail, antelope squirrel, ground squirrel, valley pocket gopher, pocket mice, kangaroo rats, beaver, mice, hispid cotton rat, white-throated wood rat, muskrat, porcupine, coyote, kit fox, gray fox, ringtail, raccoon, badger, striped skunk, bobcat, feral burro, feral horse, feral hog, bighorn sheep, mule deer.

Reptiles and amphibians: Include desert banded gecko, desert iguana, chuckwalla, zebra-tailed, collared, long-nosed, yellow-backed spiny, desert side-blotched, western brush, tree, Mojave fringe-toed, and southern desert horned lizards, Great Basin whiptail, many-lined skink, Gila monster, spadefoot, Great Plains, red-spotted, and southwestern toads, canyon tree frog, leopard frog, bullfrog, soft-shelled and mud turtles, western worm snake, desert rosy boa, glossy snake, western shovel-nosed snake, spotted night snake, California kingsnake, common whipsnake, spotted leaf-nosed snake, gopher snakes, western ground snake, desert and Mojave patch-nosed snakes, checkered garter snake, Arizona lyre snake, sidewinder, Mojave rattlesnake, western diamondback rattlesnake.

Activities

Camping: At Five Mile concessions on Topock Marsh. No camping in the Refuge except boat and tent camping on the AZ shoreline below the buoys marking the S end of the gorge; no camping in Mesquite Bay.

Hiking: On Refuge roads. No marked trails, but numerous areas are suitable for hiking, including the upland E of the gorge. On the CA side, hiking into the BLM area (see "Adjacent" section).

Hunting: In designated areas, subject to federal and state regulations.

Fishing: In all waters except as posted. Largemouth and striped bass, bluegill, crappie, catfish, rainbow trout.

Swimming: Except where restricted. No supervised area.

Boating: On all waters except as posted. Water skiing on the river only; it is not permitted in the gorge. Boat traffic has become so heavy at peak periods that regulations have been adopted to minimize accidents. Boaters should be aware of these before launching. Launching at commercial facilities: Topock Marsh, Park Moabi, Golden Shore Marina.

Canoeing: March–April is the best time to canoe the gorge. Power boat traffic is slight. Desert plants bloom. Climate is good. Power boat traffic is heavy on summer weekends.

344

Adjacent

The *Chemehuevi Mountains* (BLM): 95,400 acres. The mountains lie between US 95 and Topock Gorge. 66% is designated wilderness. Access is from US 95, Lake Havasu Rd., or on foot from the Refuge. From the Colorado River, the horseshoe-shaped range rises abruptly through a convoluted series of highly eroded washes, vegetated with smoke tree and mesquite. The mountains form a high ridge with 18 peaks over 2,500 ft. Chemehuevi Peak is 3,697 ft. The W side of the ridge drops abruptly to the desert floor of Chemehuevi Valley. The upper edge of the valley is rocky, irregular, eroded, densely vegetated with cholla, barrel cactus, small cacti varieties. Numerous ocotillo. The mountains are habitat for a small herd of bighorn sheep.

Rugged terrain makes the mountains inaccessible except on foot or horseback. The cliffs, high canyons, washes, and ridges offer ample opportunities for solitude. A popular trail is 12-mi. Trampas Wash, which bisects the wilderness and ends at the river.

Publications

Mimeo info pages on public use regulations and general information. Also on hunting, fishing, canoe and float trips.

Leaflet with map.

Checklists of birds, mammals, fish, reptiles, amphibians; partial list of plants.

Headquarters

U.S. Fish and Wildlife Service, P.O. Box 3009, 315 Mesquite, Needles, CA 92363; (619) 326-3853. Bureau of Land Management: CA Desert District, 1695 Spruce St., Riverside, CA 92507; (909) 697-5200.

. . . .

Imperial National Wildlife Refuge

U.S. Fish and Wildlife Service

See Colorado River National Wildlife Refuges and Wilderness Areas (this zone).

Imperial Wildlife Area

California Department of Fish and Game
Finney-Ramer Unit: 2,047 acres. Wister Unit: 6,000 acres.

Finney-Ramer Unit: 8 mi. N of Brawley, on Hwy III.

Wister Unit is at SE corner of Salton Sea. Visitor permits for Wister at Davis Rd., ¼ mi. S of Hwy III, 5 mi. NW of Niland.

The *Finney-Ramer Unit* is S of the Salton Sea, in the Imperial Valley, a natural habitat enclave surrounded by broad, flat farmlands. The wildlife area serves the dual purpose of supporting waterfowl populations and lessening their consumption of farm crops. The area is about 175 ft. below sea level, with sandy saline soil, in a hot desert climate. Water from the Colorado River flows in through irrigation canals, maintaining Ramer and Finney Lakes, each about 2 mi. long, and four small ponds. Lakes and ponds are surrounded by thick riparian vegetation. Common vegetation of the site includes mesquite, palo verde, tamarisk, palm, arrowweed, willow, cattail, cane.

The Unit is a strip almost 10 mi. long, about 1 mi. wide, bordered and crossed by public roads. HQ and visitor registration are on the E side of Ramer Lake, near the midpoint of the site. Two campgrounds are on Finney Lake, to the S.

The *Wister Unit* is at the S corner of the Salton Sea, not far from the Salton Sea National Wildlife Refuge (see entry this zone), close to the shore but with no frontage. Acquired in 1956, much of the land was then desert. There are now 2,700 acres of ponds, 1,000 acres of ponded watergrass and bulrush. Feed is grown on about 1,000 acres of irrigated land. Colorado River water is purchased.

Birds: Up to 50,000 ducks and 20,000 geese winter here. Checklist available for Finney-Ramer Unit. This and checklist for Colorado River National Wildlife Refuges are applicable to Wister Unit. Over 260 species identified here, including tundra swan, sandhill crane, roseate spoonbill, white pelican, bittern, white-faced ibis, wood stork, herons, egrets, rails, terns, snipe, dowitcher, dunlin, yellowlegs, phalaropes, fulvous tree duck, roadrunner, killdeer, Gambel's quail, doves, a dozen hawk species, owls, swifts, woodpeckers, and songbirds.

The first flights of returning ducks arrive in late July or early Aug. The main flights of snow and Canada geese arrive in late Nov. or early Dec. Duck and goose numbers peak in Feb. Most are gone by late March. Shorebirds are most numerous in winter, marsh birds in summer.

Summers are extremely hot, *temperatures to 120°F.* Winter weather is delightful.

Activities

Camping: Two primitive campgrounds at Finney-Ramer, one at Wister.

Hunting: At Finney-Ramer, waterfowl and upland game. Because of treacherous lake bottoms, hunting from boat only. Quota of 60 hunters. At Wister, permit and fee required; quota. Hunting 3 days per week and certain holidays, in season.

Fishing: The principal visitor activity. Warm-water species: channel catfish, bluegill, largemouth bass, carp.

Boating: Small boat ramp on Ramer Lake. No motors.

All users must have permits, available by self-registration at entrances.

Publications

Leaflets with maps, both units.

Site maps.

Bird checklist, Finney-Ramer Unit.

Headquarters

CA Dept. of Fish and Game, Star Rt. 1, Box 6, Niland, CA 92257; (619) 359-0577.

....

In-Ko-Pah Mountain Wilderness

U.S. Bureau of Land Management
29,700 acres.

On the Mexican border just E of Anza-Borrego Desert State Park. S of Ocotillo and Coyote Wells. I-8 and Hwy 98 are the N boundary.

This area was designated as wilderness by the California Desert Protection Act. The mountains rise from the Yuha Basin to the E and extend to the NW beyond the limits of this BLM area. The basin is between sea level and 500 ft. Most terrain is under 2,500 ft., with one peak in the SW rising to 4,548 ft. Landforms include pinnacles, spires, steep-walled canyons, and the gently sloping Davies Valley, strewn with huge granite boulders. Five springs are in the W portion.

Vegetation is mostly creosote scrub. Several small palm groves are scattered in Davies Valley, and the valley also has extensive stands of agave and ocotillo. A palm oasis is at Mountain Springs with a black-brush enclave nearby. The Smuggler's Cave area has an extensive growth of chaparral.

The site includes both permanent and transient bighorn sheep range, a mule deer populaton, foraging areas for golden eagle and prairie falcon, chukar, quail.

Headquarters

Bureau of Land Management, CA Desert District, 6221 Box Springs Blvd., Riverside, CA 92507-0714; (909) 697-5200. Or BLM, El Centro Resource Area, 1661 S. 4th St., El Centro, CA 92243-4561; (619) 337-4400.

Joshua Tree National Park

U.S. National Park Service
630,800 acres.

At Twentynine Palms on Hwy 62. S entrance from I-10 on Cottonwood Springs Rd., 25 mi. E of Indio.

The visitor center at Twentynine Palms, just outside the Park, is the best introduction to the area, worth a stop for at least an hour or two. The center includes a self-guiding trail through the Oasis of Mara, where birding is lively. With this orientation, the Park itself becomes an introduction to the southwestern desert. No one who has spent a few days here is likely to consider any desert region dull or monotonous.

This is high desert, in the transition zone between the Mojave and Colorado Deserts. Unlike the below-sea-level Death Valley and Imperial Valley, elevations range from 1,000 ft. in the Pinto Basin in the E to nearly 6,000 ft. in the Little San Bernardino Mountains in the W. The weather here is usually pleasant, especially so in spring and fall. At Twentynine Palms, elevation 1,960 ft., temperature peaks above 100°F about 80 days per year. Even then, nights are cool, and days are considerably cooler at higher elevations. Average annual rainfall is less than 5 in., but with considerable variation. At Twentynine Palms the driest year on record had only ¼ in. of rain, the wettest more than 11 in., and once almost 4 in. fell in a single day.

Many visitors make a 40-mi. tour, entering at Twentynine Palms, turning right at Pinto Wye Junction, and returning to Hwy 62 at the town of Joshua Tree, 15 mi. W of their starting point. Others make the 49-mi. N–S crossing to I-10. These are the principal paved roads in the Park, winding and narrow in places, adequate for trailers and large RVs with care in driving. Several dirt roads are satisfactory for autos in dry weather. Others are marked for 4-wheel-drive vehicles. No motor vehicles are permitted off established roads, and all must be registered and street-legal.

Large areas are roadless, reached only by foot or on horseback. This includes most of the high country in the Little San Bernardino Mountains as well as the Pinto Mountains in the NE. Indeed, 630,800 acres have been designated as wilderness.

Plants: The Joshua tree, a giant yucca, is abundant in the higher W half of the Park, where elevations are generally over 3,000 ft. It attains heights of 40 ft. When it blooms—in March and April, but not every year—it bears clusters of cream-white blossoms at branch tips. The similar Mojave yucca is shorter and has much longer leaves.

The Colorado Desert area, lower, in the E half, is characterized by abundant creosote with small stands of ocotillo and jumping cholla. A third ecosystem is the oasis, found where water is at or near the surface. The Park has five fan palm oases. Outside the Park, a number of communities grew up around such desert oases. Since then the water table has been lowered by pumping from deep wells, and the oases may be doomed. At the Oasis of Mara, action along the Pinto Mountain fault may have more to do with this than pumping groundwater.

Those who hike into the W mountains find the upper zone not only cooler but moister than the desert below, with patches of chaparral, the association including manzanita and scrub oak. Nearby are slopes with sparse pinyon pine and juniper.

To many visitors, "desert" means cacti, and many varieties occur here, including cottontop, calico, beavertail, mound, pancake, old-man, foxtail, fringe-flowered foxtail, barrel, fishhook, grizzly bear, Mojave prickly pear, dead, and pencil, buckhorn, jumping, silver, and golden cholla.

The blooming of desert wildflowers in spring transforms the landscape. Species found here include wishbone, sand blazing star, jimsonweed, sand mat, mojave aster, purple mat, desert paintbrush, coreopsis, gold-poppy, fiddleneck, sand verbena, locoweed, desert mariposa lily, desert mallow, primroses, desert senna, encelia, lupine, ocotillo.

Birds: Checklist available; 230 species, though many of these are casual or occasional. Seasonally common or abundant species include turkey vulture, red-tailed hawk, Gambel's and mountain quail, mourning dove, roadrunner, long-eared owl, poor-will, white-throated swift, Anna's, Costa's, and rufous hummingbirds, northern flicker, ladder-backed woodpecker, western kingbird, Say's phoebe, horned lark, scrub jay, raven, mountain chickadee, plain titmouse, verdin, common bushtit, wrens, mockingbird, California and Le Conte's thrashers, robin, blue-gray gnatcatcher, ruby-crowned kinglet, phainopepla, loggerhead shrike, warblers, western meadowlark, Scott's, hooded, and northern orioles, western tanager, house finch, sparrows.

Mammals: Checklist available. Includes several bats, California chipmunk, pocket gopher, ground squirrels, black-tailed jackrabbit, cottontail, kangaroo rats, wood rat, various mice, shrew, raccoon, ringtail, badger, spotted skunk, kit fox, coyote, gray fox, mountain lion, bighorn sheep. Mule deer occasional in the W mountains.

Reptiles and amphibians: Checklist available. Includes banded gecko, zebra-tailed, collared, leopard, horned, desert spiny, western fence, Mojave fringe-toed, long-tailed brush, side-blotched, and desert night lizards, Gilbert's skink, western whiptail, California tree frog, red-spotted toad, desert tortoise, western blind snake, rosy boa, glossy snake, western shovel-nosed snake, night snake, common kingsnake, red and striped racers, spotted leaf-nosed snake, gopher snake, long-nosed snake, western patch-nosed snake, lyre snake, sidewinder, speckled, Mojave, western, and red diamond rattlesnakes.

Features

The *Oasis of Mara* is the site of the *visitor center* and HQ.

Fortynine Palms Oasis is reached only on foot, by a 1½-mi. trail. Trailhead is off Hwy 62 about 4 mi. W of Twentynine Palms.

Keys View is at the end of the only paved road into the Little San Bernardino Mountains. At 5,185 ft., it offers a magnificient view.

Ryan Mountain, 5,461 ft., is near the center of the Park. The summit is reached by a 1½-mi. trail.

Cottonwood Spring, a palm oasis, is near the S entrance. The area includes a visitor center, campground. *Lost Palms Oasis,* reached by a 4-mi trail, has the Park's largest stand of palms.

The *Coxcomb Mountains, Sheephole,* and *Cadiz* area: 194,880 acres. At the E and NE corner of the Park, extends N across Hwy 62. The area S of Hwy 62 contains portions of two major mountain ranges, the Coxcomb and Pinto Mountains. The Coxcombs rise sharply from the desert floor on the E, grade W into an area of small boulder piles. The Pintos, on the W edge, extend into the Park, and are more rounded, although many slopes are steep. Large alluvial fans slope away from the mountains. The terrain is rugged. Vegetation is sparse, mostly creosote scrub. Two springs in the E portion of the Coxcombs are used by wildlife, including bighorn sheep.

The 136,000-acre *Sheephole-Cadiz* area is divided by Hwy 62 from the Coxcombs. The area includes two vast desert valleys bounded by steep granitic mountains: Cadiz Valley, below 1,000 ft., and Sheephole, generally above 1,000 ft. Highest point in the area is a 4,613-ft. peak in the Sheepholes. Both valleys have dry lakebeds that attract snowy egrets and other birds after heavy rains. Cadiz has a small dune system. Creosote bush, galleta grass, and mixed shrubs in the valleys. Almost no vegetation in the lakebeds and on the slopes. One spring in the Sheepholes provides water for a small bighorn sheep herd.

The *Eagle Mountains:* 55,000 acres. On the SE side of the Park. Much of this area is also part of the Park. An unsurfaced road penetrates the area. The mountains are rugged and complex, with many small canyons, interior valleys, steep slopes, washes, large boulders of quartz monzonite, and boulder piles. In some portions of the washes vegetation is thick and includes yucca, cacti, palo verde, ironwood, smoke tree, and various annuals. Most vegetation is creosote scrub, with ocotillo and cholla. Three springs in the Eagles support wildlife populations, including bighorn sheep. Chukar and quail occur in fair numbers. The area includes fan palm oases.

Interpretation

Visitor centers are at the N and S entrances and Black Rock Canyon. The one at Twentynine Palms, the N entrance, is more extensive, the preferred introduction to the area.

Nature trails at several locations: at the Oasis of Mara; Indian Cove, off Hwy 62; Cap Rock; Cholla Cactus Garden, on the N–S Pinto Basin road; Arch Rock in White Tank Campground. *Geology Tour Rd.,* 18 mi., emphasizes geology, early history. The unpaved road, suitable for cars in dry weather, offers some fine views of Park features.

Guided walks, hikes, and *campfire programs* are scheduled prinicpally in spring and fall. Notices posted.

Activities

Camping: 8 campgrounds, 535 sites. All year. Water is available at Cottonwood and Black Rock Canyon Campgrounds. Water can be obtained at Twentynine Palms visitor center and Indian Cove ranger station.

Hiking, backpacking: Many short trails for day hikes. An information sheet describes hikes of 1–13 mi. 35 mi. of the CA Riding and Hiking Trail pass through the Park. Camping in the backcountry is permitted, no closer than 1 mi. to any vehicle route, no closer than 500 ft. to a trail. Backpackers must register at backcountry boards. A few areas are restricted; these are marked on maps at ranger stations and visitor centers. The hiker is responsible for knowing about them. For all but short day trips, hikers should have topo maps, ample water, understanding of desert hiking safety.

Horseback riding: 35 mi. of the CA Riding and Hiking Trail in the Park. Horses are permitted at only two campgrounds, Ryan and Black Rock Canyon. Horse travel in the backcountry is permitted, but because of the special requirements for horses and other stock, care must be taken in planning trips. Permit required to camp with stock in backcountry. Grazing is not permitted. Manure must be removed from campgrounds and trailheads. Horses and other stock must stay on established trails, and are not permitted within ¼ mi. of any natural or artificial water source.

Rock climbing: Very popular activity here, but proceed with caution as weathering loosens rock particles. Climbers prefer Hidden Valley Campground (no water) near some of the major climbs.

Pets are not permitted on trails and must be kept on leashes at all times.

Adjacent

The *Pinto Mountains* (BLM): 26,800 acres. The Pintos lie between Hwy 62 and the Park's N boundary, just E of the Oasis of Mara entrance. Steep, generally rounded hills. Vegetation is mostly creosote scrub with smoke trees, palo verde, and ironwood in washes. Mojave yucca in interior valleys. Much evidence of past mining activity. About 11 sq. mi. of bighorn sheep range, 3 sq. mi. of desert tortoise habitat. A

BLM study concluded that the area is unsuitable for wilderness designation. It has had considerable ORV use, which will probably continue.

Publications

Leaflet with map.

Checklists of birds, cacti, mammals, reptiles and amphibians.

Park newspaper.

Headquarters

National Park Service, 74485 National Park Dr., Twentynine Palms, CA 92277; (619) 367-7511.

***

Kelso Dunes; Kelso Mountains; Granite Mountains

U.S. Bureau of Land Management
See Mojave National Preserve (this zone).

***

Kingston Range

U.S. Bureau of Land Management
270,360 acres (209,608 acres of wilderness, plus other federal, state, and still private lands).

In San Bernardino County, 50 mi. NE of Baker. From Baker on I-15, N on Hwy 127. The area lies E of Hwy 127, from Silurian Dry Lake to Tecopa.

Most land in this region, E and S of Death Valley National Park, along the NV border, is public domain, though it includes some scattered nonfederal lands. The designated wilderness area lies E of the S end of the Park, beyond Tecopa Pass.

The rugged Kingstons are the highest mountains of this desert region, Kingston Peak rising to 7,323 ft. The Range forms 17 mi. of continuous ridgeline above 6,000 ft., and seems to surface like an island in a sea of desert lowlands. To the SW, the mountain slope, steep near the ridges, gradually flattens into the broad Valjean Valley, below 1,000 ft., and Hwy 127. S of the valley are the Silurian Hills, with soft rolling topography. E of the Silurian Hills and S of the Kingstons—separated from them by Kingston Wash—are the Shadow Mountains. Here the highest point is 4,197 ft. These mountains have smooth ridges, rounded peaks.

The area contains 15% badlands, 25% alluvial fans, 20% hills and mountains, 15% dissected fans, 20% plains, plus sand dunes and other features. Less than 4 in. of rain a year, rarely as much as 1 in. in any month. The rainfall pattern is less sharply seasonal than in most of CA. May and June are the driest months, Aug. the wettest. Below-freezing temperatures are rare in the valleys. Summers are very hot. Water is scarce, but the Amargosa River has surface water most of the year. Year-round water and wetland habitat provide food for wildlife, as well as cover and nesting space for birds, fish, mammals, and insects.

The chief economic activity has been mining. Most of the past mines have been abandoned, but the region is thought to have good potential, and exploration continues. The wilderness area boundary was drawn to exclude most disturbed areas, and there are no roads within the boundary. Several primitive roadways do penetrate it, but the wilderness is closed to all vehicle traffic, including ORVs.

Plants: Over 500 plant species make this area one of the most botanically diverse in the CA Desert. In the washes, in the interior valleys, and at the base of the mountains, creosote bush and other low desert shrubs. In the higher interior valleys: Joshua tree, yucca, barrel cactus, cholla. Higher, on steep slopes, pinyon-juniper forest. There's a small white fir forest at the highest elevations in the Kingstons, a surprising occurrence. Another botanical curiosity is a stand of enormous nolinas, a yuccalike plant, this species growing as much as 15 ft. tall; it is found only here and in Joshua Tree National Park. In the SE, the area includes part of one of the densest Joshua tree stands in the Southwest. This is 1 of 4 places in CA where confirmed sightings of banded gila monster have been made.

Birds: No checklist. Species noted include yellow-billed cuckoo, golden eagle, vermilion flycatcher, gray vireo, summer tanager, prairie falcon, Virginia's and yellow warblers, yellow-breasted chat, hepatic tanager. Some 220 bird species are said to visit or reside in the Amargosa Canyon, including pied-billed grebe, great blue heron, green-winged and cinnamon teals, shoveler, ruddy duck, northern harrier, sharp-shinned, Cooper's, and red-tailed hawks, Gambel's quail, roadrunner, great horned owl, belted kingfisher, flicker, Say's phoebe, violet-green, tree, and rough-winged swallows, verdin, ruby-crowned kinglet, phainopepla, Lucy's, yellow-rumped, and black-throated gray warblers.

Mammals: Include Amargosa vole, desert chipmunk, desert bighorn sheep, bats, rock squirrel, mule deer, black-tailed jackrabbit, coyote, kangaroo rats, antelope ground squirrel, cactus mouse. Desert kit fox, ringtail, and bobcat are presumably present.

Features

Amargosa Canyon has been designated as an Area of Critical Environmental Concern. Once heavily used by ORVs, this use is now prohibited. The canyon extends S from a point about ½ mi. S of Tecopa. It is one of the few desert areas with a permanent stream and riparian vegetation. It varies in width from about 400 ft. in the N to about 2,000 ft. as it opens in the S on a broad alluvial fan. The greatest depth is 960 ft. midway through the canyon. The canyon was cut through the Sperry Hills, exposing layers of widely different ages and compositions. Most colorful are the China Ranch Beds, midway through the canyon, light-colored, mainly white to brilliant pink.

The canyon is an ecological oasis, isolated from any other watered area. Thus unique species have evolved. At the same time, it is an essential water source for fauna from surrounding areas and for migrants. Hiking and bird-watching are the principal visitor activities.

The *Dumont Dunes* lie to the south of Amargosa Canyon, the site boundary extending W to Hwy 127. The dunes are not stabilized, but move with the winds. They are both scenic and scientifically interesting because of their great variations. They have little vegetation, some on the lower slopes and on the sandy terraces to the N.

The BLM tells us that the dunes continue to be used by ORVs, but that this should not deter visitors who seek fascinating places in the winter months.

Salt Creek, like the canyon an Area of Critical Environmental Concern, follows Hwy 127. Salt Spring Hills are N of the Avawatz Mountains (see entry this zone). The creek has an exceptionally large riparian zone—for the desert—about a mi. long, up to 150 ft. wide. It attracts diverse wildlife, 82 bird species recorded.

Headquarters

Bureau of Land Management, CA Desert District, 6221 Box Springs Blvd., Riverside, CA 92507; (909) 697-5200. Or BLM, Needles Resource Area, 101 Spikes Rd., Needles, CA 92363; (619) 326-3896. Or BLM, Barstow Resource Area, 150 Coolwater Lane, Barstow, CA 92311; (619) 255-8700.

Mecca Hills Wilderness

U.S. Bureau of Land Management
24,200 acres.

E of Indio. I-10 is N boundary. On the S and SE, Box Canyon Rd., which joins I-10 25 mi. E of Indio.

The Mecca Hills are extremely colorful, deeply eroded into a maze of narrow, winding, steep-walled canyons, a badlands labyrinth. The intricate passages give the visitor an immediate sense of isolation. Immense layers have been tilted, folded, uplifted by the San Andreas fault, and exposed by erosion, often presenting color contrasts. It is considered a unique geological site, providing important information about the impact of earthquakes on the earth's crust. Elevations range from near sea level to about 1,500 ft. Sandy washes dissect the area, with limited stands of ironwood, smoke tree, and palo verde. Scattered ocotillo on the slopes.

Painted Canyon, one of the features, is outstandingly scenic throughout. Good views of the area can be enjoyed along Box Canyon Rd. Riverside County has a campground in the canyon.

Headquarters

Bureau of Land Management, CA Desert District, 6221 Box Springs Blvd., Riverside, CA 92507; (909) 697-5200. Or BLM, Palm Springs–S. Coast Resource Area, 63-500 Garnet Ave., P.O. Box 2000, N. Palm Springs, CA 92258; (619) 251-4800.

Milpitas Wash-Palo Verde Mountains

U.S. Bureau of Land Management
40,400 acres.

SW of Blythe on I-10, near AZ border. W of Hwy 78, S of the town of Palo Verde. Milpitas Wash Rd. originates at Hwy 78 about 12 mi. S of Palo Verde, turning NW, then N to Wiley Well, becoming Wiley's Well Rd. before its junction with I-10.

The Palo Verde Mountains are a low range lying W of the Cibola National Wildlife Refuge on the Colorado River (see entry this zone for Colorado River National Wildlife Refuges). Steep, colorful, jagged peaks, the highest only 1,795 ft. Small, narrow canyons lead into enclosed basins and intimate valleys. Sheer cliffs, caves, arches, often with bright colors. Scenic value rated high.

Milpitas Wash is a broad drainage S of the mountains, dropping from about 1,000 to about 250 ft. at the Colorado River. It is one of the largest virtually undisturbed examples of the Sonoran Desert in CA. The wash is actually a series of parallel washes separated by thick islands of vegetation. Water collects in temporary pools after rain or infrequent flash floods.

Creosote covers much of the area. Also mesquite, ironwood, palo verde, and catclaw. Wildlife includes several bat species, kangaroo rats, pocket mice, desert tortoise, numerous snakes, including diamondback rattlesnake. Bighorn sheep and mule deer in the mountains. Quail and chukar hunting. The area has had light to moderate recreational use, chiefly for sightseeing, hiking, rockhounding, and camping at large.

Headquarters

Bureau of Land Management, CA Desert District, 6221 Box Springs Blvd., Riverside, CA 92507; (909) 697-5200. Or BLM, El Centro Resource Area, 1661 S. 4th St., El Centro, CA 92243-4561; (619) 337-4400.

Mitchell Caverns Natural Preserve

California Department of Parks and Recreation
See Providence Mountains State Recreation Area (this zone).

Mojave National Preserve

U.S. National Park Service
1,400,000 acres.

E from Baker on I-15, the N boundary; E from Ludlow on I-40, the S boundary.

Volcanic cinder cones, slow-moving tortoises, great sand dunes, lofty mountain peaks, a spectacular sweep of spring wildflowers, rock formations holding petroglyphs from ancient times, an eagle soaring thermal updrafts, panoramic vistas framed by Joshua trees. All these comprise the Mojave National Preserve. The Desert Protection Act of 1994 served to transfer the various lands known as the E Mojave National Scenic Area from the BLM to the National Park Service, which now adminsters as a single unit these ecological, geological, recreational, and historic-cultural areas of the CA Desert. 22 areas, nearly half the Preserve, are designated wilderness.

The best months for seeing the Preserve are Oct.–May, as summer temperatures average over 100°F. Elevations range from under 1,000 ft. to nearly 8,000 ft. Wildlife is plentiful, though not always in view. The Preserve is home to nearly 300 species of animals, including desert bighorn sheep, mule deer, coyotes, and desert tortoises. Birds include golden eagles, various hawks, Gambel's quail, chukar, and mourning doves. Other birds live in canyons and washes where they find water, food, and more cover. Common vegetation includes various cacti, yucca, sage, creosote, and Joshua tree. With winter rains, colorful wildflowers fill the desert in April and May.

Evidence of earlier peoples who followed the cycles of nature is etched and drawn on rocks throughout the region. Much later, others came to ranch cattle and to mine the desert. In fact, this "empty" land has drawn humans to its particular resources for over 10,000 years. Now, historic-cultural sites and archeological features are protected by law from disturbance or removal by visitors. Those who come, however, may enjoy a picnic, a scenic drive, a bike ride, a hike, camping, birding, backpacking, or stargazing. The Park Service maintains two campgrounds in the Preserve with water, tables, and toilet facilities.

Plants: White fir, Joshua tree, pinyon pine, juniper, oak; lower down, big galleta scrub steppe, creosote, Great Basin sagebrush and other sages, mesquite, various grasses, and low desert shrubs; then, evening primrose, desert sunflower, desert lily, other wildflowers in season, cacti. In the few riparian areas, willow, cottonwood, cattail, watercress, ferns.

Birds: Include golden eagle, prairie falcon, hawks, hepatic tanager, Virginia's and yellow warblers, Bendire's thrasher, northern flicker, Gambel's quail, chukar, mourning dove, roadrunner.

Mammals: Include bighorn sheep, mule deer, coyote, Panamint chipmunk, Panamint kangaroo rat, bats, rock squirrel.

Reptiles and amphibians: Many species of lizards and snakes. Watch out for rattlesnakes. Frogs are found in times of heavy rain.

Features

Cima Dome seen from a distance seems almost perfectly round, a landform rising 1,500 ft. above the surrounding desert. Here an enormous molten mass of rock stopped rising well below the earth's surface. The dome is about 75 sq. mi. in area and is now covered by a large, exceptional Joshua tree forest. Thick undergrowth includes many varieties of cactus. Wildlife of interest include golden eagle and Swainson's hawk. This is also said to be the only CA area where Bendire's thrasher and northern flicker are known to breed. The *Sunrise Rock* area, about 6 mi. N of Cima, is a good place to explore on foot. The trail to Teutonia Peak, which rises sharply from the top of the dome, begins just N of Sunrise Rock and takes about 2 hr. round-trip. The area may be reached N of Baker on I-15 to Cima Rd.

The *Cinder Cones,* more than 30 in number, dark red and black, rise about 300 ft. above white, sandy washes and black lava flows. Terrain includes flat valleys crossed by numerous large washes. Several springs create limited areas of riparian vegetation. These are probably the best example of recent volcanic activity in the Mojave Desert. Vegetation includes good stands of Joshua tree. Located just off Kelbaker Rd., outside the town of Baker.

The *Clark Mountains* were formed by a series of thrust faults. Mining of various minerals began here in the 1860s and continues today. Clark Mountain itself is the highest peak in the Preserve at 7,929 ft. A prominent regional landmark, the mountain mesa has steep-walled, colorful rock formations. Surrounding terrain includes rugged hills, narrow canyons, sloping bajadas dissected by washes. The mountain is biologically distinctive, with 8 plant communities. These include a large stand of white fir, with many specimens over 250 years old, a Joshua tree forest, and an exceptionally rich cactus populaton. Fine seasonal wildflower displays. Wildlife is abundant and diverse. Birding is outstanding, and unusual species may be seen. Two golden eagle eyries. Breeding area for hepatic tanager and Virginia's warbler. Populations of bighorn sheep, hoary bat, desert tortoise. The Clarks may be reached on I-15 (follow signs) near the NV border.

Hole-in-the-Wall, a series of volcanic rock formations, is at 4,500 ft. It is a popular recreation site for camping, hiking, picnicking. There are 2 trails here, one of which involves a descent using metal rings and scrambling around and over many boulders. The other is 7 mi. long and winds through *Wild Horse Canyon,* where one has a good view of diverse desert landscape. Backcountry camping is available along the trail. Rock climbing on the volcanic rocks is not recommended because of their crumbly nature. The area can be reached by Black Canyon and Essex Rds.

The *Kelso Dunes* are in a vast area of 161,900 acres lying W of Kelbaker Rd. Also within the area are the sweeping valleys and the rolling *Bristol Mountains,* which are administered by the BLM. The dunes themselves are the tallest in the CA Desert, rising more than 600 ft. above the Mojave floor. They were created by SE winds blowing fine-grained residual sand from the Mojave River sink, which lies to the NW. Golden rose quartz particles color the dunes. As the sand grains slide down the steep slopes, a booming sound is heard. A hike to the top of the dunes takes about 2 hr. There are sweeping views of the *Providence Mountains* to the E and of the equally rugged *Granite Mountains* to the S. The dunes are also noteworthy for a varied assortment of plant species, more diverse than the scrub of the surrounding desert. Vegetation now somewhat stabiliizes the lower dunes. In wet years there is a fine floral display, including evening primrose, desert sunflower, and desert lily. The dunes are closed to all vehicles.

The *Kelso Mountains* extend E to Kelbaker Rd. Highest point is 4,764 ft. The mountains are part of the bighorn sheep range. This 70,700-acre area is about 40% alluvial and dissected fans, 35% sand dunes, 20% hills, 5% sandy plains. Vegetation is sparse, chiefly creosote.

The *New York Mountains* are the highest in the region. From the 1,000-ft. elevation in the Chemeheuvi Valley, far to the SE, the land rises slowly through connecting valleys into the Lanfair Valley, where the rise continues from about 3,500 ft. to the base of the mountains at 5,000 ft. Here the slopes become steeper, rising to the highest point, 7,532 ft. This is part of the mountainous central portion of the Mojave region, the Mid Hills and Providence Mountains (see Providence Mountains State Recreation Area this zone) extending to the SW. Composed primarily of granite. Erosion produced the spectacular scenery. Buff-colored jointed rocks and boulders, vertical walls of lava, steep talus slopes. NE of Ivanpah Rd. are the *Castle Peaks,* vertical red-hued spires reaching up 600 ft. above the surrounding terrain. They are volcanic in origin. Broad valleys and canyons penetrate the mountains on the SW side. The scenic and complex terrain of the interior area, combined with dense vegetation, provides many opportunities for solitude in pristine surroundings. In Fourth of July Canyon one finds a small, relict stand of white fir, only about 30 trees. Oak, not usually associated with the desert, is also seen. Unusual fern species have been found in canyons here. Lower slopes are dominated by Great Basin sagebrush, juniper, and Joshua tree. Golden eagle breed here, as do yellow warbler, prairie falcon, northern flicker. Mammals include bighorn sheep, western pipistrel (bat), Panamint kangaroo rat, Panamint chipmunk, rock squirrel. Bird watching, hiking, hunting in season. On the NV border S of I-15. The area is crossed by the Ivanpah/Lanfair Rd.

Piute Creek/Fort Piute is on the NV border, E of the Ivanpah/Lanfair Rd., about 12 mi. N of Needles. The area includes parts of the *Castle Mountains* to the N. The Piute Range runs N–S between the Lanfair and Piute Valleys. High point in the range is 4,909 ft. Vegetation is sparse. Visitors are attracted by *Piute Gorge,* near the S end of the range. This spectacular steep-sided formation, not easily seen until you reach the edge, has been heavily eroded by water draining out through the Piute Canyon fault zone. It is nearly 300 ft. deep and very colorful. An unmaintained foot trail on the SW side provides access to the bottom of the gorge. Piute Springs is the source of perennial Piute Creek, one of the few free-flowing streams in the Mojave Desert. It was an important water source for native Americans and early explorers. In the 19th century a U.S. Army fort was built, traces of which remain. At the site is ½ mi. of willows, cottonwoods, and other riparian vegetation, above which rise the steep, red canyon walls. Plants include cattail, watercress, mesquite. The water attracts wildlife. The area is closed to vehicles. The riparian creek area is closed to hunting.

Providence Mountains State Recreation Area (Mitchell Caverns) is within the Mojave National Preserve but is administered by the CA Dept. of Parks and Recreation. See separate entry this zone.

Soda Springs served as a source of water for travelers on the Mojave Trail. Today it is jointly managed by the Park Service and CA University System as a desert education and study center. An unstaffed *orientation center* is open, year-round.

Interpretation

Mojave Desert information center in Baker, CA (see below). Call or visit for up-to-date information on programs offered throughout the year. Open daily.

Hole-in-the-Wall information center is open as staffing permits.

National Park Service rangers patrol the Preserve to provide information and resource protection.

Desert Education and Study Center, managed by the Park Service and CA University System. Unstaffed orientation center. SW of Baker off I-15, Xzyzx Rd. exit.

Activities

Camping: 2 campgrounds, 61 sites. At Hole-in-the-Wall and Mid Hills. Limited water at both. No potable water at Mid Hills, and road in is not suitable for trailers. 2 group campsites at Black Canyon Equestrian and Group Campground across from Hole-in-the-Wall information center, reservations required. Roadside car camping in areas that have been traditionally used for that purpose, use only existing sites.

Hiking, backpacking: Bring plenty of water, in hot weather 1 gallon per person per day. 2 developed trails. 2-mi. trail to Teutonia Peak on Cima Dome. 8-mi. trail between Mid Hills and Hole-in-the-Wall Campgrounds. Many other routes. Old mining roads, canyons, or washes are popular for hiking. Carry appropriate topo maps. Take special care in hot or windy conditions with protective clothing and sufficient water. Flash flooding may occur, stay alert in canyons or washes. Do not enter old mine shafts. Backpackers may camp anywhere in the backcountry, ½ mi. from a road, 1,000 ft. from a water source. Pack out trash, please.

Hunting: Permitted in designated areas. Inquire.

Horse riding: Permitted in designated areas. Corrals at Black Canyon Campground.

Headquarters

National Park Service, Mojave National Preserve, 222 E. Main St., Suite 202, Barstow, CA 92311; (619) 255-8801.

Additional Information

Mojave Desert information center, P.O. Box 241, Baker, CA 92309; (619) 733-4040. CA Desert information center, 831 Barstow Rd., Barstow, CA 92311; (619) 255-8760. Hole-in-the-Wall visitor center, Black Canyon Rd., Mojave National Preserve; (619) 928-2572.

Morongo-Whitewater

U.S. Bureau of Land Management
About 20,000 acres.

Generally bounded by the N unit of San Bernardino National Forest on the W, I-10 on the S, Hwy 62 on the E, Pipes Canyon Rd. on the N. Numerous private ownerships within area. The entry concerned a block S on Pipes Canyon Rd. and Hwy 62 and another on I-10 between the Forest and Hwy 62.

On the E slopes of the San Bernardino Mountains. Landforms range from broad bajadas and low, rolling foothills to steep, rugged mountains. Elevations range from 2,500 ft. in the valley to about 6,000 ft. at the Forest boundary. Several deep, steep-walled canyons penetrate the mountains, notably Little Morongo, Big Morongo, Mission, and Whitewater. Each of these canyons is watered by natural springs and creeks that flow all year, at least in upper sections.

Vegetation ranges from Mojave yucca, Joshua tree, creosote, and mixed desert shrubs, up through a pinyon-juniper zone to ponderosa pine forest. The moist canyon habitats have a rich and diverse riparian plant community, including tall cottonwoods and willows. Scenic qualities of the canyons are rated high, especially Whitewater Canyon, which has highly eroded, colorful ridges above the pale white of the boulder-strewn canyon floor.

The canyons, because of their water, attract wildlife. Mule deer are common, as well as black bear, bobcat, raccoon. Whitewater Canyon has two prairie falcon eyries and breeding pairs of summer tanager.

The Pacific Crest Trail enters the area from I-10, following the Whitewater River N along the road to a fish hatchery, then crossing to Mission Canyon, following it into the Forest.

Nearby

A lower section of *Big Morongo Canyon* E of Hwy 62, is a famous birding site. 235 species have been recorded, of which 72 nest. Checklist available. Access is just N of the town of Morongo Valley on Hwy 62, turning right at the sign for Covington Park, then left after 300 yds. and into a parking area. *Big Morongo Wildlife Reserve* is a 180-acre county park. It adjoins the 80-acre *Big Morongo Canyon Preserve* of The Nature Conservancy. Some of the adjoining land is public domain.

Land has been acquired to round out a cooperative scheme for preservation and management of the canyon.

Headquarters
Bureau of Land Management, CA Desert District, 6221 Box Springs Blvd., Riverside, CA 92507; (909) 697-5200.

Mount San Jacinto State Park and State Wilderness
California Department of Parks and Recreation
13,522 acres.

From Banning on I-10, S 27 mi. on Hwy 243.

This State Park is within the San Jacinto Wilderness of the San Bernardino National Forest (see entry this zone) and shares a trail system, including a section of the Pacific Crest Trail. Hwy 243 is the NW–SE route crossing the Forest. Park HQ is at Idyllwild, a small community within the Forest. The Park can also be entered by the Palm Springs Aerial Tramway 3 mi. W of Palm Springs to Desert View at about 8,400 ft. elevation. The tram operates all year and the Long Valley ranger station at the top is open all year.

Two campgrounds are on Hwy 243. No roads penetrate the Park. All travel is on foot or horseback. The Park is 6 mi. E–W, 3 mi. N–S. At 10,804 ft., San Jacinto Peak is the highest in the range, second highest in S CA. Four other peaks within the Park are over 10,000 ft. Most of the Park is above 6,000 ft. The NE face of the San Jacinto Range plunges 9,000 ft. in less than 6 mi., one of the sheerest escarpments on the continent, and a good reason to use the aerial tram. The tram carries passengers over a 12,800-ft. span with a rise of 5,873 ft.

Annual precipitation is about 40 in., much of it falling as snow. Snow cover usually lasts Dec. through April, depths to 10 ft. at higher elevations. High winds and below-zero temperatures are common.

The area is mostly forested. Incense cedar, white fir, Coulter, Jeffrey, ponderosa, and sugar pines over the lower slopes, lodgepole and limber pines above. Flora and fauna are essentially the same as in the surrounding National Forest.

The Park is within a 2-hr. drive of both Los Angeles and San Diego. Not surprisingly, permits are required to enter the wilderness, and permits are on quota. Backcountry camping is in designated primitive sites only.

Interpretation
Visitor center.

Activities

Camping: 1 developed campground, 33 sites; 1 primitive campground, 50 sites. Both open all year. Reservations April–Oct.

Hiking, backpacking: Day hiking permits issued on day of entry. Overnight permits can be obtained at HQ or by writing in advance for dates as much as 8 weeks ahead.

Ski touring, snowshoeing: Many arrive by tram for ski or snowshoe touring and camping. All should be prepared for severe weather.

Horse riding: Grazing is prohibited; equestrians must pack in their own feed. Camping is permitted. Horse rentals available.

Dogs are prohibited in the wilderness area.

Publication
Leaflet with map.

Headquarters
CA Dept. of Parks and Recreation, P.O. Box 308, 25905 Hwy 243, Idyllwild, CA 92349; (909) 659-2607.

. . . .

New York Mountains
U.S. National Park Service
See Mojave National Preserve (this zone).

. . . .

Palen-McCoy Wilderness
U.S. Bureau of Land Management and others
270,629 acres.

E of Joshua Tree National Park, bounded by I-10, the Rice-Midland Rd., Hwys 62 and 177.

Between Joshua Tree National Park and the Colorado River, several small mountains stand like islands on the desert floor. Elevation of the floor is 500–1,000 ft. The mountains, averaging 10–12 mi. in length, are irregularly spaced, several miles apart, roughly but not uniformly oriented NW–SE. Ridges are generally under 3,000 ft., a few peaks higher.

These low but rugged mountains are in the S central portion of the area, rising from Chuckwalla Valley, the route of I-10. The two major peaks are 3,623 ft. and 3,831 ft. high. Palen Valley, W of the mountains, is a large alluvial outwash plain including dry Palen Lake below the 500-ft. contour, as well as extensive sand dunes. The McCoy Mountains are to the E. An extensive interior valley lies between the mountain masses, extensive rolling bajadas crossed by sandy washes.

The Granite Mountains are N of the Palen, the Little Maria Mountains are N of McCoy, and the much smaller Arica Mountains are in the far NE sector. The area offers a variety of desert scenery: jagged peaks, eroded rock formations, deep canyons, washes, valleys, dunes. Vegetation is sparse through much of the area. Sandy washes have communities of ironwood, palo verde, and smoke tree. A small stand of crucifixion thorn occurs at the far S of Palen Valley. The desert wash woodland provides a cover for burro, mule deer, mountain lion, coyote, gray fox, and bobcat. Includes some state and private land within the boundaries.

Headquarters
Bureau of Land Management, CA Desert District, 6221 Box Springs Blvd., Riverside, CA 92507; (909) 697-5200. BLM, Palm Springs-S. Coast Resource Area, 63-500 Garnet Ave., P.O. Box 2000, N. Palm Springs, CA 92258; (619) 251-4800.

Picacho State Recreation Area
California Department of Parks and Recreation
See Colorado River National Wildlife Refuges and Wilderness Areas (this zone).

Pinto Mountains
U.S. National Park Service
See Joshua Tree National Park (this zone).

Providence Mountains State Recreation Area; Mitchell Caverns Natural Preserve

California Department of Parks and Recreation
5,900 acres.

Exit I-40 at Essex Rd., 99 mi. E of Barstow, 43 mi. W of Needles, turn N, 16 mi. to Park HQ.

This attractive State Recreation Area is an enclave within the Providence Mountains of the Mojave National Preserve. Leaving I-40, the Essex Rd. crosses a broad, gently rising plain. At the base of the Providence Mountains the paved road begins to climb steeply, reaching the HQ area at 4,300 ft., overlooking 300 sq. mi. of desert and mountains.

Jack Mitchell was introduced to the Limestone Caverns in 1929 by local ranchers, filed a patented silver claim, and made his home here. He and his wife built the road and the stone houses now in the HQ complex and offered guided tours to visitors. After his death in 1956, it became a State Park. Today the visitor center has good exhibits, excellent natural history and caving documentaries on video shown daily, and, for those with serious interests, a reference library.

Mitchell Caverns, the main feature of the area, has a wide variety of formations. Two separate caves were connected by tunnel in 1970 for an easy loop through the interior of the mountain. Total walking distance is 1.5 mi., about 1¾ hr., and sturdy shoes are recommended. Paved walkways, stairs with railings, and special electric lighting facilitate viewing the caves' amazing stalagmites, stalactites, cavern coral, and flowstone. The resident five species of bat prefer that visitors leave their flashlights in the car. Tours of the caverns are offered year-round; guides may include long-time local residents who are knowledgeable about the area's history. Oct. to May are the months most visitors come. In summer, however, it is considerably cooler here than in the valley below, especially inside the caverns.

Altogether, four main hiking trails covering over 4 mi. are available in the Recreation Area and Natural Preserve. The beautiful *Providence Mountains* extend NE into the Mojave National Preserve for about 20 mi., from Granite Pass, S of Kelso, overlooking the Clipper Valley to the E. High points in the range include Edgar Peak, at 7,171 ft., and the 6,996-ft. High Fountain Peak. Landform varies, from limestone cliffs and caverns to rhyolite crags and peaks, mesas, broad bajadas, with secluded canyons and valleys.

Plants: Much creosote and blackbrush scrub, including yucca and a dozen cacti species. Higher elevations are covered with pinon pine woodland. Caverns and visitor center straddle the two vegetation communities. A profusion of flowers in wet years, stands of Mojave and banana yucca.

Birds: Checklist available. Residents include turkey vulture, Cooper's and red-tailed hawks, golden eagle, kestrel, Gambel's quail, barn, screech, horned, burrowing, and pygmy owls, roadrunner, poor-will, ladder-backed woodpecker, raven, pinyon jay, cactus, rock, and canyon wrens, phainopepla, loggerhead shrike, house finch, black-throated sparrow.

Mammals: List available at HQ. Bighorn sheep in the mountains, mule deer, Panamint chipmunk, antelope ground squirrel, rock squirrel, Panamint kangaroo rat, cottontail, coyote, gray fox, bobcat, ringtail. Bats in the caverns.

Reptiles and amphibians: Desert tortoise and banded gecko are on the protected species list. Also present are chuckwalla and spiny and side-blotched lizards. Speckled rattlesnake is the prevalent species of rattlesnake, found along rocky slopes.

Interpretation

Guided tours of Mitchell Caverns available both morning and afternoon on weekends and state holidays from Labor Day–Memorial Day. Afternoon tours only, midweek and on weekends during the off-season summer months. Groups should make reservations.

Visitor center with exhibits. Natural history and caving videos shown daily.

Nature trail, ½ mi. in length, has a printed guide keyed to signs.

Activities

Camping: 6 sites, all year. Self-contained RVs may use adjacent parking lot overnight. Park Service sites available in the Mojave National Preserve.

Hiking: Four short maintained trails. Backcountry day-hiking opportunities available, but terrain is steep, rocks unstable, and dense cover of cacti; no permanent water source available.

Hunting: Chukar and quail in a restricted area.

Closest gas station is at Cima Junction, 54 mi. away. Come prepared!

Publications

Brochure, general information.

Geologic Setting of Mitchell Caverns.

The Archeology of Mitchell Caverns.

Mary Beal Nature Trail Guide.

Checklists of birds, mammals, plants, reptiles, and amphibians.

Caverns map.

Headquarters

CA Dept. of Parks and Recreation, P.O. Box 1, Essex, CA 92332-0001; (619) 928-2586. (Staff available 12:30–1:30 daily, 9:00–3:00 on weekends; recorded information otherwise.)

Rainbow Basin–Owl Canyon

U.S. Bureau of Land Management
See Harper Dry Lake (this zone).

Salton Sea

From Indio on I-10, SE on Hwy 111. Hwy 86 is on the opposite shore.

An ancient lake once filled a huge desert basin almost to sea level. Over centuries it dried, leaving a barren salt bed that held water only at brief intervals. In 1905, during construction of irrigation works, the Colorado River, in flood, broke through and poured into the basin for 2 years. When the flow was stopped, the Salton Sea was 45 mi. long, 20 mi. wide, as much as 100 ft. deep. It dried, the level dropping until runoff from irrigated land halted the decline and the lake level began to rise again. For a time there was concern that resort communities on the shore would be inundated, but evaporation has approximated the inflow. The lake surface is now about 235 ft. below sea level.

The water is slightly saltier than the ocean, and saltwater fish species have been successfully introduced. Average depth is now

about 10 ft. The lake area is about 175,000 acres. High winds sometimes sweep the lake, making boating dangerous.

Most of the shoreline is privately owned. Several resort communities have developed, but growth is limited because of the exceedingly
hot, dry summers. Boating, fishing, and swimming are popular.

See entries for the following sites on the lake: Imperial Wildlife
Area, Salton Sea National Wildlife Refuge, and Salton Sea State Recreation Area.

Salton Sea National Wildlife Refuge

U.S. Fish and Wildlife Service
37,218 acres.
From Brawley Hwy 111 N 10 mi. to Sinclair Rd. W on Sinclair to HQ.

Since 1930, when the Refuge was established for protection of waterfowl and shorebirds, the level of the Salton Sea has risen, progres-
sively inundating all but about 2,000 acres in 2 units, both on the
shoreline, about 5 mi. apart. These remaining areas are salt marsh,
goose pasture, and freshwater marsh, and are completely flat except
for Obsidian Butte, Red Hill, and Rock Hill.

The site is about 228 ft. below sea level, in one of the hottest and
driest areas of the continent. Average rainfall is about 3 in. per year,
and summer temperatures often touch 120°F. Winters are mild and
pleasant.

The birding is extraordinary. Wintering populations include large
numbers of Canada and snow geese, great masses of pintail, along
with green-winged teal, wigeon, ruddy duck, and coot. Other winter
residents include eared grebe, great and snowy egrets, white-faced
ibis, long-billed curlew, whimbrel, willet, greater yellowlegs, long-
billed dowitcher, marbled godwit, avocet, and western sandpiper.

In the annual Christmas bird count, the Refuge often has high
scores for such species as rough-winged and bank swallows, Scott's
oriole, orange-crowned and yellow-rumped warblers, redstart, burrowing owl, mountain plover, and others. White pelican are common
in spring and fall. (In spring we saw a flight of at least a thousand,
soaring high in the sky, near the Salton Sea.) Summer visitors include
wood stork, fulvous tree duck, black-necked stilt. The Refuge has an

interesting list of accidentals, including brown booby, magnificent frigate bird, Baikal teal. It also has a black skimmer colony.

Best birding areas are off Garst Rd. and Red Hill, from Rock Hill, and along the shoreline.

Hunting: Special rules. Inquire.

No motor vehicles allowed on Refuge roads. No water, toilets, or picnic sites.

Publications

Leaflet.

Bird checklist.

Refuge map.

Hunting regulations.

Headquarters

U.S. Fish and Wildlife Service, 906 W. Sinclair Rd., Calipatria, CA 92233; (619) 348-5278.

....

Salton Sea State Recreation Area

California Department of Parks and Recreation
17,913 acres.

From I-10 at Indio, SE 25 mi. on Hwy 111.

18 mi. of shoreline on the NE side of the Salton Sea, a narrow strip of land. A popular site for water-based recreation year-round, though area is extremely hot April–Sept. We include it because of a note from the manager: "This is a tremendous bird-watching area!" No details, but see entries for the Salton Sea National Wildlife Refuge and Imperial Wildlife Area.

Interpretation

Programs Oct.–April.

Activities

Camping: 150 developed sites. Reservations Oct. 1–May 28. 3 primitive campgrounds, about 1,000 sites.

Fishing: Gulf croaker, sargo, corvina, tilapia.

Swimming: Unsupervised.

Boating: Ramp, basin, moorings. Sea is dangerous in high winds.

Publication
Leaflet.

Headquarters
CA Dept. of Parks and Recreation, P.O. Box 3166, North Shore, CA 92254; (619) 393-3052/3059.

San Bernardino National Forest

U.S. Forest Service
818,999 acres of Forest land; includes federal and private lands.

Two sections: (1) N and E of San Bernardino; (2) S of I-10 at Banning. Scenic routes through both sections.

These wild lands of the San Bernardino, San Gabriel, and San Jacinto Mountains were designated a National Forest about 10 years ago. The Forest contains a great diversity of terrain and habitat. Gentle flat-lands and rolling hills are dominated by sheer escarpments and rocky peaks higher than anything else in southern CA. In some places, snow is a rare visitor; in others it may linger half the year. There are mountain lakes, boggy meadows, quiet brooks, and rushing streams. Often barrel cactus and Joshua trees flourish in proximity to Jeffrey pines and incense cedars.

Forest statistics say that winter sports are the greatest single attraction here. Also, with 6 million visitor-days per year, this Forest has the heaviest recreation use of any National Forest. Driving for pleasure is the top use, followed by downhill skiing, camping.

On a Sat. evening in late April, we checked into a commercial campground on Big Bear Lake in the N section of the Forest. Few of the sites were occupied. Early next morning we drove W on Hwy 18.

Lines had already formed at the entrances to the several ski areas, people waiting for the ski slopes to open. Traffic was so heavy we were relieved to find our way out.

The larger of the two sections adjoins and lies E of the Angeles National Forest. About 50 mi. from W to E, it occupies the San Bernardino Mountains and the E portion of the San Gabriel Mountains. I-15 and US 395 cross the Forest through Cajon Pass between the two mountain masses. To the S, I-10 crosses San Gorgonio Pass between the San Bernardinos and the San Jacinto Mountains, occupied by the smaller section of the Forest.

The Forest includes 24 communities with over 35,000 homes, a summer population of over 120,000 people. Commercial establishments include the ski areas, campgrounds, resorts, marinas, restaurants, garages, and stores. Most of the land around Big Bear Lake and Lake Arrowhead is privately owned. Also within the Forest are the Silverwood Lake State Recreation Area and Mount San Jacinto State Park and State Wilderness (see entries this zone). There are 4 large designated wilderness areas: San Gorgonio, Cucamonga, San Jacinto, Santa Rosa (see "Features" below).

The mountains lie between the aricultural and industrial coastal valleys and the desert. Hwy 18 is called a scenic highway, but it overlooks a great sea of suburbs, shopping centers, freeways, factories, and railroads. Elevations rise from about 1,300 ft. in the front country to the mountain plateau region of 5,000–7,000 ft. Highest point is 11,501-ft. San Gorgonio Peak, highest in southern CA. San Jacinto Peak is 10,786 ft., and 5 other peaks rise above 10,000 ft. Many slopes are extremely steep.

Annual rainfall in the W valleys is about 16 in. per year. Precipitation is heavier on the high slopes, much of it falling as snow, enough to keep ski areas busy into April or later. On the E side, in the rain shadow, desert climate prevails. Most mountain streams are seasonal.

Water is the principal product here, the Forest watersheds supplying enough for the needs of a million people. Forest management practices are designed to conserve this resource, and to enhance recreation, wildlife, and other values—not for commercial production of wood.

Fire hazard is high in summer. Fire crews responded to 195 small fires in 1995, 16 caused by lightning, 179 by humans. 2,123 acres burned. Back in 1970, when conditions were especially bad, a single fire burned 53,000 acres between dawn and dusk. Substantial areas of the Forest are closed in fire season.

Both because of heavy use and fire hazard, overnight camping requires a visitor permit, for either a designated campground or back-country camping.

Plants: About 50% forested, including pinyon-juniper areas. Chaparral covers about 35%, on the lower slopes. Pinyon pine, juniper, and sagebrush cover midelevation desert slopes. Conifer and oak forests, with some stands of fine, mature trees, between 6,000 and 8,500 ft. Ponderosa, Jeffrey, sugar, lodgepole, Coulter, and limber pines, white fir, incense cedar, Douglas-fir, and black oak are found here. Above 8,500 ft., lodgepole and limber pines dominate. Some 2,000-year-old limber pines are to be found in the San Gorgonio Wilderness. The Forest claims the widest range of rare plant species to be found in the continental US. Many of these are in only one mountain range.

Birds: Checklist available. Residents include golden eagle, turkey vulture, 7 owl species, pied-billed grebe, coot, Cooper's, red-tailed, and red-shouldered hawks, kestrel, killdeer, poor-will, northern flicker, acorn, downy, hairy, ladder-backed, and white-headed woodpeckers, black and Say's phoebes, mockingbird, California thrasher, jays, dipper, brown creeper, blue-gray and black-tailed gnatcatchers, Anna's hummingbird, Clark's nutcracker, finches, sparrows, white-throated swift, brown and rufous-sided towhees, solitary vireo, wrens, bushtit, wrentit. Many waterfowl in winter.

Mammals: Checklist available. 61 species identified. Common are ground squirrel, gray squirrel, deer mouse, striped skunk, black bear, coyote, bobcat, mule deer, peninsular bighorn sheep. Many bat species, shrews, moles, mice, rabbits, and squirrels. Less frequently seen are badger, kit fox, ringtail, beaver, mountain lion.

Reptiles and amphibians: Reported as common: horned, colared, and western fence lizards, salamander, Pacific tree frog, western toad, bullfrog, yellow-bellied racer, western garter snake, western rattlesnake.

Features

San Gorgonio Wilderness: 58,669 acres. In the SE sector of the N unit, N of Banning. Trailheads on Hwy 38. The summit region of the highest range in southern CA. Peaks over 10,000 ft. with sweeping vistas of mountains and desert. Small meadows and lakes, wide expanses of bare rock; conifer forest on the N slopes. Maintained trails cross the area, and hikers are advised that only experienced backcountry travelers should go off the trails; terrain is rough and water scarce. Wilderness permits are required.

San Jacinto Wilderness: 33,408 acres. In the S unit of the Forest. See the entry for Mount San Jacinto State Park and State Wilderness, which divides the National Forest wilderness in two and has a common trail system. On the crest of the San Jacinto Mountains. The N portion is somewhat more scenic, overlooking San Gorgonio Pass and across to the mountains beyond. Wilderness permit is required, and here, too, the number issued is limited. Note that the National Forest permit does not authorize entry into the State wilderness.

Santa Rosa Wilderness: 19,803 acres. Next to the BLM's Santa Rosa Wilderness on its W boundary. The BLM lands in turn meet Anza-Borrego Desert State Park, with its own Santa Rosa wilderness. In these 3 adjoining wilderness areas, desert and mountain environments combine to form unique habitats. The Santa Rosa Mountains support the largest peninsular bighorn sheep herd in the U.S. (See entries for Santa Rosa Mountains and Anza-Borrego Desert State Park for further description of area.)

Granite Park Roadless Area: 10,600 acres. In the far NE corner of the N unit, at the boundary. Rolling mountains, rock outcroppings, elevations from 5,500 to 7,500 ft. Relatively low elevations and proximity to the Mojave Desert make this area accessible and attractive in winter and spring. Most of the area is covered with chaparral species of juniper and pinyon pine. Fine stands of Joshua trees at lower elevations. The world's largest Joshua tree is here. Arrastre Creek, an ephemeral stream, forms a large canyon at the N end.

Cucamonga Wilderness: 8,581 acres. On the W side of the N unit. This area adjoins the Angeles National Forest (see entry zone 8). Rugged terrain. Sharp peaks, steep slopes. Elevations from 5,000 to 9,000 ft. The Middle and North Forks of Lytle Creek flow all year. Otherwise water is scarce. Wilderness permit required. Area is subject to fire closure after about June 20.

Pyramid Peak Roadless Area: 10,200 acres. In the SE sector of the S unit. About 12 mi. S of Palm Springs. Elevations from 2,200 to 7,100 ft. Rolling terrain in the S; rugged mountains with numerous rock outcroppings in the N. The W boundary meets the Pacific Crest Trail. Live Oak Canyon includes 40-ft. Hidden Falls, flowing most of the year. Palm Canyon has lush riparian vegetation, including fan palm, cottonwood, rushes, ferns, grasses. Numerous springs and seeps attract wildlife.

Black Mountain Scenic Area: 7,590 acres. N of Idyllwild, between Hwy 243 and the San Jacinto Wilderness. It is a popular recreation area with numerous scenic overlooks, trails for day hikes, native American pictographs, and other points of interest.

Idyllwild County Park: 202 acres. Just N of Idyllwild on Hwy 243, has an exceptionally fine visitor center and nature trail.

National Children's Forest: 3,400 acres. Located off Keller Peak Rd. in Arrowhead Ranger District. ½-mi. self-guided paved trail tells the story of the Forest's replanting after a 1970 fire.

Interpretation

Nature walks, slide shows, ranger talks.

Nature trail in Big Bear Ranger District.

New *Discovery Center* to open in 1997.

Activities

Camping: 25 family campgrounds, 917 sites. Some open all year. Reservations recommended May 30–Labor Day.

Hiking, backpacking: 538 mi. of National Recreational Trails, wilderness trails, interpretive trails, and hiking trails. The 2,600-mi. Pacific Crest Trail has 200 mi. within the Forest. All wilderness areas except Santa Rosa require permits.

Driving: The Rim of the World Scenic Byway, through the N part of the Forest. Self-guiding auto tour guide available at all Ranger Districts for $0.50. In the S portion, the Palms to Pines Scenic Byway, a 67-mi. route through the San Jacinto and Santa Rosa Mountains, travels from desert to snow-capped mountains.

Hunting: Deer, ducks, quail.

Fishing: About 110 mi. of fishing streams, as well as lakes. Rainbow and brown trout, black crappie, bluegill, green sunfish, smallmouth bass, redeye bass, bullhead, white catfish.

Swimming: Lakes.

Boating: Chiefly from private ramps and marinas.

Horse riding: Permitted on almost all trails, except nature trails. Horse camp near Heart Bar, another at McCall in San Jacinto R.D., off Hwy 74.

Skiing: Centered around Big Bear and Arrowhead. 6 commercial ski areas, 3 with snow-making machines.

Ski touring: In the high country, depending on snow cover. 2 Nordic ski facilities in the Arrowhead area.

Biking: Mountain bikes permitted on nonprivate dirt roads and on most trails except Pacific Crest Trail, nature trails, and trails within the 4 wilderness areas.

OHVs: Trail system is one of the best in southern CA. Primarily in Arrowhead, Big Bear, and Cajon R.D.s. No "open areas."

Publications

San Bernardino National Forest Visitor map, $3.25.

Maps of the San Gorgonio, Cucamonga, Santa Rosa, and San Jacinto wildernesses, $3.25 each.

Trails to Hike, Arrowhead Ranger District, $1.10.

Plants of the Big Bear Valley Preserve.

San Bernardino County shooting map.

Headquarters

U.S. Forest Service, 1824 Commercecenter Circle, San Bernardino, CA 92408-3430; (909) 383-5588, TDD (909) 383-5616.

Ranger Districts

Arrowhead R.D., P.O. Box 350, 28104 Hwy 18, Skyforest, CA 92385; (909) 337-2444, TDD (909) 336-1626. Big Bear R.D., P.O. Box 290, N. Shore Dr., Hwy 38, Fawnskin, CA 92333; (909) 866-3437, TDD (909) 866-3233. Cajon R.D., 1209 Lytle Creek Rd., Lytle Creek, CA 92358; (909) 887-2576. San Gorgonio R.D., 34701 Mill Creek Rd., Mentone, CA 92359; (909) 794-1123. San Jacinto R.D., P.O. Box 518, 54270 Pinecrest, Idyllwild, CA 92549; (909) 659-2117.

Sand Hills

U.S. Bureau of Land Management
68,700 acres.

Extreme SE of CA. A long, narrow triangle, its base at the U.S.–Mexican border, between the Coachella Canal on the W, Southern Pacific Railroad on the E, extending NW almost 40 mi. Crossed by Hwy 78.

The area is also known as the Algodones Dunes, one of the largest dune systems in the U.S. In the N, 32,000 acres have been designated as the North Algodones Wilderness. The southern area is open to multiple-use activities. Camping is at large.

About 40 mi. long, the dune system is up to 8 mi. wide. Some of the dunes rise 200–300 ft. above their bases. The system includes transverse, longitudinal, crescent-shaped, and star dunes, many shapes and sizes, some partially stabilized by vegetation, some migrating. Where vegetation occurs, it is likely to be thick stands of mesquite and creosote. The area includes several species of rare, threatened, or endangered plants.

Birds: Include turkey vulture, red-tailed and Swainson's hawks, kestrel, burrowing owl, roadrunner, phainopepla, poor-will, black-chinned and Costa's hummingbirds, white-throated and Vaux's swifts, raven, lesser nighthawk, mockingbird, verdin, Gambel's quail, ladder-backed woodpecker, loggerhead shrike, horned lark, ash-throated flycatcher, crissal and Le Conte's thrashers, western kingbird, white-winged and mourning doves, gray vireo, black and Say's phoebes, black-tailed gnatcatcher, barn, tree, and cliff swallows, Abert's towhee, cactus wren, house finch, black-throated and white-crowned sparrows.

Mammals: Include ground squirrels, mice, kangaroo rats, black-tailed jackrabbit, cottontail, pocket gopher, striped skunk, coyote, kit fox, badger, bobcat.

Reptiles and amphibians: Lizards include zebra-tailed, leopard, desert crested, western whiptail, western banded gecko, flat-tailed horned, desert horned, desert spiny, desert fringe-toed, long-tailed brush, and side-blotched. Desert tortoise, soft-shelled turtle, desert toad, Couch's spadefoot toad. Snakes include glossy, branded sand snake, spotted night snake, common whipsnake, spotted leaf-nosed snake, gopher snake, long-nosed snake, patch-nosed snake, western ground snake, lyre snake, diamond rattlesnake, sidewinder.

Headquarters
Bureau of Land Management, El Centro Resource Area, 1661 S. 4th St., El Centro, CA 92243-4561; (619) 337-4400. BLM, CA Desert District, 6221 Box Springs Blvd., Riverside, CA 92507-0714; (909) 697-5200.

Santa Rosa Mountains

U.S. Bureau of Land Management and others
136,100 acres.

SW of Indio, on the N boundary of Anza-Borrego Desert State Park; adjoining San Bernardino National Forest on the W. Hwy 74 crosses near the Santa Rosa summit about 1½ mi. E of its junction with Hwy 371.

Adjoining the Santa Rosa Wilderness of the Anza-Borrego Desert State Park, this area has been characterized as one of the most pristine and spectacular in the desert. This despite the checkerboarding of private ownerships in much of the area. 64,340 acres have now been designated wilderness. Within it are found important lambing areas for bighorn sheep. The mountains are home to one of the largest herds in the U.S.

From the below-sea-level Salton Sea about 6 mi. E, an alluvial fan slopes gradually upward to about the 500-ft. contour. Above that the mountains rise steeply. Much of the mountain mass is above 4,000 ft., with a peak of 6,623 ft. within the site, one of 8,716 ft. just outside the boundary to the N. The mountains are rugged, strewn with boulders, cut by highly eroded canyons and washes, with steep cliffs, sheer faces, several valleys. 19 springs are scattered throughout the area.

Vegetation includes a number of plant communities, from the low desert floor to the ridges: creosote scrub, succulent scrub, desert chaparral, juniper-pinyon woodland. Spring floral displays. Wildlife includes, in addition to the bighorn sheep, mule deer, quail, chukar.

Headquarters

Bureau of Land Management, CA Desert District, 6221 Box Springs Blvd., Riverside, CA 92507; (909) 697-5200. Or BLM, Palm Springs–S. Coast Resource Area, 63-500 Garnet Ave., P.O. Box 2000, N. Palm Springs, CA 92258; (619) 251-4800.

Sheephole Mountains–Cadiz Valley

U.S. National Park Service.
See Joshua Tree National Park (this zone).

Silverwood Lake State Recreation Area

California Department of Parks and Recreation
2,400 acres.

In the San Bernardino National Forest, on Hwy 138, 11 mi. E of I-15.

The State Water Project reservoir, formed by a 249-ft.-high dam, has a surface area of about 1,000 acres. It is heavily used for water-based recreation. Campground reservations are available all year. The site map printed in the leaflet gives only a slight indication of the land area around the lake.

But it is within a National Forest, in a setting of chaparral-covered hills, at 3,200–3,800 ft. elevation, conifers on some N-facing slopes. About 130 bird species have been identified here, including bald and golden eagles, osprey, and migrating waterfowl, as well as such mammals as coyote, ringtail, bobcat, beaver, mule deer, mountain lion, and black bear.

Intepretation

Hikes and *boat tours* Jan.–March to view bald eagles and osprey. Reservations.

Activities

Camping: 128 developed sites. All year. Reservations.

Hiking: 12 mi. of paved trails. Group and hiker/biker camps.

Fishing: Trout, bass, bluegill, catfish.

Swimming: Supervised in season.

Boating: Ramps, docks, rentals. Because of heavy traffic, lake is zoned: ski area, no-ski zone, no power boats zone, etc.

Bicycling: Extensive bike trails circle the lake. Trails also go up to crestline.

Publication

Leaflet with map.

Headquarters

CA Dept. of Parks and Recreation, 14651 Cedar Circle, Hesperia, CA 92345; (619) 389-2281/2303.

Tijuana Estuary Visitor Center

California Department of Parks and Recreation
1,100 acres.

I-5 to Imperial Beach Blvd. exit W to 3rd St. Turn left to Caspian St. and the visitor center entrance.

The Tijuana River enters the U.S. W of San Ysidro and flows NW to Imperial Beach and the Pacific Ocean. While most of the river is located in Mexico, it is also San Diego County's largest watershed. Slough habitat includes sand dunes, mud flats, tidal sloughs, marshes, and riverbeds. Plants commonly found in the estuary are cord grass, wild buckwheat, toyon, and lemonadeberry. Also found here is the endangered salt marsh bird's-beak, a relative of the snapdragon. This is an excellent spot for birdwatching. The estuary is home to black-necked stilt, great blue heron, great egret, avocet, clapper rail. The visitor center features a diorama with examples of estuary plant and animal life. There are nature and bird walks, call for reservations. Junior Ranger program as well.

Headquarters

CA Dept. of Parks and Recreation, 301 Caspian Way, Imperial Beach, CA 91932; (619) 575-3613.

Torrey Pines State Reserve and State Beach

California Department of Parks and Recreation
1,750 acres.

On S-21, seaward of I-5, 1 mi. S of Del Mar.

Open: 8 A.M. to sunset.

Coastal bluffs overlooking the ocean, 5 mi. of beach, salt marsh, eroded canyons, mesa. Highest point is 400 ft. above the sea. The Reserve was established to preserve the last of the Torrey pines, a species that grows naturally only here and on Santa Rosa Island, 175

mi. away. In 1850, the Torrey pine was the rarest pine in the world. Today, it is one of the rarest in the U.S. About 5,000 of the pines are within the Preserve, the oldest about 200 years of age. The Torrey pine is not a large tree, but, especially growing exposed places, is striking—wind-blown, gnarled, and twisted.

Torrey Sandstone, the yellow, tan, and white cliffs, is estimated to be 40 million years old. Sandstone along the beach, said to be 40 million years older, contains many fossils.

The Los Peñaquitos Lagoon is at the N end, flowing under a bridge on the Coast Rd. A salt marsh and waterfowl refuge is on the inland side.

Plants: The Reserve is botanically rich, more than 400 plant species recorded. List available. Since annual precipitation is only 10 in. and summers are dry, the assortment is limited to species adapted to these severe conditions. Common trees and shrubs include scrub oak, toyon, wartystem ceanothus, lemonadeberry, laurel sumac, mission manzanita, mountain mahogany, bush rue. Also common: chamise, redberry, flattop buckwheat, redbush monkeyflower, bush poppy, deerweed, San Diego rock rose, golden yarrow, black sage, sagebrush, Mojave yucca. Barrel cactus, prickly pear, and polypody ferns in shaded canyons.

The spring wildflower display includes sea dahlia, sand verbena, mariposa lily, milkmaids, live-forever, tidy tips, lupine, beach evening primrose, blue-eyed grass, fishhook cactus.

Birds: Over 235 species recorded. Checklist available. Salt marsh attracts loons, grebes, great blue and green herons, snowy egret, mallard, pintail, lesser scaup, long-billed curlew, whimbrel, and least terns, rare in this area. Upland species include quail, brown thrasher, brown towhee, wrentit, scrub jay, roadrunner.

Mammals: Include opossum, cottontail, ground squirrel, bobcat, coyote, gray fox, mule deer. Gray whale often seen offshore during Jan.–Mar. migration. Also seen are dolphins.

Interpretation

Museum theme is a natural history. Exhibits, publications.

Guided hikes on weekends throughout the year. Schedules posted.

Activities

Hiking: Trails through the pines, to viewpoints, down to the beach.

Swimming: Surf, supervised in season. Ocean swimming can be hazardous. Some swimming in estuary, especially at high tide.

Pets are not permitted in the Reserve or on the beach.

Reserve is closed when parking capacity is reached. This happens almost every pleasant weekend. Visitors must stay on trails. No fires, smoking, picnicking, food, beverages, collecting.

Publications

Leaflet with map.

Bird checklist.

Headquarters

CA Dept. of Parks and Recreation, 9609 Waples St., Suite 200, San Diego, CA 92121; (619) 642-4200.

Trona Pinnacles Natural Area

U.S. Bureau of Land Management
19,600 acres.

At Searles Lake, E of Hwy 178 near Trona.

Searles Lake is a dry lake and a salt desert, barren of vegetation except around the edges. Elevation is about 1,600 ft. The pinnacles are one of the best examples of tufa deposits in the U.S. The more than 500 spires formed under water about 25,000 years ago, by the interaction of blue-green algae and geothermal springs. These deposits of calcium carbonate are up to 140 ft. high, and their shapes are so bizarre that the site is often used as a setting for science fiction films. The Trona Pinnacles are a National Natural Landmark.

Activities

Camping: Primitive camping is permitted, but campers are encouraged to use existing campsites and fire rings and to pack out all trash.

Hiking: ½ mi. loop trail around the pinnacles. The hike is not difficult, but it helps to have shoes with good ankle support.

Headquarters

Bureau of Land Management, Ridgecrest Resource Area, 300 S. Richmond Rd., Ridgecrest, CA 93555; (619) 384-5400.

Turtle Mountains

U.S. Bureau of Land Management
238,200 acres (144,500 acres of wilderness plus other federal, state, and private lands).

30 mi. S of Needles, CA, near the AZ border. E boundary is US 95, S boundary Hwy 62. Part of the N boundary is Turtle Mountain Rd., SW from US 95 a short distance S of Havasu Lake Rd.

The landscape ranges from broad, open bajadas to highly eroded red basalt spires. Spires and peaks characterize the scenic, steep NE half of the range, while the SW is steep but rounded. The Turtles lie in a horseshoe arrangement, parted by a large, flat interior valley crossed by many shallow washes. The NE mountains are volcanic, colorful, displaying shades of pink, gold, green, brown. Highest point in the NE is 3,804 ft., in the SW 4,313 ft., above the valley, which lies at about 1,500 ft.

The area has a number of springs. Notable among them is Mopah Springs, the most N known fan palm oasis. Names like Mohawk Springs, Coffin Springs, and Gary Wash invite the dauntless hiker. However, one should not rely on mapped springs for water. Each person should always carry a gallon of water per day. Camping is at large; there are no developed campgrounds.

Vegetation occurs throughout the area and is relatively lush on the bajadas that surround the mountains. The interior valley has dense stands of creosote, cactus, and mixed shrubs.

The region has a herd of bighorn sheep, extensive desert tortoise habitat, prairie falcon and golden eagle eyries, breeding sites for Bendire's thrasher.

The central portion of the Turtles is pristine, 144,500 acres of designated wilderness. This has no frontage on any surfaced road. Wilderness boundary maps can be obtained at district or resource area offices.

Headquarters

Bureau of Land Management, CA Desert District, 6221 Box Springs Blvd., Riverside, CA 92507; (909) 697-5200. Or BLM, Needles Resource Area, 101 W. Spikes Rd., Needles, CA 92363; (619) 326-3896.

Whipple Mountains Wilderness

U.S. Bureau of Land Management
85,100 acres (77,520 acres of wilderness including other federal, state, and private lands).

Near the AZ border. 10 mi. NW of Parker Dam, E of US 95. S boundary is the Colorado River Aqeduct and Copper Basin Reservoir roads.

The Whipple Mountains Wilderness came into being when the CA Desert Protection Act was passed in 1994. The Whipples lie E to W across the wilderness. The western half of the range has pale green formations. A low angle fault separates the formation on the W from striking brick red volcanic formations to the E. The landscape is diverse, ranging from valley floors and washes to steep-walled canyons, domed peaks, and eroded spires towering to 4,000 ft. Flowing westward from the colorful spires and domes are bajadas with isolated lava rock masses and red sandstone outcrops.

Sonoran Desert creosote scrub and thorn forest decorate the area. In addition, dense stands of palo verde, ironwood, smoke tree, cholla, saguaro (1 of only 2 or 3 such stands in CA), foxtail, and Mojave prickly pear cacti all grow here.

Activities

Camping: No designated sites. Access is by 4-wheel-drive vehicle on a powerline road in the eastern boundary.

Hiking: Private lands lie within the wilderness area. Boundary setbacks from roads on trails are 30 to 300 ft. Since potable water is scarce, always carry a gallon of water per person per day while hiking in the backcountry.

Headquarters

Bureau of Land Management, CA District Office, 6221 Box Springs Blvd., Riverside, CA 92507; (909) 697-5200. Or BLM, Needles Resource Area, 101 W. Spikes Rd., Needles, CA 92363; (619) 326-3896.

INDEX

About the Authors

The Perrys, long residents of the Washington, D.C., area, moved to Winter Haven, Forida, soon after work on these guides began. Their desks overlook a lake well populated with great blue herons, anhingas, egrets, ospreys, gallinules, and wood ducks, plus occasional alligators and otters.

Jane, an economist, came to Washington as a congressman's secretary and thereafter held senior posts in several executive agencies and presidential commissions. John, an industrial management consultant, was for ten years assistant director of the National Zoo.

Married in 1944, they have hiked, backpacked, camped, canoed, and cruised together in all fifty states. They have written more than a dozen books and produced more than two dozen educational filmstrips, chiefly on natural history and ecology.

Both are involved in conservation action, at home and abroad. They are board members of several environmental organizations.